Low Carb High Fat Barbecue

Skyhorse Publishing books may be purchased in bulk at special discounts for sales promotion, corporate gifts, fund-raising, or educational purposes. Special editions can also be created to specifications. For details, contact the Special Sales Department, Skyhorse Publishing, 307 West 36th Street, 11th Floor, New York, NY 10018 or info@skyhorsepublishing.com.

Skyhorse® and Skyhorse Publishing® are registered trademarks of Skyhorse Publishing, Inc.®, a Delaware corporation.

Visit our website at www.skyhorsepublishing.com.

10 9 8 7 6 5 4 3 2 1

Library of Congress Cataloging-in-Publication Data is available on file.

Cover photo credit: Mikael Eriksson

Interior design and photos: Mikael Eriksson, M Industries

Print ISBN: 978-1-63220-532-2
Ebook ISBN: 978-1-63220-933-7

Printed in China

Low Carb High Fat Barbecue

80 Healthy LCHF Recipes for Summer Grilling, Sauces, Salads, and Desserts

Birgitta Höglund

Photos by Mikael Eriksson

Skyhorse Publishing

CONTENTS

Meat and Poultry   97

Vegetable Dishes and Salads   125

A Sweet Ending   143

Grilling Vegetables   153

Foreword by Anna Hallén

I'm delighted to have been asked to write a few words for this book—happy and proud for many reasons. First, because you're now holding in your hands an excellent cookbook by an author who has thorough knowledge of low-carb high fat grilling; better yet, she has firsthand experience of how wonderful this way of eating is, and the vitality and strength it can bring about. I have been fortunate enough to follow Birgitta Höglund's impressive progress for a few years now. I've enjoyed seeing her grow in courage, and go from a state of pain and low energy to the Birgitta of today, who is a fantastic role model for anyone fighting heavy odds. She proves that it is indeed possible to find one's way back from ill-health and truly enjoy life to its fullest.

These are strong words, to be sure, but they aren't empty—I mean each and every one of them.

Furthermore, I'm excited to help spread this knowledge far and wide, and to as many people as possible. The low-carb eating plan, with its natural fats, is a lifestyle choice that is very dear to me. In fact, I myself eat according to LCHF dietary guidelines.

Knowledge about carbohydrates, fat, and protein, and how they work in the human body, has allowed me to finally get off the well-worn yo-yo dieter's track (which was keeping me overweight), to become the healthy, happy, and weight-stable girl I am today. Perhaps not "girl"—I'm not really sure what to call myself. In any case, this is forty-seven-year old Anna speaking.

The three nutritional building blocks (carbohydrates, fat, and protein) are what piqued my interest at the beginning. Later, it became more important for me to understand the actual balance and relationship between these macronutrients in our diet. How much of each are we supposed to eat? What are healthy foods to choose, and what does a nutritionally sound plate look like? It seems that, thanks to our current knowledge and experience, we now have a solid dietary foundation that can be adjusted to most of our individual needs, goals, and preferences.

Today even the smaller details attract my curiosity—the micronutrients such as vitamins, minerals, and antioxidants. Unfortunately, we sometimes overlook them while we're stuck in our hunt for carbohydrates. But these small details are critical if you want to feel your best, and they happen to be an integral part of Birgitta's recipes. She not only creates the tastiest dishes around, she even manages to include all those good-for-you nutrients in a varied, simple, and natural way—as it should be.

Are you ready? If so, follow me on a short tour to discover the world of our foods' tinier components.

Vitamins

Do you know what a vitamin is? The simplest way to define a vitamin is to say that it's a critical, life-sustaining organic compound that we must obtain through eating food, because we are unable make it ourselves. It is a nutrient that is not a carbohydrate, a fat, or a protein. A vitamin isn't a mineral, either. Vitamins are in fact a group of many different compounds that are collected under a single umbrella term. They can be—and often are—very different from one another.

For example, vitamin D is a hormone, whereas vitamin C and E are also antioxidants. Vitamins can be divided into two groups: water-soluble and fat-soluble. In addition, if you take too many of some vitamins, you run the risk of overdosing, while you can ingest other vitamins in virtually any amount since their toxicity levels are very low.

Minerals

In the next category of micronutrients are the minerals, which are to my mind almost more important than vitamins. It seems that lack of minerals is a more common problem than vitamin deficiency, yet it's still not highlighted to the same extent. Minerals are elements found in the periodic table—the one featured in chemistry class. Trace elements are the same as minerals, and are so-called because we need them in such small amounts. But I'm not going to nitpick here—I will just call them all minerals.

Iron, magnesium, and calcium are examples of minerals. They each play different roles in the body; keep in mind that they have multiple purposes, too, not merely one. What's more, they often work in symbiosis with one another, i.e. calcium helps you tighten your muscles, while magnesium helps them relax. The balance between the two minerals is very important.

Antioxidants

As their name indicates, antioxidants work against oxidation, which is damage inflicted by certain types of oxygen and nitrogen molecules. Other expressions for oxidation are rusting, aging, and going rancid. By consuming antioxidants, we slow down the rate at which oxidation takes place, and in some cases we can prevent it from happening altogether. A healthy body can live to between eighty and one hundred years if it ages normally. The body is amazing: it can produce antioxidants by itself, but with today's stress—whether due to environmental factors or chronic worry—it's not a bad idea to give the body a helping hand. When it's so easy and tastes so good, why not?

Certain vitamins and minerals are capable of fighting oxidation. Selenium is a very important mineral that is also a powerful antioxidant. Selenium belongs to the body's arsenal of natural defenses against cancer.

There are a lot of other elements besides vitamins and minerals that behave like antioxidants. You've surely heard of the benefits of green tea, as well as the healthful properties of colorful leafy vegetables, berries, and cacao. But, you can also find a lot of antioxidants in mushrooms, spices, and herbs.

So is it really that difficult to eat right? It does feel like a big science project to gather all the different elements onto one plate. How did things get so difficult? How did people manage to survive at all before all this information came to light?

Well, earlier on we simply ate what was good for us, we listened to our bodies, and we learned from experience. We ate to feel our best according to our needs and capabilities.

Then nutritional advice came along that turned our concepts about food on their head. We removed much of what was nutritious out of our food—such as fat, for example, which ended up causing a vitamin D deficiency in many people. We increased our food options, but with foods that decreased our ability to absorb certain minerals. Foods that hamper our ability to absorb minerals tend to contain flour, which in turn contains gluten and other lectins. If we choose to eat whole grains, we also end up ingesting phytates, which hinder the body's ability to absorb enough vitally important minerals.

You who are reading this book have probably already corrected these mistakes, and are now eating natural fats and a diet free of flour, gluten, and whole grains. However, many among the low-carb devotees have focused primarily on eliminating carbohydrates from their diets, and have forgotten that we need all these other small, critically necessary elements in our food. Many of them are building blocks essential for energy, happiness, and calm, as well as a fully functional body, and many of them can be found in foods that also contain carbohydrates. In fact, many nutrients can only be found in those types of foods, at least in appropriately beneficial amounts.

So we have to approach this matter from two perspectives: what nutrients are we most lacking in, and where do we find them? Then we turn it around and ask: where do we find all the nutrients in the food we eat to stay healthy? This is not a complete overview of nutrition, of course, but it is a start, and also a quick reference, on a topic that touches most of us.

Selenium and Iodine

Selenium and iodine go hand in hand; they are critically important for our metabolism. The thyroid produces its hormones from selenium and iodine, and if there's too little of them, you won't generate enough hormones to stay in good health. Where do we find selenium and iodine? You'll find them primarily in shellfish. Sadly, we eat less and less of it in our daily diet. Honestly, how many times do you eat shellfish per week? My guess is that it's seldom enough that I recommend you boost your intake of this important food.

What if you're allergic to shellfish? You can find selenium in Brazil nuts—two to four nuts per day is enough. You'll find iodine in iodine-enriched salt, or in seaweed at the health food store.

Folic Acid

Folic acid is also known as vitamin B9, and it is present in a variety of food. If this is the case, how can we be lacking in folic acid? The problem is that it's heat-sensitive and water-soluble, so it's often destroyed through the process of cooking. When we consume meat (or to be more accurate, the meat's protein) our bodies produce homocysteine. Homocysteine is responsible for blood clots, and as such it is more and more associated with coronary disease. How is this possible, since we've always eaten meat and it is a natural food for us? Well, it still is, so don't stop eating meat; just make sure you're getting enough folic acid, or vitamin B9.

That's not the end of it, though, and it's such a clever set up: meat contains vitamins B6, B9, and B12, all of which remove homocysteine from the body, which is a good thing. However, don't forget that folic acid is heat-sensitive, and some of it is destroyed during the cooking process—especially nowadays when we fry our meat in slices, instead of serving whole roasts as we did in the past. So where else can we get folic acid, or vitamin B9? We can find it in dark green, leafy vegetables such as broccoli, arugula, and spinach. Including leafy greens in our diet is a very smart tactic if we want to stay healthy as long as possible.

Another important point to remember about folic acid is that it is a precursor to serotonin. Serotonin is a neurotransmitter that strongly influences our feeling of wellbeing, and by extension our eating habits, so folic acid is a nutrient we should take care to always get enough of.

Magnesium

Magnesium is a bit of a troublesome element. First of all, it does an enormous amount of good in the body, and has a hand in many things. It influences how we feel, as a lack of it will make our muscles cramp; it affects the nutritional uptake of our intestines; and it is a friend to calcium.

What I think can lead to some confusion here is that the telltale signs of magnesium deficiency are often similar to the signs of a lack of vitamin D. This means that many people supplement their diet with vitamin D when they should be boosting their levels of magnesium instead.

Many magnesium supplements on the market do not work. Getting adequate magnesium through food is always the best choice, but some people still need supplements. So if you need to buy magnesium as a supplement, avoid magnesium oxide, magnesium hydroxide, or magnesium carbonate, as their bioavailability is inferior. That last word, "availability," indicates how accessible magnesium is to the body; it can only be beneficial to the body if it's easily accessible. All other combinations are good!

Your body doesn't absorb what you put in your mouth; it gets what it can and has time to absorb from your intestines.

A lack of magnesium is often manifested through fatigue, feeling out of sorts, and muscle cramps, especially in the legs. The best food sources for magnesium are almonds, pumpkin seeds, cacao powder, Brazil nuts, and basil.

Vitamin D

Vitamin D deficiency is very common in people who follow nutrition advice that emphasizes low-fat diets; research has borne this out. I doubt that anyone who has been eating fat for many years lacks vitamin D. Fatty foods are rich in vitamin D, which in turn requires fat to be properly absorbed by the body.

You can quite easily recognize vitamin D deficiency yourself. Symptoms can include depression, listlessness, pain, and infections; if you take supplements, your symptoms will disappear once your level of vitamin D is back to normal. If they don't disappear, however, some other cause is likely at the root of your fatigue and listlessness. If you choose to take supplements, it needs to be vitamin D3.

Good natural sources of vitamin D are: all kinds of fatty fish, such as eel, pike, whitefish, different kinds of herring, and salmon. Vitamin D is also plentiful in mushrooms.

So, what are our top ten food choices? These foods provide us with everything our bodies need!

1. Eggs. They contain every vitamin except vitamin C, and they are a source of perfect protein. If you're lucky enough to have access to hens that have eaten natural chicken feed instead of commercially produced pellets, the eggs will be even better.

2. Shellfish, which is full of nutrient-rich minerals and (very important) selenium and iodine. Mussels, especially green-lipped mussels, contain extra amounts of a unique omega-3 fatty acid that helps keep airways clear and optimizes lung function. But don't concentrate on the green-lipped mussels alone: it's a good thing to make all mussels a staple of your diet.

3. Fish, especially fatty fish (but all fish is good). It contains the right types of omega-3s: EPA and DHA. Vegetable omega-3, also known as ALA (as found in flaxseed oil and food-grade linseed oil) is not the same as the EPA and DHA omega-3s that are found in seafood. We need EPA and DHA.

4. Nuts. I'm always asked "Which nut is the best?" and my answer remains steadfast: "All of them." So mix them to your heart's content. This usually decreases the risk for overeating them, and you'll get all the minerals naturally without having to keep track of what minerals belong to which nut, and in what quantity. Mix them up to make it easy!

5. Dark green vegetables, including all our delicious herbs. Here you'll find folic acid, vitamin B9, and lots of powerful antioxidants as well as vitamin C. So, what to pick? Here are a few examples: spinach, arugula, parsley, basil, rosemary, thyme, lemon balm, nettles, and kale.

6. All types of vegetables, because we need vitamin C, and because we must keep our digestive system in good working order. You'll find water-soluble fiber in vegetables, which is food for the good bacteria in the colon. When they thrive, so do you. Other examples of fiber include whole flaxseed, psyllium seed, and whole psyllium husk, but these do not contain vitamin C.

7. All vegetables in the cabbage family (brassicas). White and red cabbage, cauliflower, and broccoli are the best; research has shown that cabbage has strong cancer-thwarting properties.

8. All types of onions. Onions feature generous amounts of health-giving properties. Some of these have been proven through scientific research, while others belong to the oral tradition and experience. Whatever the case may be, let onions become a natural staple in your food preparation.

9. Spices and herbs! We're talking both fresh and dried herbs here. They contain a lot

of what is good for us. Their main asset is that they're good antioxidants, and the more you include in your dishes, the less you need to know about each of them to get a healthful helping. While all spices and herbs are beneficial, you only need the right occasion to sample them all. Turmeric is unique; it's a good antioxidant, but it also has antibacterial properties and is an effective anti-inflammatory, too. Unfortunately, despite its many excellent qualities, it isn't possible to simply eat turmeric. (Honestly, how appetizing would it be to eat a bright, yellow food that always tastes the same?) So the best health tip I can offer is to spice up your food, and to sample a variety of different herbs and spices each day.

10. Variety! In the past we ate a little from a lot of different sources. Inversely, today most of us eat a lot from very few sources. This makes for a narrow selection of foods in our diet, which in turn puts us at greater risk for nutritional deficiencies. So it follows that the wider variety of food there is in your daily diet, the healthier your diet will be.

Birgitta has created some wonderful recipes here, which also contain all those micronutrients. It's nutrition at its best and most natural!

Enjoy!

All the best,

Anna Hallén

Introduction

It's given me great pleasure to write the book you're now holding in your hands. It is the culmination of a twenty-year dream of writing my very own cookbook. I'm also very happy and grateful to my friend Anna Hallén for sharing her vast knowledge about diet and all its intricate, different nutrients. She explains simply and intelligibly why it is so good for us to eat a diet comprised mainly of natural foods containing fewer carbohydrates and more natural fats.

My own body has been so much healthier and stronger since I decided, four years ago, to exclude all unnecessary carbohydrates (such as sugar and flour) from my daily meals. Instead, I began eating far more vegetables than I had ever done before, and they have proven themselves worthy complements to the varieties of fish and meat, shellfish, and eggs that I now put on my plate. My diet has become so much more varied, and tastes far better without all the different additives that are included in most commercially prepared foods.

Soon after changing my way of eating, I started to write about it in my blog, *Birgitta Höglunds Mat (Birgitta Höglund's Food)*. My budding interest in low-carbohydrate diets made me want to learn more about this lifestyle, as well as about the lives of our predecessors and their nutrition. In books and on the Internet, I sought out information about foods we've been eating since back when we started to evolve into the thinking human beings we are today, foodstuffs we hunted by simple means, or that we fished for and collected along the coastlines where early settlements took root.

That is how I came to learn about a way of eating many call LCHF (Low Carb High Fat), and others call the "Paleo" or "Stone Age" diet.

I prefer to call it, quite simply, natural nutrition, because it is prepared with as few processed ingredients as possible, and, whenever possible, with ingredients that have been raised organically.

I prefer to buy meat that comes from grass-fed animals (domesticated or wild game), and fish that is line-caught and wild, as opposed to trawled or grown in aqua farms. Eggs come from free-range hens. As much as possible, we should ensure that our food animals are raised humanely and allowed to live natural lives.

Nutritionally, there isn't a big difference between the Paleo and LCHF diet models. LCHF includes more dairy products and fewer fruits and root vegetables, while the Paleo diet excludes dairy products and embraces more fruits and root vegetables. Both diets are completely gluten-free.

Preparing and enjoying good food made from natural ingredients has been a lifelong endeavor. I grew up rurally, in the mountainous area of north Dalarna, in Sweden, around fifty years ago. There was a lot of game on our menu, as well as fish, vegetables, wild mushrooms, and berries. This was pure, tasty home cooking with very few additives.

My passion for good, natural nutrition led me to become a chef. I spent eighteen years in different restaurant kitchens, many of them featuring high quality, local produce.

But a chef's work involves a lot of heavy lifting, and after injuring my back I was unable to continue working in restaurants. For many years I needed a walking stick to get around; I also put on weight over the ensuing years and was in constant pain. All this changed for the better, however, as soon as I modified my diet, removed gluten and sugar, and started eating the kind of foods we are all meant to eat, i.e., natural ingredients and plenty of natural fat.

Over these last few years I've been fortunate enough to be able to share my culinary knowledge by writing about food. Together with physician Annika Dahlqvist I have written a book about LCHF cooking specifically for seniors, and have even contributed to several books by Anna Hallén. This past year I helped develop recipes for a restaurant called PriMaten, in Uppsala, Sweden; it's a fast food restaurant where the menu features only gluten-free LCHF/Paleo dishes.

Grilling Through the Ages

Grilling food over an open fire has been part of people's everyday existence since we left our primate relatives behind to proceed down our own evolutionary road. Long ago, small groups of hunter-gatherers congregated around open fires to share the spoils from the hunt. Nowadays, we gather around the grill in our gardens. Naturally, men grilled during the hunt too, a habit that is still evident today considering the keen interest they often still take in being the main cook at the grill.

But as common a sight it is to see men around the grill now, it was just as rare to see a woman in a restaurant kitchen in my day. While I was relatively alone in my occupation as a female chef during the 1980s and '90s, I had a great time and loved my work. So here I am again, entering a world that is still typically male-dominated, this time around the fire, by releasing this book about grilling.

As I've said, this is not a new interest in food; it has been with me since my childhood in the mountains. Food never tasted any better than when eaten by the side of an open fire after fishing, or when it was time to hunt for wild mushroom and pick berries.

My Warmest and Most Heartfelt Thanks Go to: Lennar Collin, my life partner. Without your wholehearted support, there would never have been this book.

Anna Hallén, my dear friend, and mentor in the natural foods, LCHF world.

Micke Eriksson, who adds fantastic life and tastiness to my food with the lens of his camera.

I owe a big thank you to the glassblowers of Storsjöhyttan, the craftsmen and potters at Drejeriet and Gaupa, the textile artists at Frösö Handtryck, and the kitchen boutique Cervera, all of them located in Östersund, Sweden. The organically grown herbs are from Maries Trädgård (Marie's Garden) in Västerkälen, Krokom, Sweden.

Thanks to all of you who so kindly let me use your products! With your help my book has become a thing of beauty.

Tips for Successful Grilling

The art of grilling has been appreciated over the entire span of human evolution. To start off with fresh-caught fish, some fresh shellfish, or a not-always-tender piece of meat, and end up with something that's both tasty and easy to digest, is what has kept us grilling our food over glowing coals or a pit full of red-hot stones.

Adding flavor to our food with herbs, fruits, berries, and natural spices is a very long-held tradition. Enjoying the company of friends as food is being cooked is also a throwback from times around the campfire.

Grilling is one of the most easygoing and casual of our social get-togethers today. But grilling only gets better when it's allowed to take its time, so while the coals turn to embers you can prepare a few good sauces and side dishes to go with the main course. The more dishes that make up a meal, the tastier and more nutritious it'll be, too.

How to Reach the Perfect Grilling Heat

To grill successfully, you need a thin layer of embers that are hot, but not burning. Sadly, many people are in too much of a hurry to cook, so the meat ends up getting scorched by red-hot coals.

I'll share some tips with you here so you and your guests can enjoy foods fresh off the grill as fully as possible.

I prefer to use an ordinary charcoal grill because I prefer the taste it imparts. Otherwise, gas grills are very handy and simple to use; you can select your preferred temperature simply by changing the setting.

If you own a gas grill, I'm sure you're already well versed in how it works, so I will focus instead on charcoal grilling.

To reach perfect grilling temperature, you don't need anything besides a charcoal starter, also called a charcoal chimney. Just tear a few pages out of a newspaper, crumple them into loose balls, and stick them on the underside of the chimney. Place the chimney starter and newspaper on a thin, even bed of charcoal on the grill. Now, fill the chimney with charcoal and all-natural briquettes; I usually place some coals at the bottom (as they light up quicker), add a layer of briquettes, and then fill the rest of the chimney up to the brim with charcoal.

This will give you a mix that's easy to light and that will glow over a long time. Start fire to the newspaper through the small holes at the bottom of the chimney, then wait approximately 15–20 minutes until the coals are bright red. If I'm going to grill a large quantity of food, I'll carefully add another layer of briquettes at the top of the chimney when it is really hot and the coals are starting to sink down into the chimney.

Once the coals are glowing brightly, it's time to slowly and carefully pour them into the grill. At this point the charcoal in the chimney starter will be extremely hot, so make sure that there are no unsupervised children anywhere near the grill. Spread the coals evenly with a long-handled grilling spatula, and let them burn a bit longer until their surface is covered in a layer of grey ash. Then—and not before—it's time to start grilling. Some soaked branches of juniper, sprigs of rosemary and thyme, or smoke chips placed on the grill will add an aromatic and slightly smoky flavor if you grill the food with the lid on.

If you prefer not to use a charcoal chimney, you can opt for several types of electric starters; they also happen to be a more eco-friendly way to get the grill going. This is grilling at its most natural, because you need no chemical starter fluids (which could possibly add an unwelcome tang to the grilled food). If you'd rather have your set-up be even more like an original fire pit, a bed of coal made from charred birch wood is perfect. It takes longer to heat up and requires more tending, but it makes very good embers, and the grilled food tastes fantastic.

When I cook a larger piece of meat, fish, or fowl, I push the coals to the side of the grill (with a spatula or tongs) to make an empty space under which the food will be grilled. This is called indirect heat grilling. By using indirect heat, you significantly reduce the risk of dripping fat starting a fire, and it's easier to avoid overcooking or burning the meat. But keep a spray bottle of water nearby,

to avoid singeing the meat in case the fat does catch alight.

You can also push the coals to one side of the grill so the other half is empty. In this way, the food gets a nicely charred surface directly over the hot embers, and then can be moved over to the empty side to continue cooking at a lower temperature.

Marinades, Glazes, and Rubs

I have purposely chosen to make most of the recipes in this book as simple as possible, to illustrate the fact that you can prepare a quick grilled dinner with fresh ingredients, instead of with pre-marinated, tenderized cuts that are becoming more ubiquitous at the meat counter.

Tenderizing means that the manufacturer injects the meat with a lot of salt water. The salt water bursts the meat fibers, which makes most people believe that the meat is tender. That's why I never buy any pre-marinated pieces of meat anymore: I think they taste more like fish balls than a chicken breast or a rack of pork chops.

In my kitchen, you'll find no artificial smoke flavors, no glazes loaded with sugar, and no rubs, spice mixtures, and grill oils full of glutamate (E621) or other flavor enhancers.

And, I use very few of the hotter varieties of chilies.

Instead, I emphasize the taste of grilled food itself, along with nature's own flavors. Different cold-pressed oils, herbs, spices, wine, berries, fruit, ordinary sea salt, and freshly ground pepper are common ingredients in my recipes.

Each ingredient's own character is allowed to develop and bloom in the meat, fish, shellfish, and fowl, instead of everything tasting uniformly spicy, sweet, smoked, or salty.

Most of the commercially available, bottled marinades and glazes contain large amounts of sugar, and a harmful chemical compound called acrylamide is formed when sugar comes in contact with high heat during the grilling process. So it isn't just that food tastes so much better with homemade marinades, grilled food is considerably healthier, too.

However, it does take a bit longer to infuse meat and fish with adequate flavor when using a homemade marinade, so if you have the time, by all means let the items rest and absorb the delicious flavors for twenty-four to forty-eight hours.

How Long Does It Take to Cook Something on the Grill?

I have made notes in the recipes on the time required to grill different items to my liking. But, perhaps you prefer your meat a little bit more well done, or rare? You'll need to test the recipes to discover your own particular preference.

Most meat tastes better if it's a bit on the rare side, or—according to my personal taste—lightly grilled. Keep in mind that the inner temperature of a food will continue to rise for a while after the meat or fish has been removed from the grill, so take care not to leave anything on the grill for too long.

A meat thermometer is good to have on hand if you're unsure about timing, especially if it's a bigger piece of meat, fowl, or fish. Also, remove the food from the grill and let it rest ten to fifteen minutes under loosely tented foil—this will ensure that your piece of meat will retain most of its juiciness.

Obviously, most food, with the exception of chicken, will be more tender and juicier if cooked at a lower temperature than what is typically recommended in most cookbooks, on the meat thermometer, or in the instructions.

One last thing: remember to remove all ingredients from the fridge so they have time to reach room temperature before they hit the surface of the grill—that way they'll take even less time to cook.

The recipes in the book are meant to serve four, unless stated otherwise.

While the Grill Is Heating Up

Cucumber Boats with Cream Cheese and Smoked Mussels

Smoked mussels make perfect appetizers to pair with a before-dinner drink. They're very quick and easy to prepare. You can get them ready and store them in the refrigerator under plastic wrap until your guests to arrive.

I have chosen a creamy, organic, fresh cream cheese from Castello, as it is easily piped on to the cucumber boats.

You can also make your own cream cheese—it's very simple to do. You'll find my recipe for cream cheese on page 60.

Cucumber Boats with Cream Cheese and Smoked Mussels

- 1 cucumber, preferably hothouse
- 1 tub of organic cream cheese (or homemade cream cheese)
- 1 can of smoked mussels
- parsley for garnish

Cut the cucumber in half length-wise. Scrape out the seeds with a spoon. Cut the cucumber into inch- or inch-and-a-half-long pieces. Take a small slice off the rounded side on the back of the cucumber piece to make it stable on a platter.

Place the cream cheese in a bowl and whip it with an electric beater until soft and airy. Fill a piping bag fitted with a wide tip. Pipe a rosette of cheese into the hollow side of the cucumber piece.

If you don't have a piping bag, make small eggs of cheese by using a teaspoon dipped in warm water. Leave the mussels to drain in a sieve, and then place one atop each cucumber boat. Garnish with a small sprig of parsley.

Seed Crackers and Spicy-Hot Nuts

Seed crackers, a creamy dip, and my hot and spicy nuts can convert even the biggest snack hound to LCHF.

Seed Crackers

- 1 cup + 1 tablespoon water (250 ml)
- 3½ tablespoons (50 ml) unflavored coconut oil
- 7 tablespoons (100 ml) sunflower seeds
- 7 tablespoons (100 ml) sesame seeds
- 3½ tablespoons (50 ml) flax seeds
- 3 tablespoons unflavored, whole psyllium husk*
- 2 tablespoons fresh thyme, oregano, or chives, finely chopped
- a pinch (1 ml) of cayenne pepper
- ½ teaspoon crushed salt flakes (for example, Maldon Salt Flakes), for dusting the crackers

*Unflavored whole psyllium husk can be found at health food stores or online at netrition.com or iHerb.com.

Preheat the oven to 300°F (150°C). Line a baking sheet with parchment paper.

Pour water and coconut oil in a saucepan and bring to a boil. Meanwhile, mix the dry ingredients (except salt) in a bowl. Pour the boiling water and oil mix over the dry ingredients and mix well. Taste and adjust seasoning if needed. Leave the batter to rest for 5 minutes.

Pour the batter onto the parchment paper on the baking sheet. Place plastic wrap or parchment paper on top of the batter, and roll the batter out in a thin layer with a rolling pin to cover the entire surface of the baking sheet, minimum measurement being 13" x 17" (33 x 43 cm).

Sprinkle the salt flakes evenly over the batter. Bake the batter at 300°F for 45 minutes. Lower the temperature to 125°F (50°C) and leave the crackers to dry for about 2 hours. Let the cooked batter cool and break into uneven pieces. Keep the crackers in a tin with a lid in the pantry; they should keep for a long time.

Dip with Ajvar Relish

- 3⅓ fl. oz. (100 ml) mayonnaise (see recipe on page 42)
- 3⅓ fl. oz. (100 ml) crème fraîche
- 3⅓ fl. oz. (100 ml) Ajvar (or smoked bell pepper) relish, mild or spicy
- 1 teaspoon organic garlic powder
- ¼ teaspoon (1 ml) Worcestershire sauce
- a pinch of salt

Mix all ingredients for the dip and adjust seasoning to taste. Chill.

Hot and Spicy Nuts

- 10 oz. mixed nuts (Brazil nuts, walnuts, and cashews, for example)
- 1 tablespoon coconut oil
- 1 teaspoon paprika
- ¼ teaspoon (1 ml) ground cumin
- ¼ teaspoon (1 ml) cayenne
- 2 teaspoons salt flakes

Roast the nuts in a dry skillet for a few minutes. Mix in coconut oil and spices, crush and sprinkle in the salt flakes. Stir-fry for one minute and mix well.

Gazpacho with Parmesan Crackers

My gazpacho is more nutritious with the inclusion of almond meal, which is how I ate it on the Spanish island of Gran Canaria. Parmesan cheese crackers (try using the special cheese from the Swedish northern province of Västerbotten, if you can find it) make the soup an even better starter course for those of us who eat LCHF.

Gazpacho

- 2 tomatoes
- 1 small cucumber
- 1 green bell pepper
- 1 shallot
- 2 cloves garlic
- 1¼ cups (300 ml) tomato juice
- 7 tablespoons (100 ml) almond flour
- 3⅓ fl. oz. (100 ml) olive oil, cold pressed
- 3 tablespoons apple cider vinegar
- ½ teaspoon (2 ml) salt
- ½ teaspoon (2 ml) cayenne pepper

Cut a cross into the top of the tomatoes. Submerge them in boiling water for one minute. Remove them from the boiling water and rinse them in cold water to stop the cooking. Peel the blanched tomatoes, cut them in half, and seed them. Chop the tomatoes into small dice.

Cut the cucumber, bell pepper, shallot, and garlic into evenly sized dice. Place half of the vegetables in a blender, and pour in the tomato juice, almond flour, olive oil, apple cider vinegar, and spices.

Process until smooth, and adjust the spices if you prefer more heat, or more tang with added vinegar. Divide the rest of the diced vegetables into small cups or glasses. Top with gazpacho.

Parmesan Crackers

- 7 tablespoons pumpkin seeds
- 3½ tablespoons sesame seeds
- 1 teaspoon unflavored whole psyllium husk*
- 3 oz. (200 ml) Parmesan cheese (or Västerbotten), grated
- 1¾ fl. oz. (50 ml) water
- salt flakes

*Unflavored whole psyllium husk can be found at health food stores or online at netrition.com or iHerb.com.

Preheat the oven to 435°F (225°C). Line a baking sheet with parchment paper. Mix pumpkin seeds, sesame seeds, and psyllium husk in a bowl. Mix in the grated cheese and water. Blend thoroughly with an electric mixer. Let the batter sit for 10 minutes.

Make small round balls from the batter. I managed to make fifteen out of this batter. Place them on the parchment-paper-lined baking sheet, taking care to leave some space between the balls, as they will spread when they bake.

Bake 12–15 minutes at 435°F. Let cool on rack.

Hot and Spicy Shrimp Kebabs

A quick and tasty appetizer of large shrimp marinated overnight in a spicy sauce and served with homemade mayonnaise.

The shrimp will only quickly touch the embers— just enough to heat them through but not enough to dry them out.

Place the skewered shrimp in a grilling tray or basket and hold them just above the glowing coals; at this point the coals are still too hot to cook the main dish.

Hot and Spicy Shrimps Kebabs

- 2 inches (5 cm) fresh ginger root
- 2 cloves of garlic
- 1 fresh red chili
- 1 organic lime
- ¼ cup (50 ml) mild olive oil, cold pressed
- 1 teaspoon salt
- 2 lbs (800 g) cold water shrimp in the shell
- olive oil for grilling

Peel and grate ginger and garlic. Finely chop the chili and include the seeds for really spicy shrimp, or leave them out if you prefer less heat. Wash the lime and grate the peel finely into a bowl. Juice the lime and add the juice to the peel. Mix in the rest of the ingredients, except for the shrimp, until the salt has dissolved completely. Add in the shrimp, and stir until the marinade coats them evenly.

Pour the shrimp and marinade into a plastic bag. Leave the bag on a plate in the refrigerator until the next day. Turn the bag over now and then. Put the shrimp into a sieve to drain, and thread them onto skewers. Brush with olive oil.

Place the skewers on a grilling tray or basket, and grill near the glowing coals for about 30 seconds on each side. Serve the shrimp with a green salad, mayonnaise, and lime wedges.

Set small bowls of water and a wedge of lime next to each placemat so your guests can clean their fingers as they are eating.

Serve the shrimp with mayonnaise or coconut curry mayonnaise (see recipes pages 42 and 44).

Basil-Marinated Scallops

Scallops are another delicious treat to enjoy while you're waiting for the coals to reach the right temperature for the main dish. They're called either sea or bay scallops.

Here the scallops are marinated in basil oil, quickly grilled on skewers, and served with a tangy lime aioli.

Scallop Skewers Marinated in Basil Oil, with Lime Aioli

- ¼ cup cold-pressed olive oil infused with lemon
- 1 bunch of fresh basil
- 1 teaspoon white balsamic vinegar
- ¼ teaspoon salt
- ⅛ teaspoon white pepper
- 16 scallops

Remove the basil leaves from the stalks and place them in a food processor or blender. Add oil, vinegar, and spices. Process until the leaves are finely shredded. Let stand until the next day. Pass the marinade through a fine mesh sieve to remove the leaves.

Place the scallops in a plastic bag and pour in the basil oil, saving a small amount to drizzle over scallops at the table. Close the bag and gently move the scallops around in the bag to coat them evenly with oil.

Leave the scallops on a plate in the refrigerator a few hours. Drain the scallops and thread them onto skewers. I use double skewers to make it easier to turn the slippery seafood on the grill.

Brush the grill with oil. Grill the scallops near the heat for 30 seconds on each side. Season them lightly with some salt flakes.

You'll find the recipe for aioli on page 42. Mix the aioli with finely grated peel and juice from an organic lime. Julienne-cut some basil and scatter it over the skewers upon serving.

Raspberry Lime Spritzer

Beer, cider, and sweet drinks are not compatible with the LCHF diet. However, a spritzer made from dry white wine works well because it is low in carbohydrates.

This is a refreshing summer drink to keep you cool while you wait for the embers to heat up.

White Wine Spritzer with Lime and Raspberries

- 2 cups (500 ml) dry white wine
- a scant 1 cup (200 ml) raspberries
- juice from 1 lime
- ¼ cup (50 ml) leaves of lemon balm
- 1 bottle club soda, 11⅛ fl. oz. (330 ml)

Mix the wine and lime juice with the raspberries and lemon balm in a pitcher. Leave this mix in the refrigerator for a few hours. Top up with club soda and stir lightly before serving.

I froze borage and raspberries in ice cubes. They taste nice and look pretty when added to the drinks.

Sangria

Many of us have enjoyed a glass of fruity sangria while on holiday in Spain. Unfortunately, it's often loaded with sugar from both the fruit and the added sweetened sodas.

My version of sangria has only a tiny bit of natural sweetness provided by an orange and a lemon. The drink derives a pleasantly spicy taste from cinnamon and star anise.

Sangria

- 1 organic orange
- 1 organic lemon
- 2 cups (500 ml) dry red wine
- 6 star anise pods
- 2 cinnamon sticks
- 1 bottle club soda, 11⅛ fl. oz. (330 ml)

Wash the citrus fruit and slice off a few thin slices from both. Cut the slices in half and cover with plastic wrap. Squeeze the rest of the fruit, and mix the fruit juice with the red wine, star anise, and cinnamon.

Place the pitcher of sangria in the refrigerator for a few hours to let the flavors develop.

Add the lemon and orange slices and top up with the club soda and ice. Stir lightly before serving.

Pale Green Summer Drink

Cucumber and lime are the main flavors of this delectable pale green, alcohol-free drink. Many of us who eat LCHF limit our alcohol consumption for weight management and for general health reasons. This drink also gives the green light to those of us at the party holding the car keys.

A few fresh raspberries atop a straw enhance the taste and make the drink doubly attractive. I make this with tonic water, but if you want to avoid all added sugar, substitute with club soda or diet tonic water.

Pale Green Summer Drink
- 1 large hothouse cucumber
- 2 limes
- 2 bottles tonic or club soda, 11⅛ fl. oz. (330 ml) each, sugar-free
- raspberries for garnish

Peel and slice the cucumber, and juice the limes. Mix in a blender until smooth.

Mix the cucumber and lime blend with tonic or club soda in a pitcher. Serve the drink with ice cubes and raspberries on a straw.

Iced Tea with Peppermint

Why not offer your guest a glass of refreshing iced tea while you wait for the grill to heat up? But don't drink the ready-made product sold in cans—it contains lots of added sugar.

My iced tea gets its fresh taste from lemon and peppermint leaves. I use Earl Grey tea, but feel free to choose your favorite blend. The tea bags should steep in cold water to prevent the tea from turning bitter.

Iced Tea with Lemon and Peppermint

- 4¼ cups (1000 ml) cold water
- 5 tea bags
- 4 sprigs peppermint
- juice of 1 lemon

Pour the cold water into a pitcher and add the tea bags. Leave the pitcher in the refrigerator overnight. One hour before serving, add the peppermint sprigs and lemon juice.

Add ice cubes and serve in glasses garnished with a fresh sprig of mint and a slice of lemon hanging over the rim of the glass.

Water Infused with Berries and Herbs

Ice-cold water flavored with a variety of berries and herbs is one of the most refreshing quaffs you can enjoy on a warm summer's day.

The water will absorb a lot of flavor from the berries if you leave it in the refrigerator to infuse. Frozen berries give off more juice, so if you want water with intense taste and color, opt for frozen fruit, or crush a few of the berries before adding them to the bottle.

Do freeze different berries and herbs in ice-cube trays—they look fresh and inviting in glasses and pitchers. And the carbohydrate count is very low in flavored water, especially compared to Italian sodas and pop.

Pick large, nice sprigs of herbs, rinse them well, and put them in a bottle or pitcher. Add to this about ⅓ cup (100 ml) berries, top with water, and leave in the refrigerator to chill overnight.

Here are a few suggestions for flavor combinations:

Lingonberries and rosemary

Black currants and a few young leaves from a black currant bush

Blueberries and lemon thyme

Raspberries and peppermint

Red currants and thyme

Sea buckthorn and lemon verbena

Cloudberry and young birch leaves

Cherries and lemon balm

Gooseberries and lavender

Tasty Spreads and Sauces

Mayonnaise and Aioli

It's simple and quick work to make mayonnaise and aioli, especially if you use an immersion blender. When homemade, those sauces are both more nutritious and far better-tasting than anything that you can buy at the store.

To make mayonnaise, I use mild-flavored olive oil. Cold-pressed oils have too strong a taste for this.

Aioli gets its characteristic flavor from olive oil, but I mix in some mild olive oil to make it mellower. These sauces keep for at least a week in the refrigerator.

Mayonnaise

- 2 organic egg yolks
- 1½ teaspoons unsweetened mustard
- 1 teaspoon white balsamic vinegar
- 6¾ fl. oz. (200 ml) mild-flavored olive oil
- ⅛–¼ teaspoon salt
- freshly ground white pepper
- a few drops of Worcestershire sauce

Mix egg yolks, mustard, vinegar, and salt with the immersion blender in a narrow bowl with high sides. Add in the oil very gradually, drop per drop at first, and then drizzle in a fine stream. Blend continuously.

Once the mayonnaise starts to thicken, you can add in the oil in larger quantities. Work up and down the bowl to make sure everything is thoroughly blended. Season with white pepper and Worcestershire sauce. Taste and adjust seasoning if you feel that more vinegar or salt is needed. Put the mayonnaise in a jar with a tight-fitting lid.

Aioli

- 3 cloves garlic
- ¼–½ teaspoon salt
- 3 organic egg yolks
- 5 fl. oz. (150 ml) cold-pressed olive oil
- 5 fl. oz. (150 ml) mild olive oil
- juice of ½ lemon

Grate the garlic very finely, and mix it with ¼ teaspoon salt and the egg yolks in a narrow bowl with high sides.

Add in the oil drop by drop at first, and then drizzle in a fine stream. Blend thoroughly. This is easily done with an immersion blender, but a handheld electric mixer works well, too. Season with lemon and perhaps some more salt, for a pleasant contrast between salty and tangy.

Before serving, leave the aioli in the refrigerator for an hour or so to allow the flavors to develop.

Coconut Curry Mayonnaise

Coconut cream is delicious and also a very good alternative to crème fraîche, if for some reason you wish to limit your intake of dairy products.

This rich and smooth cream is sold in small packages under the name coconut cream. But if you're unable to find this product, the creamy top layer in a can of coconut milk will do the job just as well.

Coconut Mayonnaise with Curry

- 3⅓ fl. oz. (100 ml) coconut cream, room temperature
- 3⅓ fl. oz. (100 ml) mayonnaise (see recipe page 42)
- juice of ½ lime
- 1–2 teaspoons curry powder
- salt

Mix the coconut cream and mayonnaise thoroughly for an even texture; season with lime juice and curry powder (to taste), and a pinch of salt.

Leave the mixture at room temperature for a little while to give the flavors time to develop. Store the mayonnaise in the refrigerator, but let it come to room temperature before serving.

Blueberry and Nettle Pesto

A classical Italian pesto made from olive oil, basil, Parmesan, and pine nuts complements many dishes of grilled fish, meat, fowl, or vegetables.

Here I've made two Nordic variations on this nutritious sauce, using ingredients you may be able to pick for free out in the woods. Use gloves when picking nettle shoots to avoid being stung. If you can't find nettles, you can substitute baby spinach.

Both sauces are freezer friendly if you happen to make larger quantities; this way you can defrost a container at any time and enjoy a taste of summer throughout the year.

Blueberry Pesto

- 4½ oz. (200 ml) blueberries
- 1½ oz. (100 ml) Parmesan (or Swedish Västerbotten) cheese, finely grated
- 1⅓ oz. (100 ml) hazelnut flour
- 1 bunch parsley
- 1 bunch lemon balm
- 1 teaspoon white balsamic vinegar
- about ¼ teaspoon salt
- 3⅓ oz. (100 ml) cold-pressed olive oil

Place all ingredients except the oil in a food processor. Process the ingredients to a paste. Pour in the oil in an even stream while running the processor at full speed so that everything is thoroughly mixed.

Taste to see if you need to add additional vinegar or salt. Transfer the pesto to small jars and keep them in the refrigerator (the pesto will keep for a few weeks). Let the sauce come to room temperature for a bit before serving it to allow the full flavor of the sauce to develop.

Nettle Pesto

- 2 cups (500 ml) young nettle leaves or shoots (or baby spinach)
- ⅞ cup (200 ml) Italian parsley
- a scant ½ cup (100 ml) basil leaves
- 7 tablespoons (100 ml) pumpkin seeds
- 3⅓ oz. (100 ml), aged Präst cheese (or Havarti)
- about ¼ teaspoon (1 ml) black pepper
- about ¼ teaspoon salt
- 3⅓ oz. (100 ml) cold-pressed olive oil

Parboil the nettles in boiling, salted water for 2 minutes. Drain off the water, but save it and use it to make stock for a soup later. If using baby spinach, you don't need to parboil it.

Place the nettles (or baby spinach) together with herbs, pumpkin seeds, cheese, and spices in the bowl of a food processor. Mix the ingredients until all the herbs have been chopped finely, and then add the oil in a thin stream through the feeder tube. Taste to adjust for salt. Keep the pesto in the refrigerator, but let it come back to room temperature before serving to let the olive oil become liquid again.

Nettle pesto keeps for a few weeks in the refrigerator, but make sure that it's completely covered by olive oil to stop any air from getting to it.

Sea Buckthorn Mayonnaise

The sea buckthorn berry has recently become very popular; that's not surprising since it's very tasty and beautiful, as well as extremely nutritious.

This berry contains high levels of omega-7 fatty acids, which are good for preventing skin problems. Its mineral and vitamin content is also high.

The sea buckthorn grows wild along big stretches of the Swedish coastline. It's sometimes called the Nordic passion fruit because of its intense flavor. It's a very simple sauce to put together, and it's very aromatic thanks to the tartness of the berries. If you can't find sea buckthorn berries, substitute pomegranate seeds.

Sea Buckthorn Mayonnaise

- a scant ½ cup frozen sea buckthorn berries (or pomegranate seeds)
- 5 fl. oz. (150 ml) mayonnaise (see recipe page 42)
- crumbled salt flakes

Mash the berries with a fork in a bowl to extract all their juice. Mix with the mayonnaise. Season with some salt flakes.

Leave the sauce in the refrigerator so that its flavor blooms. Serve the sauce with grilled fish, shellfish, or chicken.

Avocado Salsa

The avocado is the fruit with the highest concentration of fat. Even if you consider it a vegetable, it really belongs in the fruit family. So when you hear the recommendation to eat a lot of fruit and green vegetables, well, this is one of the best choices you can make.

If you only use half an avocado, the other half will stay unblemished in the refrigerator much longer if you leave in the pit.

Fresh cilantro has a very special aromatic taste. Start with a smaller amount of it, and keep sampling the salsa until you reach what you feel is the right amount. Even those who feel a bit ambivalent about cilantro usually enjoy this salsa.

Avocado Salsa

- 2 ripe avocados
- 10 cherry tomatoes
- juice of ½ lemon
- 2 tablespoons cold-pressed olive oil
- 1–2 tablespoons fresh cilantro, coarsely chopped
- about 1 teaspoon crumbled salt flakes
- about ¼ teaspoon white pepper

Cut the avocados in half and remove their pits. Chop the avocado flesh into cubes, and cut each tomato into four pieces.

Place everything in a bowl and pour in the lemon juice, olive oil, the chopped cilantro, and spices. Mix carefully so the avocado pieces don't get mashed.

If you need to store the salsa for a short while, add the seeds back to the salsa to prevent it from quickly becoming discolored and turning brown.

Canarian Mojo Sauce

This highly flavorful sauce is very popular on the Spanish island of Gran Canaria, where it's often served alongside tapas. This one includes almond flour and is my favorite among the different varieties.

Mojo sauce is a delicious accompaniment to different grilled dishes, and makes a fine dip for vegetable sticks and seed crackers (recipe for seed crackers on page 22).

Canarian Mojo Sauce

- 1 red bell pepper
- 1 yellow bell pepper
- 2 large garlic cloves
- 3⅓ fl. oz. (100 ml) + 3⅓ fl. oz. (100 ml) cold-pressed olive oil, separated
- 1 tablespoon red chili pepper, seeded and finely chopped
- 2 teaspoons dried coriander seeds, finely crushed
- 1½ teaspoons white balsamic vinegar
- about ½–1 teaspoon salt
- 7 tablespoons (100 ml) almond flour

Cut the bell peppers into smaller segments, and finely chop the garlic cloves. Heat 3⅓ fl. oz. (100 ml) olive oil in a sauté pan.

Add the chopped vegetables and the chili to the sauté pan; season with coriander, vinegar, and salt. Let the vegetables brown slightly, and then let them simmer for half an hour, stirring occasionally. Keep an eye on the pan so the contents don't scorch.

Place the bell peppers in a food processor and blend until smooth. Add in the almond flour and remaining olive oil, and process in a few more short bursts. Adjust the seasonings if the sauce needs more salt or vinegar.

Keep the sauce refrigerated—it'll be fine for a few weeks—but bring it to room temperature before serving.

Tzatziki

Tzatziki is one of the classic sauces on a summer buffet table by the grill—a delicious gustatory memory from a vacation in Greece, maybe? Whatever the case, it's a sauce that's easy to prepare that goes well with meat and fish.

I mix Greek yogurt with crème fraîche (or Smetana for a Nordic taste) to get a higher percentage of fat and to give it a creamier texture. Use the larger quantity of garlic if you want tzatziki with more bite. Finely chopped dill or mint makes a nice contrast.

Greek Tzatziki

- 1 hothouse cucumber
- 2–4 garlic cloves
- 1 teaspoon salt
- 3⅓ fl. oz. (100 ml) Greek yogurt (10% or full fat)
- 3⅓ fl. oz. (100 ml) crème fraîche (or Smetana)
- 2 tablespoons cold-pressed olive oil
- 1 teaspoons lemon juice
- black pepper
- dill and/or mint, finely chopped (optional)

Coarsely grate the cucumber, press the garlic, and mix the two with salt in a bowl. Leave for 30 minutes. Meanwhile, stir together the yogurt, crème fraîche (or Smetana), olive oil, lemon juice, and pepper.

In a sieve, press the cucumber and garlic to remove the excess liquid, and then add it to the yogurt mix. Taste and adjust for salt, if needed.

Turkish Carrot Sauté

The inspiration for this appetizing sauté comes from the Turkish kitchen. In Turkey, it's often served on the meze buffet table among other small appetizers.

Carrots have a higher carbohydrate content than the other vegetables in this book. But with the addition of butter, which draws out the fat-soluble vitamins in carrots, this becomes a very nutritious and satisfying side dish.

This mix goes well with both fish and meat.

Turkish Carrot Sauté

- 2 large carrots
- 4 oz. (100 g) butter
- ½–1 teaspoon salt
- ¼ teaspoon cayenne pepper
- ¼ cup (50 ml) Turkish yogurt
- ¼ cup (50 ml) crème fraîche (or Smetana)

Peel and grate the carrots coarsely. Melt the butter in a sauté pan and add the grated carrots. Season the carrots with salt and cayenne. Let the carrots cook in the butter until softened, about 10 minutes, stirring occasionally.

Remove from the carrots from the heat and stir in yogurt and crème fraîche (or Smetana). Taste and adjust the seasonings if needed. The sauté can be served as is or blended with an immersion blender until smooth. It is best enjoyed lukewarm.

Sorrel Dressing and Vinaigrette

To walk in nature and forage for fresh ingredients for cooking and eating is a luxury we really enjoy here in the Nordic countries. Just make sure that what you pick grows far away from busy roads so it will be free from pollution, and tasty.

I always snack on sorrel leaves during my walks in the woods—their fresh tang is especially nice in very early summer. Don't miss the opportunity to pick and freeze them for later; that way you can then enjoy a delicious green dressing any time of the year.

The other salad dressing is a richer variation on a French vinaigrette, which is typically made from three parts olive oil to one part red wine vinegar, seasoned with salt, pepper, and occasionally a dab of Dijon mustard.

Here I've used cold-pressed, lemon-infused avocado oil and some fine, dark balsamic vinegar. Dressing enhances both the taste and nutritional value of a green salad; it makes a great difference from just eating the leaves plain.

Sorrel Dressing

- 1¼ cup (300 ml) tender sorrel leaves
- juice from ½ lemon
- 2 teaspoons white balsamic vinegar
- ¼ teaspoon salt
- 6¾ fl. oz. (200 ml) mild, cold-pressed olive oil

Rinse the sorrel leaves and remove the stalks. Place them in the bowl of a food processor and add lemon juice, vinegar, and salt. Process until the leaves are finely shredded.

Pour the oil carefully through the tube feeder while continuing to process. Keep blending until you have an intensely green dressing, and then let it stand for a while to let the flavors develop. Pour the dressing through a fine-mesh sieve to remove the leaves, and store it in the refrigerator. Let it come to room temperature before serving so the olive oil returns to liquid.

Vinaigrette with Avocado Oil and Balsamic Vinegar

- 3 tablespoons cold-pressed avocado oil, infused with lemon
- 1 tablespoon best-quality, dark balsamic vinegar
- pinch of salt
- pinch of coarsely ground black pepper

Mix oil and vinegar with the spices. Taste and adjust seasoning if needed. Pour the dressing into a small bottle with a cork stopper (this will make it easier to shake the bottle before adding the dressing to the salad). This dressing keeps for a long time at room temperature.

Fresh Cream Cheese with Capers

This spread is delicious alongside fish, or as a dip with vegetable sticks and seed crackers (see recipe page 22).

It also makes an excellent spread for Parmesan crackers (see recipe on page 24).

This spread is best made from a natural cheese — you'll get the best taste using a fresh cheese made from tangy and fat-cultured mountain milk. If you can't find this at your local store, you can use full-fat cultured milk (or buttermilk or yogurt) instead.

You can vary the flavors in many ways by, for example, using grated horseradish, chives, garlic, chili, cumin, olives, walnuts, or black pepper.

Fresh Cheese from Cultured Milk
- 2 cups (500 ml) cultured (filmjölk) milk (or buttermilk or yogurt)
- ¼ cup crème fraîche
- salt to taste

Heat the milk to 122°F (50°C) while stirring. Pour the milk into a coffee filter, and let it drain, resting overnight in the refrigerator.

Pour the cheese into a bowl, stir in the crème fraîche, and season with salt.

Fresh Cheese Spread with Capers and Dill
- 5 fl. oz. (150 ml) homemade cheese, or 1 jar organic cream cheese
- 1 tablespoon capers, finely chopped
- 1 tablespoon dill, finely chopped
- 1 teaspoon mild olive oil infused with lemon
- salt and pepper

Mix all ingredients, except salt and pepper, in a bowl. Mix thoroughly with a wooden spoon or an electric whisk until you have a smooth spread.

Season it with salt and pepper. Go easy on the salt, as capers are already salty.

Form small egg shapes with a spoon dipped in warm water.

Rhubarb Chutney

Most chutney recipes contain a lot of sugar, but mine are naturally sweet from the fruit.

I have used rhubarb, pear, and apple in my recipes, but it's also delicious with cherries, melon, mango, or pineapple. The fruit adds a lot of flavor and some sweetness. If you're very sensitive to sugar, simply decrease the amount of fruit you use to your own preference.

If you serve a spicy butter or butter sauce with this chutney, the carbohydrate content will stay pretty low overall.

Rhubarb Chutney

- 8¾ oz. (250 g) rhubarb
- 1 shallot
- 2 tablespoons water
- ½ tablespoon acetic acid (spirit vinegar), 12% acidity
- 1 tablespoon chili pepper, finely julienned
- 1 tablespoon fresh ginger, grated
- 1 teaspoon curry powder
- ½ teaspoon salt
- 3½–7 oz. (100–200 g) ripe pear
- 1 tablespoon lime juice

Cut the rhubarb into thin slices and finely chop the shallot. Bring it all to a boil in a saucepan with the water and spirit vinegar. Let simmer for 10 minutes until the rhubarb is soft.

Stir in the chili, ginger, curry powder, and salt. Let simmer over low heat for 20 minutes, stirring occasionally to prevent the mixture from burning.

Peel and cut the pear into small chunks, add it to the saucepan together with the lime juice, and let it come to a boil. Remove from the heat and pour into warm, thoroughly sanitized jars. The chutney will last about a week in the refrigerator. It also freezes well if you want to make a larger batch.

Bell Pepper Chutney with Apple and Pink Peppercorns

- 1 yellow bell pepper
- 1 tablespoon yellow chili pepper
- ½–1 green, tart apple
- 2 inches (5 cm) of the white part of a leek
- 2 tablespoons mild-flavored olive oil infused with lemon
- 1 tablespoon pink peppercorns
- ½ tablespoon apple cider vinegar
- ¼ teaspoon salt

Seed the bell pepper and chili pepper, and dice them finely. Peel the apple, and along with the white section of the leek chop it into small, equally sized dice. Quickly fry the peppers, apple, and leek in the oil and let cook over low heat for 10 minutes, or until the mixture has softened.

Stir in the pink peppercorns, vinegar, and season with salt. Bring the chutney to a boil, and then transfer to warm, dry jars. Screw the lids on tightly and store them in the refrigerator.

Spiced Béarnaise and Chili Hollandaise

Classic butter sauces can make a marvel out of the simplest grilled offering. Here, the sauces' seasonings have been slightly updated.

Reduction for the Béarnaise Sauce

- 2 tablespoons white wine vinegar
- 2 tablespoons water
- 1 tablespoons yellow onion, finely chopped
- 5 whole white peppercorns
- sprigs of parsley

Mix all in a saucepan. Bring to a boil and let the liquid reduce until half is left. Strain through a cheesecloth and pour into a jar.

Spiced Béarnaise Sauce

- 10½ oz. (300 g) butter
- 4 egg yolks
- 2 tablespoons reduction (see preceding recipe)
- 2 tablespoons finely chopped parsley
- 2 tablespoons French tarragon (estragon) in vinegar, chopped (or 1 tablespoon dried tarragon soaked in 1 tablespoon white wine vinegar for a couple hours)
- ½ teaspoon sweet cicely (or dried dill, aniseed, or chives)
- 1–2 teaspoons lemon juice
- a few drops of Worcestershire sauce
- ¼–½ teaspoon salt
- a pinch cayenne pepper

Melt the butter in a saucepan over low heat. Heat some water in another saucepan until simmering, lowering the heat as low as it will go. The water should not boil, as it will be too hot for the yolk mixture.

Mix the yolks with the reduction in a bowl. Place the bowl over the water bath (bain-marie) and whisk until the yolk mixture is as thick as a custard sauce. Make sure the whisk reaches the entire surface of the bottom of the bowl as you're mixing.

Once the mixture has thickened, set the bowl on a dishcloth that's been wrung out in warm water. That way the bowl stands steadily, which makes it easier to whisk.

Pour the yellow clarified butter into a large (4-cup) measuring cup, to make it easier to simultaneously whisk the béarnaise and add the melted butter. Be careful not to add the white sediment at the bottom of the pan.

Pour the butter slowly into the yolk mixture in a thin stream while whisking vigorously. Stir in the chopped herbs, the lemon juice, and the spices. Start with the smaller amount of lemon juice and salt, taste, and adjust the seasonings if needed. Pour the sauce into a sauce bowl or gravy boat, and keep warmed on the side.

If the sauce curdles, start by whisking a new yolk and a teaspoon of water in a bowl over a water-bath. Then add the curdled sauce to this mix gradually, a little bit at a time.

To make my garlic Béarnaise, I season the finished sauce with 1 tablespoon finely minced garlic, 1 tablespoon finely chopped chives, 1 tablespoon finely chopped lemon balm, and 1 tablespoon French mustard.

Chili Hollandaise

- 10½ oz. (300 g) butter
- 4 egg yolks
- ¼–½ teaspoon salt
- 1–2 teaspoons red chili flakes
- 2 tablespoons lemon juice

Melt the butter over low heat. In a stainless steel bowl over a water bath, whisk together the yolks and the lemon juice. Whisk vigorously until the yolks have thickened.

Follow the instructions in the recipe for Béarnaise sauce on how to add the clarified butter to the egg mixture.

Season with salt and chili flakes, and perhaps some added lemon juice. Leave out the chili flakes if you want a classic Hollandaise sauce.

Flavored Butters

Herb butter is wonderful with just about any savory dish. Feta butter is seasoned with Ajvar relish grilled bell pepper spread that can be found in the vegetable aisle of a well-stocked grocery store or ethnic food store.

Café de Paris butter is typically loaded with ingredients. I've made a simpler version here.

Herb Butter with Feta Cheese and Ajvar Relish

- 5¼ oz. (150 g) feta cheese
- 8¾ oz. (250 g) butter, room temperature
- ¼ cup (50 ml) Ajvar (or red pepper) relish
- a pinch of cayenne pepper

Mash the cheese with a fork in a bowl. Add the butter, relish, and cayenne. For best results, whisk thoroughly with a handheld electric mixer.

Fill small bowls with the butter, or roll it into a log and store in the refrigerator or freezer.

Café de Paris Butter

- 2 tablespoons chopped parsley
- 2 tablespoons chopped chives
- 2 tablespoons chopped thyme
- 2 tablespoons chopped French tarragon (estragon)
- 1 tablespoon finely chopped capers
- 1 tablespoon finely chopped shallot
- 1 tablespoon tomato purée
- 1 tablespoon lemon juice
- 1 garlic clove, finely chopped
- ½ tablespoon paprika
- 1 teaspoon Dijon mustard
- 1 teaspoon Worcestershire sauce
- 1 teaspoon ground turmeric
- about ½ teaspoon salt
- ¼ teaspoon cayenne pepper
- ¼ teaspoon ground white pepper
- 2 anchovies filets, cut into smaller pieces
- 17½ oz. (500 g) butter, softened
- 1 egg yolk

Put all ingredients, except butter and yolk, into the bowl of a food processor; mix at full speed until they become a smooth paste. Transfer to a mixing bowl, then mix in the softened butter and egg yolk with an electric handheld mixer until it becomes light and fluffy.

Pipe small roses of the butter or fill small bowls. Store the butter in the refrigerator or freezer, but leave it out a little while before serving to allow the flavor of the herbs to shine through.

Herb Butter with Roasted Garlic

One tasty way to enjoy herb butter is to stuff it in seeded, long, pointy sweet peppers (or larger bell peppers cut into segments).

Remove the stalk and scrape out all the seeds from the pepper with a teaspoon. Cut off a small piece at the end of the pepper to make it easier to fill the entire pepper with butter.

Fill the pepper with softened herb butter using a spoon, or pipe it with a piping bag. Press hard on the butter to make it fill the whole pepper without leaving any air pockets. Leave the peppers in the refrigerator a few hours to chill and solidify. Slice with a sharp knife.

Herb Butter
- 8¾ oz. (250 g) butter
- ⅓–½ cup (100 ml) chopped herbs (parsley, lemon balm, thyme, and/or chives, for example)
- 1 teaspoon dried red chili flakes
- ½ teaspoon Worcestershire sauce
- ¼–½ teaspoon crushed salt flakes

Leave the butter at room temperature to soften. Place the butter in a bowl and add the rest of the ingredients.

Mix the butter until light and fluffy with a handheld electric mixer; then stuff bell peppers or add to small bowls. Make a large batch and keep it in the freezer; the butter will keep a long time.

Pan Roasted Garlic Butter
- 4 large garlic cloves
- 1 tablespoon mild-flavored olive oil
- 1 tablespoon lemon juice
- ¼–½ teaspoon crushed salt flakes
- ¼ teaspoon ground white pepper
- 8¾ oz. (250 g) butter, softened

Peel and chop the garlic into small pieces. Brown the garlic lightly in the olive oil for 4–5 minutes, without letting it get too dark. Squeeze the lemon juice into the pan and let it cook; season with salt and pepper.

Let the garlic cool and then whisk it into the softened butter. Fill peppers as above, or roll the butter into a log in greaseproof paper, as described below.

Place the butter in one long line in the middle of a piece of parchment paper. Fold the paper over one side and use a broad-blade or chef's knife to nudge the butter into the shape of a log. Roll the paper together and twist the ends in the shape of a holiday cracker. Store the log in the refrigerator or freezer. Allow it to come up to room temperature for a little bit before serving, as it will enhance the flavor more than if it's served chilled.

Chili Sauce and BBQ Sauce

Store-bought chili and BBQ sauces often contain lots of added sugar, whereas mine only have the natural sweetness of tomatoes and bell peppers.

These sauces will only keep for about a week since they don't contain any sugar. Freeze what you're not using in small containers to enjoy later.

Chili Sauce

- 1 red chili, finely chopped
- 2 tablespoons butter
- 2 teaspoons paprika
- 1 teaspoon garlic powder
- 1 teaspoon onion powder
- ½ teaspoon ground white pepper
- ¼ teaspoon ground cloves
- 17½ oz. (500 g) canned crushed tomatoes
- 6¾ fl. oz. (200 ml) water
- 2 tablespoons white balsamic vinegar
- 1 teaspoon salt

Cut the chili pepper in half and remove the seeds (leave the seeds in if you prefer a really spicy chili sauce). Heat the butter in a saucepan and add the chili and spices (except the salt). Let this cook lightly for a minute while stirring, to let the flavors develop. Keep a careful watch on this so it doesn't burn.

Add the tomatoes, water, vinegar, and salt. Bring to a boil, reduce the heat, and let it simmer for half an hour, until the sauce has thickened a little. Stir occasionally so the sauce doesn't stick to the bottom of the pan. Turn off the heat and blend with an immersion blender directly in the saucepan. Taste and adjust seasonings if needed.

Pour the sauce into a quart-size measuring cup, and then with a funnel fill very clean, warm bottles or jars with the sauce. Screw the lid on immediately. Store the sauce in the refrigerator or freezer, depending on how often you plan to use the sauce.

BBQ Sauce

- 1 red bell pepper
- 1 red onion
- 2 garlic cloves
- 2 tablespoons coconut oil
- 6¾ fl. oz. (200 ml) tomato juice
- 1 tablespoon Worcestershire sauce
- 1 tablespoon tamari soy sauce
- 1 tablespoon balsamic vinegar
- 1 teaspoon unsweetened mustard
- 1 teaspoon chili flakes
- ½ teaspoon coarsely milled black pepper
- ¼–½ teaspoon salt

Cut the bell pepper into sections, and coarsely chop the onion and garlic. Quickly fry the vegetables in the coconut oil. Add the tomato juice and other ingredients, using the smaller amount of salt at first.

Let the sauce cook down on low heat for half an hour, stirring occasionally. Taste and adjust the seasonings if you prefer more salt or spice.

Marinated Vegetables

Marinating vegetables is a wonderful way of preserving all the best flavors of summer. The tart, spicy chunks of vegetables make a perfect combo with grilled dishes or a salad.

These vegetables are also good as a fresh, green addition to tapas. As long as the vegetables are completely covered in olive oil, they'll keep for several months in the refrigerator.

Garlic-Marinated Baby Portabella Mushrooms

- 8¾ oz. (250 g) baby portabella mushrooms
- 2 garlic cloves
- 1 fresh chili pepper
- 6¾ fl. oz. (200 ml) cold-pressed olive oil
- 1½ tablespoons white balsamic vinegar
- 2 teaspoons salt flakes
- 5 sprigs thyme

Cut each mushroom into quarters. Place the pieces in a saucepan and cover with cold water. Add 1½ teaspoons salt. Bring to a boil and let boil for 5 minutes. Meanwhile, put together the marinade.

Thinly slice the garlic cloves. Cut the chili in half and remove the seeds (or leave the seeds in if you prefer more spice in the marinade).

Stir the olive oil, vinegar, and remaining salt flakes together in a bowl. Add the sprigs of thyme (chopped fine), and add in the chili.

Drain the mushrooms in a colander and then add them, still warm, to the marinade. Stir so everything is thoroughly mixed.

Ladle the vegetables into jars, and make sure the olive oil covers them completely. If it doesn't, add some more oil. You can use any kind of edible mushroom for this marinade.

Pickled Bell Pepper and Garlic

- 2 red sweet, pointy peppers
- 2 yellow sweet, pointy peppers
- 8 garlic cloves
- 1 fresh chili pepper
- 3⅓ fl. oz. (100 ml) water
- 3⅓ fl. oz. (100 ml) apple cider vinegar
- 1 teaspoon salt
- 6¾ fl. oz. (200 ml) cold-pressed olive oil infused with lemon

Remove the seeds and cut the peppers into even, one-inch pieces. Cut the garlic cloves in half length-wise. Cut the chili pepper in half and remove the seeds, or leave the seeds in if you prefer spicier pickles.

Place the vegetables in a saucepan and pour in the water, vinegar, and salt. Bring it to a boil, lower the heat, and let it simmer 20 minutes.

Remove the saucepan from the heat, and let the bell peppers cool in the liquid overnight.

Place the vegetables in a jar, pressing down firmly on them with a ladle. Pour in ¼ cup (50 ml) of cooking liquid and top to cover with olive oil. Screw the lid on tightly, and shake the jar to mix contents thoroughly.

It's important to prevent oxygen from seeping into the jar and destroying the peppers. You may have to add more oil to cover the vegetables completely.

Marinated Oven-Dried Tomatoes

- 17½ oz. (500 g) cherry tomatoes
- 2 garlic cloves
- 2 teaspoons salt flakes
- 2 tablespoons chopped fresh oregano or thyme
- about 6¾ fl. oz. (200 ml) cold-pressed olive oil

Cut the tomatoes in half and place them, cut side up, in an ovenproof pan. Slice the garlic thinly and scatter over the tomatoes.

Sprinkle salt flakes and herbs over the tomatoes and garlic. Oven-dry the contents of the pan at 170°F (75°C) for 6 hours. Put the tomatoes in a jar and cover, while still warm, with olive oil.

Three Gratins

It is said that all good things come in threes. That certainly applies to these gratins, which are flavored with three different kinds of cheeses.

First comes a broccoli gratin, covered in creamy blue cheese.

Gratin number two features many Mediterranean flavors: thin slices of grilled zucchini layered with marinated tomatoes, herbs, garlic, lemon peel, and grated Halloumi cheese. On the island of Cyprus—Halloumi's birthplace—it's common practice to serve grated Halloumi with different types of warm dishes.

Last but not least, a creamy daikon radish gratin. It's similar to a potato gratin in both taste and texture, but has only a tiny amount of carbohydrates compared to the starchy potato.

Broccoli Gratin with Creamy Blue Cheese

- 2 heads of broccoli, approx. 4¼ cups (1000 ml) broccoli florets
- 6¾ fl. oz. (200 ml) crème fraîche
- 6¾ fl. oz. (200 ml) grated blue cheese
- ½ teaspoon grated nutmeg
- ¼ teaspoon salt
- ¼ teaspoon ground white pepper

Cut the broccoli into small florets. Save the stalk in the refrigerator for later use (as a good flavoring for soup stock, for example).

Place the florets in a bowl and mix in the crème fraîche and the grated cheese. Season with nutmeg, salt, and pepper, and mix well. Place the mixture in a large, buttered casserole dish or into individual ovenproof dishes, one per guest. Bake for 30 minutes at 350°F (175°C). The salty creaminess makes this a great side dish for fatty fish, pork, or chicken.

Zucchini Gratin à la Mediterranean

- 14 oz. (400 g) zucchini/summer squash, preferably both green and yellow
- 3⅓ fl. oz. (100 ml) julienned, marinated cherry tomatoes (see recipe page 72)
- 3⅓ fl. oz. (100 ml) julienned leeks
- 2 tablespoons chopped parsley
- 2 tablespoons chopped thyme
- grated peel from 1 organic lemon
- olive oil
- 3½ oz. (100 g) Halloumi cheese, grated
- salt and black pepper

Slice the zucchini into ½-inch thick (1 cm) slices. Salt the slices lightly on each side. Let them sit for 5 minutes to draw out their liquid. Rinse off the salt, and leave them in a colander to drain thoroughly.

While the zucchini is being salted, mix together the tomatoes, leek, herbs, and lemon peel.

Brush the zucchini with olive oil and grill 1 minute on each side; season lightly with black pepper.

Butter a gratin dish and place half of the zucchini in a tile pattern on the bottom of the pan, layering the yellow and green slices.

Spread a layer of the tomato mix over the zucchini, and sprinkle half of the grated Halloumi on top. Continue with the rest of the zucchini, tomato mix, and finish off with the Halloumi.

Bake for 20 minutes at 395°F (200°C). Serve with grilled fowl or fish.

Daikon Gratin with Aged Präst (or Havarti) Cheese

- 17½ oz. (500 g) daikon radish
- 1¼ cup (300 ml) heavy whipping cream
- ½–1 teaspoon salt
- ¼ teaspoon ground white pepper
- 2 shallots
- 2 garlic cloves
- 1¼ cups (300 ml) grated aged Präst (or Havarti) cheese

Peel and slice the daikon radish into quarter-inch (1/2 cm) slices. Place the slices in a saucepan and add the cream, salt, and pepper. Bring to a boil and let simmer for about 10 minutes. Meanwhile, slice the shallots and the garlic; add them to the saucepan and let the mixture cook for 5 minutes more. Taste the contents of the pan and add more salt if needed.

Layer the daikon with the grated cheese in a buttered gratin dish. Finish with a layer of cheese to cover. Bake 10–15 minutes at 395°F (200°C) until golden. This gratin is very good with grilled rib-eye steak, roasted pork belly, or hamburgers.

Faux Potato Salad

Before I adopted the low-carb lifestyle, potato salad was a perennial side dish for any grilled fare on the menu.

Today, I don't miss the carbohydrate-laden white tuber at all, as there are so many other tasty veggie alternatives out there.

The following recipe is my version of a "faux" potato salad, made with lightly fried zucchini/ summer squash. Together with homemade mayonnaise, Smetana (or crème fraîche), onion, and capers, it's even more appetizing than its original incarnation.

Smetana is a cultured heavy cream with a fat content of 42%, originally from Russia. Crème fraîche will work if Smetana is unavailable in your area.

Zucchini Salad

- 1⅔ cups (400 ml) of diced zucchini
- 2 tablespoons butter
- ¼–½ teaspoon salt
- ¼–½ teaspoon freshly ground black pepper
- 2 teaspoons lemon juice

Salad Dressing:

- 3⅓ fl. oz. (100 ml) mayonnaise (see recipe on page 42)
- 3⅓ fl. oz. (100 ml) Smetana (or crème fraîche)

- ¼ cup (50 ml) finely chopped onion
- 2 tablespoons finely chopped parsley
- 2 tablespoons finely chopped dill
- 2 tablespoons capers

Peel and dice the zucchini into ½-inch (1 cm) cubes. Fry them lightly in butter for a few minutes; season with salt, pepper, and lemon juice.

Start off with the smaller amount of salt and pepper, and adjust the seasoning if needed after the salad has been mixed.

While the zucchini cools, mixing the dressing. Then combine the two. Place the salad in the refrigerator for a while to let the flavors develop.

Fish and Shellfish

Herb-Stuffed Brook Trout

My favorite of all seafood dishes is herb-filled brook trout. Its delicate pink flesh has a flavor like no other. I'm very fortunate to have relatives whose fishing rights in the northern mountain rivers of the Swedish province of Jämtland allow me a much-appreciated top up from time to time. Here, I've brushed a large brook trout with melted butter and stuffed it with herbs, salt, and pepper. That's all you need to put a real gourmet dinner on the table.

Although I wouldn't turn down a generous side portion of chanterelle mushrooms, quickly fried in butter, and along with some fresh cheese spread!

Whole Grilled Herb-Stuffed Brook Trout

- 1 large brook trout, weighing about 2 lbs. 10 oz. (1200 g)
- 3½ tablespoons (50 g) melted butter
- 1 bunch lemon balm
- 1 bunch thyme
- 2 teaspoons salt
- ½ teaspoons ground white pepper

Rinse the fish thoroughly inside and out, and dry with paper towels. Brush the whole fish cavity generously with melted butter; season well with salt and some pepper. Stuff the fish with as many herbs as you can fit into its cavity.

Brush both sides of the fish with butter, and season with salt and pepper. Place the fish in a fish basket or holder that has first been greased with butter.

Grill the fish for one minute on each side, near the embers. Then lift the grid a little higher, and grill the fish about 10 minutes more. Turn the basket or holder several times and brush the fish with more butter at each turn. Cover the fish with aluminum foil, and place it beside the embers to let it cook on indirect heat for 5 minutes.

A meat thermometer should read 118.4°F (48°C) when the fish is ready. If you're not using a thermometer, lightly tug the dorsal fin: if it loosens easily, the fish is ready to eat.

Plate the cooked brook trout with fresh herbs and lemon wedges. Serve with chanterelles sautéed in butter, and fresh cheese with dill and capers (see recipe on page 60).

Hot-Smoked Whitefish on the Grill

Hot-smoked fatty fish is delicious grilled over glowing coals; it's amazing, fast food with lots of flavor. Simply let the fish heat through so it stays moist.

I often have whitefish, but other delicious options are brook trout, salmon, rainbow trout, mackerel, or kippers—the latter being the English name for smoked herring.

I think that 6¼ oz. (175 g), skin and bones included, is a good portion of fish per person for an entrée, and 2½ oz. (75 g) is enough for an appetizer.

Cut the fish into portions, or grill it whole. Brush it with mild-flavored olive oil, put it in a fish basket or holder, and grill it over direct heat: 1 minute per side if the fish isn't too thick, otherwise 2 minutes per side.

Here, I serve the freshly grilled whitefish with a tasty sea buckthorn mayonnaise (recipe on page 48), and a chard and pumpkin seed salad.

Cod and Fennel Wrapped in Foil

A good way to prepare a cod filet on the grill—to keep it really moist and flavorful—is to cook it wrapped in foil together with some tasty vegetables.

Cod is a very lean fish, but I've increased the fat content of the dish by adding a generous dab of butter and almonds to the foil packet.

This dish can be served with a bowl of aioli or a big dollop of herb butter to make a truly satisfying meal.

Filet of Cod Baked in Foil with Fennel, Asparagus, and Cilantro

- 1 bunch white asparagus
- 7 tablespoons (100 ml) almonds
- 4 cod filets, 5¼ oz. (150 g) apiece
- ¼–½ teaspoon salt
- ¼ teaspoon ground white pepper
- 3 tablespoons melted butter (for brushing the foil)
- 6¾ fl. oz. (200 ml) julienned fennel
- ¼ cup (50 ml) julienned leek
- ¼ cup (50 ml) coarsely chopped cilantro leaves
- 4 pats of butter (to place on top of the fish)

Break off the woody base of the asparagus spears, and peel the spear from just under the top and down. Cut the asparagus into 1-inch pieces and parboil them in salted water for 2 minutes. Drain well. Cut the almonds in half lengthwise.

Lay out four pieces of heavy-duty foil, each measuring 12 inches x 18 inches (30 cm x 45 cm). Fold the edges in about 1 inch to make them stronger for when the foil is pressed together. Season the fish on both sides with salt and pepper.

Brush melted butter down the middle and on one half of the sheet of foil; place a small mound of julienned fennel, leek, and asparagus on the foil. Salt lightly. Place the fish on top of the vegetables, and scatter almonds and cilantro over the fish. Cut a few slices of butter and lay them on top of the fish. Fold the other half piece of foil up over the fish so that their edges meet. Fold in the three open edges of foil together, a quarter inch at a time, until you're up against the fish.

Set the parcels on the grill, with the grate set a little above the embers. The fish will be ready in 10–12 minutes. You can open a packet of foil after 10 minutes to see if the fish is white and firm. Place the packet on a plate, cut a cross in the foil, and open it up when it's time to serve it.

Serve with aioli (recipe on page 42) or butter.

Fish Skewers Marinated in Saffron

Saffron yellow skewers with salmon and pollock become party fare when paired with creamy chili hollandaise sauce. Here, I've chosen the back piece—it makes nice even cubes to thread on the skewers.

I only have fish on these skewers, because it grills far more quickly than vegetables; they wouldn't have time to cook. If you still want some grilled vegetables to go with this dish, make up a few vegetable skewers with, for example, bell peppers, onion, and mushrooms; make sure to grill those skewers separately from the fish.

Grilled slices of blanched fennel also make a very nice side dish.

Salmon and Pollock Skewers Marinated in Saffron

- 1 teaspoon saffron threads
- 3⅓ fl. oz. (100 ml) mild-tasting olive oil
- 2 tablespoons finely chopped dill
- 2 tablespoons lemon juice
- 10½ oz. (300 g) filet of salmon, preferable wild caught
- 10½ oz. (300 g) filet of pollock
- salt and pepper

Using a mortar and pestle, grind the threads of saffron with a pinch of salt. Mix it with the oil, dill, and lemon juice. Cut the fish into 1-inch (3 cm) cubes. Place the cubes in a plastic bag and pour in the marinade.

Carefully move the cubes around inside the bag to coat the fish evenly with the marinade. Place the bag in a bowl in the refrigerator, and let sit as long as 8–10 hours. Turn the bag over a few times during this time.

Place the fish in a colander and let it drain. Thread the cubes on skewers. Brush the fish and the grill basket or holder with oil. I often use a holder or a basket for grilling fish, because the meat can be more delicate and thus easily fall apart when turned.

Place the skewers in the basket or holder; season with salt and pepper. Grill over direct heat for 2 minutes, turn the basket/holder and finish grilling the skewers 2 more minutes on the other side. Leave the fish a short while over indirect heat to finish cooking it without drying it out.

Sever with chili hollandaise (recipe on page 65).

Serrano Ham–Wrapped Pollock Filets

Pollock belongs to the cod family of fishes, but the flesh is a bit tougher so it's very good for grilling.

As it's a very lean fish, I brushed it with flavored olive oil and wrapped it in Serrano ham.

A garlic béarnaise sauce and radishes sautéed in butter enhance the flavor and fat content of this dish even further.

Filets of Pollock Wrapped in Serrano Ham

- 4 pieces of pollock, 5¼ oz. (150 g) each
- 2 tablespoons cold pressed-olive oil infused with lemon
- 1 teaspoon salt
- ½ teaspoon freshly ground black pepper
- 4 large slices of Serrano ham
- 1 bunch of radishes
- 3 tablespoons butter, browned

Remove the skin from the fish with a filleting knife. Brush the fish filets with olive oil and season with salt and pepper. Wrap the Serrano ham tightly around the filets, and fasten with toothpicks. Now, brush the ham with more oil.

Brush the grates of the grill with a bit of oil. First grill the filets for 1 minute on each side over direct heat. Raise the grate up, and grill the fish on slightly lower heat for about 8 minutes. Turn a few times during this time.

If you want to use a meat thermometer, the fish is ready at 122°F (50°C). Keep in mind the temperature will continue to climb a bit after you've removed the fish from the heat.

Cut a bunch of radishes in half lengthwise, and sauté them for a minute in 3 tablespoons of browned butter; season lightly with salt and pepper. Grilled broccoli is also a very tasty side dish to this fish. Try serving the fish with garlic béarnaise sauce (recipe on page 64).

Grilled Tuna Steaks

Tuna's texture is so different from other types of fish that it's more reminiscent of a slice of turkey breast. Tuna belongs to the mackerel family and contains nearly as much fat as salmon.

The steaks need only a short spell on the grill, so this is really fast food once the prep work is done.

Skewers of Grilled Tuna Steak and Halloumi

- 4 tuna steaks, 5¼ oz. (150 g) each
- 3⅓ fl. oz. (100 ml) mild-flavored olive oil infused with lemon
- 1 bunch green asparagus
- 4 thin slices of hot-smoked pork belly
- 3½ oz. (100 g) Halloumi cheese
- 4 long sprigs of rosemary
- 1 teaspoon salt
- ½ teaspoon ground white pepper

Place the tuna on a plate. Brush both sides generously with the lemon-flavored olive oil. Don't salt the fish until it's on the grill, as the salt might dry out the fish.

Snap off the woody ends of the asparagus and blanch the stalks in salted, boiling water for 1 minute. Drain. Rinse the asparagus in cold water to stop the cooking.

Make 4 asparagus bundles by wrapping the asparagus with the slices of smoked pork belly, and secure them with toothpicks.

Cut the Halloumi cheese into even, inch-wide cubes (2 cm x 2 cm).

Scrape off the leaves from the sprigs of rosemary, leaving some at the top. Thread the cubes of Halloumi onto the sprigs, doing this as carefully as you can so as not to break the cubes of cheese.

First, set the asparagus and the Halloumi on the grill, and let them get good color all over. Keep them warm on a sheet of foil on the side of the grill with indirect heat while you grill the tuna. Brush the hot grill with oil and place the fish onto the grill; season with salt and pepper.

Grill the fish for 1 minute on each side over direct heat. The fish should still be red on the inside or it will be too dry.

If you want your fish cooked a bit longer, leave it for short while on the side of the grill with indirect heat; this will help it stay moist.

Serve the tuna immediately with the skewers of Halloumi, the asparagus, and a bowl of bell pepper chutney (see recipe on page 62).

It is, of course, always nice to serve fish with a flavorful herb butter. (You'll find recipes for several varieties on pages 66 and 68.)

Mussels in Cream

Moules marinière is a hearty, Belgian dish made from fresh mussels cooked in white wine, butter, garlic, and herbs.

This absolutely delicious starter course works well on the grill, too. I've added heavy whipping cream to my variation, so we'll call the dish moules crème instead.

Cook the mussels in a cast iron pot that has warmed up on the grill while the coals were being lit.

Moules Crème

- 1 mesh bag of fresh mussels weighing about 2.2 lb (1 kg)
- 1 shallot
- 2 cloves of garlic
- 2 oz. (50 g) butter
- ⅔ cup (150 ml) dry white wine
- 6¾ fl. oz. (200 ml) heavy whipping cream
- ¼ cup (50 ml) finely chopped thyme
- ¼ cup (50 ml) finely chopped chives
- ¼ cup (50 ml) finely chopped parsley
- about 1 teaspoon salt
- ¼ teaspoon ground black pepper

Scrub the mussels thoroughly with a bristle brush. Discard any mussels with broken shells. Some mussels might be slightly ajar but will close if you press the shells together. If they don't close, discard them as well, as you don't want to run the risk of having a bad mussel in the pot.

Chop the shallot and garlic finely. Brown the butter lightly in the cast iron pot, without browning it too much. Add the shallot and garlic, and sauté for a few minutes until they're translucent but not browned. Pour in the wine, bring to a boil, and add the mussels. Cover with a lid and bring to a rapid boil for about 5 minutes, until all the mussels have opened.

Fish out the mussels with a slotted spoon, and place them in a stainless steel bowl, keeping them warm on indirect heat next to the embers. Discard any mussels that did not open.

Pour the cream into the pot, bring it to a boil, and let simmer for 5 minutes. Stir in the chopped herbs, salt, and pepper, taste, and season with more salt if needed. Serve the broth in bowls with the mussels placed around the edge. Garnish with a few sprigs of fresh herbs.

If you don't have a cast iron pot, you can also make the broth in a saucepan on the stovetop. Heat the broth later in small bowls made from folded foil, one per guest. Place 3 sheets of foil one on top of the other, and crush the edges together to mold into the shape of a pot. Place it on the grill's grate nearest the embers, then fill it with a ladle of broth and add in the cooked mussels to be heated.

This dish is also excellent served as entrée. Simply double the recipe and use two bags of mussels instead of one.

If you prepare the dish in the paleo style without cream, it will be even more delicious if served with an aioli (you'll find the recipe on page 42).

Grilled Crawfish

We humans have eaten shellfish since time immemorial, which has helped us evolve into the thinking beings we are today. That's why they're also a good choice nowadays for those among us who wish to follow a diet similar to that of our ancestors. Here is a recipe for an appetizer that uses traditional crawfish, but prepared with a twist.

Grilled Crawfish with Browned Chive Butter

- 16–20 large crawfish
- 3½ oz. (100 g) butter
- 3⅓ fl. oz. (100 ml) finely chopped chives

Horseradish Chili

- 3⅓ fl. oz. (100 ml) chili sauce (see recipe on page 70)
- 2 tablespoons grated horseradish
- 1 tablespoon lemon juice

Place the crawfish on a cutting board, backs on the board. Grip the crawfish firmly and cut it in half lengthwise with a sharp knife. Place the crawfish on a platter.

In a saucepan, lightly cook the butter until it's golden; remove it from the heat and add in the chopped chives.

In a separate bowl, stir together the ingredients for the horseradish chili.

Grill the crawfish, meat side down on the grill's grate, over hot coals for 30 seconds. Turn the crawfish and brush the tail with butter. Grill for another 30 seconds (if you leave the crawfish on too long they'll become dry and tough).

Serve the crawfish alongside the butter and the horseradish chili in small bowls. Use a small fork to spear the crawfish and dip them in the sauces. Parmesan crackers are good with this dish (recipe on page 24).

Meat
and Poultry

Grilled Rib Eye

I typically like to grill fatty cuts of meat, because the marbling adds so much flavor and juiciness compared to filet mignon or other types of steak, which can often be rather lean. If you can buy meat from grass-fed, free-range animals, its flavor and nutritional profile will be far superior.

I season these slices of rib eye simply with salt and freshly ground white pepper, which enhance the meat's own flavors; a spicy marinade could easily overwhelm this dish.

I prefer cuts to be on the thick side so they're as juicy as possible. The weight per portion will consequently be a bit higher than your typical rib eye, which is usually around 5¼ oz. (150 g), but don't pass up the opportunity to enjoy some of the best food you can throw on the grill.

Grilled Rib Eye with Café de Paris Herb Butter

- 4 thick slices of rib eye, 7 oz. (200 g) each
- 2 tablespoons cold-pressed olive oil, for brushing
- a generous amount of salt and freshly ground white pepper

Place the meat on a cutting board and let it to come to room temperature. Brush with olive oil and season with salt and pepper.

Brush the hot grates of the grill with some oil, and set the meat down on the grill over direct heat for 2 minutes. Turn the meat and cook on the other side for 1 minute if you want the meat to be rare. Grill the cuts for 2 minutes on each side if you prefer your meat medium, and 2 additional minutes if you want it well done.

Good side dishes for rib eye include grilled mushrooms, a few chunks of bell pepper with slightly charred skin from the hot coals, and a green salad.

By all means, serve the freshly grilled meat with a flavorful Café de Paris herb butter (recipe on page 66).

Spareribs with Chili Glaze

In contrast to most store-bought specimens, my glaze is made entirely without sugar. It'll keep for a few weeks in the refrigerator.

Spareribs with a Chili Glaze

- 3⅓ fl. oz. (200 ml) chili sauce (see recipe on page 70)
- ¼ cup (50 ml) cold-pressed olive oil + more for grilling
- 2 tablespoons gluten-free tamari soy sauce
- 2 teaspoons Worcestershire sauce
- 1 rack of thin spareribs, approx. 2⅔ lbs (1.2 kg)
- salt and pepper for seasoning

In a bowl whisk together the ingredients for the chili glaze. Brush the glaze on both sides of the spareribs, saving about ¼ cup (50 ml) for grilling.

Put the meat in double freezer bags and set it on a platter. Marinade for 24 to 48 hours in the refrigerator for the best flavor. Turn the bag now and then, and remove it from the fridge plenty of time before grilling.

Wipe off most of the marinade from the meat with paper towels; season with salt and pepper, and brush generously with oil. Move the coals toward the sides of the grill, leaving an empty space in the middle for the spareribs. Let the coals get covered in gray ash before setting the ribs down above the empty spot, meaty side down.

At the beginning, the grate should be set down close to the embers so the meat can develop some color. Grill the spareribs for 3 minutes, turn them, and grill on the other side for 3 more minutes. Repeat this step once more (6 total minutes).

Brush some saved glaze onto the meaty side of the spareribs and grill them for another 2 minutes. Now move the grate to the highest level up from the coals, turn the ribs, and cover them with heavy-duty foil. Let them rest for 10 to 15 minutes.

Separate the ribs with a sharp knife. Serve them with the "faux" potato salad (page 76) and chili sauce (page 70).

Pork Collar
with Black Currant Glaze

Bottled, store-bought glaze typically contains a lot of sugar. This is a double-whammy when you take into account its high carbohydrate load, in addition to the carcinogenic chemical compounds that develop in the meat when this added sugar heats up over the grill.

This glaze, however, is made from black currants and lime, and is totally free of added sugar. It infuses the pork with a delectably tangy flavor.

Grilled Pork Collar with Black Currant Glaze

- 1 organic lime
- 6¾ fl. oz. (200 ml) black currants
- 1 teaspoon Worcestershire sauce
- ½ teaspoon coarsely ground black pepper
- 4 slices of pork collar, 5¼ oz. (150 g) each; if bone included, 7 oz. (200 g)
- salt and pepper for seasoning
- mild-flavored olive oil for brushing

For the glaze, wash the lime and grate its peel. Squeeze the juice into a saucepan. Add the lime zest, black currants, Worcestershire sauce, and black pepper, bring to a boil, and let simmer for 10 minutes. Pass the contents of the pan through some cheesecloth, and pour the glaze into a glass jar.

Season the meat with salt and pepper, and brush it generously with black currant glaze on both sides, making sure to save some for the grilling. Place the meat in a plastic freezer bag and leave it to marinate for a few hours (preferably longer) in the refrigerator.

Wipe the marinade from the meat with paper towels and brush it with olive oil. Brush the grill's grate with some oil before setting the meat on it over direct heat.

Grill the meat for 2 minutes on each side, and lightly season again with salt and pepper. Brush the glaze on the slices, turn them, and grill for 1 additional minute on each side.

If you're grilling bone-in pork collars, leave them for a few minutes more on the side of the grill, over indirect heat, or under cover over low heat, to give the meat a bit more time to cook through along the bone.

Serve the pork collars with the remainder of the glaze, a green salad, and some grilled slices of daikon radish. Herb butter also works well (recipes on page 66). Another excellent side dish for the glazed pork collar is a broccoli gratin with blue cheese (recipe on page 74).

Greek Souvlaki

For us Swedes, souvlaki and tzatziki are the two dishes that bring to mind a vacation in Greece. I learned this simple recipe when I worked in a Greek restaurant here in Sweden.

I use fresh pork tenderloin, which I marinate in lemon and oregano. Buy two larger tenderloins so you'll get nice even slices for the skewers.

Souvlaki

- 1 lb. 5 oz. (600 g) pork tenderloin
- juice of 2 lemons
- ¼ cup (50 ml) cold-pressed olive oil
- 2 tablespoons dried oregano
- salt and freshly ground black pepper

Trim the membranes off the tenderloins. Slice each tenderloin into 8 even slices, about 1 inch (3 cm) thick. Freeze the end pieces for use at a later time. Set the meat on a platter and squeeze half the lemon juice over it. Drizzle on some olive oil and half the oregano; season lightly with salt and pepper.

Turn the meat and sprinkle it with the remainder of the lemon juice and oregano; season with some salt and pepper on this side, too. Cover with plastic wrap and leave the meat to marinate at room temperature for one hour to let the lemon and herb flavors infuse the meat.

Thread the slices of meat onto skewers, brush with olive oil, and grill 2 minutes per side over direct heat. Season with some more salt and black pepper.

Pork tenderloin can dry out very quickly if it's grilled for too long, so let the skewers rest for a little while over indirect heat on the side of the grill to keep the meat juicy.

Pair this dish with grilled slices of eggplant and bowls of tzatziki sauce (recipe on page 54). A Greek salad with lots of feta cheese, olives, and finely sliced red onion also makes a perfect LCHF side dish.

Coffee-Marinated Pork Belly

This fresh pork belly derives its taste from a different type of marinade, one that combines coffee with cinnamon. It imparts a very full flavor to the pork.

I like to bring a whole slab of pork belly with me on my trips to the berry-laden woods by my cottage, which is located up north in the Swedish province of Dalarna. The meat grills slowly over nice embers left over from an open birch wood fire.

The process of cooking pork belly can't be hurried, but once it's ready to eat there is nothing left to do but slice it and eat it with a cup of coffee. It certainly has an edge over the ordinary hot dog, and is an absolute delight after a long day spent in the woods.

Grilled Pork Belly Marinated in Coffee

- 3⅓ fl. oz. (100 ml) strong, brewed coffee
- 2 tablespoons tamari soy sauce
- 2 tablespoons cold-pressed mild-flavored olive oil
- 2 teaspoons cinnamon
- ½ teaspoon ground white pepper
- 1½-lb. (700-g) slab of pork belly, in one piece with the rind attached

Mix the ingredients together for the marinade in a bowl. With a sharp knife, make closely spaced incisions in the pork rind. Set the pork belly in a plastic freezer bag and add the marinade. Close the bag tightly, and gently rub the pork belly to make sure the marinade gets into the cuts in the rind.

Leave the pork belly in the bag on a plate in the refrigerator to marinate for at least 24 hours, preferably longer.

When ready to cook, wipe off the marinade with paper towels, and cut the meat into ¾-inch (2 cm) thick slices. Grill them over direct heat for 2–3 minutes on each side to give the meat some color.

If you want to grill the pork belly in one piece, do so over indirect heat, or over low heat on a gas grill. Move the coals to the sides of the grill and make an empty, coal-free space for the meat. Turn the meat several times while grilling to prevent it from scorching. Cooking will take about 30–40 minutes, depending on the thickness of the pork belly.

Use a meat thermometer if you like, and insert it into the middle section of the meat. When the temperature reads 149°F (65°C), cover the meat with foil and let it rest next to the grill for 10 minutes.

Cut the meat into slices and serve them with a blue-cheese broccoli gratin (recipe on page 74).

Lamb Chops Marinated in Red Wine

I often look to the kitchens around the Mediterranean for inspiration. These lamb chops soak up all the flavors of a red wine, olive oil, garlic, and coriander seed marinade.

This recipe comes from the island of Cyprus, where these spices are very commonly used in long-cooking stews made with tougher cuts of meat, making them taste heavenly. The bell pepper sauce, Mojo, is a souvenir from a trip a bit further south, to the Spanish island of Gran Canaria.

Grilled Lamb Chops with Mediterranean Flavors

- 2 garlic cloves
- 6¾ fl. oz. (200 ml) dry red wine
- 3⅓ fl. oz. (100 ml) cold-pressed olive oil + more for grilling
- 2 tablespoons crushed coriander seeds
- 1 teaspoon coarsely ground black pepper
- 8 double-cut lamb chops
- salt for seasoning

Peel and slice the garlic cloves. Mix all ingredients for the marinade in a bowl. Place the lamb chops in double plastic freezer bags and add in the marinade; it's safest to double-bag all this to avoid losing any of the tasty marinade if the bones of the chops poke a hole in one of the plastic bags.

Close the plastic bags and rub the chops a little to coat the marinade evenly. Place the bags of chops on a platter and keep them in the refrigerator for a few hours, preferably overnight if you have the time.

Drain the meat thoroughly and wipe the marinade off with paper towels. Brush the chops with olive oil, and brush the grill's grates with olive oil too.

Grill the chops 2 minutes per side over direct heat; season with salt. Move the grate up to a higher, slightly cooler spot, or reduce the heat on a gas grill. Grill the chops until ready, about 6–8 minutes, depending on if they're cut thick or thin. Turn them a few times while cooking.

Place the chops, covered with foil, next to the grill. Let them rest for about 5 to 10 minutes to give the meat time to cook up around the bone. The meat will be at its best if it's slightly pink inside, so don't over-grill it. If you use a thermometer, the meat is ready when it reads 131–140°F (55–60°C), depending on how well done you like it.

Serve the lamb with avocado, browned garlic butter (recipe on page 68), and Canarian Mojo sauce (recipe on page 52).

Turkish Lamb's Liver

Alanya, in Turkey, is my home during several winter months, and one of my favorite restaurants there serves this well-spiced lamb's liver. The diced liver is sautéed in butter and served with a salad of arugula, red onion, and lemon. At home, I occasionally prepare it as finger food to go with a glass of wine.

For this dish, I slice the liver and leave it to absorb the flavors of the spices before I take it on a quick trip over the hot grill. If you can't find lamb's liver, calf's liver is a fine substitute in this case.

Grilled Liver the Turkish Way

- 1 lb. 5 oz. (600 g) lamb's or calf's liver
- 2 lemons, cut in half
- 1 tablespoon chili flakes
- 2 tablespoons dried oregano
- 2 teaspoons salt flakes
- olive oil for brushing

Slice the liver into ¾-inch-thick (2-cm) slices. Place them in a bowl and squeeze lemon juice over them. Season with chili, oregano, and crumbled salt flakes. Mix thoroughly. Cover the bowl with plastic wrap and leave it in the refrigerator for a few hours.

Place the liver in a colander to drain thoroughly. Remove most of the oregano with a paper towel so that it doesn't burn while grilling. Brush the slices with olive oil.

Preferably, grill the liver in a grill basket brushed with olive oil, 1 minute per side, very close to direct heat. Then let the liver rest for a while away from the heat so it retains its juices and stays slightly pink inside.

Serve the liver with grilled eggplant and onion, with garlic butter or herb butter on the side (recipes on page 68).

Elk Burgers

Elk and other wild game are among the most nutritious foods available. In the woods, the animals subsist on branches, herbs, and leaves that are a part of their environment. This diet produces both extremely flavor- and nutrient-rich meat.

Ground meat of wild game is often very lean, so to make it juicier and more filling we need to mix it with some ground pork.

Remember not to overcook it on the grill, or it will quickly dry out.

Grilled Elk Burgers with Goat's Cheese and Blueberry Pesto

- 1 organic egg
- 1 tablespoon unsweetened mustard
- 1 tablespoon finely chopped parsley
- 1 tablespoon finely chopped rosemary
- 1 teaspoon salt
- ½ teaspoon coarsely ground black pepper
- 14 oz. (400 g) ground elk meat
- 7 oz. (200 g) ground pork
- oil for grilling
- 4 slices goat cheese

Whisk together the egg, mustard, herbs, and spices in a bowl. Crumble the ground meat into smaller pieces. Work all ingredients together quickly and thoroughly to get an even mix, and let it rest in the refrigerator for about half an hour.

With the mix, make up four burgers and flatten them. Brush the heated grate with oil and place the burgers on top.

Grill the burgers quickly, 2 minutes per side, over direct heat. Leave the burgers, higher up and at lower heat, for 5 minutes so they stay juicy. Add more salt and pepper while grilling.

Just before serving, open the grill basket and cover each burger with a slice of goat cheese.

Side dishes that work well these burgers are slices of grilled cauliflower, blueberry pesto (recipe on page 46), and aioli (recipe on page 42).

Hamburgers Wrapped in Bacon

For many, a juicy hamburger on some crusty warm bread, slathered with mayonnaise and chili sauce, is a perennial favorite meal from the grill. Prepared my way, it will also be a very good choice if you've stopped eating unnecessary carbohydrates and breads made from cereals.

Here, the hamburger bread is baked with almond meal, the chili sauce is entirely sugar-free, and the mayonnaise is homemade; this will make it a dish you can enjoy often.

Grilled Hamburgers with Classic Side Dishes

- 1 lb. 5 oz. (600 g) ground chuck with high fat content (preferably freshly ground)
- 1 egg
- 2 teaspoons salt
- 1 teaspoon ground black pepper
- 1 teaspoon Worcestershire sauce
- 4 slices bacon or hot-smoked pork belly
- 2 tablespoons mild-flavored olive oil for brushing

Crumble the ground meat into small pieces in a bowl and mix it well with the egg, salt, pepper, and Worcestershire sauce. Let the mixture rest for half an hour in the refrigerator; this will allow it to hold together better while grilling.

Dip your fingers in cold water, and shape the ground meat into four, somewhat thick patties. Wrap the slices of bacon all around the edge of each patty and fasten with a toothpick. Flatten the burger slightly with your hand.

Brush the burgers generously with oil on both sides. Brush some oil onto the hot grate of the grill, too. Use a grill basket if you have one—it'll make grilling the burgers easier.

Place the burgers on the grill and cook for 3 minutes on each side over direct heat. Then place them over indirect heat, or lower the temperature on a gas grill. Let them cook for 2 more minutes on each side.

If you're unsure if the hamburgers are cooked through, use a thermometer; it will register 136°F (58°C) when the hamburgers are cooked medium. If you want them well done wait, until the thermometer reads 149°F (65°C).

Taste-test a hamburger grilled to medium. They are far juicier than the ones that have been grilled longer.

Serve the hamburgers in freshly toasted buns with crisp lettuce and tomato. Grilled onion slices are good too, unless you prefer raw onion rings.

For an even more flavorful burger, melt a slice of cheddar over the patties toward the end of grilling the meat.

Mayonnaise, chili sauce, and salted cucumbers make great sides (recipes for the sauces on pages 41 and 70, respectively). Coleslaw is also very tasty (recipe on page 134).

Hamburger Buns

Preheat the oven to 350°F (175°C). Line a baking sheet with parchment paper.

- 3 eggs
- 6¾ fl. oz. (200 ml) almond flour
- 3 tablespoons unflavored, whole psyllium husk*
- 1 teaspoon baking powder
- ½ teaspoon salt
- ¼ cup (50 ml) cold water
- sesame seeds, for garnish

*Unflavored whole psyllium husk can be found at health food stores or online at netrition.com or iHerb.com.

Beat the eggs thoroughly with a handheld electric mixer. Stir together all the dry ingredients, except for the sesame seeds, in a bowl. Mix the water with the egg batter, and then add in the dry ingredients. Mix well.

Leave the batter to rise for 5 minutes. Use two wet spoons to form four round bun shapes on the prepared baking sheet. Wet your hands and shape them evenly. Flatten them to give them the authentic appearance of hamburger buns. Sprinkle them generously with sesame seeds.

Bake at 350°F (175°C) for 20 minutes. Let cool on a baking rack. Cut the buns in half and grill the cut surfaces just before serving.

Lamb Sausage with Skagen Shrimp Salad

Many of us in Sweden have enjoyed a grilled sausage with a side of shrimp salad, bought from a food truck as a late night snack. A somewhat strange combination perhaps, but it's still a very enjoyable treat. My make-at-home version, however, will guarantee that the sausage and small Swedish Skagen shrimp salad are a cut above. I consider this dish a poor man's surf and turf.

Grilled Sausage with Skagen Shrimp Salad

- 6¾ fl. oz. (200 ml) homemade mayonnaise (see recipe on page 42)
- ¼ cup (50 ml) finely chopped dill
- 1 tablespoon finely chopped shallot
- 14 oz. (400 g) cooked peeled shrimp (small shrimp if you can find them)
- juice of ½ lemon
- salt and pepper
- 4 sausages with high percentage of meat and fat
- olive oil for brushing

Mix mayonnaise, dill, and chopped shallot. Chop the shrimp coarsely and fold them into the mayonnaise. Season with lemon juice, salt, and pepper. Place in the refrigerator for a while to let flavors meld.

Slash the sausages on the diagonal, making slits just shy of ¼ inch (1 cm) deep. Place them on a hot grill and brush on some oil. Grill for 2 minutes on each side over direct heat.

Move the sausages to a cooler side on the grill, and leave them a few minutes until they are completely warmed through.

Serve the sausages with a dollop of shrimp salad, and why not add a tangy cabbage salad with cumin seeds and bacon (see recipe on page 134)?

Rosemary-Marinated Turkey Skewers

I often make these skewers on winter evenings in Turkey; we eat a lot of turkey meat during our stay there. Turkey breast has a coarser meat texture than chicken, and both the consistency and flavor are reminiscent of fresh ham.

Turkey meat is excellent for grilling, either on skewers or in slices.

Grilled Turkey Skewers Marinated in Orange and Rosemary

- peel and juice from 1 organic orange
- ¼ cup (50 ml) olive oil infused with lemon
- 2 tablespoons finely chopped rosemary
- one turkey breast, 1 lb. 5 oz. (600 g)
- 2 yellow bell peppers
- salt and pepper
- olive oil, for brushing

Grate the orange peel finely, and mix with the juice from the orange and the olive oil. Stir in the rosemary. Dice the turkey breast in 1-inch (3 cm) cubes. Place them in a plastic freezer bag and pour in the marinade. Close the bag and mix the turkey cubes and marinade to coat.

Place the bag in a deep plate and leave it in the refrigerator, preferably for 24 hours. Turn the bag a few times during this time.

Dice the peppers evenly, also in 1-inch (3-cm) cubes. Place the turkey pieces in a colander to let the marinade drain thoroughly.

Alternately thread turkey meat and bell peppers onto the skewers. If you use wooden skewers, you'll need to let them soak in water for about half an hour before using them, or they can easily catch fire from the heat of the grill. Season the skewers with salt and pepper, and brush on some olive oil.

Brush some oil on the hot grill. Cook the skewers over direct heat, 1½ minutes per side, 6 minutes altogether. Place the skewers on the side of the grill, over indirect heat, for 5 minutes. If you use a meat thermometer, the meat is ready when the thermometer registers 158°F (70°C).

Serve the turkey skewers with avocado salsa (recipe on page 50) and feta cheese butter (recipe on page 66).

Chicken Schnitzel

During the winters in Turkey I often buy fresh produce at the local vegetable markets and grass-fed meat at the butcher. There I'll find nice chicken schnitzels made from chicken breast, or boned chicken thighs that have been pounded flat.

Each shop has its own special recipe for spice rub, which is used to season the meat. Unfortunately, a lot of the rubs contain MSG (monosodium glutamate), so I buy my chicken unseasoned and then make my own spice mix, which I keep in a jar. The spice mix is perfect for rubbing onto the chicken, which I then brush with some oil and set on the grill. It's fast, good, and simple food.

Grilled Chicken Schnitzel with Turkish Spice Rub

- 2 tablespoons dried thyme
- 1 tablespoon chili flakes
- 1 tablespoon paprika
- 2 teaspoons organic garlic powder
- 4 chicken breasts, 5¼ oz. (150 g) each
- salt
- olive oil

Mix the spices for the rub and pour it into a jar with a lid. This batch will make enough rub for several meals; it's particularly good with pork.

Place the chicken breasts on a cutting board, and place your hand on top with a steady grip. With a sharp knife, slice the breasts along the middle, from the thinner end toward the thicker, long side. Don't cut straight through the meat; leave about ¼ inch (1–2 cm) attached.

Fold out the meat and flatten it with your hand. If the chicken breast is very thick, place a piece of plastic wrap on top and hit it hard with the bottom of a saucepan to flatten the meat. Season both sides of the meat with about 2 teaspoons of the spice rub and work it in thoroughly on both sides. Salt and brush on olive oil.

Brush some oil onto the hot grill, and set the chicken schnitzels on top. Grill for 2 minutes on each side over direct heat. Move the grate up to its highest position, or turn off the heat if you're using a gas grill. Leave the chicken on the grill for 2 minutes.

Serve feta cheese butter (recipe on page 66) and, why not, a coleslaw with pesto (recipe on page 135) as side dishes to the chicken schnitzel.

Stuffed Chicken Thighs Wrapped in Parma Ham

Boneless chicken thighs are very juicy and flavorful when served fresh off the grill. Here I've concocted a stuffing of Parmesan, herbs, and almond flour. All is then wrapped in Parma ham, so this dish has many flavors typical of the Italian kitchen.

It's a slightly more sophisticated dish to prepare compared to the other recipes in this book, but it is well worth the time and prep work.

Chicken Thighs Stuffed with Parmesan and Almond Filling, and Wrapped in Parma Ham

- 3 ⅓ fl. oz. (100 ml) finely grated Parmesan
- 6¾ fl. oz. (200 ml) almond flour
- 1 egg yolk
- 2 tablespoons finely chopped thyme
- 2 tablespoons finely chopped basil
- 8 boneless chicken thighs
- 1 teaspoon salt
- ¼ teaspoon coarsely ground black pepper
- 16 slices of Parma ham
- olive oil for brushing

Mix together the grated Parmesan, almond flour, yolk, and herbs to make the filling. Knead the mixture into firm dough. Shape the dough into 8 balls equal in size. Flatten them slightly into oblong shapes.

Season the chicken thighs inside and out with some salt and pepper. Place a piece of the filling into the hollow from the removed bone, and firmly press the meat around the dough to cover.

For each chicken thigh, set two slices of Parma ham down on a cutting board in the shape of an X. Place a chicken thigh in the middle of the X.

Fold the edges of the ham over, alternating the slices, to make a parcel around the chicken thigh. Secure the edges with a toothpick, and pinch the edges to make sure that the packet will hold together. Place the wrapped chicken thighs in the refrigerator for an hour to firm them up so they hold their shape once they're on the grill.

Brush the packets with olive oil, and grill each side for 2 minutes over direct heat. Move the grate up one step and grill them for 15 minutes on lower heat. Turn them several times while they cook. Then let the chicken rest on the side of the grill over indirect heat. Cover with foil and let the chicken cook for another 5 minutes. If you want to check for doneness with a meat thermometer, the chicken will be ready when the thermometer reads 176°F (80°C).

Slice the packet on the diagonal to expose the stuffing. Serve with aioli (recipe on pages 42), marinated cherry tomatoes (recipe on page 72), and broccoli. The zucchini gratin (on page 74) is also a good complement to the meal.

Vegetable Dishes and Salads

Grilled Beefsteak Tomatoes

These tomatoes are very easy to prepare, but the addition of cheese gives them added complexity. They make an excellent side dish or appetizer.

Select your favorite cheeses and let them melt a little over the warm tomato. I choose a blue cheese and a goat cheese from a local dairy here up north in the Swedish province of Jämtland.

Grilled Beefsteak Tomatoes with Melted Cheese

- 4 slices of blue cheese
- 4 slices of goat cheese
- 4 beefsteak tomatoes
- olive oil for brushing
- salt flakes and coarsely ground black pepper
- 2 tablespoons roasted sunflower seeds
- 2 tablespoons chopped chives
- 2 tablespoons cold pressed olive oil
- 1 tablespoon balsamic vinegar

Leave the cheese out of the refrigerator so it comes up to room temperature. Slice the tomatoes into ¾-inch (2-cm) slices from their thicker, middle section. Brush with olive oil. Season with some crushed salt flakes and pepper.

Grill the tomatoes for 1 minute per side on a hot grate brushed with olive oil. Turn the slices over carefully with a frying spatula. Season lightly again, and place the cheese on the tomato. Grill for 30–45 seconds, just enough to get the tomatoes heated through, then move them carefully to a heated platter. Sprinkle with sunflower seeds and chives, and drizzle with olive oil and vinegar. Serve immediately.

Feta Baked in Foil

This delicious dish is one of my wonderful souvenirs from a vacation in Greece. There, restaurants often serve this dish as an appetizer, either grilled in foil or as a gratin in a ceramic bowl.

Feta Cheese Baked in Foil, from the Grill

- 1 green bell pepper
- 1 red bell pepper
- 1 small yellow onion
- 2 blocks of feta cheese, 5¼ oz. (150 g) each
- 1 small bunch of fresh oregano
- ¼ cup (50 ml) cold-pressed olive oil

Tear off four sheets of foil approximately 10 inches (25 cm) square in size.

Slice bell peppers and onion thinly. Cut the blocks of feta in half and place one half on each piece of foil. Pile the slices of bell pepper and onion onto the feta. Sprinkle with oregano leaves, and finish with a drizzle of olive oil.

Pinch together the edges of the foil to make packets, and grill them for 7–8 minutes, until the cheese is warmed through. Place the packets onto plates and let your guests savor the cheese straight from the packet.

Oyster Mushroom Burgers

This mushroom burger is beloved by vegetarians and meat-eaters alike. With its satisfying combination of Halloumi cheese, oyster mushrooms, egg, and ground hazelnuts, the texture isn't far off that of an ordinary hamburger, but it is far more flavorful.

Mushroom burgers can be a bit tricky to grill because they burn easily. To avoid this, I grill them on a buttered piece of foil placed on the grate of the grill, and not too close to the embers. You can also pre-cook them in a sauté pan and then finish them off in a grill basket over the embers.

Mushroom Burgers

- 7 oz. (200 g) oyster mushrooms
- 2½ inches (5 cm) of leek, white part only
- 2 garlic cloves
- ¼ cup (50 g) butter, for sautéing
- ¼ teaspoon salt
- 1 teaspoon chili flakes
- 1 cup + 1 tablespoon (250 ml) hazelnut flour
- 8¾ oz. (250 g) Halloumi cheese
- 3 egg yolks + 1 whole egg
- ¼ cup (50 ml) coconut flour
- ¼ cup (50 ml) chopped parsley
- 2 tablespoons French tarragon
- butter, for brushing

Chop the mushrooms into small dice, and finely chop the leek. Mince the garlic. Brown the butter lightly and sauté the leeks for a few minutes to sweat them, not to brown them. Add in the mushrooms, season with salt and chili flakes, and let cook over medium heat for 5 minutes, stirring occasionally to avoid burning. Pull the pan from the heat, and mix in the hazelnut flour. Let cool.

Meanwhile, grate the Halloumi coarsely. Mix the cheese, egg yolks, and the whole egg, coconut flour, and herbs in a bowl and mix well. Add in the sautéed mushroom-leek mix, a little at a time, and make sure that everything is thoroughly mixed.

Taste and season it with more salt if needed, although you might not have to, as Halloumi is already quite salty. Let the mixture rest for half an hour. Wet your hands and then shape the mix into eight burgers. Flatten them so they're approximately 1¼ inches (30 mm) high.

Tear out two big pieces of foil, place one on top of the other, and fold in the edges to make the sheets stay together. Brush the sheets generously with melted butter. Place the foil on the grate of the grill, and let the butter brown slightly. Place the burgers on the foil, and grill for 2–3 minutes on each side; season lightly with salt and pepper.

If you want more color on the burgers, place them directly in an oil-brushed basket and grill 1 minute per side over direct heat. Serve the burgers between slices of grilled zucchini and onion rings that have been soaked in cold water.

Turkish carrot sauté (recipe on page 56) and garlic butter (recipe on page 68) are both delicious accompaniments to these burgers.

Grilled Portabella Mushrooms

The portabella is a type of mushroom that is allowed to grow very large before being harvested. The segments on the cap's underside give the mushroom its dark brown color. I leave them on when grilling because they contribute to the rich, meaty flavor.

This firm mushroom is excellent for grilling, but it needs to be brushed with a generous amount of melted butter so it doesn't dry out while cooking.

Here, I'm serving it with side dishes that are full of flavor and high in nutritional value.

Grilled Portabellas with Asparagus, Garlic Butter, and Toasted Macadamia Nuts

- 3½ oz. (100 g) garlic butter (see recipe on page 68), divided in half
- ¼ cup (50 ml) cold-pressed olive oil
- 8 portabella mushrooms
- salt and pepper
- 1 bunch tender, green asparagus
- 1¾ oz. (50 g) macadamia nuts
- 3⅓ fl. oz. (100 ml) nettle pesto (see recipe on page 46)

Melt half of the garlic butter and mix with olive oil. Brush the top and the underside of the mushroom caps; season with salt and pepper.

Snap off the woody ends of the asparagus stalks, and brush the asparagus with the melted butter/olive oil mix. Salt lightly. Place the fresh macadamias in a dry pan, and roast them in a 400°F (200°C) oven for 10 minutes.

Grill the mushrooms for approximately 5 minutes on each side, until they're nicely colored and well cooked through, which intensifies their flavor. Brush them a few times with the garlic/oil mixture.

Grill the asparagus next to the mushrooms. They'll be ready after about 1 minute on each side.

Take two portabella caps and press them together with macadamia nuts and a slice of garlic butter, which will melt into the caps. Place the asparagus on the side and drizzle over them with nettle pesto.

A mixed salad with marigold leaves and lemon juice makes a beautiful counterpoint to these mushrooms.

Cabbage Salad x3

There's plenty of room for different varieties of cabbage salad in a diet low in carbohydrates. White cabbage was often recommended to diabetics as a replacement to potatoes, as it doesn't raise blood sugar.

Cabbage salad with hot-smoked pork belly comes from Austria, where it's popular to season both sauerkraut and fresh white cabbage with cumin seed.

Cauliflower salad is common in countries around the Mediterranean, too, and a variation of it features a bit of heat contributed by chili pepper.

The third salad is influenced by America. It's a mild-tasting, creamy, green coleslaw with our nettle pesto.

White Cabbage Salad with Hot-Smoked Pork Belly

- 4 slices hot-smoked pork belly
- 1 teaspoon cumin seeds
- 4¼ cups (1000 ml) finely shredded white cabbage
- 6¾ fl. oz. (200 ml) finely julienned leek
- 3 tablespoons mild-flavored olive oil
- 1 tablespoon apple cider vinegar
- ¼ teaspoon salt
- ¼ teaspoon coarsely ground black pepper

Cut the pork belly in thin strips, place them in a cold frying pan, and turn the heat on under the pan. Sprinkle in some cumin seeds. Fry the pork strips until they're nicely browned; stir them occasionally to prevent the strips from burning. Remove the pan from the heat and let it cool a little.

Meanwhile, mix the shredded cabbage and leek with oil, vinegar, salt, and pepper in a bowl. Fold in the browned pork strips together along with the rendered fat from sautéing, and mix well. Taste for added seasoning, if needed.

Cauliflower Salad with Paprika and Chili

- 4¼ cups (1000 ml) cauliflower florets
- 2 red long, pointy bell peppers
- 1¾ oz. (50 g) butter
- about 1 teaspoon salt
- ½–1 tablespoon chili flakes
- 2 tablespoons apple cider vinegar
- 3⅓ fl. oz. (100 ml) chopped Italian parsley
- cold-pressed olive oil, for drizzling

Drop the cauliflower florets in salted, boiling water and parboil for 2 minutes. Drain well.

Seed and cut the bell peppers into four sections lengthwise, and then cut the quarters into strips.

Brown the butter in a pan and add in the bell pepper strips and the cauliflower.

Season the vegetables with salt and the smaller amount of chili flakes. Sauté them for a few minutes, shaking the pan from time to time.

Pour in the apple cider vinegar and let it cook in. Taste and add more salt and chili, if needed. Let cool and then, just before serving, stir in the chopped parsley. Drizzle some (preferably) cold-pressed olive oil over the salad for extra flavor and nutrition.

Coleslaw with Nettle Pesto and Mayonnaise

- 4¼ cups (1000 ml) finely shredded white cabbage
- 3⅓ fl. oz. (100 ml) mayonnaise (see recipe page 42)
- 3⅓ fl. oz. (100 ml) nettle pesto (see recipe page 46)
- ¼ cup (50 ml) toasted sunflower seeds
- salt and ground white pepper to taste

Place the shredded cabbage in a bowl. Knead the cabbage thoroughly with your hands to make it softer and easier to mix with the mayonnaise. Mix in mayonnaise, pesto, and sunflower seeds; season with salt and pepper.

Brie and Strawberry Salad

This is a flavorful and fresh salad that's also a nutritious and satisfying side dish. You get all these benefits by adding brie, walnuts, and pumpkin seeds to the salad.

The slightly tangy taste of sun-ripened strawberries fully enhances the greens. Oak leaf lettuce is full of flavor and adds both nutritional value and beautiful color, turning this salad into a small work of art.

Oak Leaf Lettuce Salad with Brie and Strawberries

- 1 head oak leaf lettuce, washed
- 3½ oz. (100 g) brie cheese
- 8 strawberries
- 3⅓ fl. oz. (100 ml) walnuts
- 2 tablespoons pumpkin seeds
- ¼ cup (50 ml) Italian parsley
- 2 tablespoons cold-pressed olive oil
- 1 tablespoon lemon juice

Line the sides of a bowl with beautiful oak leaf lettuce leaves. Shred the rest of the lettuce and set it in the middle of the bowl. Cut the cheese into small slices and the strawberries in quarters.

Scatter the cheese and strawberries evenly over the lettuce. Sprinkle the nuts and pumpkin seeds over the top. Strip the parsley stalks of nice leaves and sprinkle them over the salad. Drizzle on some good olive oil and lemon juice right before serving.

Smoked Pork Belly and Mozzarella Salad

My daily meals include all manner of vegetables in different colors and shapes. When the summer heat is in full swing, salads make the best side dishes.

A satisfying green salad is a nice complement to many grilled dishes, or makes a great starter while the coals are heating up. Eating different types of green leaves is a very simple way for us to take in a lot of important vitamins.

Good fats and proteins are present in the mozzarella and hot-smoked pork belly. I often add some fruit for an extra touch of flavor to my salads, but this one works even for those of us following the strictest LCHF regimen.

Green Lettuce with Asparagus, Mini Mozzarellas Balls, and Smoked Pork Belly

- 4–5 thin slices of smoked pork belly
- 1 bunch tender, green asparagus
- 1 package mini mozzarella balls
- 4-inch (10-cm) piece of leek
- 8 cherry tomatoes
- 1 head green lettuce (Lollo Bianco, Lollo Rosso, or romaine lettuce work well)
- ½ bunch of basil
- 3 tablespoons of mild-flavored olive oil
- 1 tablespoon apple cider vinegar

Cut the pork belly into very thin strips and place them in a cold frying pan. Turn the heat to high. Brown the strips until they're really sizzling. Remove the pan from the heat and let cool.

Snap off the woody ends of the asparagus and boil in salted water for about 3–4 minutes. Drain and rinse in ice-cold water to stop the cooking. Drain thoroughly, and then cut on the diagonal in strips of 1 inch (3 cm).

Set the mozzarella in a colander to drain. Rinse and julienne the leek, and cut the tomatoes into quarters.

Line the edge of a salad bowl with pretty lettuce leaves taken from the heart of the lettuce. Shred the rest into smaller pieces and place inside the bowl, alternating with basil leaves, tomatoes, asparagus, mozzarella, pork strips, and leek.

Garnish with a few nice asparagus tips. Sprinkle with pork strips and basil leaves. Drizzle on some mild olive oil and vinegar right before serving.

Grilled Halloumi and Pomegranate Salad

Halloumi is one of my favorite cheeses. Here, its chewy saltiness is paired with pomegranate, one of my favorite fruits.

I always bring back pomegranate vinegar from my trips to Turkey, but it is available in ethnic food shops that sell Middle Eastern foods or olive oil/vinegar shops. Make sure you get true vinegar made from reduced pomegranate juice. Unfortunately, there are many types of pomegranate vinegar that are loaded with added sugar.

Pine nuts are not nuts—they're seeds from pinecones. Many who are allergic to nuts can therefore still eat pine nuts.

Halloumi, Pine Nut, and Pomegranate Salad

- 1 head of romaine lettuce
- 8 yellow cherry tomatoes
- 3 tablespoons pomegranate seeds
- 3½ oz. (100 g) Halloumi cheese
- 2 tablespoons pine nuts
- 2 tablespoons cold-pressed olive oil
- 1 tablespoon pomegranate vinegar
- fresh parsley leaves and mint leaves

Place lettuce leaves on a platter. Cut the tomatoes into quarters and place them on top of the lettuce.

Remove some seeds from a pomegranate. The easiest way to do this is to slice off a piece at the top and then make two vertical cuts, approximately 1½–2 inches (4–5 cm) apart. Place the pomegranate in a plastic bag and break off the wedge that has been cut out. This will make it easy for you to pick out the seeds without having the juice squirting all over.

The pomegranate will keep for quite a long time if you keep it in the plastic bag in the refrigerator. When you need some more seeds, simply make a new cut and break off the piece.

Grill the Halloumi cheese and add it on top of the lettuce; sprinkle pomegranate seeds and pine nuts all over the top. Drizzle olive oil and pomegranate vinegar over the salad, and garnish with parsley and mint.

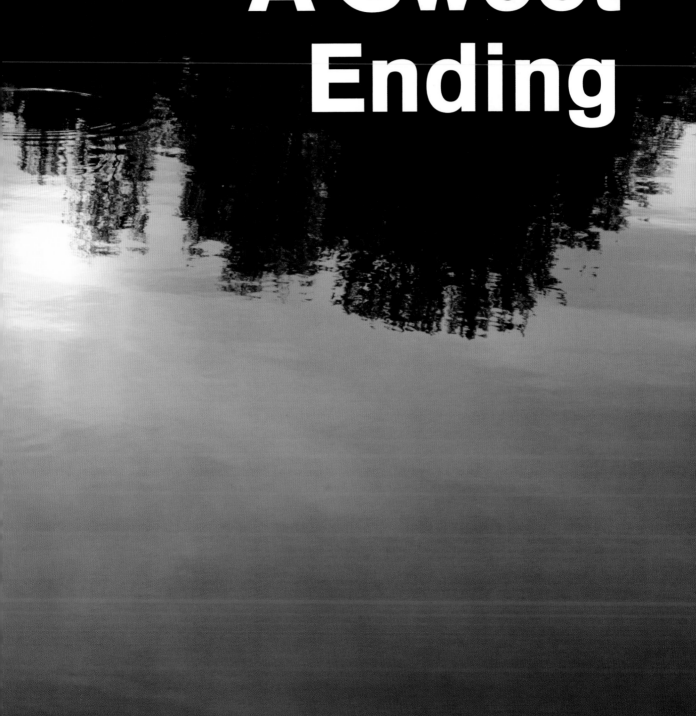

A Sweet Ending

Ice Chocolate Truffles with Cloudberries

This truffle is a real treat to pair up with a cup of coffee after a grilled meal. It's also a genuine health food made from the darkest chocolate, cold-pressed coconut oil, egg yolks, and cloudberries from a mountain swamp.

Even dark chocolate often contain lots of added sugar, so make sure that you opt for varieties with the highest cacao content you can find.

Ice Chocolate Truffles with Cloudberries

- 3½ oz. (100 g) dark chocolate (85–90% cacao)
- 1⅓ fl. oz. (40 g) cold-pressed coconut oil
- 2 organic egg yolks
- 3⅓ fl. oz. (100 ml) cloudberries (or yellow raspberries)
- a pinch of crumbled salt flakes
- unsweetened cocoa powder

Break the chocolate into small pieces and melt it together with the coconut oil over low heat. Meanwhile, whip the egg yolks until very thick with a handheld mixer.

Mash the cloudberries lightly and mix them in with the salt and the chocolate/coconut oil mixture. Salt brings out the chocolate flavor even more, thereby making the truffles even more delectable.

Stir some of the chocolate into the yolks and keep stirring until smooth. Then fold in the remaining melted chocolate; the truffle mixture thus becomes nice and smooth. Fill small confectionary paper cups with the chocolate, as you would for ordinary candy preparation.

You can also leave the truffle mix to sit for a few hours in the refrigerator until it thickens. Use a melon baller or a teaspoon dipped in lukewarm water to make small balls. Place the truffles on a platter and put them back in the refrigerator to chill again. Sift some cocoa powder over the truffles through a tea strainer just before serving.

Store the truffles in the refrigerator or freezer, and remove them a little before they are to be enjoyed. Sift some more cocoa powder over them at that point.

Grilled Berry Dessert

I have the luxury of making delicious desserts with berries that I have picked myself. We are so fortunate in Sweden to have a law called the "right of commons," which among other things allows people to pick all kinds of edibles such berries, nuts, fruits, and mushrooms that grow in the wild, as long as they're not on the endangered species list. It's a benefit we've enjoyed and taken advantage of since way back in time. And not only do we get to glean edibles outside or from our gardens, the exercise we take while harvesting is free of charge, too.

This dessert is as easy to put together as can be, and yet its flavor is exquisite. A LCHF lifestyle can accommodate berries in small amounts, as they aren't as loaded with carbohydrates like other fruit.

Warm Berries with Dark Chocolate and Cardamom Cream

Set out one piece of foil per guest measuring approximately 8 inches (20 cm) square, and place 3⅓ fl. oz. (100 ml) fresh berries in the middle of each piece of foil. I used wild raspberries, bilberries (blueberries), red currants, and sea buckthorn in my packets.

Place a few pieces of coarsely chopped dark chocolate (85–90% cacao) on top of the berries, which will add smooth sweetness and intricate flavors when it melts down into the fruit.

Fold the foil over the berries and pinch the ends to close the parcels. Place them on the grate of the grill over cooling embers, and leave to heat up for about 2–3 minutes, depending on how many embers are still left. The berries should reach no higher than lukewarm temperature, and all the chocolate should melt.

Place the berry packets directly onto dessert plates, open them, and serve with a bowl of crème fraîche seasoned with some ground cardamom and vanilla powder.

Cheese Platter

A tray of fine cheeses is the perfect dessert for those of us who follow an LCHF lifestyle. If the cheese (preferably from sheep's or goat's milk) is locally made, so much the better. A well-ripened, sharp, hard cheese would work well here, too.

To change things up from the usual combo of crackers, pears, grapes, and marmalades, I choose to serve cheese with black currants, radishes, and tart bell pepper chutney, which is naturally sweet from the inclusion of a bit of diced apple (the recipe for the chutney is on page 62). My seed crackers (on page 22) are also a nice addition; bake them without any seasoning except salt, so when they're served with cheese, the cheese flavors take center stage.

Coconut and Vanilla Pannacotta

Many of us associate pannacotta with intensely sweet desserts. This particular pannacotta, made in the LCHF way, derives its natural sweetness from coconut cream and vanilla bean.

This dessert is also fine if you follow a paleo/stone age diet, because the pannacotta is dairy-free.

No sugar and no cream, and yet it still tastes like pannacotta—everyone who has tasted it has declared it delicious.

Coconut Pannacotta with Vanilla Bean

- 2 packets coconut cream, 1 cup (250 ml) each
- 2 sheets of gelatin (or about 1½ teaspoons powdered gelatin)
- 1 vanilla bean

Coconut cream can usually be found with Thai foods at well-stocked grocery stores. Otherwise, use the thick layer of cream at the top of canned coconut milk.

Soak the sheets of gelatin in a bowl of cold water for 5 minutes. If using gelatin powder, follow the instructions on the packaging. Pour the coconut cream into a saucepan and let it melt over low heat. Cut the vanilla bean in half and add it to the cream. Bring the cream to a boil, and let it simmer over low heat for 5 minutes, stirring occasionally.

Remove the saucepan from the heat and remove the vanilla bean. Scrape out the vanilla seeds and return them to the cream while whisking. Wring out the gelatin (if using sheets) and add the gelatin to the warm coconut cream.

Let cool for a little while, stir thoroughly and pour the cream into glasses or dessert cups. Chill in the refrigerator for 3–4 hours until it has gelled.

Serve with fresh berries.

Grilling Vegetables

In this chapter you'll find tips on cooking vegetables that didn't fit in with the veggie recipes; these vegetables are delicious when grilled all the same. Most vegetables are very tasty simply when grilled as is, while others need to be salted or blanched or parboiled first.

Ordinarily, I grill vegetables in a foil pan or a basket specially made for grilling vegetables. There are several types of metal baskets, complete with holes that let the vegetables char without falling into the embers.

Brush the vegetables and the pan with mild-tasting olive oil, preferably one flavored with lemon. Plain oil with added crushed cloves of garlic, some finely chopped chilies, crushed saffron threads, or fresh herbs is also good to add to whatever vegetable is going on the grill.

Drizzle on some fine vinegar and sprinkle salt flakes onto the grilled vegetables; this brings out the flavors even more. Or simply squeeze on some lime or lemon juice. A pat of butter, plain or seasoned, adds a final, satisfying mouthfeel.

Apple – Cut the apples into quarters, and cut out their core so the pieces lay a bit flatter. Brush with melted butter, add a pinch of salt, and grill for 3–4 minutes on each side. Grilled apple is excellent with all kinds of pork dishes.

Asparagus – Both green and white asparagus make a great side dish for any grilled main course. First, snap off the woody end of the stalks. White asparagus stalks need to be peeled from just under the top and down the stalk. They also need to be parboiled for 3–4 minutes in boiling, salted water, slightly longer if the stalks are thicker.

Green, tender asparagus can be grilled directly; simply brush on some oil, season with a bit of salt, and place them in a vegetable grill basket or directly on the grill's grate. Roll the stalks on the grate to ensure that they color evenly all around. Grill green asparagus for 2–3 minutes; do the same with parboiled white asparagus.

Bell Peppers – All types of bell peppers become intensely flavorful when grilled whole until the entire surface of their skin turns black. Once charred, place the peppers in a bowl and cover with plastic wrap for 15 minutes. This makes it easy to remove the blackened skin and get at the juicy flesh.

Bell peppers can also be quartered, seeded, brushed with oil, and grilled for a few minutes on each side. Or, dice them and slip them onto skewers.

Broccoli – Separate the broccoli into florets and cut the larger ones in half. Brush with oil, and season with salt and pepper. Grill the broccoli as you would cauliflower, but this time be a bit more cautious when using the direct heat. The small broccoli florets tend to burn easily, and then taste slightly bitter.

Cauliflower – Separate the cauliflower into smaller florets. Brush with oil and season with salt and chili flakes, which adds a lot of color and flavor to an otherwise rather pallid vegetable.

Grill the florets over direct heat for 5 minutes. Turn the florets with a frying spatula a few times during cooking. Leave the cauliflower over indirect heat until it is as soft as you like.

Daikon Radish – Daikon does well when grilled, but requires parboiling for 5 minutes in boiling, salted water. Then brush with butter or oil, season with salt and pepper, and grill for 8–10 minutes, depending on the thickness of the slices.

Eggplant – Cut eggplant into slices ½–¾ inch (1–2 cm) thick, across or lengthwise. Salt generously on both sides, and let them sit for half an hour. Wipe off the collected liquid; this removes the eggplant's bitter taste, and makes it even tastier when grilled. Brush the slices with seasoned oil and grind on some pepper. Grill 5 minutes on each side over direct heat or until the eggplant is soft, which is when it's at its best.

Small eggplants are very nice when left intact and grilled. Poke a few holes in the skin with a toothpick. Grill them over direct heat for 15 minutes, turning several times while cooking (the eggplant's skin will turn completely black). Move the eggplant to the side of the grill to finish cooking, 30 minutes over indirect heat. Keep turning it now and then to grill it evenly. When it's done, cut it in four pieces length-wise, drizzle with some olive oil, and sprinkle with salt flakes.

Last but not least, here is another very common way to eat eggplant in Turkey: Let the eggplant cool, slice it lengthwise, and scoop out the flesh with a spoon. Cut the flesh into smaller chunks and combine it with oil, lemon juice, and minced garlic. This eggplant dish acquires a deliciously smoky flavor when grilled.

Fennel – Parboiled slices of fennel are tasty as a side dish that goes particularly well with fish and chicken. Cut the fennel in half lengthwise, and place the pieces in boiling, salted water.

Parboil the fennel for 3 minutes; drain well. Brush with oil, preferably seasoned with saffron, and season lightly with salt and pepper. Grill over direct heat for 3 minutes on each side.

Garlic – Garlic baked in foil tastes wonderful. Cut the head in half, place a pat of butter and some salt onto each cut side; wrap in a small sheet of foil, one for each half of garlic. Pinch the foil together to close securely, and grill the packets for 20 minutes near the embers. Serve the grilled garlic straight from the foil, accompanied by extra butter and salt flakes.

You can also parboil whole heads of garlic in boiling, salted water for 3 minutes. Cut the heads in half, brush with olive oil and place the cut side directly against the surface of the grate. Grill for 3 minutes on each side.

Place the garlic on a platter. Drizzle some olive oil on top and season with salt flakes and finely chopped herbs. Use a fork to pluck the grilled garlic straight from the skin. This is a superb accompaniment to grilled lamb, beef, or pork.

Green Beans – Trim off the pointy ends. Place the beans in boiling, salted water. Blanch them for one minute, then pour the green beans into a colander and rinse them immediately in cold water. Make bundles of six or seven beans by wrapping them in a slice of bacon and fastening the bundle with a toothpick. Brush with oil and grill over direct heat, 2 minutes per side.

Lemon – Cut organic lemons into 1-inch (3 cm) thick slices. Brush with oil and sprinkle generously with salt flakes. Grill over direct heat until the slices are quite colored, at least 5 minutes on each side. Let them sit for a while over indirect heat, until they become very soft. Grilled lemon is exceptionally tasty when squeezed over fish, shellfish, fowl, and pork.

Miscellaneous Mushrooms – Mushrooms are at their tastiest when they're brushed with butter before hitting the grill, but seasoned oil works perfectly well, too. Mushrooms absorb a lot of fat while cooking, so brush on more butter or oil as you go.

Larger mushrooms such as portabellas and oyster mushrooms are delicious when grilled whole. I usually cut button mushrooms and wild mushrooms into smaller pieces. Season them with salt and pepper.

Larger mushrooms need 3 minutes on each side over direct heat, but then let them cook for a while on indirect heat. Grill smaller mushroom pieces in a vegetable basket or in a foil pan for 5 minutes over direct heat. Turn the pieces a few times with a frying spatula.

Onions/Scallions/Spring Onions – Grilled onions lose a lot of their sharp taste and become very mild and sweet. Peel large onions, yellow or red, and cut them into ¾-inch (2-cm) slices. Brush with oil and season with salt and pepper. Grill the slices for 3 minutes on each side over direct heat. Leave the slices over indirect heat for a while to finish cooking.

Scallions, also known as spring onions, are very good to grill whole. Cut off the top of the green part, and grill as you would slices of onion. Smaller onions can be parboiled unpeeled in boiling water for 2 minutes. Drain them thoroughly in a colander. Brush with oil and grill for 10 minutes until the outer skin turns black. Turn the scallions several times while cooking.

Tomato – Grilled tomatoes have a delectably tangy flavor. Cut them in half or in thick slices and season with salt and pepper, chili pepper, or herbs. Grill for 2 minutes each side, or less if you are grilling slices. Don't allow them to get more than just warmed through, or else they'll turn mushy. Cherry tomatoes can be grilled whole, still on the branch, in a vegetable basket.

Zucchini/Summer Squash – Cut slices ½–¾ inch (1–2 cm) thick across or lengthwise. Brush with oil and season with salt and pepper. Some squeezed lemon, chili pepper, and/or garlic are also good for seasoning these slices. Grill over direct heat, 2–3 minutes on each side, until the slices have developed a nice color but are not too soft.

Recipe Index

The Late Norman M. Glass
1894 – 1976

Happy Birthday
mum Joy
helping you remember your
war time memories
Love Ailsa x

CAITHNESS AND THE WAR 1939~1945

A RECORD

Written and compiled by

N. M. GLASS

WICK

PUBLISHED BY:
*NORTH OF SCOTLAND NEWSPAPERS, 42 UNION STREET, WICK,
CAITHNESS, SCOTLAND*

ACKNOWLEDGEMENTS

The Publishers acknowledge with gratitude the assistance afforded by Mr Peter Glass, Wick – son of the late
Norman M. Glass, author of Caithness – And The War, 1939 - 1945.
We are also indebted to Mr Robert Begg, Wick.

COVER

A scene of devastation following an Air Raid on Bank Row, Wick. This dramatic photograph was taken on
the 2nd July, 1940, the day after the raid which claimed the lives of 15 (including 7 children) and injured
22 people. Photograph from the Johnston Collection, courtesy of the Wick Society.

PRINTING HISTORY

Peter Reid & Co. Ltd, Edition Published 1948.
North of Scotland Newspapers, Edition Published 1994.
Set in 10/10½ pt Bembo Regular

A Catalogue Record
for this book is available from
The British Library

ISBN 1 871704 10 3

Typeset by North of Scotland Newspapers
42 Union Street, Wick, Caithness, Scotland.
Printed by Highland News Group Limited,
Henderson Road, Inverness, Scotland.

INTRODUCTION

FEW books merit the compliment of being reprinted in their original form more than 45 years after their first publication. Those who possess a copy of the original "Caithness - and the War" by Norman Glass treasure it. For others who seek a copy there has been only the rare opportunity to see them sold at a high price in auction rooms throughout the county. It is this continuing public interest which has prompted North of Scotland Newspapers to undertake the large task of reprinting this book.

An examination of any few pages of "Caithness - and the War" can identify one of the major reasons for the book's enduring popularity. It is a book not merely of how the war affected the county of Caithness but also how it affected the people of Caithness. Page after page tells some part of the story of Caithnessians who lived through the last war. Coverage of each of the war fronts contains the personal stories of local lads involved in the action. In the absence of any official record, Mr Glass compiled a Roll of Honour which gives the personal details of each of those Caithnessian servicemen who were taken prisoner of war, wounded or killed in action. This book is a valuable record of how the war affected individual servicemen from Caithness.

In addition the Second World War was one which affected civilians on a grand scale and the civilians of Caithness were to be no exception. Working on the "John O'Groat Journal", Norman Glass was in a position to be aware of how the waves and ripples of warfare entered into almost every aspect of the Caithness Home Front. Mr Glass pays due respect to this in his "Our Folks at Home" section. The sheer carnage displayed by the photographs of Bank Row taken a day after the fateful visit by a lone German bomber vividly portrays the trauma which the Home Front endured. Yet the personal story is never far away. Mr Glass includes an essay, written by a "lad of 14", George Cameron, which tells of the teenager's experiences when a German bomber obtained a direct hit on his house in Hill Avenue resulting in the tragic death of his brother, sister and a female lodger.

This book deals with the effects of the Second World War on Caithness at a personal level. In addition it is comprehensive. It looks at life on the military and civilian fronts. The book has an interest for every Caithnessian. Few members of the older generation will be able to pass over the pages without recognising names and events or recalling their own memories. For those of the younger generation, many of whom will also be able to recognise the names or deeds of their elders, it will give an insight into how the Second World War brought disruption, destruction and death to the county of Caithness. The message that war is evil is a timeless one and Mr Glass shows clearly the dreadful cost which it took on the people of Caithness during the Second World War.

A classic book is one which attracts lasting interest over many years and across different generations. "Caithness - and the War" by Norman Glass truly fits such a description.

ALLY BUDGE,
Wick, Caithness, 1993

PREFACE

CAITHNESS found herself in a strategic position of some consequence in the 1939-45 War, and the county had a share to bear – apart from the proud part taken by natives of both sexes who served at sea, on land, in the air. There were those who served, too, in the vital role of food producers through our main industries, farming and fishing, and in many other different ways as well. It is the County's share as a whole that this Record seeks to cover.

Sometime in the year 1942 the idea occurred to the writer to compile the names of Caithness folk who lost their lives or were injured during the war years. That seemed simple - but to trace and keep pace with an ever-mounting list of victims was not quite as simple as it seemed. There were snags - many of them. Hence the lists were published in order to have inaccuracies corrected and details supplemented if relatives considered as inadequate the particulars given. Reliance was placed on the interest of our county folk. The response was gratifying indeed, and it is hoped the unheeding were insignificant in number. Even so, there is no suggestion that the casualty lists given herein can be accepted as "official" – there is no official list in existence. In several instances it was difficult to distinguish between Caithness men and those connected with the county, and there may well be errors in judgement.

Newspapers were forbidden to record war-time happenings, and this was another handicap in the compilation of this Record. The drawing aside of the censorship curtain after years of black-out revealed a dimness on the "stage" and there was some peering to be done where events were reviewed in retrospect.

Four articles by Police-Sergeant Neil D. Sutherland, whose interest in Civil Defence was beyond praise, are included in the Home Front section. Two of the articles cover in part incidents already recorded but are given here because of the additional and authentic information they contain.

Finally, the writer would like to thank Sergt. Sutherland, Mr James Campbell (for prints of bomb damage), and all who supplied information or photographs to make this Record possible, also the many correspondents who wrote him personally when several of the articles were published in the "John O'Groat Journal". Most of the letters received were unanswered, but were nevertheless appreciated.

N.M.G

CONTENTS

PHOTOGRAPHS

FOREWORD

THIS Record of the War of 1939-45 as mainly affecting the County of Caithness was written up by Mr Norman M. Glass, foreman and principal linotype operator in the "John O'Groat Journal" Office. He wrote it from time to time as events developed, and also compiled the Rolls of Honour printed herein. On his part it was truly "a labour of love".

Several of the chapters and Rolls appeared in serial form in the pages of the "Journal" during 1946; and Mr Glass has since reviewed the whole, up to the time of printing off the sheets. So highly appreciated was the work that, while the Record and Rolls were appearing in the "Journal" many communications were received from readers expressing gratification at the announcement that the work would eventually be issued in book form. Mr Glass had this intention in mind all along; and I feel sure that the Record as now completed will be regarded as in every way excellent. Alike from the literary, technical and patriotic points of view, it is not only a credit to the author, but also a worthly local WAR MEMORIAL in itself.

As showing how the terrible struggle affected one particular county of Scotland, it is probably unique among War Books so far published. I have said "as affecting one particular county". In a map of the world the county of Caithness could be covered by a pencil point, and even in a map of the British Isles it occupies only a small space away up in the far north-eastern corner. Its population is round about 24,000.

Reading the following chapters and perusing the Rolls of Honour, one can realize how splendidly and loyally and with what sacrifice the people in this small corner of the kingdom, in common with those elsewhere, played their part so that human liberties and Christian civilization might be preserved on the earth. Multiply these efforts and sacrifices to cover practically every country in the world and one gets a vivid idea of what the great conflict cost our nation and our Allies. And if one observation may be permitted in this Foreword, we would say: Surely only madmen, drunk, like Hitler or Mussolini and their henchmen, with visions of world domination, would so act in the negotiation of Peace settlements as to risk bringing another, and even more dreadful, catastrophe upon the world. In Mr Glass's own fine closing words (page 59) let our prayer be: "May it be an enduring peace – peace for all time, please God – bringing freedom and security with consequent prosperity to all peoples."

Every Caithnessian anywhere who procures a copy of this book, will, we feel certain, value it highly and be proud of its possession.

R. J. G. M.

THE UNKNOWN

No man holds the key that will unlock to-morrow,
No one can foretell the future, or what lies in store;
Human eyes can't penetrate the veil or see
The end towards which we move along the roads of destiny,
For God in His great mercy has withheld these secret things.
We know sufficient for the day, and every moment
Brings its promise and its hope;
It is enough that now, today, we have the strength
With which to climb, and light to see the way.

Lines by a Canadian airman who later lost his life flying
somewhere around our coasts.

CAITHNESS – AND THE WAR

Hitler had made up his mind.

Changing from Peace to War.

WE ARE AT WAR. These four fateful little words were broadcast to the people of Britain on the forenoon of Sunday, September 3, 1939. The speaker was Neville Chamberlain, the Prime Minister who had striven strenuously to avoid such a catastrophe – the man who had pocketed his pride and gone abroad three times to meet the dictators of Germany and Italy in efforts to preserve peace. No policy of appeasement proved workable.

Germany under Adolf Hitler had annexed Austria; claimed Sudetenland (within Czecho-slova-kia) and when Britain had recognised the claim, Hitler marched in and took over the whole country. . . . .And now (a few months later) the powerful German Army had begun the invasion of Poland.

So ticks the clock in this immortal hour,
The fate of nations hangs by slender thread;
And War, the arbiter of earthly power,
Describes the paths of duty to be led.
– H. FAINT (Wick)

"This morning," said Mr Chamberlain in his broadcast, "the British Ambassador in Berlin handed the German Government a final note stating that unless we heard from them by 11 o'clock that they were prepared at once to withdraw their troops from Poland, a state of war would exist between us. I have to tell you now that no such undertaking has been received and that consequently this country is at war with Germany. . . Up to the very last it would have been quite possible to have arranged a peaceful and honourable settlement between Germany and Poland, but Hitler would not have it. He had evidently made up his mind to attack Poland whatever happened.

"We have done all that any country could do to establish peace. The situation in which no word given by Germany's ruler could be trusted and no people or country could feel themselves safe has become intolerable. . .

"May God bless you all. May He defend the right. It is the evil things we shall be fighting against – brute force, bad faith, injustice, oppression and persecution; and against them I am certain that the right will prevail."

* * * * *

The country had come through many months of anxieties, alarms, crises. No sooner was one international problem seemingly solved than another flared up. The clamour of Germany and Hitler's demands were unceasing; and Mussolini by a show of might had added Abyssinia and later Albania to the Italian Empire. The defenceless peoples of these countries had been bombed without warning (and the Ethiopians poisoned by war gases) into submission to his rule. He, too, was howling again. Italy demanded Tunis, Corsica, Nice.

The world rocked. The dictator countries were armed to the teeth and had the backing of Japan. Where were demands, followed by undeclared war, to cease? What country next to be "annexed"? Britain to an extent had heeded the warning and was preparing quietly if inadequately to meet the challenge. Talks, notes, messages, appeals had all been useless. Mr Chamberlain's declaration of war simply had to come, but clearly the other countries of the world did not believe in Britain's strength to overcome the might of Germany. Little nations were afraid to move. They hoped to be spared the agonies of war but they knew they might be swallowed. They waited – and swallowed they were. The day came when Germany had almost all Europe in her relentless clutches.

* * * * *

War! The shadow was ever lengthening – growing bigger, darker, heavier; overcasting the lives of mankind from end to end of an unsettled country. No one could escape its tentacles. Weeks beforehand even far-away Caithness was fully conscious of the preparations going ahead, amid a mass of rumour and speculation. Special trains had arrived at Thurso with Navymen recalled to their ships stationed at Scapa; from various parts of the county Royal Naval Reservists were called up, as were men of the Territorial Units. There were appeals for men and women to join national defence companies and auxiliary services.

This war was to be different from all previous wars – it was to bring the civilians into the front line. Britons were not to be secure in their island home: "there were no longer any islands" and, said the Prime Minister, "it will strike the workman, the clerk, the man in the street or on the bus, his wife and children in their homes" – a prophecy that was to be fulfilled.

Air raid precautionary services had been organised for every district, and gasmasks had been assembled and distributed to every resident, old and young, by the wardens in their area. Caithness had a small army of voluntary workers in the precautionary services which had undergone training quietly but regularly over a period of many months beforehand. The services included air wardens, special constables, decontamination squads, first-aid detachments, fire fighting and rescue squads, ambulance drivers, centre personnel, etc. These fellows knew what to expect when the warning siren sounded and always readily answered the call. When the day came – as come it did in Wick – that their services were required, they faithfully performed their allotted tasks – helping the homeless, removing the sick, the injured, the dead; guarding shattered property until rightful owners recovered what they could from the wreckage.

Main roads in the burghs and county were given a white centre strip for the guidance of traffic under black-out conditions. Paving kerbs were whitened and lamp standards given white bands to help guide pedestrians after darkness fell. Municipal and local government buildings were sandbagged. There was an order compelling all fishing boats to remain in port – a ban that later was lifted and the boats issued with permits for fishing.

★ ★ ★ ★ ★

Sunday, September 3, 1939, was a dull, depressing day in Caithness. The sky was overcast as Mr Chamberlain spoke – then came heavy showers of rain. Groups of people assembled in the streets to discuss the situation. The strength of Germany and her air power filled the conversation. Enemy propaganda had encouraged this – it had sought to spread a spirit of depression, of defeatism – and partially succeeded. But there were braver hearts as well: men with faith in the Empire's strength and resources, and faith also in the justice of her cause.

Appropriate references were made in the church services to the trials and tests the nation was about to undergo, but on the first day of war the evening services were cancelled by order because of the danger of light penetrating through insufficiently darkened windows. Territorials guarded the wireless station and special constables took over the cable-house at Reiss, the post-office and other vulnerable points.

The change-over from peace to war meant "Orders," and these came concerning the effective obscuring of lights, the early closing of shops, a curfew for children (indoors by 8 p.m.), and there was a call for volunteers for the fire brigade. Altogether, there were said to be 7000 war-time Orders.

Within a week more than 600 men had said farewell to their native Caithness to join the Services – Territorials, R.N.R.'s, and volunteer transport drivers. The clarion call "To arms" reached every corner. Men answered from the heights of Benechielt to the gray crags of Duncansby and from Drumholistan to the Ord; they came from farms and crofts in out-of-the-way places along the countryside, from the hamlets and the villages; they came from the offices and the workshops of the towns – gathering in to "Battle for Britain." The little island of Stroma had a quarter of its population of about 130 on war service, and 15 per cent of its Servicemen gave their lives for their country.

Large crowds assembled at Thurso to witness the departure of the T.A. Anti-Aircraft unit, then only lately returned from a month of training in camp. The men were under Major Potter, and sang like good soldiers as the buses took them off to Scrabster.

The 5th Seaforths entrained at Wick and Thurso on September 4 for Dornoch and Evanton. At Thurso friends were not permitted to bid them good-bye on the station platform. This was regarded as a heartless restriction. About 80 of the Wick Company were posted to Stromness and took their departure by bus from the Drill Hall in Dempster Street. The buses passed along a street lined by people and the soldiers had a good send-off. Who then thought that our lads were destined to chase the enemy over burning sands from El Alamein to Sicily and later fight their way over bloody battlefields from the coast of France to Germany? How many of those smiling faces were never to return? – who among them privileged not to feel "the grinding tread of grim Misfortune's heel"?

Caithness had a front seat.

Early Raids on Scapa Flow.

SIX weeks after the opening of hostilities Caithness came close to the realities of air attack – and Wick had its first war scare.

Scapa Flow and the ships therein came in for early attention from the *Luftwaffe*. This great naval base was reckoned as of much strategic importance and its proximity brought the whole North of Scotland into the danger zone. There were five sharp bombing attacks on Scapa in the early stages of the war.

Fourteen 'planes were engaged in two attacks on October 17, 1939, and the *Iron Duke* , a depot and training ship, was damaged. Two enemy bombers were shot down.

Despite the danger from exploding bombs and falling shrapnel, hundreds of Kirkwall and Stromness people watched the fighting. Actually, they set a bad example as children took the same risk – a risk that finally led to casualties.

The weather was very fine on that October day, and it was an awe-inspiring spectacle as, amid thunderous droning of planes, the guns of ships and shore batteries rattled up hundreds of rounds and produced curtains of bursts in the sunny and almost cloudless sky.

★　★　★　★　★

That day at 2 p.m. Wick had its first air raid warning – sounded on the John O'Groat Laundry buzzer (then the town's only siren). 'Planes had been sighted flying over Caithness at great height. The warning caused much speculation and apprehension in the royal burgh, and wild rumours went around. One alleged that there were casualties by poison gas in Bower and Thurso – the names of victims were circulated and added credence to the tale. Confusing rumour was Hitler's best ally and how willing we were to help him!

Few people in the streets were carrying gasmasks when the warning came and many hurried home for the protecting facepiece. Police patrolled the streets in steel helmets and with gasmasks at the alert position. The police cars, too, were busy careering through the streets and ringing bells as a warning of danger. Excitement was everywhere – everyone believed the war had come to the county. Forty minutes elapsed before the "All clear" signal was given.

★　★　★　★　★

The control of school children became a problem. When first the siren sounded the schools were instantly dismissed and the children crowded the streets in rushing breathlessly to their homes – a perfect target for machine-gun fire. What casualties there could have been! Country pupils accompanied the town scholars and took refuge wherever they were welcomed.

Next day (October 18) the schools were again dismissed, following a report that enemy 'planes were heard over Caithness; the A.R.P. authorities decided to keep the Wick schools closed for the remainder of the week, and for a period thereafter education was hampered by irregular schooling – a redistribution of pupils, the scattering of scholars, the departure of male teachers, and shorter hours all contributing to an unsettled state, "disturbance" it was termed officially. The town council made representation regarding the provision of shelters at the schools, but these did not come till long afterwards. The Education Authority were pardonably unwilling to accept responsibility regarding the safety of the pupils. Schools are big buildings and were likely targets for the enemy – and a solitary bomb could create a catastrophe should it fall in the vicinity of 500 children. Fortunately, that did not happen here, though other towns had harrowing experiences.

★　★　★　★　★

Residents along the north coast and on Stroma island had a grandstand view of the first raid on Scapa, particularly the attempted bombing of ships in the Pentland Firth. A Stroma motorboat fishing east from the island found itself within the danger zone and quickly made for harbour. The realities of war had come to a quiet countryside. Those with good telescopes had a clear view of one of the German raiders falling in flames and a man descending by parachute.

Advocating the installation of an improved telegraph service in the island of Stroma, Mr G. Manson, schoolmaster there, wrote to Mr Robertson, county clerk:– "We have to-day witnessed two aerial attacks on Scapa Flow. The approaching aircraft were clearly visible to us, coming in over the Skerries from an easterly direction – seven aeroplanes in close formation and one in the rear. We identified these as German machines, although they were flying at a high altitude . . .

"There were a Belgian trawler, a small steamer, and a Stroma fishing boat in the firth. A bomb fell quite close to the trawler, but fortunately did no damage. It might have been otherwise, however, but we could not have given immediate notice had anything serious happened . . ."

★　★　★　★　★

The third attack on Scapa Flow (there was a small raid on March 31) by German bombing 'planes was at dusk on April 2, 1940. The enemy had to evade British fighters and gunfire from ships.

They found it difficult to penetrate the defences – defences which became more formidable with each attack and which later were described by Mr Churchill (then First Lord of the Admiralty) as "the heaviest protective anti-aircraft in the world."

The third raid did not last long, but casualties included two civilians and a Serviceman injured by splinters. One Nazi machine was shot down into the sea.

Visibility was good that April evening and in the twilight two German raiders were recognised as they flew over John O'Groats at a comparatively low altitude.

The raid was less spectacular than usual. Either the barrage of fire from the Orkneys made them hesitate to develop an attack or else it was the rapid approach of British fighters in pursuit. At any rate, before the bombers were half-way across the Pentland Firth they turned in an easterly direction.

Two trawlers were at the time proceeding in the direction of Duncansby Head, and one of them was subjected to a burst of machine-gun fire from one of the raiders. Flying low over Duncansby Head this raider also treated the lighthouse to another burst of machine-gun bullets. The lighthouse-keeper who was on duty saw the 'plane pass quite low between the watchtower and the foghorn.

★　★　★　★　★

The fourth raid on Scapa Flow (on 8th April, 1940) was a determined attack, and the alarm lasted from 8.30 till 11 p.m.

The island of Stroma had an air alarm that evening and the wardens were on duty. The people of the island and along the north coast were thrilled by the proceedings and witnessed much of the battle from the moment the first five Jerry 'planes flew comparatively low across the firth. Amid a fusillade of bursting shells the movements of one enemy machine became erratic and it disappeared from view leaving behind a long trail of black smoke. German 'planes passed over Stroma several times during the desperate struggle (British fighters were out in force) and the whine of bullets and shrapnel was clearly heard. Some pieces of shrapnel landed on the island, and some shells passed over and fell into the sea on the south side of the island.

Three German airmen were picked up at sea after having been twelve hours adrift in a rubber dinghy; the *Luftwaffe* were not altogether masters of the skies. They lost five machines that night over Orkney.

★　★　★　★　★

Wick got a prize that evening – an intact German Heinkel. This machine was damaged in the engagement over Orkney, pursued by Hurricanes from Wick 'drome and chose to land there rather than to perish in the sea. Two of the crew were killed and two uninjured were made prisoners, passing their first night in Scotland in the police cells at Wick before going south to an internment camp. One was an officer aged over 30 who could speak English and the other a young airman in his early twenties. Both were smart-looking and well dressed.

And here a wee bit story: Quite a number of German airmen passed through police hands at Wick in the earlier stages of the war. There they were searched and possessions removed, and lodged in the cells. They were interrogated by the Intelligence service. Two such were a tall, young and haughty ober-lieutenant (a swaggering Nazi) and an older airman who showed much concern for the welfare of his "master." The men occupied separate cells.

In the evening they were served with tea and when collecting the empties a women courthouse attendant spoke to them without receiving an answer. "Was it go-o-d?" she inquired off the older airman, and repeated the question slowly and deliberately, as she might to a child: "Was it g-o-o-d?"

"Yes,", he smilingly acknowledged to her astonishment, "I think it was Lipton's." He had been some years in America.

★　★　★　★　★

Scapa was the target of sixty bombers in the most intensive raid of all on the evening of 10th April, 1940. The machines flew very high and attacked in successive relays. Meant as a knockout blow, it failed completely in its object, and cost the enemy seven valuable 'planes in addition to those which must have hirpled home in a crippled state. The total cost must indeed have been extremely heavy because Scapa as a target was pretty well dropped thereafter.

Caithness was made vividly aware of this raid and alarms were sounded in Wick and Thurso. From practically every part of the county, and particularly from the coast, the sounds of gunfire and explosions were heard and the sky was lit up with shellfire and the groping fingers of searchlights concentrated on enemy aircraft. Visibility was so good that barrage balloons were readily spotted from our coasts.

The wail of the warning sirens caused considerable uneasiness in both Wick and Thurso, although only a precautionary measure. A.R.P. personnel promptly manned all posts, but happily their services were not needed. Danger threatened, however, and the townspeople were made aware of this because of the great air activity over Wick – flights of Hudsons flying around continuously. Large numbers of people flocked to the sea-fronts (foolishly it might have been) to gaze upon the distant scene. Flashes of gunfire were frequent – sometimes low in the sky, sometimes high in the heavens. There was also heard the booming of guns and the crash of explosives, some of them sounding uncomfortably near.

The enemy was indeed at our doorstep.

★　★　★　★　★

Luftwaffe raiders came again to Orkney at 9.30 on the evening of April 24, and were met by intense anti-aircraft fire and attacked by fighter 'planes of the R.A.F. Shooting was brief but heavy. Air raid warnings were sounded and the "All clear" signal was given after about an hour.

Two bombs fell on a heather-clad part of the island of Hoy. A roadway was strewn with machine-gun bullets but no casualties were reported. The explosions on Hoy caused houses in Stromness (six miles across the water) to shake as if by earthquake.

Days in a northern town.

Experiences in and Around Wick in War-time.

FIVE years of war produced many memorable days for the people of Wick – days of terror, trials, and tragedy; days of anxiety, accidents, and anger; days of stress, sorrow, and sympathy; days of partings, patience, and of pride; days of danger and of courage; days demanding all qualities from a community – and all occasioned by the awfulness of "man's inhumanity to man" as practised in warfare. Drawing memory's chord, we can trace again some of the experiences.

Days in a northern town – unforgettable days. There were days when the railway station was the scene of much activity; where friends took farewell of each other for a time – perchance for all time. The Territorials went away; men of the auxiliary services were called to the colours. Hundreds of Naval Reservists went to help man Britain's great

Fleet and to the merchant service; many volunteered to do battle against and to destroy the enemy's secret weapon, the treacherous sea-mine. Young men and girls continued regularly to go away under the group system to all the Services. There were times when soldiers or airmen stationed here took their departure as units or as individuals.

These were all memorable days – for someone. Think of the passenger platform scenes when all these brave fellows bid good-bye to their dearest friends. The men generally went laughingly; the women returned home to their everyday duties, in most cases sad at heart but showing no outward sign of the sorrow with which such partings are ever tinged.

★　★　★　★　★

Those who live in a town by the fringe of the sea become attached to it in all its moods. They know it can be bountiful, they know it can be pitiless: their interest is ever centred in all who "go down to the sea in ships" and there existed a comradeship that seemed unbreakable. But ruthless war respected nought – it multiplied the dangers. Shuddering sounds and woeful and saddening sights brought it very near in the first years of conflict. Yet the people remained calm; they sought only to be helpful, to care for the sick and injured, to assist and succour brothers from our own country or abroad whose ships had gone down with all they possessed; and they buried the dead with honour.

Night-time came with a storm raging at sea. Morning brought the news that a guardian vessel had gone down outside the bay. The body of a sailor was washed ashore; others followed, mainly handsome fellows wearing lifebelts and some in dungarees, until at one point 18 were laid side by side for burial with military honours in a common grave. Had they escaped by boat or raft only to be tossed by relentless waves against which the human frame was helpless? Had cruel fate been doubly unkind to them? No one could tell, but all could surmise. The townspeople turned out to the funeral and women lined the streets on a bitterly cold afternoon to watch the sad procession – and to weep.

That was another memorable day in this little corner of the country but it was only the forerunner of similar scenes to follow. The bodies of foreign seamen, too, came from the icy waters to be buried here. Poor souls, they or their country at the time had no quarrel with the Nazis, but Nazi pirates had made targets of their ships and sent them to their

5

grave. Neutrality was not respected.

There are 155 war graves in the cemeteries at Wick and Thurso, and there are others scattered throughout the county. Wick cemetery is the last resting-place of 120. Known servicemen number 88, made up of: – Navy 34, Army 3, Air Force, 51; there are six local men – two from each of the three Chief Services. The "unknown" buried at Wick number 22 – 21 sailors and an airman. Four German airmen are also interred here. Servicemen buried at Thurso number 35 – 2 Army, 13 Naval Services, 19 Merchant Navy, and one Polish soldier. (There are

they are posted as "missing." One who perished was within sight of his home. The injured went to hospital; the haggard, oil-bespattered sailors to an institution to be cared for by kindly hands. The ship moved slowly on, blazing for days.

Around about mid-day the townspeople heard the sound of gunfire at sea – sharp sounds and dull thuds. They suspected the Navy was demanding an eye for an eye – that the destructor was being destroyed.

That was a memorable day.

Some of the war graves in Wick Cemetery.

two bodies in some of the graves).

Huge flames lighting the sky at sea in the early morning indicated a gigantic tragedy. And so it proved. Oil was burning over a mile wide radius at sea and in the centre of the conflagration was a stricken ship – stricken by the enemy. Survivors picked up by fishermen came into port – and the story spread around the town, whose streets the fire reflection had lit as if by daylight through all the dark hours of night. The survivors presented a picture sufficient to soften the hardest heart. They had come through a fearsome experience, some clad only in underwear as they hurriedly left their bunks to leap into small-boats to row as they had never rowed before to keep outside the quickly spreading flames on the sea surface and to get away from the infernal heat. They rowed with oily oars in a thick, oily surface. Their desperate struggle lasted fully half-an-hour. But they won through, exhausted by their efforts. Thirty men scrambled (as it were) from the gates of hell to safety – eleven were left behind:

Two white Danish fishing boats throbbed their way into the harbour. A glance showed that they carried more lifeboats than usual and their arrival at the quayside revealed another sad tale – another dash for life. They had on board 39 seamen saved from foreign ships: some required medical attention, others went to a centre to await arrangements for their transport south. Few of them could speak English but their very appearance showed the haste with which they were compelled to part from their belongings. They had only minutes in which to save themselves. Twenty of their friends, including a woman stewardess, had perished. They had rowed for nine hours in open boats. They had "walked with death" but luckily for them the sea was in a friendly mood.

These are sad stories of the sea that come readily to mind; they will pass on for they, and others like them, will often be recounted in homes around the Caithness coasts.

* * * * *

Peace and quietness prevailed in the town on the first afternoon in July of 1940. Everyone in the little town was engaged in daily tasks – men and women moved around, some stood chatting in the streets, others scrutinised the contents of shop windows; here and there, children were at play.

Heavy low clouds hung over the town that afternoon and dipping from above them an enemy 'plane released a couple of bombs in the vicinity of the harbour.

The like had never happened in the country in day-time before. The missiles exploded as they crashed on the hard surface of the roadway, and the explosions shook the town and its people. Dwellings in the near neighbourhood collapsed, crumbling in a moment into a mass of wreckage; window panes in a whole area flew from their sockets as if by magic – there was a mess that baffled description. Peace was replaced by pandemonium.

Men and women were killed instantly, as were little children playing innocently in the streets. Many suffered from shock and injuries. Three hours later a mother who had lost one child was still searching for another of her family – and finally found her in the mortuary. Identification was not always easy.

Truly, the civilian had taken a place in the front line – a memory that will remain for ever.

That was the first but not the last awful experience of attack from the air that came to Wick.

* * * * *

There was a day (some time later) when people in the streets gazed skyward as the clock was about to strike the noonday hour. High above the town was an intruder machine, and higher still but to its rear were specks in the sky – moving ever closer to the fleeing enemy. Some were quick to grasp the situation; they guessed that something unusual was happening above them; the rattle of machine-gun fire confirmed the conjecture of a chase. Quickly they passed over the town – over the town but not so far away. Those who lived on the outskirts saw a machine crash into the sea and the Hurricanes circle to return.

Two hours later the body of a German airman was taken into harbour and conveyed to the mortuary. He was pale in death, slim of build, and young in years. Now and again one tried to picture the airmen above dealing death and destruction – could it

be that we would ever meet? Here was one (probably not a true specimen) who was to be buried in a strange land by people he had been drilled to despise. Yet we looked upon him as somebody's son and he got a resting-place alongside other unreturning airmen who, sent out to destroy, had been themselves destroyed.

That evening an official communique stated that an enemy machine (a Dornier) had been brought down off the north coast of Scotland. We will leave it at that, but keep it as a memory.

* * * * *

A convoy! Everyone around the coasts of Caithness had at times cast an eye seawards to admire a procession of massive ships move seemingly slowly on, guarded against attack by high-speed destroyers. To the man on the coast these mighty merchantmen gave an impression of strength and defiance – they were the links between great nations and their war-time needs. "The convoy must go through" was a living command.

There was one convoy, however, which Caithnessians did not see but which dwells indelibly in the memory: Far out in the Atlantic were 38 merchantmen escorted by the armed merchant cruiser *Jervis Bay*. Late on a November afternoon (in 1940) a mighty German battleship appeared on the far horizon. Here was the prize the raider sought: valuable targets for her heavy guns.

Monument erected in Nova Scotia in honour of the captain and crew of the "Jervis Bay".

But the *Jervis Bay* had a duty to perform and it was undertaken without hesitation. Throwing a smoke-screen around the merchantmen, she went forth to do battle against the giant. Her commander knew she could not survive, but by engaging in battle hoped to gain sufficient time to enable the convoy to escape.

Early in the unequal fight the *Jervis Bay* had her bridge, engine room and steering-gear badly damaged, but she went on with her job – drawing the enemy's fire. With rent bows, the gallant ship, ablaze and sinking, fought on, her flag still flying defiantly – fought until she could no longer fight. Her task was nobly done: 34 of the merchantmen came safely through.

That was an epic action that thrilled the world – a fight against impossible odds that saved precious ships, lives and cargoes. Caithness shared in the nation's pride, pride mingled with sorrow, because she had shared in the sacrifice. Nine of her 18 sons on the *Jervis Bay* were lost. Comdr. Fegan was posthumously awarded the Victoria Cross – a signal honour reflecting on the men who so gallantly fought under him.

Caithness will remember!

SOULS OF THE BRAVE.

Hats off! unto their memory,
Brave, gallant heroes of the sea;
Salute the Flag at half-mast high:
They showed us how to fight and die . . .

Though great the odds against them were,
They closed in mortal combat there,
And, with a grim, determined smile,
And in the true old British style.

Who says the race is in decay
That breeds such men as them to-day?
Who says we do not rule the waves,
Or that our sons would live as slaves? . . .

Caithnessia, as a mother, weeps
Her valiant dead, the while she keeps
Sad vigils by the wailing wave,
The sheltered creek and wide-mouthed cave;
There's gloom and sorrow on her brow,
Yet pride lights up her eyes somehow,
Her tears are like the salt sea spray,
Her proudest memory – "Jervis Bay."
That wild sea fight, fifth of November.
Britannia sure will aye remember.

–H. Henderson (Reay).

War-time Wrecks Around the Caithness Coasts.

WAR-TIME restrictions were manifold, and at points these pinched according to the customary tendencies of the individual. What we were "used to" in the way of food, raiment and necessities in and around the home was not always easy to forgo; but the grasp of the greedy had compulsorily to be checked in order to provide for the needy, and the control of commodities aimed at an equal distribution and generally was accepted as ample.

There was one restriction, however, that applied particularly to Caithness and was at times tantalising. That was the censorship of mail, all of which went direct to Inverness for examination; at one period letters and packages for delivery within the county were given the same official scrutiny and business transactions were consequently much delayed. A letter from Wick or Thurso to any neighbouring district took four or more days to arrive. For instance, the County Council circularised its members enclosing timeous notice of meeting. Away to Inverness went the correspondence, and it has been known that the date of meeting passed ere the notices intimating same were received by the members. Everything was delivered by way of the Highland Capital – even medicine posted by a chemist – and consequently there was annoying delay. This imposed a needless hardship and was rightly resented, until finally the authorities (after many protests) permitted mail within the county to be delivered direct.

"Thou shalt not" was the slogan of the censor – thou shalt not mention a ship, a 'plane, or an army lorry, or anything that happened to them; thou shalt not comment on the weather or give the whereabouts of the boys from home, nor give particulars of Service personnel met or entertained; neither any clue whatever likely to be of value to the enemy. Dare not say that a bomb or mine exploded in your district. "Thou shalt not" made letter-writing a confined and trying affair.

And what applied to the individual applied likewise to the Press – only stories for publication had to be submitted to London. There they went through the mill and we were to learn that the censorship mills "grind slowly and grind exceeding small " – so small sometimes that what was left was worthless as news. "Thou shalt not" reigned here, too, and permission to publish was frequently withheld altogether.

The war is over, censorship is raised and freedom reigns again. What is written now can be of no value to the enemy, but may be of interest to the people. Here then is an attempt to re-write some of the outstanding stories.

★ ★ ★ ★ ★

A terrific gale swept in from the sea on Saturday, 24th January, 1942. It was so fierce that in exposed places the pedestrian had to struggle desperately to make headway against it: the full blast brought him to a standstill. That night a ship was smashed to pieces in Wick bay and all her crew perished. Until now nothing has been published concerning this disaster.

The vessel was a coasting steamer named the *Isleford*, believed to have 15 on board. Said to be plying between Orkney and Invergordon, she had passed Wick earlier that awful night going south but developed engine trouble and became the plaything of merciless waves. Distress flares from her when off Sarclet were picked up at 10.30 by coast-watchers and the coastguard station at Wick informed. The severity of the storm precluded the launching of the lifeboat but the rocket apparatus crew were ordered to stand-by.

The storm-tossed ship was picked up in the beam of a searchlight off Wick, where the fury of the wind and wave carried her into the bay, which was a seething mass of broken water with mountainous waves dashing on the shores. Here the steamer was whirled hither and thither on an erratic course to death. Anticipating her ultimate doom, the rocket crew took up position on the north shore, and miraculously the ship survived only finally to be flung on to the jagged rocks under the cliffs. Exposed to the full force of the heavy seas, the ship broke in two – the forepart was swept away.

The figures of five men were seen near the bridge and others many have been sheltering in the wheelhouse. The rocket crew went into action: at the first attempt it was lifted high in the air and over the mast; a second met the same fate, only the line fell across the steamer – but out of reach of the seamen.

When hope was high, rescuers and spectators were horrified to see two men and the wheelhouse washed away; another man went to his doom with the next wave.

The battle for life went on. Two survivors clung desperately to the rigging. A rocket whipped round the mast which was swinging dizzily and violently from side to side, plunging the clinging victims into the sea. Above the men's heads was the life-line. Did they know it? Human voices were lost in the storm. The man nearest struggled forward. Everything was against him: the sweeping wind, the bitter cold, his drenched condition, his precarious hold, and the higher he got the wider the swing of the mast and the greater the chance of being mutilated on the rocks. There was that one chance – no, he was exhausted. His shipmate below released his grip – and was gone in a flash; the last man was soon his companion in Fate.

Early that Sunday morning – midnight had gone – the rocket crew returned from valiant but vain attempts to save brothers from the sea and praying ne'er again to have such a sad experience.

Wreckage was plentiful when daylight dawned and some bodies were recovered. One held tightly an empty box in each hand. That pointed to hope of being washed ashore but man could live only for moments in such a sea.

★ ★ ★ ★ ★

All war days were more or less sad days. Tragedies on the doorstep, however (though insignificant compared with happenings elsewhere) cling closer in the memory. There were particularly saddening sights in Wick in early 1940 when on two occasions some 15 British sailors were buried in a common grave. The coffins were draped with the Union Jack and borne on Service lorries. A party of bluejackets preceded the hearses, and a detachment of the R.A.F. and Army formed the escort party.

Two Admiralty vessels went to their doom off the Caithness coast early in 1940. These were the destroyer *Exmouth* and the minesweeper *Sphinx*. The casualty lists were heavy and the bodies of many of the dead were later washed ashore and some of them buried in our county with military honours.

The *Sphinx* was attacked by two German 'planes with bombs and machine-guns and capsized and sank with the loss of 54 men. The ship received a direct hit by bomb, and, said a survivor (there were 46) "the whole forecastle seemed to lift up and fold back without breaking into fragments . . . The seas were very heavy, and it was with difficulty that another vessel got us in tow. Early next day the tow-rope parted, and the *Sphinx* was left almost helpless in the rough seas. The engines were out of action.

"A huge wave hit the *Sphinx* broadside and the vessel capsized. It all happened suddenly – I could not even shout before I felt myself in the water. Heads kept bobbing up all around, and men kept calling out odd words about their families at home. Then a searchlight showed on the water amidst us. I struck out and caught hold of a line that had been thrown out. I was pulled aboard a ship absolutely exhausted."

The *Sphinx* came ashore on the coast at Clyth, thrown keel up on the beach. Some 30 bodies of Navymen belonging to the minesweeper were washed ashore along the Caithness coast and 20 were buried in Wick Cemetery.

★ ★ ★ ★ ★

H.M.S. *Exmouth* was lost in January, 1940, with all hands – 15 officers and 173 ratings. Nothing was known locally of the tragedy until the sea began to give up its dead. Many of the bodies were identified, a few remained unknown warriors, but whatever the circumstances all were carried to their last rest-ing-place at Wick with full military honours and fol-lowed by a mourning civilian population. The first mass funeral took place on the last day of January. The scene was most impressive. As the coffins were carried from the temporary mortuary in Huddart Street to the waiting funeral wagons a pronounced hush fell on the crowd. It was indeed a solemn moment.

Fifteen ratings from the destroyer *Exmouth* were laid side by side in one grave at Wick. One of the men buried here – Petty Officer Joe O'Brien, of Harrogate (aged 27 years) – had a distinguished ath-letic career and possessed an amazing collection of trophies and certificates, including 200 medals and cups for swimming, and 39 trophies for other sports.

★ ★ ★ ★ ★

Days later a lady in black stepped into the police station at Wick. She believed her husband had been lost in this area and had come north from London. But she had had no official intimation. She described a mascot given him on his departure for service. The Police sergeant on duty was mystified but sympa-thetic. Reference to police details of the "unknown" buried here showed that one sailor did carry a mascot such as that so minutely described. The name of the ship had also been given. There were no survivors to give information. What led her

north? – how did she know? Intuition, maybe? Anyhow, apparently her belief was founded on fact.

Subsequent funerals, although on a smaller scale, were carried through on identical lines and much care was taken that the lairs in the cemetery were simply but suitably marked and recorded to facilitate easy recognition during the visits of relatives at later dates.

Attacks on shipping were by no means confined to large vessels and fishing boats and all coastal craft were considered of sufficient importance for enemy bombing: the little ships, of course, also shared the perils of mines. Some of them, like the *Noss Head*, sunk about the end of February 1941, were lost with all hands and without much information being procurable as to how they had gone down. In other cases the crews were wholly or partially rescued by local lifeboats or by Service craft and brought to shore for short periods of recuperation before returning to the Battle of the Seas – that battle on which, perhaps more than any other, Hitler had pinned his hopes of a victory against our Island Home.

Stories the censor would not pass.

Sea Tragedies Beside the Caithness Coast.

THE oil tanker *Gretafield* (10,191 tons) was torpe-doed nine miles off Wick Bay on February 14, 1940. The first torpedo crashed into the tanker just beyond the midnight hour; the second ten minutes later. The submarine crew must have judged that the first missile only crippled the tanker and that she would be capable of limping home to port with a precious cargo. They grew impatient in awaiting the ship's doom and launched another deadly blow – a blow that caused the *Gretafield* to burst into flames – indescribable flames that lasted for days. The skele-ton of the ship finally broke and drifted to rest at Dunbeath, 20 miles away.

Trawlers fishing in the vicinity were first to the aid of the stricken ship, and picked up survivors to land them at Wick. The trawlermen were kind to their ill-fated brothers of the sea; one skipper indeed took the socks from his own feet and gave them to a needy survivor. Wick lifeboat also patrolled in the vicinity.

The crew were smeared by burning oil and had to launch boats and fight a way to safety through a raging inferno. Three boats got away. The men rowed frantically, sweating from heat and toil, but progress was mighty slow over sea thickly covered by black oil. Worse, the oil was ablaze and fire was spreading rapidly over a wide sea surface. This truly was a struggle against envelopment by flame – an uneven struggle because even the oars were made slippery by oil. The battle for life lasted 30 minutes. The trawlers had seen their plight and went to the rescue. Doctors and ambulances awaited their arrival at the quayside, and most of the seamen were taken to hospital where they had injuries dressed. The youngest member of the crew was a boy of 15 on his first voyage. He was among those saved. Thirty men were rescued; 11 perished – one of them within sight of home, for he belonged to Wick.

* * * * *

Three charred bodies were recovered when the burnt-out shell of the *Gretafield* drifted ashore at Dunbeath days later but identification was impossible. The coffins were taken to Ross Church, Dunbeath, where a memorial service was held. The unknown sailors were buried in Latheron Churchyard. At either end of the bier each time stood Mr James Sinclair, fisherman, Wick, and his son William, father and brother respectively of a lad of 20 among the missing.

The funeral service was impressive, and was conducted in ministerial robes by Rev. Alan Macdonald, Latheron. Before performing the committal service, he said:– "In the days of old the Norse seafarers, the Vikings, came to Caithness. It was their custom when one of their heroes died to place his body on board a galley. Then setting fire to the ship they launched it from the shore, to be carried away by the sea's tides. In such a fashion the bodies of these seamen drifted past our shores the other day on their floating pyre. They, too, were brave men, dying in the service of their country. We honour them, and, although their names be unknown, we will keep their memory fresh while they take their last rest in our midst."

Beautiful wreaths were laid on the grave, including one with the following inscription: "Unknown but honoured. – From the people of Latheron."

The Newcastle oil tanker *Dagheston* was also sunk off the Caithness coast. This happened on 25th March, 1940. There are no particulars but there was only one body recovered.

* * * * *

Four Danish steamers were torpedoed off our coasts early in 1940. Two of these cargo ships, the *Rhone* and the *Sliepner* (both 1060 tons) went to their doom together. The *Rhone* was first attacked and sank within two minutes. There was no time to launch the lifeboats and the 20 souls aboard had to jump into the water in the darkness before midnight. Eleven were saved from a watery grave.

The *Sliepner* was alongside the *Rhone* and within a quarter-of-an-hour she, too, was attacked and sank to the bottom. This vessel carried a crew of 23 and 18 passengers – Greek seamen going to Denmark to join a ship. Seven seamen and six passengers were reported missing. Three of the *Sliepner's* small-boats engaged in rescue work of both crews – men were said to have died as they were picked up, and one of the three boats disappeared in the darkness never to be seen again. Among the victims was a woman stewardess.

The two remaining boats, heavily laden with 19 and 20 respectively, were rowed for nine hours before being sighted by the Swedish fishing boat *Standard* 35 miles from Wick. The *Standard* came into port with the survivors, and doctors and ambulances awaited her arrival. Four men were slightly injured. The others enjoyed the hospitality of the Deep Sea Mission before going south by rail.

* * * * *

About a month later (on March 20, 1940) two more Danish ships were destroyed in the same vicinity. U-boats were ever lurking in the shipping lanes looking for likely prey. The vessels were the *Bothal* (3000 tons) and *Viking* (1500 tons), both bound for Britain in ballast. Circumstances surrounding their destruction were similar in most details to those concerning the *Rhone* and the *Sliepner,* only the percentage of casualties was uncommonly high. The *Bothal* lost all but five of her crew of 20, and only two of 17 on the *Viking* were rescued.

The attack was made in the early morning. The impact of the torpedo explosions severed the *Bothal,* covering one portion of the ship with the other in clam fashion and falling wreckage caused havoc among the crew, some of whom were killed outright. Rafts were scrambled overboard but few of the men reached them. Those who did heard the cries of their shipmates but were unable to save them as the rafts drifted rapidly further from the awful scene. One 20-year-old seaman swam desperately for an hour to overtake a raft and finally succeeded, and was hauled on board by his comrades.

Twenty hours later the seven survivors were picked up by Wick lifeboat. The rafts had been observed by a patrol 'plane and the lifeboat responded. Four of the survivors were injured (one had both legs fractured) and were taken to hospital. There one remained for many months before going elsewhere. His ultimate fate I do not know, but I do know that over a long period he was continually sending letters home and was much perturbed because he received no answer. He always lay in one position and sometimes suffered severe pain, but generally he could smile. Among the rescued was an Estonian and a seaman belonging to Faroe.

★　★　★　★　★

A fifth Danish steamer was sunk off the Caithness coast about the same time (February, 1940). The vessel's name was *Tekla* and she came into contact with a mine. Nine members of the crew lost their lives. The body of one, Verner Savenson, Fredericia, was later washed ashore and was buried at Wick. Representatives of all Services and local public bodies attended the funeral, as well as a large number of Danish fishermen who worked from Wick during the war years.

The body of Captain Tangen (of Oslo), of the 2000-ton Norwegian steamer *Navarra*, was also recovered from the sea and buried at Wick. The *Navarra* was torpedoed on 5th April, 1940, without warning by a German submarine, and the captain and nine of the crew perished. There were 14 survivors, rescued by a Finnish ship.

★　★　★　★　★

Thurso, too, had more than glimpses of the tragedies of war. Probably the worst was in January, 1945, when 19 bodies (of 26 taken from the sea) were removed from the mortuary and interred in Thurso Cemetery. The bell of St. Peter's Church was tolled during the funeral, which was preceded by a touching and impressive service attended by more than 300 people. Some of the bodies were unidentified; some were taken south for burial.

These ill-fated seamen were members of the crew of s.s. *Ashbury*. The steamer was driven ashore during a heavy gale and foundered on a reef of rocks on the west coast of Sutherland. The vessel was in ballast and caught the full blast of the storm. Altogether the crew numbered 41, and all were believed to have perished. The ship sank in deep water.

The tragedy caused widespread sorrow in the North. At Talmine and Tongue, where the bodies were recovered, the local inhabitants rendered much-appreciated assistance.

★　★　★　★　★

About a year earlier (in February, 1944) a radio message received by Thurso lifeboat also revealed a tragedy at sea. The message stated that rafts containing men had been observed off the West coast. The lifeboat (under Coxswain Macleod) responded to the call and when proceeding west came into contact with a raft. Men were huddled on it and although the sea was stormy two of the lifeboat crew (Wm. Sinclair and David Thomson) leaped on to the raft at much personal risk. They found five men – five dead men who had perished from cold. The bodies were transferred to the lifeboat.

Later the lifeboat encountered a smaller raft off Melvich containing two survivors in a most exhausted condition. They also were removed to the lifeboat and given dry clothing and nourishment. The men were Anders Lovaas, second mate, and Oddbar K. Clausen, seaman, of the Norwegian steamer *Friedig,* bound from Aberdeen to Liverpool with a cargo of grain.

The steamer had foundered 14 miles off Cape Wrath the previous forenoon and the survivors revealed that 16 members of the crew were in the ship's boat when launched. The lifeboat cruised around for a long time without tracing the small-boat, and returned to Scrabster in the evening.

Here it may be added that it was on the local police and mortuary departments that the burden of work fell in connection with all bodies washed ashore on our coasts. At best it was a trying and gruesome work, but it was something which had to be done, and the officers concerned with its fulfilment carried it out in the humble knowledge that it was small recompense to those gallant men who had given their all. Relatives of deceased men, in letters to the police department, frequently expressed thanks.

Stories the censor would not pass.

When Wick was Bombed.

THE German air force was in the ascendancy in the earlier years of the war. It was the weapon reckoned by the Nazis as powerful enough to smash into submission every country that dared oppose

Hitler's will to domination.

England suffered dreadfully and continuously in these air attacks; Scotland had only a lesser share of the *blitzkrieg*. Altogether some 250 air operations were carried out by the enemy against Scotland, and in these 6400 high explosive bombs and 300 parachute mines were dropped. The casualty list was given as: killed (or missing, believed killed), 2298; injured and detained in hospital, 2167; slightly injured, 3558 – a total of 8023. No statistics of incendiary bombs were given, but in some of the raids most damage was caused by fire.

The heaviest enemy raids North of the Tweed were on Clydeside and Aberdeen, although there were a number of bad incidents elsewhere: at Paisley, for instance, where a direct hit killed 100 people in a first-aid post. For a long period Scotland's front line towns were Aberdeen, Peterhead and Fraserburgh. The majority of the raids on these north-east towns were in the nature of tip-and-run attacks, though several of the 31 raids on Aberdeen were determined and damaging, and we can sympathise with the people there.

Wick was the object of most enemy attention in the far north and was attacked six times. It was given officially that 222 high explosives fell in the northern district. Sutherland was the only Scottish county, and Inverness one of the five large burghs, in which no bombs were dropped.

From the summer of 1940 onwards enemy reconnaissance activity was of daily (or almost daily) occurrence, and offensive action was frequent in the North. The primary objective was shipping, and as many of the raids were small and ill-directed it seems reasonable to assume that coastal towns such as Wick served as secondary targets when more valuable prizes at sea escaped.

The conquest of Denmark and Holland, and especially the occupation of Norway, demanded much shipping activity by the enemy if Germany was to garner all the plunder these unfortunate countries could provide. Railways and canals leading east were overtaxed by traffic and a distribution by sea among Baltic ports eased the problem. But if Germany increased shipping activity, Britain was gathering strength in the air and our 'planes made the Nazi sea routes precarious by means of bombs and mines, twin sisters of destruction. This the enemy did not relish and determined to attack the bombers at their base. This is where Wick came into the picture because of its airfield's comparative proximity to the Norwegian coast.

★ ★ ★ ★ ★

Wick's bitterest experience of the war fell on the first day of July, 1940, when an enemy 'plane released two bombs in the vicinity of the harbour. Fifteen citizens lost their lives, and 22 sustained injuries. The dead comprised seven children, five men, and three women. Houses and shop property in the neighbourhood were demolished or damaged, some beyond repair.

According to official records this was the first daylight attack of the war on this country.

German 'planes were far from Wick thoughts that Monday afternoon (the time would be about 4.40) when there was an alarming explosion that could be heard for miles around. The bombs fell within yards of each other on a hard road surface in Bank Row. The craters made were neither wide nor deep and the surface explosion gave great play to blast. The bombs falling and exploding simultaneously gave the effect of one crash – the loudest the townspeople had ever heard. A pall of black smoke rising skywards marked the spot.

★ ★ ★ ★ ★

The 'plane came in low from a westerly direction flying seawards and was seen by many – indeed it was fired at by an alert gunner at a South Head battery as it passed over the bay on its homeward way.

There was an unforgettable scene. Buildings in Bank Row comprising four shops and four dwellings were shattered completely and property in Rose Street also suffered badly. Dead and injured lay among the debris, and those able to struggle clear staggered away – dazed. Window panes were wrenched from their sockets over a wide area. A peaceful scene was in a moment replaced by ruin, wreckage, dust; tears, blood, excitement.

Wick's Civil Defence services (particularly rescue, first-aid and ambulance parties) responded quickly that afternoon and undertook much helpful work. The large number of casualties imposed heavy additional work upon the regular staff of the Bignold Hospital, but with the aid of medical practitioners (one came 20 miles to help) and a number of ladies (formerly trained nurses) who volunteered for service, the injured received due attention.

★ ★ ★ ★ ★

The next serious attack on Wick was on 26th October, 1940. This was a much heavier raid, but fortunately caused much less loss of life.

13

BANK ROW (LOOKING WEST) – JULY 2, 1940

BANK ROW (LOOKING EAST) – JULY 2, 1940

CAITHNESS – AND THE WAR.

This attack was directed against the aerodrome by three Heinkels and more than 20 high explosives were dropped on the north side of the town. The weight of the bombs shook the town considerably though the greater portion failed to explode. Happily, one-third were "duds" until afterwards exploded by bomb disposal personnel.

A bungalow in Hill Avenue received a direct hit and adjacent bungalows and houses were seriously damaged, also house property in Rosebery Terrace, Henrietta Street and George Street. Ceilings and plasterwork collapsed and window panes took flight as if by magic. Altogether 140 dwellings were damaged.

Three civilians were killed (a woman, a boy and a girl) in the bungalow, and the injured in the raid numbered 13.

★　★　★　★　★

Flying very low, the Heinkels zoomed over the housetops, machine-gunned parts of the town, and then dropped a cargo of high explosive bombs on or near the 'drome. There was a series of loud explosions. A Hudson machine was set ablaze and the rattle of ignited machine-gun bullets added to the alarming noises.

It was Saturday evening about six o'clock and shops in the centre of the town vibrated as the bombs exploded. People in the streets scurried for cover, some with children in their arms. Quite a number had remarkable escapes from machine-gun bullets and in houses which were completely wrecked internally.

Again the Civil Defence services responded splendidly, and some were on duty all night. The houseless, and those resident in property rendered precarious from damage or unexploded bombs, were removed to the High School where accommodation and all facilities were in readiness for just such an emergency. Round about the midnight hour men and women were called out to supervise arrangements, and the writer will ever remember how cheerfully those volunteer workers left bed and home and stepped out into the cold and darkness of the night prepared to accept all duties. As in the earlier raid, special constables guarded evacuated property from dusk till dawn.

The fire brigade extinguished two outbreaks of fire which followed the explosions and had to work within a few yards of an unexploded bomb.

★　★　★　★　★

Bailie Duncan Sinclair stepped off a train that evening to find his home in Rosebery Terrace wrecked. "Nothing but the stairs standing," was how he put it, "but the old grandfather clock was still ticking in the lobby although its hands were blown away." What was true of this grandfather clock applied to many another trusty timepiece as well, for in many a damaged home clocks ticked nonchalantly away on the mantlepiece when all around was wreckage. The secret of the survival of such delicate mechanism baffled me.

The Bignold Hospital was within a hundred yards of some of the explosions and its windows were shattered, doors torn from hinges, and plaster stripped from the walls and ceilings by blast. Yet that evening the hospital staff gamely continued an uninterrupted service for casualties. The patients had to be evacuated and went to the new school at Lybster which was converted into a hospital for the remainder of the war.

★　★　★　★　★

Lone German raiders attacked Wick 'drome on four occasions but although damage was caused there were no civilian casualties. Air Force casualties were not revealed.

Just after tea-time on the evening of June 4, 1941, Wick folks were startled by a raider that attacked with bombs and machine-guns. It sprayed the streets before and after attacking the 'drome, where a hangar was set on fire. Shells from the 'plane penetrated houses here and there, and one pierced the bonnet of a stationary motorcycle in Northcote Street. Across the way in the children's playing-field the youngsters panicked and soldiers and others in the vicinity rushed to pacify them, shielding the youngest till danger passed. Bowlers on St. Fergus green were also disturbed and quickly sought the protection of a surrounding wall.

Not long after the raider had passed, two alerts were sounded in quick succession. Both were of short duration and neither added to the confusion.

★　★　★　★　★

Caithness should have been "in the news" in the spring and summer seasons of 1941 – but the censor would not permit. It was then the German warplanes were frequent visitors and Wick's siren belched forth by day and by night the screaming notes indicative of the approach of danger – maybe of death. Oft we knew that "Jerry" was somewhere in the stratosphere overhead, for the "chug-chug" of a foreign engine could be clearly heard though no 'plane was actually visible.

The German airman stooped to small prizes at times such as on February 22, 1941, when off our coast he made a motor seine-net craft and lighthouses on the coast targets for machine-gun fire. The crew of the fishing boat adroitly took available cover and only one member was slightly injured by a flying splinter although bullets smashed into the engine-room and wheelhouse.

Two lighthouses in the Pentland Firth were attacked in the same way on the same day but the damage caused (chiefly by broken glass) was not worth the visit. A return visit was made to Duncansby lighthouse in the early hours of June 23, 1941, when a bomb was dropped by the raider. Fortunately, it missed the lighthouse and plunged into the sea.

During the war the German air force destroyed or damaged 2,750,000 houses in Britain. In the Far North, however (apart from gunning streets) the enemy airmen rivetted attention on military objectives only, and where mistakes were made these were understandable. Luckily for Wick, it did not experience indiscriminate bombing otherwise the town would have been a shambles. But while we give the *Luftwaffe* credit for sparing the town, the attacks on fishing craft and lighthouses are unforgiveable. For longer than the living can recall the lighthouse has been a friend to men of all nations. Its striking whiteness is symbolical of its untainted record of service.

★ ★ ★ ★ ★

The people of Wick saw a German 'plane pass over the town at low altitude on the afternoon of March 17, 1941, and quickly learned it was on a bombing mission. The 'drome was the objective, but it did not forget to spray parts of the town with machine-gun bullets. Children playing at the Riverside escaped injury miraculously, and one laddie retrieved as a souvenir a bullet-shell from within inches of his foot. The 'drome was bombed again in the evening of the same day.

Taking advantage of low clouds, a German aircraft made a surprise attack on Wick 'drome about two o'clock on January 16, 1942. Pupils were returning to school and workers were on the move following dinner, and some recognised the swastika markings. Three bombs fell on the 'drome but only one exploded.

Eight aircraftmen and a corporal were working

that afternoon in an armoury shack on the aerodrome. Discussion was going on among them as to whether there were good Germans as well as bad and only a glance was made at the approaching 'plane. They did not even suspect it to be enemy. The discussion was violently disturbed. A massive bomb (the huge shell may be still at the 'drome) came to earth not so far away from the shack. It came to earth and bounced again and again before penetrating the roof of the shack and tearing the tunic and underclothing on the corporal's back in its downward clatter. The force of the impact flung all the occupants to the ground. Surprise! Every armourer made a hasty exit, seeking any available dip as protection and strategically moving ever farther away ere the expected explosion came. But come it did not, for the bomb remained a dud. That was indeed a miraculous escape, as only the corporal (a Leeds lad) suffered slightly from shock. The upholder of good Germans changed his mind! He came from Windygates.

★ ★ ★ ★ ★

In those unhappy siren days the A.R.P. personnel manned their posts at every call. Twice at least church services were interrupted on the Sabbath day and congregations given the option of remaining in church or returning home. The first occasion was on May 12, 1940, when air raid alarms were sounded in both Wick and Thurso because enemy aircraft had been observed approaching the coast. Hurricanes rose from Wick 'drome to intercept the enemy.

About a year later (May 18, 1941) the quiet of the Sabbath day in Wick was broken again by the siren's wailing notes, and ministers continued the services for those who elected to remain in church. The weather was good and children had gone for walks, and anxious mothers hurried in search of their own. In those days the siren was treated as an alarm, later it became an alert. To cease work every time the siren sounded was more than industrial areas could afford and southern firms introduced roof-watchers or look-out men to spot real danger.

★ ★ ★ ★ ★

The only bomb dropped in the locality of Thurso landed on the town's refuse dump, about a mile outside the burgh boundary. It made a crater 30ft in diameter and 15ft in depth. The only result reported was the rattling of doors and windows. The incident occurred late on the night of April 7, 1941.

Thurso, however, was an important centre during the war years, thousands of Servicemen passing through its streets on the way to Scrabster and Scapa. Hundreds of prisoners of war, too, were landed by this route and commenced their journey to internment camps from Thurso railway station. Such scenes attracted much interest locally.

* * * * *

The marshy ground at Redmire, Thrumster, was converted into a decoy 'drome – at a bit of expense – and dotted over it were dummy 'planes to draw the enemy's attention and his bombs. Householders in the neighbourhood were provided with Anderson shelters. This 'drome was surrounded by anti-aircraft batteries, so that the scheme was double-sided. In Thrumster district (at Tannach) important wireless stations were erected, and a radiolocation station was nearby on the coast at Ulbster.

German airmen were quick to spot the little 'drome at Thrumster and squandered much precious ammunition there. Several of the bombs dropped went deeply into the mirey ground and some at least were probably never recovered although bomb disposal squads were engaged for days at a time.

* * * * *

The first enemy airman to bomb Thrumster arrived about 8.30 on the morning of Sunday, March 30th, 1941, and dropped several bombs before machine-gunning houses in the district. The target may really have been an unused wireless station, the standards of which were left in the ground. There were two explosions (heard very clearly in Wick) but apart from damage to houses in the Sarclet district the result was negative. A schoolboy asleep in one house was rudely awakened by a piece of plaster falling on the bed, and another laddie had a remarkable escape when a bullet narrowly missed his head and embedded itself in the wall.

Three days later (and again at eight in the morning) "Jerry" paid a second call to Thrumster. There was one explosion and again there was little damage and no casualties.

A third raid on Thrumster 'drome (perhaps mistaken for Wick) was made in the wee sma' hours of May 17, 1941, when there were several loud explosions and the whole neighbourhood was alarmed. Windows and doors were shattered here and there but there was no serious damage. During the next two months Thrumster had further unpleasant visits from units of the *Luftwaffe*, and bombs exploding there were always heard very distinctly in Wick.

* * * * *

The total number of bombs dropped on Caithness soil was approximately one hundred and well over 50 per cent of these exploded in country areas causing little or no damage although they caused alarm. Areas "up 'e coast" had most of these, but Castletown also had a visit from the enemy raiders. Sometimes outlandish places were attacked, Strathmore, for instance; again, a bomb (a big one) was dropped on the moor at Acharole, Watten, on April 10, 1940 (the first enemy high explosive to be dropped on the mainland of Britain and believed to have been dumped by a machine scurrying from a Scapa raid).

These widespread war incidents are worthy of more detail and this will be given later in a section dealing with Civil Defence activities and events on the Home Front.

Victim of a bombing raid.

The Greatest Experience of My Life.

THE following article is taken from a schoolboy's essay. It was written by a lad of 14 (George Cameron), a victim of a bombing raid on Wick during which a high explosive demolished the bungalow in which along with him were his mother (badly injured); brother, sister and a lady friend (all three of whom were killed). The lad himself came near to death so that he had something to write about under the popular school-essay heading: – "The Greatest Experience of My Life":–

On October 26 last year (1940) the enemy attempted to bomb several large buildings outside the town of Wick. Three Heinkels roared over the roof-tops, releasing their bombs a split second too soon.

The first indication I had of enemy air-action was when two of the bombers zoomed over the house at a terrific speed. The Nazi bomb-aimers' judgment was poor, for the bomb exploded in a field – yards away from the target. The 'plane which passed directly over our house released its first bomb so that it landed on the roadway, ten yards from our front door. It proved to be a "dud." The second bomb landed on our neighbour's door-step with a clang. It also did not explode.

My mother, who was standing in the centre of

the living-room floor, said in a hushed voice – "We'd better go to the shelter." Time forbade, however, and all five of us made hurriedly for the lobby, where there was no glass. There we stood in something like a circle wondering what was to happen next.

★ ★ ★ ★ ★

I now come to the tragic part of my story. A death-like silence prevailed for about five seconds,

blood. All the power had gone out of my body and it was only by a determined effort that I moved my arm across the ground to find that I was lying on a heap of stoney rubble. The air around me was filthy with gas fumes.

I then felt tired and helpless. I had a queer feeling that I was going to die. It was then that I heard the cries of my brother and sister. My mother's voice came to me from what seemed miles away.

Wreckage of the Bungalow in Hill Avenue – October 27, 1940.

although it seemed at that time more like an hour.

Suddenly there was a terrific flash, accompanied by a dreadful explosion. My brain seemed to snap and everything became blank for a brief moment. I then had a terrible sensation. It seemed as if an electric current had been put into my body. My skin began to tingle while my chest and throat gradually began to tighten – tighten – tighten. I could feel myself being thrown into the air. Several times I felt searing pains in my legs as if a naked knife had been thrust into them. Suddenly everything became black and faded away.

When I regained consciousness my eyes were clamped shut and it seemed they would never open. My face was wet with blood while my hair was plastered down on my head with a mixture of lime and

She was saying something like: "Lie still, somebody will come in a minute and help us." Although I did not know it, my father was first on the scene . . . If he had not come it is doubtful if any of us would have survived.

The next thing I can remember is being lifted by a man with a purely English accent who carried me to a hospital, only a short distance away. I heard my rescuer ask a question and tried to answer, but my tongue and lips were so swollen with the explosion that only a meaningless sound could have escaped.

★ ★ ★ ★

When we reached the hospital, it was then I began to shiver. I shivered and shook uncontrollably. I realised I was hurt, terribly hurt. My clothes were hanging in tatters on my battered body . . . . A little while after I felt a needle prick my arm and everything faded away. It was not until two days later that I saw daylight again. My neck was horribly stiff and my face – well, it was unrecognisable. My arms and my face, not to speak of my legs, had been badly burned and a purple liquid had been painted on them. This liquid had become solid, so you can imagine what I was like. The next three days were simply awful. Every morning my legs had to be dressed. The dressings had to be pulled off my woulds, but as I was still somewhat dazed I didn't feel that much.

Next day my foot, which had been cracked by a boulder, was put in plaster. The doctors and nurses were all very nice and I don't think I will every forget them.

Two days later my mother and myself were transferred to an auxiliary hospital in the country because the hospital we were in had itself been damaged in the raid, and as we both were very ill we needed a place which was both quiet and comfortable. I was delighted to see my mother again that afternoon . . . I spent three months in the auxiliary hospital . . . I shall never forget my helplessness when first I attempted to walk again, but once I got going I had some fine times . . . I hope and pray that no one will have the horrible experience that I had – of being only ten feet away from a high explosive bomb when it bursts.

The Royal Air Force.

Night and day their vigil keeping,
  Over our beloved isle,
Swift they go, their pulses leaping,
  Into action with a smile.

Flashing past across the skyway,
  Over heath and over hill,
Over busy town and highway,
  Seaward with unshaken will.

And some go, no more returning,
  Dashing lads and debonair,
Death and danger ever spurning,
  Seeking but to do and dare.

Heroes Britain shall remember,
  And in memory adore,
Dying that they might defend her,
Give her freedom evermore.

– ELLA R.C. MACDONALD
(Montrose).

They helped to shape European history.

Wick was Proud of its Airmen.

THERE were four aerodromes in Caithness when the war terminated. These were at Wick, Skitten (Killimster), Castletown and Dounreay (nearing completion).

Wick aerodrome was in a sufficiently advanced state to merit a place on pre-war maps. Such publicity may have been flattering as to its readiness, but the 'drome figured among the few in Scotland at the time – and consequently its existence was no secret to friend or foe. The spacious airfield was situated on the north side of the town. It incorporated the new £20,000 North School as headquarters and later acquired the Bignold Hospital for the treatment of ill and injured personnel.

There was much work to be completed even after the declaration of war, and very many local men found employment there. As showing prevailing wages at the time, it may be worth recalling that 300 labourers went on strike in mid-July (1939) demanding 1/2d per hour instead of the shilling paid, and returned to work when granted an increase of three farthings. With the coming of war, however, wages quickly soared, and it would be interesting to know the total cost of construction and maintenance for the first six years of the aerodrome. (In 1938 the Government couldn't afford to support on a percentage basis a projected Caithness road improvement scheme estimated at £300,000).

Skitten aerodrome was constructed in 1940, and was quickly in commission. The Castletown airfield came later and was mainly for the fighter types of 'planes. Dounreay was still under construction when Germany collapsed and was a more extensive airfield, understood to be for the use of the Fleet Air Arm. Here and there throughout the county war-time stations appeared – at Tannach, Ulbster, Warth Hill, Noss, Dunnet, Geise, Bower – all mainly in connection with radio and radar and all more or less "Hush, hush." Some of these isolated posts were centred in lonely moorland, and were reached by shaggy winding tracks that became quagmires in wet weather. Some of them developed into big affairs.

★ ★ ★ ★ ★

To these aerodromes and outposts came thousands of workmen and thousands of airmen (and thousands of Servicewomen too), during the war years. Most of them had not previously even heard of Caithness, and maybe most of them departed wishing they had never seen it! The airmen hailed from all parts of the country and of the Empire; some indeed were of foreign nationality – men whose countries had been pillaged by the foe and now allies in the fight. The Caithness climate chilled and displeased many; the wintry winds harassed them and the bare surroundings depressed them. They missed home and life as they knew these things – endless traffic, road beacons, the pubs, the clubs, and the choice of entertainments – and they groused annoyedly. Happily would they applaud were I to parody the poet to sing:–

Snell are the winds of thee, strong are the blasts of thee,
  Foul are the rains of thee – more ever to come;
  Bare are the lands of thee, dull are the towns of thee,
Oh! to get away from thee – Caithness, by gum!

Contentment is within the heart, and there were airmen who found in Caithness "a strange old land beyond the mountains," men who loved its open spaces, thrived on the pure, bracing air, and did not scoffingly rank its climate as akin to that of Siberia. These fellows mixed with the natives in their pastimes and their homes, found the people intelligent, happy and hospitable – and here they passed pleasant days, exploring the countryside in the warmer weather and enjoying to the full the endless daylight in this summer "land of never night." These fellows will come back again. Romance flourished in wartime and quite a number of our visitors were quick to prize the charms of our northern lassies. They made themselves at home here and will probably return to build a home. The county's somewhat confined list of surnames will be expanded and, by the way, quite a number of our own lads and lasses on Service found life partners elsewhere – so that the balance was kept fairly even.

Whatever opinions airmen formed of Caithness and its people, this much the people will say honestly of visiting airmen as a whole: "They were good fellows and remarkably well behaved. Good luck be with them."

★ ★ ★ ★ ★

Some day there may be published the official story of the part taken in the war by 'planes stationed on Wick aerodrome. The civilian does not know, accurately at anyrate. Certain things we do know. The 'drome was prematurely in commission, and the early days are memorable on account of the machines, men and mud – mud that was carried on to the burgh roadways and became a nuisance. Billeting quarters were unready and pilots and other personnel had accommodation in the hotels and private houses. What excitement there used to be when aircrews hurriedly answered a call! Ground staff, too, had sleeping accommodation in every quarter of the town over a lengthy period and this hastened and cemented friendships. The "wifies" were uncommonly kind to the poor boys (as they called them) and many were little less than "adopted" for sixpence per night! The Noss wireless ops., too (about 130 of them) were billeted in the town, but on more favourable terms.

The squadrons which came and went flew different types of aircraft from the early days when Ansons and Skuas were predominant. Aeroplanes were a rare sight in northern skies up till then. The first Service machine that landed here occasioned much curious attention and inspection. The day came, however, when natives would hardly give them a passing glance. Prominent among the machines at different times were Hurricanes, Spitfires, Grumans, Hudsons, Whitleys, Wellingtons,

Typical bomber crew – lost, and buried in France. Second from right – F.O. A.S. Middleton, Watten.

Hampdens, Beaufighters, Warwicks, Liberators, Mosquitos and Fortresses. There were other types as well. For years companies of the R.A.F. Regiment protected the airfield against attack and some of the test manoeuvres indulged in were of interest to the inhabitants.

★　★　★　★　★

The station was under Coastal Command. The 'planes undertook much reconnaissance work (particularly photographic), played an important part in conquering the U-boat campaign, the bombing of targets in Norway and enemy shipping off the Norwegian coast and U-boat dispositions in the fjords. Many of the operational flights were successfully performed, not always without loss and sometimes at heavy cost.

Latterly Wick and Skitten were two of 14 stations between Yorkshire and the Faroes that came under Group 18 Bomber Squadron (with headquarters in Fife). This Group accomplished some of the most remarkable flights of the war during its ceaseless operations over northern waters. Planes from 519 Squadron at Wick, for instance, flew long range sorties that took them 100 miles inside the Arctic Circle and at heights of 2400 feet on meteorological flights to obtain advanced weather information. Temperatures recorded were as low as minus 58 degrees, equal to 90 degrees of frost. The reports returned decided the date of D-Day and were of considerable help throughout the invasion of Normandy. Meteorological flights were sometimes undertaken when conditions were such that other aircraft were compelled to be grounded. Spitfires used for vertical ascents went up to 43,000 feet and pilots in pressurised cabins recorded temperatures of minus 99 degrees or 131 degrees of frost. The work of the Group (stated an official report) represented a tremendous effort in human endeavour, and the results were achieved only by the courage, fortitude and unselfishness of the aircrews, fighting the enemy day after day in fair and foul weather, and often in the face of intense opposition. Wick was proud to share in such a record.

★　★　★　★　★

The honours conferred on airmen stationed here were many and varied. Two of the early awards were won by Squadron-Leader Richard A. M'Murtrie – the Distinguished Flying Cross for gallantry and devotion to duty in the execution of air operations, and (when Wing Commander) the Distinguished Service Order. The official intimation stated: – "During a period of five days in December,

1940, he led three separate bombing missions against a target over sixty miles inside Norway. On the first occasion, despite heavy cloud over sea and land, he successfully located and attacked his objective. He then remained flying in the target area with his lights burning in order to assist subsequent aircraft in finding the target. In the next two raids he again bombed the target heavily. He has taken part in 76 operational flights." This officer became known to many in the community. He began for Wick Aerodrome a record of faithful and gallant service that was maintained throughout the years.

Described as the most brilliant shipping attack of the war by a single squadron (nine aircraft were engaged) an operation carried out from Wick on 29th October, 1941, sunk or damaged seven enemy ships and bombed and set ablaze a fish oil processing plant and harbour installations in Norway.

Several enemy submarines were destroyed by aircraft operating from Wick, and on at least two occasions, after attacking aircraft were damaged and forced to "ditch," the crews were recovered by Air-Sea Rescue along with survivors from the sunken U-boats.

★　★　★　★　★

Mr Peter Fraser, a Ross-shire man who had become Prime Minister of New Zealand, visited Wick 'drome in August, 1941, to dine with members of his country's forces stationed here. At lunch he sat between two medallists, each holder of the Distinguished Flying Cross. The Officers were Flt.-Lieut. S. M'Hardy, Waipawa, Napier, who won his decoration for operations over Norway, during which he shot down two enemy 'planes (a Messerschmitt and a Heinkel) in one day; and Flying Officer J. T. Swift, Invercargill, who won his cross in action over Germany.

During his brief stay in Caithness, the N.Z. Premier visited Lybster School and gave the children a fascinating account of his journey to London. He presented the school with some Maori songs and photographs, and signed the school log-book. Teachers and pupils appreciated the privilege of meeting this famous son of Scotland, and memories of his visit will remain.

★　★　★　★　★

More than 7000 people visited Wick R.A.F. Station on a Saturday afternoon in September, 1945, when it was opened to public inspection to mark the fifth anniversary of the Battle of Britain. The visitors were much impressed by the immensity of the place and the genial reception extended by all ranks.

They were impressed, too, by an exhibition of aircraft in action, particularly when a squadron in battle formation swept across the sky above the 'drome conveying in some measure the power concentrated in an attack and the helplessness of the ordinary mortal to stay that power.

They trained, they fought, and they conquered.

Army Units in Caithness.

THE tread of tacketty boots re-acted in our northern streets shortly after the evacuation from Dunkirk, that milestone in the progress of the war. Soldiers were sent to train in Caithness where they occupied many buildings (including schools and halls) and erected camps in rural districts, the largest probably being at Watten. They swarmed in the towns, too. Highland regiments predominated – Camerons, Seaforths, Black Watch, H.L.I., Lovat Scouts; but there were dozens of others as well, including Artillery, Royal Engineers, Cameronians, Pioneers, Army Service Corps, Army Medical Corps, and so on. There were "sodgers, sodgers, sodgers everywhere". Ayrshire Yeomanry batteries were stationed in Caithness principally as a mobile striking force with positions at vulnerable points. It is recorded that one troop carried out a remarkable march on foot whilst in the county, travelling 85 miles in three days, and covering 38 miles on the last day. Every man completed the course. Army transport filled our roadways, the speed of light vans contrasting with the ponderous movement of heavy vehicles. Accidents there were, some of them regrettable, but probably few in proportion to the amount of traffic.

There were soldiers from every corner of the globe among these fighting men. There were complete units of Polish forces. Generally, the soldiers settled happily here during their stay and mixed freely with the natives. Canteens were opened under the auspices of the Church of Scotland, and the Seamen's Mission at Wick, too, was kept particularly busy. These social centres (the canteens), where services were maintained in a praiseworthy co-operative spirit by voluntary workers from various churches and other religious and social organisations, were "home from home" for the Servicemen. These canteens were an inestimable boon and provided hot meals, light refreshments, indoor recreation, and reading and writing rooms. Entertainments such as concerts were arranged, and the spiritual welfare of the men was not forgotten. The work undertaken without reward was enormous, and were this spirit uppermost in other directions what a happy country this would become! Here surely was the foundation for a "new order."

* * * * *

The Seamen's Mission is worthy of more than a mere "mention" for its services to the Forces. This institute tended the needs of distressed seamen whether they arrived by day or by night, and there they were clothed and fed in an atmosphere of Christian kindliness. Seamen saved from sunken ships arrived cold, hungry and bereft of all personal possessions; the Mission cheerfully supplied all the answers, and the men went on their way again appraising the merits of goodly, kind-hearted, brotherly men who found a real pleasure in serving the deserving. Skipper Stewart and Mr Willie Craig did a big job – quietly, efficiently. They helped to soothe the sorrows of the sea by comforting words and ready and helpful action. They catered for the needs of Servicemen as well and at one period had (and appreciated) the voluntary services of quite a number of local lady helpers.

* * * * *

Air Force personnel stationed in the county set a precedent by bringing their wives and families to reside here. Soldiers followed suit. There was a persistent door-to-door search for accommodation until finally the population figures were swollen beyond recognition. This was especially true of Wick which was crowded out with 20,000 inhabitants instead of the customary 7,000. There were advantages in bringing north a wife: not only was a monetary allowance available but it made conditions more like home as Servicemen in such circumstances were permitted to sleep outwith the camps; again, many of these visitors hailed from vulnerable areas and were glad to come to a countryside where quiet contentment lingered, where queuing for food was unknown, and where slumber was undisturbed. Happily, the available rations sufficed for all although (be it admitted) at one stage the resident housewife complained of shopkeepers giving alleged preferential treatment to the incomers. Quite a number of wives remained in the North even after their husbands were posted elsewhere.

* * * * *

Like the airmen, these visitors held mixed opinions on the county and its people. Some were

23

happy, very happy, here; others not so happy and glad to get away. Some appreciated the hospitality extended to them, and to this day communicate with friends found in the North in war-time. Ofttimes did letters come from far-away places conveying kindly thoughts expressed in words. There was something grand and touching about a Southerner (even men from Eire) soldiering in the desert or in the broiling heat of the East thinking again on kindness he had received in Caithness and writing to keep afresh the friendship. There are kindly folks in the towns and in the "wee hoosies 'mang the heather," a statement that could be substantiated by many instances. One may suffice, told by a Cockney when billeted in Pulteney Distillery. Six of his company of Pioneers were travelling on a lonely road in the Reay district one forenoon. They had forgone their morning rations because of a shortage at Loch Loyal and were hungry. Coming upon a little wayside house they decided to ask for a cup of tea to tide them over until they reached town. An old lady answered their knock on the door and readily agreed to supply their need, only they would have to "wait outside until she was ready". When the call came they found themselves ushered into her best room where the table was covered with a white cloth and on which were plates of eatables, and there were two boiled eggs for every man.

"We knew it was her best room, her whitest tablecloth, her silver spoons – but she seemed to think nothing was too good for us," said the Pioneer, "and her kindness brought a tear to my eye." The old lady refused to accept any reward, but it so happened that in the course of conversation the scarcity of chocolate had been mentioned. It so happened also that weeks later the same men were passing the same way, but in the opposite direction. When the house was reached the conveyance stopped. One man went to the door and knocked. The old lady with the shawl around her shoulders answered – and she received a present from the six soldiers, a present of chocolate to which they all had contributed. No doubt the old lady wondered why! "A present for you, mother," was all the soldier said. Should this meet her eye, she will know the gift was in return for unexpected but appreciated kindness.

* * * * *

Naval forces that visited the county (apart from those which passed through Thurso) were less than expected. Minesweepers put in occasionally to Wick, as also did Tank Landing Craft, and there was a small number of resident shore personnel. For a time a few foreign sailors were at Wick. A submarine did not appear until the war was over.

But the Navy was still the popular service in the Far North. A visit to the picture-house was convincing on this point whenever a march-past was depicted. The Army got a cheer, the Air Force got a cheer, but the Navy – well, you have heard of the Hampden roar! "The sea" is still in the blood of the Northman and the young ever yearn to follow "out where the crested billows foam, out where the fresh winds blow."

An Admiral who happened to appeal to the county on behalf of a Naval fund did not disguise his surprise when the response was a cheque for something like £1200.

Followers of the sea are found in all corners of our county. Caithness men have ever been noted seafarers, but it is questionable if any part of the country produces more brilliant seamen than the stretch between Dunnet and John O'Groats. Men from this area hold important posts afloat, carrying the banner of the county across the further seas to the uttermost parts of the earth. Dunnet, Mey and Scarfskerry have a great record in that respect. It is indeed the proud boast of these hamlets that they hold pride of place, over any other of the same size – a worthy record, and one that was maintained in the war years.

* * * * *

Many Service visitors to Caithness who were taken ill in the course of their sojourn in the county will have pleasant memories of Forse House, which had been used as an auxiliary hospital. The Latheron mansion, the home of the Baird family, had a reputation second to none for hospitality and kindness. The local folk saw to it that the patients (mostly convalescent) did not lack for the little extras that count, and a good matron and staff added to its popularity. Ordinary visitors were given a glimpse of the thoughtfulness bestowed on patients, as county folk who had relatives as inmates know full well.

* * * * *

In taking leave of our war-time visitors and assuring them of our goodwill, let me conclude with a brief but true tale of a young man in a hurry. He had arrived in (to him) far-away Caithness and had concluded his first evening meal in his new-found northern billet after coming off the train. "Can I see the northern lights here?" he queried, and on being informed that he might he startled his new landlord when he asked, "Where can I see them now?" Weeks elapsed ere the young man's curiosity could be satisfied, when there happened to be some good displays of this remarkable phenomena.

★　★　★　★　★

During the last year of the war the camp at Watten was converted into an internment camp for German prisoners of war. There would be approximately 1600 of them, and they were given labouring work in and around the camp. These prisoners were also made available to farmers as agricultural workers, and proved very useful when there was a shortage of labour at harvest time. The prisoners travelled around in motor lorries, were "delivered to farmers" and collected again seven hours later. Those who engaged them were not allowed to give food or cigarettes or to reward them in any way, except to supply to each a mug of tea or other hot drink about 12 noon. Fraternisation was not permitted, yet our ex-enemies moved freely around the farms and the fields. Generally, they worked well. The charge for their services was 1/3p per man hour.

The Germans found much employment, too, on the aerodromes, and were inclined to be friendly – not the fellows who had been led to believe they were a race superior and destined to rule the world and all its peoples. The prisoners had an orchestra which earned high praise. Frequently it performed at Service entertainments but up to the time of writing it had not appeared in public.

This much can be said, however. It is no uncommon occurrence to meet unguarded German prisoners on the streets of Wick. They are probably hired as gardeners. Each morning they come into the town, and, like the village blacksmith, each night return.

★　★　★　★　★

Though maybe at heart unwilling guests, the German prisoners generally were docile in captivity, and only one attempted escape is recorded (up till the end of 1945). Early on a Sunday morning in August of that year a tall, young fellow (he was 6ft. 3in. in height) made a bid for liberty. He escaped from the camp at Watten and walked across country on foot, reaching the main road to the south about ten miles away.

Police and special constables were on the lookout for him long before he covered this distance, and his adventure ended quietly and abruptly. He was observed, still wearing his prison camp uniform, seated by the roadside near Rangag on Sunday morning. He offered no resistance when arrested by the police.

Since the above was written there have been more determined attempts at escape. Three prisoners got beyond Lybster, three to Loth, two as far as Aberdeen, and one to Glasgow before he was recognised and recaptured. So all of them (or maybe any of them) cannot be altogether happy in their new-found home at "Voton."

They also serve who only stand and wait.

Home Guard Formed in Desperate Days.

THIS country was in a desperate plight in the summer of 1940. The capitulation of France and the evacuation from Dunkirk of what could be salvaged of the British Army are tales for the historian. Suffice it here to say that, as in 1914 so in 1939, the British Army was "contemptibly" small and the nation ill-prepared for warfare. The collapse of France robbed Britain of practically all she possessed in armour and weapons and (be it never forgotten) it was in that dark hour that Mr Winston Churchill accepted the leadership. "There were few applicants for the job," he has said.

Britain stood alone against the might of Germany and boastful Italy, and the swaggering conquerors had practically all Europe in their grip. Japan was being nasty, too. How long would Britain survive? The coming of Churchill changed the tone. We will fight, he declared, anywhere and everywhere. "We will never surrender," was the challenge he issued in the nation's darkest and loneliest hour, and proceeded to build for defence and attack on a gigantic scale. By means of rousing speeches and inspiring leadership he rallied the nation and knitted the Empire, and drew all men and nations of goodwill to his side. He and his colleagues in the Cabinet (of which Sir A. Sinclair of Ulbster was a member) set to work with unbounded energy and encouraged everyone everywhere to work. Blood, sweat, toil and tears, said Mr Churchill, were all he had to offer; and blood, sweat, toil and tears were in the forefront on the home front for years to follow.

★　★　★　★　★

The threat of German invasion o'ershadowed Britain for long, weary months, for years indeed. How would the Germans come – by parachute, aeroplane or ship? seemed the only point to be determined. Civilians were issued with instructions on how to beat the invader. Among these were two main orders – "Stand firm" and "Carry on." Do not crowd on the roads in cars, in carts, on bicycles and on foot; do not believe rumours and do not spread them; keep watch for anything suspicious and report; do not give any German anything, do not tell him anything, do not help him in any way; make sure that no invader will be able to use your cars, petrol, maps or bicycles; be ready to help the military in any way; think before you act, and take advice and orders from policemen and A.R.P. wardens. The ringing of church bells (from then on these were silent in war-time) was to be a warning to the local garrison that enemy troops had been seen landing from the air in the neighbourhood of the church whose bell was used.

That summer (1940) saw the formation of a new defence arm – Local Defence Volunteers, known as L.D.V., and later christened Home Guard. Men of the 1914-18 army quickly volunteered, and companies were formed everywhere. Altogether there were 1,700,000 doughty volunteers. "Grandfathers in battledress" was an apt description, but these men had been in emergencies before and would have been "tough."

The initial appeal for a Home Front Army under the rather unwieldy name of Local Defence Volunteers was made in May, 1940. Caithness was not behind. Here the appeal was for "useful men – stalkers, gamekeepers, shepherds and others" who knew the outlying districts of the county. These men were specially required "for detection of enemy attempts to land forces in the county by parachute or otherwise." Enrolment was open to men between 17 and 65 years, and forms were obtainable at the police stations.

Caithness rightaway made a good response, some 400 men enrolling; six weeks later there was a force of more than a thousand volunteers. Observation posts were established in various parts of the county and much patrol work was undertaken.

> They left their homes to man the posts
> That netwise stretched from coast to coast.

Captain (later Lieut-Colonel) Ian M'Hardy was appointed to command and organise the company. He was in command during the years 1940-43. Platoon leaders were also appointed. These were:– Southern and eastern area, Admiral Sir E.S. Alexander-Sinclair, Dunbeath; Wick and district, Comdr. R.R. Gore Browne Henderson of Bilbster; Central and western area, Major Wm Reid, Halkirk; Thurso and district, Colonel D. Keith Murray, Thurso; Northern and eastern area, Major D. M.

Mackenzie, John O'Groats Hotel. The Post Office had a separate section of Guardsmen (at Wick, under Capt. R. Bremner).

In July, 1940, Captain M'Hardy had 1540 volunteers under his command and the unit was given battalion status, becoming the 1st Caithness Battalion Home Guard with 40 training centres in the county. The formation period was one of many difficulties. Among the drawbacks were lack of accommodation for stores and drill, and shortage of supplies, uniform, arms, equipment etc. There was no transport in the early days. Although Companies at first were ill-equipped they passed on from crude beginnings to the intricacies of the Sten gun and Spigot mortar under the guidance of regular officers and n.c.o.'s. Likewise the humble armlet of early days was superseded by complete service uniform.

Service in the Home Guard later became compulsory for all men between 18 and 50 years not already on military service; only certain sections of Civil Defence were exempted. Full-time administrative and instructional staff was provided for every area. Indeed the Home Guard throughout the country developed into a force numbered in millions, ready to take over the defence of our island home when armies of trained troops went on duty overseas.

★ ★ ★ ★ ★

The Caithness sections attended drill twice weekly and gained proficiency in the use of arms. Now and again all-night exercises resembling actual warfare took place. For instance, on a Sunday morning in April, 1942, Lybster Home Guard were called upon to hold their village against a strong attack by sections from Wick and district. It was a realistic assault, starting at dawn and made from various points. The "battle" waged for a few hours on the outskirts and finished in the streets of Lybster. Later the combatants paraded in the village square, where they were addressed by a Staff Officer and mistakes and successes reviewed.

Now and again, too, exercises were carried out against, or in conjunction with, regular forces. By far the biggest of these were week-end affairs at both Wick and Thurso in November, 1942, when Civil Defence units were also given important tests. The town shops and places of business were closed all Saturday afternoon, and the exercise continued until mid-day on Sunday. At Wick it took the form of a large-scale attempted invasion by regular forces, the town first being *blitzed* by our own aircraft

(Wellingtons). Gases were let loose in the streets and the whole exercise was uncannily realistic. Even Civil Defence made mistakes! Early on Sunday morning the "enemy" were observed on the outskirts of the town, and were promptly engaged by Home Guard and military forces holding outposts. The assault, however, was carried on into the streets – by "dead men," the Home Guard alleged. Anyhow, the "fighting" gave scope for the use of varied weapons.

★ ★ ★ ★ ★

The Home Guard was composed mainly of men who had been under fire in trench warfare; they made good use of weapons and were quick in initiative. That much umpires conceded.

One of the oldest members fooled a sentry one Sunday morning and "destroyed" a headland battery. Dressed as a civilian with a bag in hand, he approached the sentry in seeming haste, explaining he was a vet, and had an urgent call to a farm beyond. Could he go direct? The sentry believed the tale and let the innocent vet go by. The camp was asleep. Judge their surprise on finding a "bomb" on each gun emplacement.

Another point worth recording is that quite a number of our county Home Guardsmen cycled miles to attend parades, and were most regular in attendance.

★ ★ ★ ★ ★

The last parade of the Home Guard before the official "Stand down" was on Sunday, 3rd December, 1944. A Scottish contingent of 400 (representative of all battalions) attended a special parade in London where the King took the Salute during the march past. Caithness was represented by Sergt. James Sutherland, Scrabster, Thurso; Corpl. J. Sutherland, Lybster; and Pte. D. C. Henderson, Watten.

At Wick that Sunday more than 700 Home Guardsmen paraded to the Old Parish Church, headed by the company pipe band, where an appropriate service was conducted by Rev. G. Moore, B.D., and on the march back the Salute was taken at the Town Hall by Colonel D. Keith Murray, V.D., V.L., the first Commandant of Thurso platoon.

Addressing the men later, Colonel K. R. Palmer of Banniskirk, Commanding Officer in Caithness, read a message from the King in which he stated that by "patient and ungrudging effort you have built and maintained a force able to play an essential part in the defence of our threatened soil and liberty. History will say that your share in the greatest of all our struggles for freedom was a vitally important one. You have given your service without thought of reward. You have earned in full measure your country's gratitude."

Col. Palmer referred appreciatively to the wonderful spirit and organisation of the Home Guard from its early days. It had become efficiently trained for the defence of the country, and he thought the position of the Home Guard could most appropriately be stated in the well-known quotation: "They also serve who only stand and wait."

★ ★ ★ ★ ★

Thurso was one of the few companies of Home Guards where in the early days each man managed to get a rifle. It was probably the first platoon formed in the county and started off with a strength of 30, and in six months reached 140. Successive platoon commanders were – Col. D. Keith Murray, Major James Bremner, and Lieut. John Sinclair.

Lieut.-General Sir Andrew N. Thorne, G.O.C.-in-C. Scottish command in December, 1944, approved the award of certificates for good service to the following members of Caithness Home Guard:– Major J. Mackintosh, Coy.-Sergt.-Major J. Campbell, Sergeants W. Cormack, D. Fraser, D.A. Mackay, D. Manson, M. Nicolson and J. G. Sutherland.

★ ★ ★ ★ ★

Wick Home Guard (A Coy., No 3 platoon) distinguished itself by winning the championship cup open to Home Guard rifle teams in Britain. The award was the Macworth Praed challenge trophy, presented by the S.M.R.C. Some 1600 teams competed; 25 qualified for the final, Wick taking third place with a score of 981 (possible 1000). Wick returned an even higher aggregate in the grand final (983), and this gave them the coveted championship.

The team that brought this national honour to our town and county was:– Lieut. William Murray, Stirkoke; Sergt. Jack Steven (team leader), Wick; Corpl. W. Manson, Wick; Corpl. D. Nicolson, Sibster; L.-Corpl. A. Clyne, Noss; Ptes. W. Bain, Stirkoke; Joe Sutherland, Haster; D. Macivor, Haster; D. Ross, Reiss; and S. Macdonald, Wick.

The Home Guard rifle team repeated this outstanding performance in marksmanship a second year in succession, scoring 976 in the final shoot.

The trophy won on the second occasion was the Kent-Philips challenge cup. The winning team showed only one alteration from the previous year, H. Waters, Stirkoke, taking the place of Lieut. Murray.

Well done, Wick Home Guard!

They braved the perils of the sea.

Work of the Lifeboats in War-time.

"THE survivors were taken into port by a lifeboat." Such a sentence often appeared in print in war-time, and hidden behind it might be a story of untold hardship heroically endured. The survivors might be from sunken ships or lost aircraft, for the lifeboat answered every call.

The lifeboats at Wick and Thurso responded readily and between them rescued scores of perishing men. (Unfortunately, I cannot give authentic figures.) Although there were Air Sea Rescue craft (speedboats, we called them) at Wick, the seas were

Coxswain Neil Stewart

often against them, and the lifeboat was called upon to move out into the storm. Yes, into the storm – in daylight or darkness. Wick lifeboat put out at the height of south-easterly gales on three occasions when the seas in the bay were fearsome, and twice on the blackest of nights when authority had to be sought to switch on the harbour guiding lights for a few minutes. On these occasions the lifeboat dared not to return because of weather conditions and temporarily went to Scrabster. Let us salute the lifeboatmen around our coasts, among whom there are none better than our own Caithnessmen.

The coxswains at Wick and Thurso (Neil Stewart, jun., and J. Macleod respectively) were awarded medals for their skilful work, and the Lifeboat Institution's thanks on vellum was given Mr Wm. J. Mowatt, motor mechanic at Wick. "I deem it an honour not only for myself but for the crew and the boat," said Coxswain Neil Stewart on receiving the Bronze Medal for a daring rescue.

Conditions were against them when at three o'clock on a morning in September, 1942, the lifeboat was summoned. "A north-easterly gale was blowing and a heavy sea was running with a dangerous cross swell. It was raining in torrents," said the official description. The lifeboat knew the vessel was on the rocks 15 miles away. The coxswain steered by compass for the awful darkness did not allow of any guide. A radio message was sent out, and the answer came that the wreck was on the Ness of Duncansby. The lifeboat got there as the first streak of daylight appeared; she daringly went in among the rocks and by expert and bold handling rescued 31 men, exhausted with cold and fatigue, and brought them safely back to port. The trip took six hours, by no means the longest mission.

The lifeboat's most spectacular services were to the Irish steamer *Dromara* whose entire crew of 13 were saved just before the vessel foundered near the Old Man of Wick. It was a rescue accomplished by skilful seamanship and not a little daring.

* * * * *

Wick was given a new lifeboat (the *City of Edinburgh*) on the eve of the outbreak of war. The boat had a wonderfully active first year: 22 calls were answered and 43 lives saved. The first call came on October 23rd, 1939, and the boat was launched five times in the following six days. On one occasion the boat was at sea for $9\frac{1}{2}$ hours. That was only the beginning of the lifeboat's work. *The City of Edinburgh* was launched eleven times in her second year and rescued 18 lives; seven times in her third year and saved 31 lives. Often the call was to assist or search for R.A.F. aircraft which had come down in the sea, but from all the many searches only one live airman was rescued.

Five members of the lifeboat crew were awarded the 1939-45 Star, presented to all who were 25 or more times at sea on lifeboat service during the war. Recipients were:– 1st Coxswain Neil Stewart, jun.; 2nd Coxswain John Sinclair jun.; Bowman John Elder, 1st Motor Mechanic Wm. J. Mowatt, and 2nd Motor Mechanic George Mackay. (Bowman Elder retired early in 1946 after 24 years' lifeboat service).

★ ★ ★ ★ ★

Under the heading "Sea Tragedies" brief reference has been made to actions by Thurso lifeboat, for one of which three members of a gallant crew were honoured. They were Coxswain J. Macleod (Bronze Medal), Messrs William Sinclair and David Thomson (thanks on vellum). The official account of the men's work stated:–

"A gale was blowing, with a high, confused sea, and snow squalls, when the lifeboat put out at three in the afternoon to the help of what were thought to be two dinghies. These were twelve miles away, and drifting inshore. The coxswain set his course accordingly, and at 4.30 saw two rafts being carried rapidly towards the shore. One was still a mile and a half away, the other was less than 200 yards from the rocks. He made at once for the second raft, got between it and the rocks, and saw that two exhausted men were clinging to it. In the high and confused sea he ran great risk of losing the lifeboat, and her crew, but he manoeuvred her alongside the raft, and took off the men. It was very quickly done, and he had rescued them in the nick of time.

"Then he made at all speed for the other raft. He could see men lying on it, evidently beyond the power of helping themselves, so he went along the weather side, secured the raft with ropes at each end, and fended it off with boat hooks. Sinclair and Thomson jumped on to the raft, at great danger to themselves of being washed away by the heavy seas or crushed between the raft and the lifeboat.

"There were five men on the raft, and all had died from exposure. They were huddled together, and their arms and legs were so interwined that it was difficult to separate them. They were all put on board the lifeboat, where the two men from the first raft had been stripped, revived and given warm clothing. The lifeboat got back just after seven in the evening, having been out for over four hours. An ambulance was waiting for the rescued men, and they were taken to hospital, where they recovered."

Coxswain Macleod was also honoured by the King, being made a Member of the British Empire in the 1945 New Year Honours List.

★ ★ ★ ★ ★

To conclude this inadequate tribute to the men of the lifeboat service, a little story: A foreign ship had struck the rocks on our northern coast and got into a stormy sea again, damaged below the waterline. The night was dark and rainy and the seas were high when (about midnight) the lifeboat reached the crippled ship. Climbing aboard the unknown vessel, the rescuers espied two women, both in tears. 'Twas then that a stalwart young lifeboatman rose

grandly to the occasion. He began to sing and dance, seized one of the sobbing women in his strong arms, and whirled around with her. She could not understand his language but she understood his actions, and his apparent happiness and sense of safety dispelled all sense of fear, and although the ship was doomed the crew were landed safely.

★ ★ ★ ★ ★

Around our threatened coasts auxiliary coastguardsmen (or coast-watchers) were stationed ever after Dunkirk. This was a service that got no publicity but did valuable work. Generally it was maintained by hardy veterans; and they required to be hardy because in the early days they had no adequate shelter, protective clothing, boots, torches or equipment necessary for duties in such arduous and exposed conditions. Later (probably 1941) these coast-watchers came under the jurisdiction of the Admiralty; they were given battledress, armed with automatic weapons, and served under improved conditions generally.

Another organisation was the Observer Corps, trained in the recognition of aircraft at a distance and to pass on the information by telephone to a reporting centre maybe many miles away. Here the movements of aircraft were traced with coloured counters on a table map until they became "out-of-date" to the sector.

The approach of enemy aircraft was the chief concern of the Observer Corps. The "make" of the 'planes, number engaged, and direction of flight was useful information in drawing a picture of a raid. With these facts known, appropriate defensive measures were taken to prevent its full development.

Observer posts were generally in out-of-the-way places, maybe in a field or on a moor – but all were important. These posts were manned in the North by farmers, coopers, gamekeepers, fishcurers, labourers, and others, who all became proficient in the work. The Corps badge carried the motto, "Forewarned is forearmed."

Danger on the beaches, too.

Perhaps the greatest source of danger to the civilian, apart of course from bombing, lay in (or near) the innocent-looking and familiar beaches round the coast. Beach-combing in war-time was a particularly dangerous pastime, for not only had one to contend with the multifarious devices which the enemy dropped in the sea with the ultimate aim of these objects reaching the shore somewhere and sometime, but account had to be taken of British mines, both land and sea.

The beaches were indeed alive with danger and the public were repeatedly warned not to handle any unfamiliar objects found there or anywhere else. "Leave it," was the caution, and inform the police. Unfortunately, this advice was not always accepted, and there were tragic consequences.

★ ★ ★ ★ ★

Probably the first serious incidents on the coast occurred at John O'Groats on February 23, 1941, where a cylindrical object (no doubt of German origin) was washed up on the beach and discovered by a lad of 16. He lifted it and carried it for some distance along a pathway, when he was met by a friend who advised him to leave the thing severely alone. The lad laid it down but unfortunately returned later along with his father. On this occasion he must have touched the object in its most delicate part for it exploded, killing him outright and so injuring his father that he died shortly afterwards.

A little more than a fortnight later two soldiers, walking on the beach at Shorelands, touched off a pear-shaped object lying on the sand; the explosion which followed killed one of them instantaneously and so injured the second that he succumbed to his injuries the following morning. And on the 2nd of May a soldier picked up an innocent-looking cylinder off the beach at Reiss; the cylinder at once exploded and the soldier was killed outright.

All these incidents occurred during what might be termed a phase of the war – a phase in which German ingenuity showed itself in one of its most spiteful moods against the civilian population of this country; in Caithness alone about 40 reports of objects on the shore were received by the police. The incidents referred to were tragic ones, all the more so when one thinks that a wider appreciation of the danger involved in touching these objects might have prevented them all.

There was carelessness, too, on the part of those aware of the danger of leaving unguarded unexploded ammunition on the ground. There were casualties among innocent children in quiet places, but there were more lucky escapes. Here is an outstanding instance from the South Head Range at Wick: a shell failed to explode when fired and its whereabouts were surrounded with red flags as a warning to passers-by. When the military returned to collect it the shell had gone – but where? The police were informed, and its removal was traced to two young boys. They had taken it into the town, even into their homes, and when recovered was stored in a shed. What might have happened!

Throughout the years soldiers and airmen stationed in the county met their end in different ways, chiefly by accidents on the roadways and the 'dromes, and one was drowned while bathing in Watten Loch. Misjudgement on the part of an attacking aircraft on manoeuvres with the military caused a tragedy on the road near Watten. Diving at high speed to attack transport, a fighting machine came in contact with telephone wires and went off its course to crash into an army lorry, cutting away the cab and killing the occupants. That was the end of the pilot as well.

Protective measures against enemy landings.

Caithness Coasts Were Mined.

MILITARY-MINDED men believed in the probability of Germany invading the North of Scotland. An enemy army landed here by air or sea (it was contended) would have several advantages, such as cover for their movements, maintenance and food. There was only a single-track railway from Inverness north and this could easily be rendered unworkable; there were valuable airfields to seize, and such invasion (if successful) would interfere seriously with naval movements to and from Orkney and Shetland. Then there was the added prize of submarine bases in close proximity to the shipping route. The mounting of heavy guns along the coast would close the Pentland Firth. There must have been some reliance in this theory, judging by precautions taken officially. Indeed it is said that such an attack was actually at an advanced stage as regards planning but was abandoned for some reason. Anyhow, it was not a pretty picture that was painted for Caithnessians in the days when the nation was waiting on the enemy's arrival.

Caithness certainly figured in some German plan. This much was later discovered by a native officer, and may be verified by a visit to Wick Library. When the British Second Army liberated Brussels (1944) amongst the documents left behind by the Germans were numerous maps of parts of the

British Isles on an inch-to-a-mile scale. These were obviously printed for the guidance of the German Army during the intended invasion of Britain, and had German explanations and data on each sheet (printed significantly in 1940). The Second Army required maps of Germany for the invasion of that country and the collection found was converted for this purpose the reverse side being used.

During the course of the battles that followed an officer from Caithness, on turning over his map of Hanover and Bremen, discovered to his surprise he also had one of his own county with Wick, Watten and Lybster much more prominently marked than the towns and villages of Germany on the other side of the sheet.

★ ★ ★ ★ ★

The Links at Reiss were regarded as a likely landing spot. What more suitable place? The attack could be real or just a feint to compel the movement of forces from more coveted centres. The only hitch in the suitability of Reiss was that Wick 'drome bordered on the ground, and assumed indeed the major role of defence for the whole North of Scotland.

Sinclair Bay was heavily mined by Royal Engineers in the early months of 1941 – indeed the sands here were said to constitute the largest minefield in the United Kingdom. Between Keiss and Ackergill there was a continuous belt three and a half miles long and about 50 yards wide. These mines were originally laid in three rows and 20 feet apart. They were of the large anti-personnel variety known as beach mines, containing a heavy weight of explosive, and had been buried with the lid about six inches below ground level. Steel anti-tank defences were also erected around the whole bay. The invader was not to come in unchallenged.

★ ★ ★ ★ ★

When peace returned the mines had to be removed. Recovery work was made difficult in Reiss Bay because of shifting sand. Sometimes mines were found perched on the tip of a windswept sand dune; others were buried very deep in drifted sand or sands moved by the tides during the years – so deep (15ft in extreme cases) as to be out of range of detectors. Foot-high grass, too, was a handicap to the use of these helpful instruments.

Heavily armoured jet-throwing carriers were assembled to set fire to the grass and to wash away sand. The work of removing the mines was estimated as a two-years' job. Bomb disposal detachments have been active there for 18 months and although more than 2000 mines have been located and destroyed the whole area is not yet (1946) regarded as "safe." The removal of fences and sweeping of doubtful sectors has yet to be undertaken and is likely to occupy the remaining six months of the estimated period.

Reiss was a popular picnicking place in pre-war years, where many hundreds of parents and children gathered on public holidays. When will it regain such popularity?

★ ★ ★ ★ ★

Those responsible for anti-invasion measures at Wick must have expected the Germans to come in by the front door, so to speak. Batteries (including searchlights) were stationed on the headlands surrounding the bay, and flame-throwers were installed at the harbour entrance – not at small expense, it was said. The harbour quays were mined, ready for destruction, and road blocks were erected on all streets leading from the harbour and on the bridges. Reinforced blockhouses were constructed at vantage points overlooking the bay and along the roadsides. [To-day (February, 1946) German prisoners of war are demolishing them, but progress is remarkably slow. Maybe a tribute to the workmanship of British engineers.] The old steam-drifters *Lottie* and *Isabella Ferguson* were held in readiness for many months at the entrances to the old and new harbours, to be sunk there and so block the channels in the event of an attack. Troops were trained for this protective manoeuvre – and then sent abroad!

Barb wire entanglements (which remain as a nuisance) were thrown around the coasts and the burgh boundaries, and poles were erected in all fields considered useable as landing grounds for 'planes and gliders. Another precaution taken was the removal of all road signs.

Mined areas were fenced on the land side during the war years and generally people moving in the locality sensed danger and did not venture beyond. Sheep and dogs were not so wise! There were casualties among humans too, but these have been referred to elsewhere.

There were happenings that would in peacetime have caused a local or even wider sensation that never got beyond official files; and incidents which received some vague publicity quickly faded into the realm of things forgotten.

Sea mines drifted ashore.

Sea mines were frequently washed up on the Caithness shores at different places – to the alarm and discomfiture of nearby residents. Happily, a Naval demolition squad dismantled most of these ugly weapons without accident; other mines blew sky-high on coming into contact with the rocks. How brave these demolition fellows were! The Spring of 1941 saw the mine danger at its height and for two or three months the responsible authorities had daily, sometimes hourly, reports of unexploded mines on the beaches all the way from Helmsdale to Duncansby Head. The village of Keiss was probably the hardest hit of any coastal community, with Papigoe coming close behind. Windows in some Keiss property were as often out as in. Never will some of us forget an officer up almost to the neck in water wrestling with a mine near the village of Keiss. That was the night (March 15-16, 1941) special constables were conveyed from Wick to evacuate the inhabitants from the threatened end of the village by direct order from the Naval authorities. The good people of Keiss responded readily to the unusual instructions, even although these came at eleven o'clock at night, but within two hours the most dangerously placed mines had been courageously dealt with by mine disposal officers. The officers won – and the incident closed.

Several mines floated into Wick Bay. Most of these were rendered harmless, or exploded harmlessly, but two at least gave trouble. The second of these floated in during a high sea on a bitterly cold Saturday afternoon in November, 1941. Some watched the progress of the unwelcome visitor on its passage around the rocky coast towards the harbour where it almost came into heavy contact with the seaward end of the south pier. The sea clutched it away again and guided it on to the beach at Shaltigoe. There it was hurled to and fro by advancing and receding waves. It rolled on its horns – and nothing happened. Watchers believed it to be a "dud." Everyone had not taken police advice to get to the rear portions of houses along the sea-front.

The mine rolled again and the "dud" exploded with a terrific bang that shook the town. Houses vibrated and slates from the roof-tops clattered to the ground in Smith Terrace and Bexley Terrace. Windows went west on a wholesale scale and the roadways became a mass of broken glass. Other streets in the vicinity did not escape unscathed. The explosion flung showers of stones from the sea-shore on to the streets above the brae. The electricity power station suffered severely, and about 150 houses were damaged.

The most remarkable feature of the incident was that no person was injured. Some tenants, however, had to be evacuated owing to the unsafety of their homes; going temporarily to Rest Centres or the High School, or to the homes of friends.

Next day the area had many sight-seers. There were but two windows intact in all Bexley Terrace and one fanlight survived! More than a thousand window panes had to be replaced.

That Sunday municipal workers were busy sweeping glass from littered streets, and every willing joiner was given a job to help remedy the damage – a work that went on for days.

Memories of that unhappy Saturday will remain with many. That evening Pulteney had one of its worst outbreaks of fire. About eight o'clock the Co-operative bakehouse was found to be ablaze and despite the all-night efforts of three fire brigades against a conflagration whipped by a semi-hurricane wind the bakery, a storehouse, and club premises were wholly destroyed. The damage amounted to several thousand pounds.

A reasonable explanation of this outbreak of fire was that the explosion of the mine nearby flung open the oven doors and scattered burning cinders on the bakehouse floor.

★　★　★　★　★

Tragedy came to Wick in the first hour of April 26, 1941, when a Whitley bomber collided with the Town and County Hospital buildings. The administrative block was totally destroyed. Two young maids asleep in an attic bedroom lost their lives, and other members of the staff escaped from bedrooms in an upper storey by dashing through flames to a window on the ground floor. Exit by the door had been cut off.

The 'plane circled the town several times flying low preparatory to landing. A wing of the machine was wrenched away by coming into contact with the main hospital building, which instantly became a mass of flames, and the 'plane crashed into an adjoining field. All six of the air crew perished.

The fire became fearsome and lit up brilliantly the whole town and countryside. The fire brigade had much assistance from teams of Servicemen and civilians in its all-night struggle and succeeded in keeping the fire confined to the main building.

Patients in adjacent wards were removed for safety. The nursing staff lost all personal belongings but remained on duty.

This was only one of many 'plane crashes in the county but the only incident of the kind in which civilians were involved.

Looking back over the events recorded above, two interesting facts were noticeable: firstly that, providentially, there were few casualties in incidents that might have resulted in many deaths; and secondly, that during the two major fires no enemy 'planes were in the vicinity. What havoc would have ensued had one or two hostile aircraft dropped bombs among the dense crowds of sight-seers who watched the proceedings. Truly, Wick had a guardian angel on these nights.

With our boys abroad.

Fifth Seaforths' Long Trek.

whereabouts were always easily placed. It was the county battalion. More than two-score of our boys fell in its ranks, and there is an attachment that Time will not wither. The remainder of Caithness Servicemen were scattered over many units in all theatres of war and not so readily followed, but we will see what the review produces; where it falls short, others can step into the breach.

The 5th Seaforths did much travelling and much training in this country before going abroad. For the first 18 months of the war duties were centred mainly in the three northern counties, the battalion or companies being stationed at (in some semblance of order) – Wick, Cromarty, Invergordon, Dingwall, Scapa, Strathpeffer, Lybster, Castletown, Staxigoe, Edderton, Lyth, Ackergill, Keiss and Dornoch. Dingwall was again their headquarters round about the New Year of 1941, but four months later they moved to Oldmeldrum, Aberdeenshire, and in September to Stonehaven. From there the battalion was transferred to Fleet and Heckfield Heath, Hants, until June, 1942.

Mr Churchill visits the 5th Seaforths in the Desert.

SOMEWHERE in these articles reference has been made to the going-away of the 5th Seaforths and now battalion doings come under review again. Why the 5th Seaforths? it may be asked. The answer is understandable: Caithness lads were grouped in this Territorial battalion and its

The battalion embarked at Gourock on the *Bergensfjord* for an unknown destination. What thoughts ran through the minds of the men when the gangways were removed? Maybe similar to those so musically expressed by Henry Henderson of Reay in days of long ago as the ship rode at anchor and the traveller stood by the sea "in its rise and its fa'":–

When I'm sailing far ower the blue sea,
I'll heave a long sigh for Scotland and thee;
When around me the waves in mid-ocean shall roar,
I'll think on the friends that I left on the shore;
I'll think on the auld folks, I'll think on the heart
That was bursting with grief and nigh breaking to part,
The heart o' my Nannie, the dearest o' a',
When the winds and the waters shall waft me awa'.

★ ★ ★ ★ ★

Eight weeks later (in August, 1942) the battalion set foot on a dusty quayside near Port Suez, and eventually arrived at El Tahag. The German Afrika Corps was at the gates of Egypt at that time and were expected to attack strongly in an effort to annex the Suez Canal. Generals Alexander and Montgomery had accepted command of the British Forces in the Middle East but few envisaged that the stage was set for the utter rout of German and Italian arms in North Africa.

To get a true perspective of the world situation at the time it is necessary to mention Russia. That country was in a bad way militarily. Leningrad was surrounded and Moscow menaced; Sebastopol had fallen and the Germans were marching on in the Caucasus. The eyes of the world had been focussed for weeks on the swaying, bitter, epic struggle for Stalingrad, where broadcast as victories was the capture of a street or even a factory. Could Russia possibly hold on? was the question.

Another feature of the war at that time was the onward rush of Japanese forces, capturing islands and strongpoints and sweeping through countries with seeming ease. Australia and India were faced with the prospect of invasion and prepared to meet it.

Submarine warfare was taking dreadful toll of our Atlantic shipping, and the Mediterranean, so vital to British interests, was all but under enemy control. That was zero hour. They were brave-hearted men indeed who planned to save the Allies from so many perils.

★ ★ ★ ★ ★

The Eighth Army heartened the wavering nations of the world by launching a staggering attack. The Battle of El Alamein (opened 23rd October, 1942) was heralded by the thunder of the biggest barrage in history. The Eighth Army rested only to rebuild and regather strength on its victorious way through Libya, Cyrenaica, Tripolitania, on to Tunis to link with the Forces (Free French, British and American) pushing east from Algeria.

The 5th Seaforths took their old-time place as a unit of the 51st (Highland) Division, a division that previously had been sacrificed in heroically covering the retreat to the coast in France in the summer of 1940. Now the Division had been re-formed and was again destined to get more publicity than any other.

The mind of every 5th Seaforth turned towards Home on the final day of October, 1942. Each thought on his Nannie and the auld folks at home and all were diligent as letter-writers. That was Hallowe'en but to them it was the eve of battle (the battalion's first real battle) when they went through to attack near Tel-el-Eisa. The night of November 1 was dark (visibility was only a few yards), the moon rose but even then the dust and smoke of bursting shells hampered vision.

Four Caithness Seaforths in Sicily.
C.Q.M.S. Wm. Reid, Thurso; Sergt. D. H. Sinclair, Halkirk; Pipe-Major Gordon Asher, Halkirk; and C.S.M. Donald Macleod, Castletown.

But the attack went well and objectives were gained and held. The way had been opened for the passage of armoured columns. That was part of the begin-

51st Divison Memorial in Sicily (overlooking battlefield).

ning of the Eighth Army's pursuit of the enemy, who stopped to fight back at every vantage point – and he knew his job, did "Jerry."

★ ★ ★ ★ ★

Other place-names linked with the Seaforths' trek were Mersa Brega, Hous-Corradini, Mareth Line, Wadi Akarit, Roumana Ridge, Sfax, Enfidaville, Takrouna (each the scene of fighting). The Seaforths said good-bye to the limitless desert. "We needed a change of air, more men and a bit of respite" (wrote the late Major J. H. Davidson, D.S.O., in his North African Diary).

"The first two we got, but respite did not come our way. The war was not finished yet . . ." The battalion moved to "a place called Djidjelli." The journey took three days and came to an end at a small Algerian village called Cavallo – a pleasant place to see after the countless desert war-strewn miles. But in this paradise there was much to do: coming events were casting a shadow. The Seaforths had to become expert mountaineers, learn the art of village fighting, the technique of assault landings, and be

fully fit physically – there was a job to do.

The Seaforths' training was preparatory to the invasion of Sicily, a task which was successfully undertaken on 10th July, 1943. Sicily did not long survive the onslaught (little more than a month) but some of our lads are buried there. Major Davidson himself died of wounds on this Mediterranean island.

British forces from Sicily crossed the Straits of Messina to the heel of Italy to help in the conquest of that country. One Brigade only (which did not include the 5th Seaforths) of the 51st Division made the crossing for a short period to protect the right flank of the Eighth Army. The Allies also made a landing at Anzio. This landing became a thorn in the Axis' side and was desperately attacked. The beach-head warriors suffered heavily, it is true, but remained a pain to the opposition and finally linked up with our forces on their northward push. Where were Mussolini's boasted eight million bayonets? Even Rome came into Allied hands and Mussolini fled. Churchill had vowed to "tear his empire to shreds" – and did it.

★ ★ ★ ★ ★

The 5th Seaforths returned to this country about 14 months later (October, 1943) when they were given a fitting reception. As a unit of the 51st (Highland) Division they had bravely upheld the traditions of Scotland, said Colonel D. Keith Murray, Thurso, and their deeds will be recorded in the historical annals of the war.

The men returned home for a few weeks' rest. They were bronzed by the heat of the desert sun and appeared healthy, and they wore that symbol of the desert, the Africa Star.

But there was yet another job to do.

With our boys abroad.

Fifth Seaforths in France.

THE 51st Divison had been much in contact with the enemy on the unending road from El Alamein to Italy, and returned to this country with other war-tested Divisions to prepare for the biggest undertaking of the war – the landing in Normandy.

The Division crossed the Channel in support of the storming D-Day troops and took part in some of the toughest fighting. These battles will go down in Divisional history, and the story of the 5th Seaforths' warfare will likely be written separately. Meantime we follow their adventures with snatches gleaned from military observers and other sources. These generally relate to incidents that could be termed "favourable," but there was another side to the picture, for the German soldier was well-trained and well-equipped and did not lack in cunning or in skill.

Among incidents reported by an officer observer with the 51st Division in Normandy was a meeting he had with Major George Green, 5th Seaforths, headmaster of Bilbster School, who later was awarded the Military Cross. This observer was tickled by Major Green telling him on a July day in 1944 that there was "not a thing doing," and added:– He'd been bombed and shelled, mortared and machine-gunned; there had been German patrols prowling round tanks, creeping up within range and firing. The Division had moved from one area to another amidst an air raid. But he was quite all right. This was the normality of war, concluded the observer. It was the ordinary things that seemed out of place.

★ ★ ★ ★ ★

Germans tumbling out of red-hot *douvres* shrieking for mercy, Nazis lying cowering in their slit trenches, afraid to move, and fighting Seaforth Highlanders in hand-to-hand combat with crack enemy troops – these were some of the incidents in a short but fierce battle in which 5th Seaforths smashed through and captured the heavily defended strongpoint in the Troarn "triangle," key to Troarn, as told by a military correspondent.

The Seaforths completely routed a battalion of crack Nazi troops. They took 80 prisoners, and nearly 200 Germans were killed and wounded.

"For six weeks we had been forced to sit and take it, unable to hit back. When we got the chance it was no wonder our lads went fighting mad," was the comment of Sergeant Donald Sutherland, of Halkirk. His company had run into fierce opposition before coming to a crossroad.

"It looked like being a pretty tough battle," C.S.M. Alistair Doull, Latheron (later killed in action), told the correspondent. "As we approached the Germans were firing from their *douvres* with their *spandaus*. Our bullets made no impression on their *douvres*. These had resisted the earlier shelling."

★ ★ ★ ★ ★

The name of St. Valery-en-Caux will ever be sacred in the annals of the 51st Division, for it was there in the summer of 1940 that the original Division terminated the heroic rearguard action that made possible the evacuation from Dunkirk. The remnants of the Division were made prisoner.

Four years later the re-formed "51st" made a tri-umphant re-entry into St. Valery. The first infantry to enter was our own county battalion. Wick men formed the advance patrol into the town and found it unoccupied except for the civil population. The Seaforths passed on, leaving behind them an excited throng of French civilians waiting to welcome the return of the Highland Division, still led by some of the pipers who had played them into battle at El Alamein.

★ ★ ★ ★ ★

Four 5th Seaforths were out on patrol and had reached the corner of a hedge when, about a hundred yards away, they saw a German patrol approaching. The Nazis were advancing cautiously with ten yards between each soldier.

"Get into cover," snapped Lieut. G. Lisle, Yorkshire. L.-Cpl. Jimmy White, Thurso; Pte. Sydney Harris, Chatham, and Pte. J. Leake, Boston, Lincs., concealed themselves in the hedge. The first Nazi soldier came round the corner. A hand was laid on his shoulder. He turned to face the Sten gun held by Jimmy White (who had been a barman in the Pentland Hotel) and collapsed quietly into the hedge. A whistle and a nod of the head backed up by the Sten guns accomplished the same feat with every man in the Nazi patrol. Without a word being spoken fourteen Nazis were thus taken prisoner, each man ignorant of the fate of his predecessors till he had rounded the hedge.

"It was a bloodless victory," L-Cpl. White said, "it wasn't till they were all in the bag that it began to dawn on them that they had been well and truly foiled, and then it was too late."

★ ★ ★ ★ ★

A patrol of 5th Seaforths, moving forward after an attack, came on a German strong-point. There were ten Germans there – everyone, including the sentry, fast asleep. The Seaforths wakened them up, and removed them to the British lines to continue their dreams in a prison camp.

"It was like one of these mad parties," said a Glasgow soldier. "We came to the corner of a farm-yard, and sitting against the wall, fast asleep, was the German sentry. I tapped him on his steel helmet, and it took a good few taps to rouse him. Even then he didn't know he was a prisoner."

"Take it quietly, boys, and we'll get the others,' said Sergt. Hamish Gunn, Thurso, in charge of the patrol. "So we tip-toed into the farmyard, and dug in beneath the haystacks we found another nine Germans sound asleep."

An amusing illustration of the uncertainty of war

occurred shortly after a company of the 5th Seaforths captured a village, wrote S.-Sergt. G. Bannerman, Wick.

"The company commander and another officer were on a walk through the village street after the place had been taken. They hadn't gone far when a car passed them heading towards our lines. The car stopped a short distance down the street, and the officers, a little suspicious, retraced their steps towards it. Imagine their consternation when they discovered it was a 'Jerry.'

"By this time the occupants of the car had disappeared into a house, and the officers crouched behind the vehicle and waited for them. When the 'Jerries' came out they were held up in true highway fashion. On investigation, it was found that the car was in charge of an enemy quarter-master-sergeant, who was bringing up a special meal for 200 of his men. The Seaforths appreciated such unexpected rations!"

★　★　★　★　★

The Seaforth Highlanders holding a bridge-head across a frozen river in the Ardennes had to live in the open for three days and two nights in case of a German counter-attack. With 28 degrees of frost – so cold that the clothes froze on their bodies and men's hands stuck to the metal of their rifles – it took every ounce of endurance to hold out.

Sergt. William Macleod, Castletown, told a military correspondent: "We were issued with self-heating soup, but it was frozen solid and wouldn't heat. It was not so bad during the day, for we built huge log fires and melted snow on these to brew a cup of tea. But at night – we just had to run up and down."

The main body of the Seaforths had gone on to surprise a German stronghold. A bridge spanning the river had been destroyed and the attack was delayed for hours. The men dug *douvres* in the frozen ground, but sleep was impossible. The Company headquarters were in a ditch and five inches of ice. Cold feet were a big problem. At dusk the attack was made when the "Terriers" mounted the crest leading to the village and advanced along a narrow, winding road. Soon they bumped into and made prisoner an enemy patrol, wrote Sergt. Thos. Sutherland, Wick, and continued with this description of their movements:– Voices were heard from a house ahead and the Seaforths crept stealthily forward and encircled it. A challenge rang out, followed almost immediately by a hasty shot. Moving still closer, the Caithness "Terriers" heard the alarmed and trembling voice of a woman say that

only the family were present. When entry was forced a German officer and six men were captured. The enemy in the village had no idea that we were in their midst so we carried on silently, clearing each house in turn and taking many prisoners with as little fuss as possible. Few shots were fired. Most of the Germans (180 were taken prisoner in the operation) were sheltering from the elements in houses, and warming themselves by the stoves.

Next day a strong patrol of infantry, accompanied by tanks, which by that time had crossed the new bridge, pushed on to some woods and returned the proud captors of seven armoured vehicles and about a dozen rather bedraggled looking Germans.

Country and landscape around this particular area in the Ardennes brought one's thoughts flashing back to places like Berriedale and Dunbeath braes (concluded Sergt. Sutherland), "and one wishes more than ever for better luck in the next leave list."

With our boys abroad.

Fifth Seaforths Cross the Rhine.

THE third phase of the 5th Seaforths' war adventures centres on the crossing of the Rhine and the advance into Germany.

A task given the battalion in the campaign between the Maas and the Rhine was to render the road from Geunep to Goch safe for traffic by capturing Siebengewald, a village some three miles to the south. The operation was successfully completed. The enemy withdrew from Bluementhals and the Seaforths advanced through Siebengewald on parallel roads, cleared the village with little opposition, and thus linked up the Divisional front. The area was heavily mined.

★　★　★　★　★

The Highlanders were for nineteen days engaged in bitter fighting through the Siegfried defences. The men lived under appalling weather conditions, slept in the open in slit trenches, sometimes with their clothes soaking wet. They swam rivers, battled hand-to-hand in the forests, swarmed across the plains, and fought in the streets of Germany. These Highlanders had been against the best German paratroopers, soldiers who died rather than surrender. Sometimes eyes were weary from lack of sleep. It was "a cruel fecht weill foughten" but they gained every objective, had been bitterly counter-attacked yet never yielded ground.

In a message to Major-General Rennie, Divisional Commander, the Corps Commander (Lt.-General B. S. Horrocks) said the Division had never fought better than in the offensive into Germany. He continued:– "You breached the enemy's defences in the initial attack, fought your way into the southern part of the Reichsvald, overcame in succession several strong points of the Siegfried Line, such as Hekkons, etc., and finished clearing the southern half of Goch, a key centre in the German defences. You have accomplished everything you have been asked to do, in spite of the number of additional German reserves which have been thrown in on your front. No Division has ever been asked to do more, and no Division has ever accomplished more. Well done, Highland Division."

★ ★ ★ ★ ★

From Goch the Brigade Group returned to Nijmegen, where a week was passed in reorganisation. They were visited on the first Sunday in March by Mr Churchill and General Crerar. Again coming events cast an indicative shadow when the battalion moved into training quarters – intensive study being given to the passage of a major river obstacle and to street fighting. When they moved into the concentration area at a point where the river was only some 450 yards broad, the Germans were active in showering unwelcome attention on the west bank of the river. The Seaforths did not cross in the first flight: their task was to get into the storm boats in the moon-light of next morning and to maintain the impetus of the assault and enlarge the bridgehead. The river was under shell and mortar fire, and frequently the boats were rocked by explosions in the water. Prospects were uninviting when the Seaforths made the passage, following a Canadian battalion as dawn was breaking.

Disembarking was a slick operation, and the Seaforths found the route to the assembly area clearly marked by a trail of discarded lifebelts. They moved to a position south of Esserden. Shelling and mortar fire were very heavy, and it was in this area that General Rennie, the Divisional Commander, was killed. The battalion later moved by Speldrop to the factory area north of Rees, which was already in British hands. The Seaforths had an unpleasant journey as, in addition to heavy long-range fire, there were enemy snipers and *spandau* posts which had not been cleared on either side of the road. The route

was tortuous and difficult to follow as the battalion moved forward using the sideway ditches.

★ ★ ★ ★ ★

The assault on the village itself was delivered by "A" Company on the left and "C" Company on the right. The leading platoon of the latter occupied the cheese factory buildings at their first rush, but were immediately heavily counter-attacked and one section was overrun. "A" Company cleared their objectives and "C" Company captured a central group of houses but were unsuccessful in their attempts to retake the cheese factory. "D" Company were ordered to exploit the success of the left flank by passing through "A" Company and seizing a group of houses south of the village astride the main road from Rees to the east, which was most important to the success of the operation. The Company went in with tremendous dash, and, after a very sharp fight, stormed their objective, taking 50 tough young paratroopers prisoner in one position which consisted of a loopholed white farmhouse with a trench system behind it sited to cover the approaches. This assault (wrote the Colonel in command) clinched the issue and the last platoon had little difficulty in recapturing the cheese factory which was by then cut off.

The Seaforths had attacked and held the heart of the enemy positions and cut off the German escape route. For two days they held out, surrounded by Germans, and captured 250 Germans trying to get out of Rees.

★ ★ ★ ★ ★

"We certainly caught the Germans by surprise," said Major Roderick Mackay, "for we had hardly got dug-in when the first batch of paratroopers came sloping up the road with their weapons. They were fighting Nazis, coming to form defensive positions further back. We took about 30 of them, but some of the others coming up took warning and formed a ring round us with their *spandaus*. When morning came we found there were Germans all round us, even on the road by which we had come. We couldn't get tanks across for the road was blown. Anti-tank guns, however, were used pretty effectively against the snipers' houses. The rest of the snipers we gradually winkled out, using smoke from our two-inch mortars to cover our approach. And when the tanks came up – well, it was just like Sunday. These Germans varied a lot, of course. The ones who gave us all the trouble were real dyed-in-the-wool Nazis, paratroopers and others. They fought on till we were right on top of them. But the

Volksturm type had no heart for fighting."

To the east of Groin the main road from Rees crosses a stream which had been canalised to form a water obstacle. A brickworks and the mansion house of Hollands Hof commanded this section of the road.

The Seaforths spent next day in patrolling outwards and mopping up. A counter-attack was expected but did not develop. The enemy long-range fire on the area slackened.

The Seaforths were relieved by another battalion of the Division, and on 28th March moved forward to a position behind the *Autobahn*, which was under construction south of Isselburg. The Camerons had occupied this town during the night almost unopposed. This was the first sign of a crack on this front which up till then had been stubbornly contested yard by yard by the remnants of the German 1st Parachute Army, supported by the 116 Panzer Regiment. There was some further successful fighting before the troops saw our armour thrusting forward to crack about in the plains of Northern Germany – and on to final victory.

★ ★ ★ ★ ★

The Highland Division celebrated VE-Day in bomb-wrecked Wesermunde when the pipe band proudly led five thousand marching men in the first parade in occupied Germany. Marching with the Divisional Headquarters party (wrote a military observer) was Pte. William Miller, Seaforths, Wick. "I marched with the Division in the Tripoli parade and I am proud and thankful to be with them in this victory march through Wesermunde," said this territorial soldier.

Leading the massed pipes and drums of the Division was Drum-Major George Macdonald, whose wife resided in Lybster village. "It was a bit of a strain, especially in the terrific heat, but it was the biggest moment of my 14 years in the Army," said this tall, regular soldier.

With our boys on service.

Adventures in Far-Away Lands.

LOOKING over a souvenir number of S.E.A.C. (a publication for the troops in South East Asia Command) one learns rightaway that Japan seized in a hundred days the widest dominion on earth. Produced for men of the "Forgotten Army" ("forgotten" maybe because their remarkable endurance, deeds and fighting qualities were overawed for a time by the major events much nearer home) it recalls the great battles by land, air and sea that contributed so much to the ultimate downfall of a mighty Eastern enemy.

First dealt with is the Battle of Arakan, in which a British division was completely encircled for 22 days, yet was supplied all that time with rations, ammunition, medical supplies, and even the daily newspaper, by the Air Transport Command.

Space is given to the historic story of Wingate's moonlight invasion of Burma by air, when 12,000 troops, with 1200 mules, guns, jeeps and even oxen, were put down by glider and transport 'plane 200 miles inside Japanese-held territory to conduct a crippling attack in the rear of the Japanese front as they advanced to the invasion of India.

Then there was the great march of General Stilwell's army over the Ledo Mountains towards Myitkyina, and the building of the miraculous Ledo Road over the mountains and across the jungle.

The souvenir copy recalls, too, the bloody bat-

KOHIMA MILITARY CEMETERY.

tles of Kohima and Imphal, two sieges far greater even than Arakan, which were eventually broken by the Fourteenth Army, and which, in fact, broke the back of the Japanese Army in Burma in 1944.

That is an unvarnished outline of the Burma campaign – a campaign of endurance against a wily enemy, against disease, against hardships and heart-breaking conditions, generally; a campaign of long marches, lonely patrols, and fearsome battles. For three years the men lived in the open, without a roof above their heads. The fighting in Burma has been described as a "merciless grapple in the jungle shadows" and those who took part are ever worthy of the profound admiration of a grateful country.

Caithness was well represented in the various units engaged.

The 101st Heavy A.A. Regiment consisted largely of Scottish Territorials. The 226 Heavy A.A. Battery mobilised in Thurso in August, 1939, and was at its station about ten days before war was declared. This Battery was formed early in 1938, and was divided between Caithness and Orkney with one-half of the battery with headquarters in both Thurso and Kirkwall. The Battery was the only one deployed in Orkney for A.A. defence of the Fleet for the first two months of the war and had the honour of being the first battery to bring down an enemy 'plane in Great Britain on October 17, 1939, when the German Air Force first raided Scapa Flow.

The Battery remained in the Orkneys until May, 1941, when it moved with 101 Heavy A.A. Regiment to sites on the mainland. The headquarters of the regiment was made up almost entirely of Caithness personnel, and Major Hugh Macdonald, of Thurso, was its adjutant for a considerable period. Altogether there were 82 Caithnessmen (six of them officers) on service with the battery. The first three years of the war were spent on lonely gun sites and, apart from defensive action in the Orkneys, these were mainly wearisome and monotonous days.

★ ★ ★ ★ ★

The Regiment (including 226 Battery) changed from a static to a mobile role in 1942, and sailed for India where it disembarked at Bombay on July 1, 1943. It served with the 33rd Corps. It underwent intensive training and finally arrived at Imphal on October 15. It advanced to Tamu where it had its first A.A. engagement abroad. The Regiment was first employed in an ack-ack role in defence of forward airfields, but its best use was as medium artillery, utilising the great range of its 3.7-inch guns. In addition, one troop was re-equipped with four 7.2-inch howitzers capable of hurling a 200lb shell over nine miles.

The gunners first took part in battle in support of East Africans in the forcing of the River Chindwin. They aimed the first shells on Kalewa at a range of 20,000 yards. Advancing to Ye-U, the Regiment moved to Shwebo and later helped to force the crossing of the Irrawaddy at Singu and in the battle for Monywa. The accurate and devastating shooting of the ack-ack men won admiration and they were christened "the twelve-mile snipers."

★ ★ ★ ★ ★

The greatest task came when the Regiment was ordered to deploy near Myinmn in support of the main crossing over the Irrawaddy. It was in this battle that the mighty 7.2-inch howitzers went into action for the first time. The battle raged for three weeks. Stripped to the waist, they fired their guns night and day, using over 2000 rounds of 7.2-inch and 12,000 rounds of 3.7-inch ammunition – a total weight of approximately 350 tons. Crossing the Irrawaddy, the Regiment was actively engaged in support of Divisions operating against the Japs still holding out in Mandalay and in the subsequent mopping-up. It is noteworthy that the first shells to fall in the city were "ack-ack." The Regiment also had experience as infantry, patrolling the jungle in the escape route from Mount Popa, and taking several prisoners and much Jap equipment.

The final scene of the Regiment's adventures was in the Toungoo area where, going into action for the last time, they took heavy toll of the enemy attempting to escape across the Sittang.

During the 226 Battery's campaign in Burma the guns were moved through some of the wildest and most difficult country in the world, drivers taking them over steep hills, appalling road, flooded chaungs and seemingly impassable tracks.

Brigadier G.D.K. Murray, O.B.E., M.C., T.D., A.D.C. , of Borgie House, Castletown, Convener of Caithness, had the unique distinction to command the 226 Battery and the 101 Regiment. He also had the command of the 5th Seaforths. A notable record indeed.

★ ★ ★ ★ ★

After four and a half years' service abroad, starting when he joined his regiment in Shanghai, Captain B. M. Manson, Wick, of the Seaforth Highlanders, is completing what he hopes will be his last six months of foreign service by killing Japs on the Assam-Burma border (wrote a military observer in the summer of 1944).

On one of his recent adventures his two sections were holding isolated positions when the enemy suddenly launched a two platoon attack. One section post was over-run and the other section could not get its gun through the hail of fire. Captain Manson worked his way alone through a *nala* with the aid of kukri and came behind a party of the enemy which he put to flight. Later he discovered that the Japs had laid an ambush and again worked up behind them and gave them a taste of their own medicine by a surprise attack with grenades. In this scrap he received grenade splinters in his right side and right arm but he certainly looks none the worse.

Captain Manson was headmaster of Staxigoe school, was called up with the Territorials, and had

5½ years' service abroad. He belongs to Keiss. He brought home with him several interesting souvenirs, including a signed document (in Japanese) conveying the sentence of death to him.

*　*　*　*　*

One of the first Caithness men to arrive home after liberation from a Japanese prisoner-of-war camp was Lac. James Donn, Lybster. He was a prisoner for 3½ years.

Lac. Donn went overseas in the summer of 1941, and was in Malaya when the Japs invaded it. Along with others, he went back to Singapore. Shortly before the fall of this naval base he escaped by sea to Java. Here he and other airmen, Allied and British, fought as ground troopers with whatever weapons could be mustered. They held out on the beach for about a month, and then were captured when Java fell to the enemy. He was held prisoner in Java until October, 1943, following which he was removed to the infamous "hell camp" at Sumatra. Later, the Japs removed the prisoners to Singapore. While in camp, Lac. Donn's weight (normally 10st. 7lb) was reduced at one stage to 7st. 3lb.

The first news that he and his fellow prisoners had of the Japanese surrender was a letter dropped by a friendly Chinaman, forced labourer for the enemy. The Chinaman, cycling past, dropped a letter behind him. "We read that the war was over," said Lac. Donn, "but we did not believe it, and tore up the letter. Later, the Japs told us we were free, and they treated us much better after that."

The 140th L.A.A. Battery.

ANOTHER Service unit in which Caithness was particularly interested was the 140th Light A.A. Battery. Our county War Record would be incomplete without an outline of its formation, its training, and its experiences abroad.

Captain (later Colonel) K. R. Palmer of Banniskirk was (on 18th September, 1939) asked to form a local Anti-Aircraft Battery, and recruiting commenced forthwith in Caithness and Sutherland. There was a good response and 40 men were attested on 29th September, a large percentage of whom were ex-Servicemen of the 1914-18 war. The 301 Troop was formed with headquarters at the Rifle Hall, Wick.

After preliminary training at Dechmont Camp and South Queensferry and advanced training and firing practice at Cark, the Troop was transferred to the Orkney Defences and during the six months' manning of A.A. guns at Flotta and other vital points played a notable part in thwarting enemy designs on the Orkney stronghold. The 301 Troop returned to Wick and along with two other Troops made up by incoming recruits formed the 140th L.A.A. Battery. Vital points at Wick, Castletown and Skitten Aerodromes, and also at Thrumster, were manned, and, as Caithness was at that time listed as No. 1 Invasion Area, the newly-formed Battery was at the alert day and night for many months. It was brought up to strength and became proficient in the handling of A.A. guns of various kinds.

*　*　*　*　*

In April, 1942, the 140th Battery, along with two other batteries, forming the 40th L.A.A.

Six members of the Battery:— Gnr. MacDougal, Inverness; Sgt. A. Brown, Wick; Sgt. Goddard, Glasgow; Gnr. H. Durrand, Wick; Bdr. W. Bain (whose wife resided in Castletown); and Gnr. Murray, Glasgow.

Regiment, was selected to provide A.A. protection for the re-formed 51st (Highland) Division. The Regiment sailed on June 21, 1942, from Gourock for service in North Africa. Freetown, Cape Town, Durban and Aden were ports of call *en route,* and the Regiment finally arrived in Egypt on September 7, 1942, at an area in the Western Desert from which operations were shortly to commence which were to bring the 51st Division the glories and honours of El Alamein and other victories in the North African campaign. The 40th Regiment was with the Division through Libya, Tripolitania and Tunisia, and had an important part in the successes of our arms in that trying campaign. At Bougie, Algeria, training in amphibious operations was carried out preparatory to the landing in Sicily (July, 1943), and with this second campaign successfully completed the Regiment embarked for home from Augusta, Sicily, on 11th November.

While in England, a process of re-equipping was carried out in preparation for D-Day. The Regiment landed on the beaches of France on 6th June, 1944, a day that paved the way to a long and arduous campaign through France, Belgium, Holland and Germany. The Regiment was disbanded at the end of March, 1945.

Throughout the various campaigns it brought down numerous enemy aircraft – six in as many minutes seems to have been the highlight of its shooting – and very valuable protection was afforded to the infantrymen of the Division.

Caithness folk may excusably be proud that to those veterans belonging to the county and neighbouring Sutherland who enrolled in its ranks in the early days of September, 1939, the 140th Battery owed much which stood it in good stead when the younger members faced the enemy overseas.

With our Men at Sea.

BRITISH Naval losses were heavy in the first three years of war. These were given as three battleships, two battle cruisers, five aircraft carriers, 22 cruisers, 14 merchant cruisers, 83 destroyers, 38 submarines, and 248 smaller craft, including trawlers, minesweepers, drifters, etc. Quite a number of Caithness Naval Reservists served on the armed merchant cruisers, and though our county had saddening news in connection with the sinkings the toll of the sea could have been even worse. Already reference has been made to the *Jervis Bay,* and here is reviewed briefly experiences of some of our Naval Reservists and other seamen on ill-fated auxiliary cruisers.

Four Caithness men were aboard the *Rawalpindi* when that merchant cruiser was sunk off Iceland in November, 1939. Three of them were lost, the fourth taken prisoner.

The *Rawalpindi* (15,000 ton former P. & O. liner) went down in an uneven battle when attacked by two German battleships (*Scharnhorst* and *Gniesnau*) but fought to the last and sank "with guns firing and flags flying." This was about the first surface encounter of the war at sea. The merchant cruiser was caught in a desperate position with no possible chance of escape, but her example was true to Navy traditions.

★ ★ ★ ★ ★

The *Scotstoun* (formerly the Anchor liner *Caledonia*) was another armed merchant cruiser sunk by the enemy. Among 340 survivors were seven Naval Reservists from Caithness and one from Embo. Most of them were attached to gun crews. This vessel was torpedoed without warning by a submarine in June, 1940. The U-boat periscope had been sighted and although the merchant cruiser was sinking by the stern, the gunners remained on duty and, with water rising to their waists, kept firing at a probable target to avenge their fate. It was a dying kick. Later the gunners were picked up by some of the eight lifeboats that had been launched. Several hours later all the survivors were taken aboard a British ship and landed in this country.

Caithnessmen serving on board the *Scotstoun* were:– Leading Seaman John Harper (later lost); Able Seamen J. Henderson, Huddart Street; D. Gunn, Oldwick Road; J. Connor, Willowbank; W. Taylor, Shore Lane; D. B. Cowper, jun., Cairndhuna Terrace – all of Wick; and Able Seaman S. Coghill, Keiss.

★ ★ ★ ★ ★

The *Salopian* was an armed merchant cruiser lost about a year later (probably in May, 1941). Six Caithness Naval Reservists were members of the crew, and were among the 300 men who got away on boats and rafts. The ship went down in the hours of darkness, and the survivors were three days and three nights in open boats before being taken aboard a British vessel.

Four of the Caithness men serving on the *Salopian* belonged to Wick. They were Seamen James Bain, Vansittart Street; James Manson, Cairndhuna Terrace; Alexander Plowman, The Shore; and Archibald Coffield, Vansittart Street. The other two were David Gunn, John O'Groats, and

John Rosie, Keiss.

One of the Caithness survivors said:– "I was in a boat with 50 men. We had very little food or water, but it might have been worse. The water was shared out a little to each man per day. We had some biscuits which did for food. The morning after the ship was sunk we rowed about in the vicinity looking among the wreckage to see if we could find any food, but got nothing."

★ ★ ★ ★ ★

The armed merchant cruiser *Comorin* unaccountably took fire at sea and was lost in the spring of 1941. There were three Wick naval men aboard: – Seaman Alexr. Fraser, 1 Henrietta Tce.; Jack Oman, 24 Oldwick Road; and William Swanson, Dunvegan Street. Two destroyers rescued a large proportion of the crew. Seaman Fraser was in another section and among those picked up from a raft after being five hours afloat. The raft was sighted by a passing vessel, but she was outward bound and landed the survivors at Freetown. Some time elapsed ere the men found a ship returning to this country, and consequently this section of the crew were several weeks behind their comrades in returning home.

The auxiliary cruiser *Patroclus* (11,314 tons) was sunk in going to the help of the *Laurentic* (18,724 tons) when that vessel was torpedoed (November, 1940). Two Wick sailors were on the *Laurentic* – Peter Miller, 31 Smith Terrace, and Robert Clyne, 40 Nicholson Street – and both were saved. It may be, however, that a soldier from the same town was less lucky and lost his life when the ship was attacked. A Wick seaman (Qmr. James Davidson) went down with the *Patroclus,* and Sub-Lieut. St. John Bernard V. Harmsworth, Thrumster House, was among those saved.

★ ★ ★ ★ ★

H.M.S. *Edinburgh* had to be abandoned and sunk (March 1942) after being damaged by the enemy. Seaman-Gunner Donald M. Rosie, son of Pte. H. Rosie, Seaforths, and of Mrs Rosie, 22 Willowbank, Wick, was a member of the crew. He had joined the Navy six years previously. Seaman Rosie was married and resided in Barnsley.

The most notable ship of the war was perhaps the British aircraft carrier *Ark Royal* (22,000 tons). The enemy had repeatedly claimed the sinking of this great ship and though she had narrow escapes she survived until November, 1941, when she was attacked by U-boats in the Mediterranean. There were 1600 officers and men on board but only one

lost his life. A member of the crew at the time was Sub-Lieut. John Ross, a native of Lybster who formerly was on the teaching staff at Wick High School. There was a Wick officer on the corvette that avenged the loss of the *Ark Royal* by destroying the U-boat believed to be responsible for the attack.

★ ★ ★ ★

H.M.S. *Danube* (of the Examination Service) was lying off the Thames on the night of October 12, 1940, waiting for a convoy. There was an air raid in the early hours of next morning – a mine-laying expedition to the Thames Estuary. The *Danube* engaged the raiders with machine-gun fire and the aircraft dropped mines around the ship, two of which exploded but caused no severe damage on board though they "shook the vessel a bit."

Later in the morning the *Danube* moved in towards the Thames and a Wick Naval Reservist (Able-Seaman Hugh Fraser, Breadalbane Terrace) was among the crew below for breakfast when "something happened." He was out for the full count. When he regained his senses he found himself wallowing about in the sea and was astonished to find that he was lying on a lifebelt with his right arm stuck on a large nail in a log of wood. He was dazed and without feeling at first but when he recovered somewhat he wrenched his arm from the nail and started to swim towards a yacht. As it turned out, he was the last of the survivors to be picked up – only 13 were saved.

No wonder Seaman Fraser didn't know what happened or how he came out of it! He had been leaning against the bulkhead at the moment a mine exploded forward – the first of three mines to explode within seconds of each other – and the ship, with boiler burst, went down in a couple of minutes. The Wick Reservist was the only one below decks to escape death.

The rescuing ship collided with the boom and had to be run ashore as she was taking water. Naval boats from Sheerness completed the rescue.

Twice saved in one day, Fraser spent that night in sick quarters at Sheerness and next morning was removed to the R.N. Hospital. There it was found that his back was broken but luckily no damage had been caused to the spinal nervous system. When he had been in bed for two weeks, blood began to come from behind the nostrils and did so night and day for a week, despite the efforts of medical men. It was a week of spit, swallow and vomit blood, and hope of the patient's recovery was running low. It was an unforgettable week for him but he "got used to it" and doing without sleep. Examinations disclosed that the base of the skull was cracked. He was then put in plaster from the neck to the hips and was four months in bed. In July, 1941, he was discharged as medically unfit for further service.

★ ★ ★ ★ ★

Able-Seaman Angus Mackay, Royal Navy, who belonged to Blackburn, Dunbeath, had some thrilling experiences at sea. Three times his ship was torpedoed – twice on trips to Russia and again at the landing in North Africa. He escaped unharmed on each occasion.

★ ★ ★ ★ ★

Seaman David Bruce, Wick, was a member of the crew of a rescue ship which had picked up a number of survivors from two merchant vessels. Next day the rescue ship was attacked and sunk by a German bomber. Several men, including the captain, were killed, and many were wounded.

In getting away from the sinking vessel, the lifeboat into which Seaman Bruce had gone overturned, and the occupants were thrown into the sea. All clung to the upturned boat, and were eventually rescued by a naval corvette which had speeded to the scene. Aboard the corvette was Lieut. W. S. Macdonald, a Wick lad who became well-known in Scottish football, and there was a happy ending to a trying experience.

★ ★ ★ ★ ★

Donald Laird, Midtown, John O'Groats, was a seaman with a story to tell when he reached home in the closing days of 1940. He had been a prisoner in Nazi hands at sea. He was one of fifty of the crew of the merchantman *Davisian* sunk by the German raider *Narvik* 400 miles out in the Atlantic.

The merchantman was on her way to Barbados with a cargo of patent fuel when a 10,000 ton cargo vessel steering across their course hove into sight, flying the Swedish colours. Suddenly these friendly colours disappeared and were replaced by a large canvas bearing the dreaded swastika. Camouflaged flaps, hiding four 6-inch guns, were let down, and the formerly innocent-looking goliath fired half-a-dozen salvos. The *Davisian* was struck by shells at least ten times; the vessel was considerably damaged and six of the crew seriously injured. The crew abandoned the ship and were taken aboard the raider. The *Davisian* was finally sunk by scuttling – a favourite German method.

The men were kept prisoners aboard the *Narvik* for three days, and were on the whole fairly well treated. They were kept between decks, however, and found the new quarters extremely hot and disagreeable, although given a short period for exercise each day. On the third day of their internment the raider destroyed another merchantman, the *King John*.

The crews of the two sunken vessels were transferred to their own boats, but the captains, chief engineers, and ten wounded seamen were retained. The small-boats lost touch with each other during the night. The boat Laird was on carried 25 men and their provisions were only dry biscuits and half a pint of water per man each day. The boat's regular store of provisions had been removed.

The boat had been riddled by shrapnel, was leaking badly, and had to be constantly baled. After seven days' privation in the open boats, they were picked up by the Norwegian picket boat *Lief* which landed them on the island of San Domingo. There they remained ten days before being taken to Kingston, Jamaica. A fortnight passed ere they secured a passage to New Orleans, and on the homeward journey the ship was bombed unsuccessfully by a German 'plane.

★ ★ ★ ★ ★

The men of the minesweeping flotillas (mainly fishermen) swept the seas under conditions which were bristling with perils, but little glory came their way. Now and again tributes were passed to their services, one of which (culled from *Chambers's Journal*) is worthy of inclusion here:

"Words cannot adequately express what we owe to these men – fishermen all, from the Hebrides and Mallaig, Wick and Peterhead, Aberdeen and Grimsby, Lowestoft and Yarmouth. Call them heroes, and they would jeer at you; yet they are nothing else. Theirs is, at once, the most lonely, monotonous, and dangerous of all our Empire Forces' tasks, and one indispensable for the maintenance of danger-free sea-lanes for the Merchant Service, our lifeline with the world beyond. They put to sea in the morning, gay or grave, according to their work . . . and some do not return. But they close their ranks, and carry on. They sweep the seas."

★ ★ ★ ★ ★

A special correspondent of *The Times* in Malta (in Novr., 1943) wrote in high praise of the work of our small craft in the Mediterranean. These small craft, seen from a destroyer or tank-landing ship, he said, have the brave and impudent air of Aberdeen terriers among bulldogs. Indeed, without such qualities as bravery and impudence they would hardly have reached here, as most of them have done, under their own steam . . .

Of long voyages by small craft there is a fine record of 16,000 miles to the credit of a minesweeper which was built at Seattle, supplied at Vancouver, came down the Pacific through the Panama Canal, along the South American coast to Pernambuco, across the Atlantic to Freetown, up the West African coast to Dakar and Casablanca, and by way of Gibraltar to the Mediterranean and Algiers and Malta.

This minesweeper's three officers were former trawlermen . . . Among the crew was a young Wick seaman, who was engaged in seine-net fishing before joining the Navy.

★ ★ ★ ★ ★

A year before the outbreak of war Lieut. Francis Bremner, R.N.R., went out to Hong-Kong on Admiralty service. He was accompanied by his wife and young daughter, Catherine. Everything was o.k. until Japan entered the war and quickly over-ran Eastern territory. It then (for thousands of our people) became a case of trying to keep a step ahead of the onrushing enemy. This was not always easy; even sea transport was often subjected to heavy air attack.

When Hong-Kong was threatened, Mrs Bremner and little Catherine were among the civilians evacuated to Australia. Later, following the transfer of her husband from Hong-Kong to Singapore, Mrs Bremner and her daughter left Australia and rejoined him in Singapore.

But they were not long in the great naval base when danger threatened, and once again they were evacuated. This time, Lieut. Bremner went along with his wife and daughter. They went to Colombo, and from there to South Africa.

They landed in Cape Town without any personal belongings. After a three months' stay in Cape Town, the Wick family, along with other evacuees, boarded a ship which brought them to Britain.

★ ★ ★ ★ ★

Two other well-known Wick fishermen and Naval Reservists went to Singapore immediately prior to the outbreak of hostilities. They were Skipper Alex. Adamson, Vansittart Street, and Skipper William Bain, Macarthur Street. Three years later they reached home again after a round-about and lengthy voyage.

Both Skipper-Lieutenants, they were in charge of boom boats, practically the last Naval vessels to leave the stronghold of Singapore. After getting away they made for Batavia, and from there to Mombasa, calling at island stations on the way.

Ultimately they reached Cape Town where they boarded a ship for the Homeland.

The homeward passage was long, slow and trying. Their friends at home had endured months of anxiety ere they both arrived in the old country and were glad to see them again.

With Our Men on Service.

SOME of our Caithness men had a number of adventures while on service. Such were the experiences of Flight-Lieut. James B. Dunnett, Wick, who joined the R.A.F. before the war, qualified as a navigator, and was 4½ years overseas before returning home in December, 1944. He served in Malta, Egypt, the Western Desert and Libya. He transferred for service in Greece, and from there went to Crete, and from that island escaped only in the nick of time.

Behind these bare statements are many trying experiences. Here are a few: (1) While on his way overseas by air early in the war, Flt.-Lieut. Dunnett was caught in an electrical storm that lasted for four hours. His 'plane was the only one which reached Malta (their destination en route) and they made it with petrol tanks uncommonly low. (2) He was attached to the famous 211 Squadron, which earned the reputation of being the best bombing squadron in the Middle East. Along with the late Sergt.-Pilot D. Gordon, D.F.M., Newton, he took part in the attack at Cape Matapan which sealed the fate of the Italian Navy as a striking force. (3) One of the most unusual raids he carried out was against an Italian Red Cross Hospital. This hospital was suspected as a fake, and when bombed blew up with its hidden ammunition. (4) He was twice shot down in three days, and luckily escaped injury on both occasions. Later Flight-Lieut. Dunnett became a bomb-aiming instructor.

★ ★ ★ ★ ★

An American newspaper claimed that the first soldier of the Allied army to enter Tunis was Sergeant William Budge, attached to the Tank Corps. He was a volunteer from Argentina, and had been manager of a sheep farm near Puerto Descado. Caithness interest in this American claim was that Sergeant Budge belonged to Lybster, where his parents (Mr and Mrs James Budge) resided at Mavsey.

When the Cameron Highlanders crossed the river Dives and entered the town of St. Pierre (October, 1944) they were greeted with flowers and kisses by the inhabitants. German soldiers were still entrenched in houses in the town, but the natives readily helped in placing them and they were routed out. Amongst the first Camerons into St. Pierre was Pte. Ben. Groat, Heather Inn, Thrumster.

Sergt.-Observer George Flett, R.A.F., had an unusual experience after a year's service in the Middle East. The 'plane on which he served crashed into the sea when on an operational flight, and all the crew were lost with the exception of Sergt. Flett and the pilot. Indeed, the pilot owed his survival to the swimming capabilities of the observer from Wick, who, although suffering from a serious eye injury, helped him to keep afloat.

Sergt. Flett after rescue was in hospital for two months and then set sail for Britain on leave. On the voyage, however, the ship was torpedoed by a German U-boat, and the lifeboats launched were crowded with survivors. There were 72 in one boat. The commander of this submarine was unusually kind to his victims. He hovered in the vicinity of the survivors for five days and saw that they were well fed – at one stage he had five lifeboats in tow. He also sent out a wireless message concerning the sinking and giving the position. A French warship ultimately came along and picked up the survivors, who were sent to an internment camp in French Morocco. Nine weeks later the Allies invaded North Africa and the prisoners were released. Sergt. Flett and others sailed in a ship to America and were in New York before reaching England.

* * * * *

A Naval Reservist had a somewhat similar experience in Algeria for ten months prior to the Allied invasion. He was leading Seaman George Munro, a native of Thurso, who was married and resided at 57 Henrietta Street, Wick.

He was serving on an armed merchant cruiser escorting convoys to Malta. Early in 1942 the ship was attacked and badly damaged by enemy aircraft while in the Mediterranean. She succeeded in reaching Malta, but sank at the harbour. Along with other members of the crew, Seaman Munro sailed as a passenger to Britain on another ship, but on the voyage it was torpedoed and driven on to the beach "somewhere in Algeria." All were sent to an internment camp in the desert, where already there were men from the other Services. Chief hardships here were the heat, and lack of proper food and clothing before the arrival of Red Cross parcels relieved their position.

Dunkirk.

The surrender of the Belgian Army early in June, 1940, changed the situation on the Western front from grave to critical. This collapse enabled the Germans to divide the Allied armies and drive hurriedly to the Channel ports. The British Expeditionary Force was placed in grave peril of complete annihilation through incessant frontal, flank and aerial attacks. Though it was a "colossal military disaster," the retreat to Dunkirk was yet the greatest and most spectacular performance in the history of warfare. The Allies' losses amounted to 30,000 killed, wounded or missing, and a vast amount of material and equipment. Everything was abandoned.

Heroic rearguard actions, however, enabled 335,000 to get away. The men swarming the beaches at Dunkirk were pounded relentlessly for days by German artillery and airmen, and casualties were heavy. The difficult operation of embarkation was successfully undertaken only through the tireless efforts of naval units of every kind and with the unfailing support of the Royal Air Force. This remarkable evacuation was accomplished with the help of fleets of large and small craft, including tugs and paddle steamers and rowing boats. Soldiers waded or swam to the smaller craft. By some miracle the seas were calm, an unusual state on that coast.

Dunkirk was a disaster transformed into a triumph, for the bravery of our fighting men inspired the nation and there was a rebirth of an admirable spirit under the threat of invasion.

* * * * *

Many Caithness soldiers came through the trials

Eight sergeants of 6th Seaforths on troopship bound for Madagascar. Extreme right (behind) – Sergt. W. Miller, Nybster (late of Lyth), later killed in Italy.

of retreat and the awful ordeal on the beaches. A member of the Field Ambulance Corps related how the section to which he was attached was ambushed by the Germans. All their motor vehicles were destroyed and they escaped as best they could. Nine of them (he said) crawled about a mile before they got clear of the enemy, and then got hold of a motor lorry, and, unaware of the evacuation arrangements, made for Dunkirk. The vehicle had to be abandoned about 14 miles from the coast and they walked the remainder of the way.

They found the beach crowded with men, but the party was very lucky, having to wait less than an hour for a boat. They waded through the water until picked up by a small boat and placed aboard a destroyer. The ship was attacked from the air by an enemy 'plane, which dropped a bomb near the stern but caused no damage. The ship made Dover in safety. The men were sent to Halifax where (as everywhere) our returning men were given every hospitality.

★　★　★　★　★

Four Wick soldiers on leave:– James Durrand (later killed), Murray Harper, Alexr. Sinclair and Harry Davidson.

Two of our Royal Engineers were less lucky when they reached the beach at Dunkirk. They were there for three days and found it was a case of every many for himself. Food was scarce. They caught a glimpse of another townsman on the beach, tried to connect with him, but lost trace of him in the moving throng.

Sticking together all the time, the two Engineers ultimately got away in a boat among a party of 30. The boat capsized, but all clamoured safely aboard a ship . . ." and we were just in time because a heavy

enemy bombardment began as we got clear."

Another of our soldiers who had been for days on the bombarded beach said he was almost a mental wreck, and was loud in praise of the Navy's qualities. A high-ranking Naval officer, he said, calmly maintained an orderly procession of troops at the point he embarked, showing no concern for personal safety. Indeed, he might have been on holiday! Order, however, meant that many men got away quickly.

This Caithness soldier found himself huddled among others on the deck of a destroyer which was attacked by aircraft. To use his own expression, he "had the wind up," but he was alongside a typically jolly tar who was busy on an anti-aircraft gun. He was working away unconcernedly and each time assured anyone who cared to listen – "I'll bet I'll bag a fellow this time!" His complete self-possession and assurance were a tonic to our weary Caithness friend (and others) who had been already shaken by the bombardment of the beaches. The aircraft followed the ship determinedly. The destroyer put up a smoke screen, suddenly swung round and turned back into it – and was lost to all her enemies!

★　★　★　★　★

Buried alive when a German shell knocked down his trench (March, 1943), John Ross, former driver, of Hamilton Cottage, Thurso, suffered no ill effects. "I was lying in the trench, heard the bang of the gun, and the next thing I knew I was covered with sand," he told a military correspondent. "I was helpless, couldn't move, felt I was suffocating. Opened my mouth to shout. It filled with sand. What did it feel like? Well, what it must feel like if you are dying and frightened. I felt myself choking, didn't know that my hands were uncovered. I seemed to be that way for ten minutes. Couldn't have been, I know, or I wouldn't be here to-day. But first there was acute discomfort, the awful feeling of helplessness, and then a kaleidoscope of confused thoughts of home and things past. Then I was in the air again. I could breathe. I was still alive."

The man who rescued him was Sergt. William McGechie, Edinburgh. "The shell buried me, head and shoulders, for I was just lying on the ground," said McGechie. "I shook myself free, ran to the top of the trench, saw two hands sticking out of the sand. I got hold of them and pulled – it took all my strength to get John out. When I did, I had to pull him back quickly into a trench, for the stuff was coming over thick and fast."

And the shell, five foot long, 210 m.m. in diameter, had failed to go off. It was dug out later.

★ ★ ★ ★ ★

Recalling incidents and jobs well done, "after the enemy had been beaten and fighting in North Africa was over," a military correspondent supplied this in May, 1943:–

The Colonel's car drew up with a squealing of brakes. He signalled the C.M.P. over. "Can you tell me. . . Bless my soul, I've seen you somewhere before! Have you ever been in my battalion?" L.-Cpl. Alistair Mackenzie smiled. "Were you ever in John O'Groats, sir?" The Colonel gave a start. "Good heavens, it's Mr Mackenzie, the manager of The Hotel, John O'Groats!" "Used to be, sir," said L.-Cpl. Mackenzie. "Now I'm trying to manage traffic – a much more difficult job" . . . .

L.-Cpl. Mackenzie's worst experience was when he was doing guard on one of the tracks at Alamein. The dust swirled so fast and furious that he couldn't see a yard in front of him. And a ten-tonner truck hit him – slap into a slit trench, and he went over. He escaped with scratches, but much prefers to be shelled! He has had plenty of that all the way up, for the C.M.P. s are right in the front line, laying tape, and lighting tracks, and guiding traffic. In fact, the only time L.-Cpl. Mackenzie is known to have lost his temper was at Sollum, where in the dark he was asked if he belonged to a non-combatant unit.

A snap from Egypt (1944). Behind (left) – John M'Lean, Wick.

"That's fighting talk!" said L.-Cpl. Mackenzie, dashing his hat on the ground and making ready for battle. But his interrogator had been a senior officer and the battle didn't eventuate! . . .

"Tunisia is all right, but give me the snell breezes of Scotland," said L.-Cpl. Mackenzie.

A neat war-time comment, written in the dark days of the late 1941, has clung in my memory throughout the years. It was only an expression in a letter to the editor of the *John O'Groat Journal* but it was tinged with humour and revealed something of the spirit that was to carry the nation through. No situation daunted our forces in the field.

The letter came from far-away, forbidding Abyssinia and was penned by Captain W. D. Sinclair, a native of Berriedale, who was attached to a South African Motor Transport Company. "My boys," he wrote, "have now done an aggregate of five million miles (150 vehicles)." And in conveying his greetings he concluded: "The *Groat* still reaches me – we're surely winning!"

★ ★ ★ ★ ★

Edinburgh had a fleeting glimpse the other day of "the only official beard in the British Army," stated a writer in a national newspaper in December, 1943, and continued:– It belongs to Pipe-Major Gordon Asher, of the Seaforth Highlanders, who was passing through the city on leave. A stalwart figure in kilt and balmoral, Pipe-Major Asher was wearing the ribbon of the Africa Star, for his battalion is in the 51st Division. Though the 51st played a great part in the Battle of El Alamein, a more strenuous battle for the Seaforths was Wadi Akarit, which resulted in the collapse of the Mareth Line and opened up the Eighth Army's way to Tunisia. In conversation with an Edinburgh journalist Pipe-Major Asher spoke of his battalion's share in the Akarit fighting, and referred particularly to a very gallant episode in which Major Jack Davidson – an old Edinburgh Academy boy – figured with a mere handful of men.

In a difficult and critical stage of the battle, Major Davidson and nine others held on to a commanding ridge. The Germans tried all they could to dislodge them, but the gallant ten simply refused to give away. Their stand helped materially to win the day and win the battle. Major Davidson – who was later mortally wounded in Sicily – was awarded the D.S.O. "But Seaforths will tell you," said the Pipe-Major," that he deserved the V.C."

Seaforth losses at Akarit were considerable, and to-day there is a bit of ground on the plain below the main ridge which will for ever have its place in the regiment's history. A cemetery was made there, and in it were buried those who had fallen so far from the hills and moors of their homeland.

One of Pipe-Major Asher's happiest memories of the campaign is of the reunion in Sicily between the Seaforths of Scotland and the Seaforths of Canada. The celebrations took place at Catania, and for the time being the war was forgotten; it was a "gathering of the clans." Seaforths poured into Catania from all directions and in all manner of conveyances. The pipes and drums of the battalions assembled near the city park – 41 pipers and 22 drummers – and, headed by the drum-major of the 5th Seaforths, swung through the streets. All traffic was stopped, and great throngs of Italians stood agape with wonder and admiration as the kilted phalanx made its way to the city stadium. There the massed bands played "Retreat" . . . It was a famous night, and went on till four next morning. [Peculiarly enough, the leader of the Canadian band had friends in Wick and enjoyed a "leave" in our northern town before going to Italy.]

Another of Pipe-Major Asher's happy memories is of his meeting with Sir Archibald Sinclair when the Air Minister paid a visit to North Africa. Sir Archibald was M.P. for Caithness and Sutherland and knew the Pipe-Major well. He hardly recognised him at first with his beard, but once recognition was made there was a very friendly talk between the two.

★ ★ ★ ★ ★

Pipe-Major Asher (concluded the article) is a Thurso man, but is no stranger to Edinburgh, for he received some of his schooling in the city. The son of a Thurso doctor (now deceased), he has been in the Territorials some 20 years. As a piper he gained renown long ago. Incidentally, he was taught the pipes by his mother.

As for his beard, he grew it because he felt inclined to, and because it was permissible. He is paid sixpence a day extra because of it. There was another bearded piper in the 51st Division – the pipe-major of a Cameron battalion – but he was severely wounded, and had his beard shaved off in hospital. [Pipe-Major Asher appears in a group photograph on page 34.]

★ ★ ★ ★ ★

The commanding ridge referred to by Pipe-Major Asher was undoubtedly Roumana Ridge, an action that brought much tribute to Major J. H. Davidson and his handful of men. They held on defiantly to one of the hottest spots imaginable.

Writing at the time (April, 1943) a military correspondent stated:– With Germans so close they could lob grenades at them, and pinned down by mortar fire, a company of the 5th Seaforths held the crest of the Jebel Manara against all comers.

"We had bagged dozens of prisoners coming up the slope," Sergt. D. Chisholm, Stornoway, told the correspondent. [Prisoners taken included at least 70 hapless Italians – surprised in bed, and too terrified to do anything about getting dressed.] "And although there was a lot of mortar fire when we got on the ridge, it was clear of the enemy. But Jerry must have slipped back, for when it got light a machine-gun opened up from 200 yards away. It was a nuisance, so Corpl. Thomson, Ptes. Smith and McGarth and I went out to finish him off. The German counter-attack came some time after that. We saw them coming on both sides of the hill. . . and it got a bit hot."

"There was a sniper on a ridge above us, and four or five Germans just over our heads," said Pte. James Smith, former ghillie, of Wester Cottage, Keiss. "They were so close they could lob grenades down on us. One just missed the company commander. But they hadn't many of these, thank goodness. Then we could see some jouking round our back, and managed to shoot some."

★ ★ ★ ★ ★

Major Davidson in his *North African Diary* reviews fully the action at Roumana. Here are snatches from his modest account: In front of us (he wrote) loomed darkly the shape of Roumana Ridge with the highest point – our objective (Point 198) – standing out sharply against the blue of the heavens. On we went – slowly, silently . . . Now and then there was a sickening crash amongst us as an enemy mortar bomb burst on our line of advance. . . L.-Cpl. Durrand at my side all the time . . . on and up we went, seeking the best possible route through the rocks that rose sharply above us . . . accompanied by the increasing thunder of the guns echoing and re-echoing among the crags and precipices. At 7 a. m. Point 198 was transformed into a smoking volcano. Crash after crash of mortar bombs came down; those devilishly accurate German mortars had found a target . . . and mingled with the incessant chatter of machine-guns – the din was hellish.

★ ★ ★ ★ ★

At 9.15 (continued Major Davidson) I met the C.O. who appreciated our plight and went off to get some support for us. Shortly after we were enfiladed from a post 400 yards to our immediate right, and our position became untenable. I ordered a defensive position on Point 198. This was occupied by the remnants of the Company – about a dozen in all – just enough to man the flanks and watch the front. . . I became aware that the enemy had penetrated right forward and had at least two positions within 40 yards of the Company immediately above our heads. We tried to climb the last few yards of the crest to get at them, but were at once machine gunned from the right. From then on it was a case of hanging on and being as offensive as possible. . . Pte. Smith from Caithness and myself watched the crest above our heads. Sergt. Mackenzie moved about from place to place and was a tower of strength. About 12.30 hours a determined German attempt was made to get round our left flank. . . . about 15.00 hours the situation was getting desperate. I could hear German voices above me, and I knew my right was vulnerable. Just then Captain Willock appeared with a Bren and helped a lot, but the Germans above us had crawled forward silently and started to let us have a shower of stick grenades. I gradually moved the Company back about 150 yards to another position, where we succeeded in re-establishing ourselves and managed to prevent the enemy getting Point 198. The reinforcing battalion arrived about 16.00 hours and took over. We relaxed and heaved a sigh of relief!

In Enemy Hands.

Four Caithness soldiers escaped from captivity, namely; – Dvr. John Cormack, R.A.S.C., 33 Girnigoe Street, Wick; Pte. Alexander Crowe, R.A.S.C., Willowbank, Wick; Pte. James R. Mowat, R.A.O.C., Portland Arms, Lybster; and Pte. John D. Sutherland, Camerons, Freswick Gardens, Thurso. The story of their adventures *en route* to freedom would be interesting. Unfortunately, only snatches of their escapades are known to the writer.

Dvr. Cormack was made a prisoner by the Italians at Tobruk, a place that was occupied and surrendered by the opposing forces several times before finally falling to the Eighth Army when the enemy was ousted from North Africa. Dvr. Cormack was sent to Italy by way of Benghazi. When that country capitulated prisoners thought they would be free, but instead the Germans moved quickly and took over much of the country and all therein. There was much confusion though, and thousands of internees took advantage of the chance to say good-bye to the camps.

Dvr. Cormack got away along with a companion and although they were separated for a time they came together again later. They obtained civilian clothes and this helped them to move around more freely – almost too freely on some occasions. For instance, they were in an estaminet one evening when German soldiers entered. They departed quickly to avoid questioning. The Italian women were good to the fleeing prisoners and when asked readily provided food. Dvr. Cormack ultimately reached Switzerland and about a year later arrived back in Britain.

Pte. John D. Sutherland had somewhat similar experiences. After forsaking a camp in North Italy he took to the hills there and wandered for ten months in enemy-occupied territory.

★ ★ ★ ★ ★

Pte. Crowe and Pte. Mowat were captured by the Nazis at the fall of France in June, 1940. The former escaped with three companions and reached Wick in March, 1941. He had been interned in a camp in France where there were many prisoners but few of them British. With him, however, were three Englishmen. The four were employed as bakers and worked during the night-time. This helped their plans to escape. September had come when the four bakers made their daring break, evaded the guards and got away. They ran into several parties of Germans but a bold front and a little luck carried them through. Weeks passed ere they reached a place of safety and months of patient waiting followed before they were able to get to the homeland. Behind their escape was said to be a thrilling story. Later Pte. Crowe obtained commissioned rank.

★ ★ ★ ★ ★

Pte. Mowat was only a few days in German hands when he made his escape from prison quarters by descending a rhone pipe, the lower part of which he found (to his dismay at that moment) had been shot away. He made his way from Belgium to freedom mainly on foot, although on occasions he was given a "lift" by unsuspecting Germans. He found the French people kindly and helpful, and it was he who met a Latheron man then resident in Calais. Like the others, he found the homeward journey a slow and uneasy undertaking and he took about the same time – a twelve month. Nevertheless, they arrived; and the time taken testifies to a spirit of endurance, initiative and determination.

In December, 1945, Mr Mowat made a return visit to his French war-time friends in the little village of Northerque, near Calais. Actually, he had been one of three starving soldiers "adopted" by Emile Daniel and other villagers who, at much personal risk, brought food and news every night to a little hut of straw and reeds in the middle of a swamp, where the escapees stayed for ten months. The villagers had the Germans to hood-wink – and succeeded. Mr Daniel collected 750 francs and passed the money to the soldiers when they set out on a final bid for freedom.

Mr Mowat found his old French friend (Daniel was 72 years of age) an invalid but the reunion was a happy one and it was reported that the joy of the poor man was great when his ever-grateful and sympathetic Scottish visitor fell in his arms and kissed him. Altogether Mr Mowat made more than 60 calls in the district. Later it was stated that a street in the village of Burbure was named *Rue de Mowat* in honour of the Lybster soldier.

Serg. Harry Sutherland, 1st Worcestershire Regt., was twice reported missing (in Abyssinia and in Greece) yet on each occasion he rejoined his regiment after a period of weeks. He served with the Seaforths in Abyssinia and there fell into Arab hands. Later Sutherland was taken prisoner at Tobruk and ultimately removed to Germany. He returned home in May, 1945. He was a regular soldier with 15 years' service. Home address – 7 Whitehouse Lane, Wick.

★ ★ ★ ★ ★

The first repatriated Caithness prisoner of war to return home was a Territorial who had been drafted to another battalion of the Seaforths. He was Pte. Peter Keith, Hoy, and was among the disabled repatriated late in 1943.

During the continuous retreat following upon the German break-through in France, Pte. Keith was severely wounded in both legs by machine-gun bullets. He lay where he fell for three days without food or water, and exposed to fire from the opposing armies – his only protection a shallow trench he had made with his bayonet. Eventually he was picked up by a German doctor and removed to a military hospital in Cambria by motor cycle and sidecar. From that day he was in and out of hospitals for over a year when, recovering sufficiently, he was sent to a war camp.

Pte. Keith was three days in the prisoners' camp before he discovered that another Caithness soldier was there: one who had served with the same battalions – Pte. Alexr. Mackay, Stirkoke. The partnership was broken after three months, when Mackay was transferred to another camp. Keith was much thinner owing to his experiences and both had

beards, as razors had not been issued to prisoners. This made recognition very difficult and their surprise the greater. They had much to say to each other.

Pte. Keith was among the prisoners to be repatriated in 1942 and was actually on board ship at Rouen when the arrangements were cancelled. He was transferred to a camp in Poland and there he met another Caithness lad, Piper John Mackay, a native of Thrumster who also had been wounded and was to have been repatriated. Their association continued until they reached England: Mackay went to Aberdeen, where he had made his home. Like all returned prisoners, Pte. Keith spoke in high praise of the parcels received through the Red Cross – parcels that meant everything to the interned men.

★ ★ ★ ★ ★

Concentration camps, more than anything else, condemned the Nazis as something worse than tyrants. Into these camps were flung all nationals who rejected the Nazi creed, many thousands of Jewish people and their children (for no real reason), and all suspected of any act of hostility, even in an occupied country. The Nazis extolled patriotism within the Third Reich, but that was the only patriotism they recognised. The Patriot of any other country was counted a traitor and punished accordingly, generally in camps where the treatment was bestial and brutal, where death by gunshot, by poisonous gas, or by lingering starvation under unbelievable conditions of cruelty was the fate of a multitude of souls. The fact that the British public executioner passed a whole day in hanging German men and women found guilty of inhuman deeds – of wholesale murder – against defenceless internees denotes the scale on which such crimes against hunanity was committed. The Germans were condemned by British justice after a prolonged and patient trial.

The story of a Caithness man who died in a German concentration camp began when a Dunbeath man emigrated to Canada and later served with the Canadian Forces in the 1914-18 war. He was Mr Mackay Macleod, Latheronwheel. In France he fell in love with a French girl and brought her home to Dunbeath as his wife in far-away 1918. Two daughters and a son were born before the Macleods returned to reside in Calais.

When France capitulated in 1940, Mr Macleod (then 54) assisted British soldiers to escape, and probably was helped by his wife and daughter, Helen. Anyhow, all three came under Nazi suspicion and were arrested. Mr Macleod was condemned to death, but was reprieved and sentenced to life imprisonment. The sentences passed on his wife and daughter were 15 and three years respectively. All of them were sent to different concentration camps. Relatives in Caithness had no news of them throughout the war years but afterwards it was learned that Mr Macleod died in a prison camp in August, 1944.

Mr James Mowat, Lybster, who was captured after the fall of France and later escaped, was in the Les Auchel (Calais) area for two months, and met and spoke to Mr Macleod frequently. Their first meeting was a great surprise to both – two men from Latheron parish meeting in France under German occupation. "I know that he helped a good many soldiers to escape," said Mr Mowat.

★ ★ ★ ★ ★

Unforgivable atrocities were committed in the name of war, and history will record crimes that should taint the name of the Axis countries in our time – indeed for all time. Japan was more than an imitator of Germany's total warfare. Here briefly is the tale (extracted from official documents) of a party of civilians murdered in Borneo. Among the victims was Mr R. F. Sinclair, a Latheron man who held office in Sarawak at the time war overshadowed the East.

The Report (issued 1946) explains that it was known that considerable doubt existed in the minds of many regarding the fate of certain Government officers and others who tried to avoid capture in Sarawak at the time of the Japanese invasion, but for security reasons information had to be kept confined to official quarters.

There were three different cases of tragedy . . . and of the people concerned in these tragedies no hope whatsoever can be entertained for their survival. The first concerned a party led by Mr A. Macpherson which left Sibu on December 27, 1941, for Long Nawang, in Dutch Borneo – reached on January 22, 1942. Here the party remained (together with a number of Dutch Europeans) until on August 20, 1942, the station was stormed and taken by Japanese Marines, who had come from Samarinda. Some Sarawak Europeans were killed on this occasion and the remainder were murdered during the course of the next month. The Japanese withdrew their main forces to Tarakan on September 25.

There were no survivors, either British or Dutch. All persons were buried in four graves.

The name of Mr R. F. Sinclair, Div. Supt. of Trade and Customs, appears among the Sarawak Europeans murdered at Long Nawang. The names

of 16 adults are given; including an R. C. priest and three married women; there are also two children and an infant.

After reviewing the adventures of others of the Sarawak party, the Report concludes: – It is of interest to note that the chief Japanese perpetrators of these murders at Long Nawang very considerately left their names written on the walls of one of the Dutch Government bungalows. The dates of their arrival at and departure from Long Nawang were also carefully recorded in like manner, all of which information was subsequently checked. The proper authorities for the apprehension and trial of war criminals were informed.

★ ★ ★ ★ ★

Incredible hardships were experienced by a missionary, his wife and two children after the Japanese invasion of the Philippine Islands and relatives did not hear from them for 3½ years. No wonder – their home was in the jungle.

The missionary was Mr A. M. Sutherland, whose parents belonged to Wick, and whose wife was an Orcadian. Even before the war Mr Sutherland had remarkable experiences among pagan natives, some of them cannibal tribes.

When the Japanese invaded the island, the missionary and his family went into the jungle to avoid capture, preferring the hardships of such an existence rather than undergo ill-treatment in the hands of an enemy who showed no measure of sympathy even to native people. Though ill-clad and sometimes hungry, sometimes fevered (Mrs Sutherland had malaria more than a hundred times) there the parents and their two children survived for three years. At times they came into contact with American soldiers who had escaped from prison camp, and one particular soldier became their friend.

Sometimes Mr Sutherland would wander as far as 20 miles in search of food of any kind, returning perhaps with a handful of bananas. "We had to learn to do without the things which you count as necessary," he said when he revisited the homeland. "We never saw bread or butter for two years, and never had a cup of tea."

Mr Sutherland related that he had noticed that his little boy always whispered something after his "bedtime" prayer. Enquiring what the boy was saying, the answer was: "Hush! this is a secret. I am asking the Lord to send a submarine to rescue us." Months later, survivors from an American submarine which had struck a mine came ashore and made contact with the missionary and other refugees in the district. By means of radio the captain of the submarine got into communication with an Australian base, and a submarine was sent to their rescue. The whole party went ten miles out to sea in little boats, were picked up by the submarine, and set out on the long voyage of 2000 miles to Australia. The little boy's prayer had been answered.

With Caithness Women.

MANY Caithness lasses assisted in the war effort – in the Services, on the land, in the factories, and in the noble role of nurses. Some of them travelled much, had unusual experiences or responsibilities, and came under the eye of official correspondents. Here are some paragraphs culled from different sources:–

Junior Commander Antoinette (Ann) Elizabeth Robertson, of the A.T.S., was described as "the girl who helped Lieut.-General F. E. Morgan plan the D-Day invasion." Ann came from Watten, a few miles from Wick, stated the writer and added: – She was used to keeping secrets and had already proved that she could be trusted with affairs of State during 1941-42 when she worked as a temporary Civil servant in the Intelligence Department of the War Office.

In 1942 she volunteered for the A.T.S. In two years she had risen from private to the rank of Junior Commander, equivalent to a captain in the Army. In 1944 she was drafted from Scotland to the staff of combined operations. Later she joined the staff of S.H.A.E.F. under General Eisenhower and specialised in amphibious warfare.

Comdr. Robertson is a daughter of Colonel J. J. Robertson, D.S.O., and Mrs Robertson, *Norwood*, Wick, who resided at Watten during the war years because of damage to their Wick residence. Ann is a graduate of Edinburgh University and later studied at a secretarial school in London. She became a Senior Commander in 1945 and was awarded the American Bronze Star for her services. By the way, her brother, Flt.-Lieut. Robert D. Robertson, served with the Royal Air Force and earned the D.F.C.

A Wick girl who has seen half the world in the last three years (wrote a military observer in October, 1944) and has done most useful work on the way is Barbara Miller, a nursing officer of the Q.A.I.M.N.S., who is now with a forward hospital near the Burma front. She is tending the wounded and the sick of General Slim's 14th Army, whose brilliant campaign of this year resulted in the complete defeat of the Japanese divisions that attempted to invade India. A cheery girl, she lives philosophically the none too luxurious life of a forward 14th Army area. She likes it well enough, though inevitably she has moments of longing for the rugged beauty of Caithness.

Barbara, who is a daughter of the late Mr and Mrs John Miller, Barns of Hempriggs, Wick, was training at the Glasgow Royal Infirmary before the war and volunteered with a true Scottish pioneer spirit to go to Africa in 1942. She saw South Africa, went to Kenya, and, after two months at Nairobi, moved on to Italian Somaliland. There she nursed in conditions of great comfort, living in a former Italian school at Mogadushu and enjoying the work enormously.

★ ★ ★ ★ ★

An impressive row of ribbons, headed by the distinguished decoration A.R.R.C., shows that Senior Sister Janet Brims (eldest daughter of Mr and Mrs J. H. M. Brims, 14 Oakbank Road, Perth) knows as much about army life as most regular soldiers (wrote an Army observer). Joining in 1939 Senior Sister Brims began her Army life the hard way, in West Africa for two years. Returning to England with a touch of malaria, her next trip abroad was on "D plus 7," and as Sister Brims seems to be attracted to the tough spots she went to Bayeux, working night and day for the wounded from one of the fiercest battles of the whole war.

The last phase of the European war found her in Holland, but she was soon on her way out East, and arriving at Singapore on the *Karea,* she was at once busy tending the sick men released from Japanese prison camps, to many of whom she was the first white girl they had seen in $3\frac{1}{2}$ years.

Where there is work there is Senior Sister Brims, so now she is in Batavia, Java, in charge of a contingent of British girls out there to look after sick and wounded British and Indian troops doing one of the most difficult and important jobs ever handled by British Forces in peacetime. Living comfortably in a typical Batavia bungalow, with plenty of work but with time for dances now and again, Sister Brims finds life in Java pleasant and interesting. The problem of what to do in her spare time is not difficult. She has no spare time.

Sister Brims is a grand-daughter of the late Mr and Mrs Sinclair Brims, and a niece of Councillor D.S. Brims, Bilbster.

★ ★ ★ ★ ★

Mrs James Sinclair (a native of Keiss) was on her

way to Australia to rejoin her husband in Sydney in the early days of the war. She reached there two years later.

The ship on which Mrs Sinclair was a passenger was attacked by the German battleship *Admiral Scheer,* and this Caithness lady was among those made captive by the enemy. She was transferred four times from one ship to another before being finally landed at Bordeaux. Two years elapsed before she was released (end of 1942), and during her internment in Germany she lost 2½ stones in weight.

Looking back over her experiences, Mrs Sinclair wrote that it all seemed a nightmare to her. Life in the concentration camps she described as terrible, and paid high tribute to the worth and work of the Red Cross service. Mrs Sinclair belongs to Stroma.

★   ★   ★   ★   ★

A Dunbeath man's wife was among 120 people, including many women and children, who cowered in the hold of a ship for almost four days while the vessel, pursued and attacked by Japanese bombers, fought its way (not without mishap) from Singapore to the open sea and ultimately to safety. The lady was the wife of Mr Lewis Kennedy, of Sarawak and Dunbeath. She had undertaken duty as an auxiliary nurse and was evacuated with sisters and nurses from various hospitals. The party had but arrived at the docks in motor cars when the Japs launched an air attack. Everyone got out and took any available cover – some in drains full of filthy water, and some flinging themselves flat on the ground.

Following this escape, the party boarded a ship. Immediately they set out to sea enemy 'planes tried unsuccessfully to dive bomb the vessel. At dawn next morning the ship joined a convoy, with two escort vessels. There was a large number of passengers, including many troops. Water was scarce and washing was difficult. The raids were resumed and the ship's gunners were kept active. The first attacking 'plane went off with one engine on fire; the second received the same hot reception, and a third was compelled to turn away before it could do any damage. Unfortunately, the ship was hit, and this resulted in casualties. Some persons were killed and others wounded, and hospitals were rigged out on board. One fire broke out, but the crew promptly had it under control.

Raids continued for 4½ hours, when the vessel was subjected to a mass attack by 24 'planes, in three formations of eight, from different directions. Down in the hold Mrs Kennedy and the others, while hearing the 'planes roaring overhead, the crack of

the bombs in the sea, and the barking of the ship's guns, could not see what was happening, but their feelings can be imagined. Every time the ship rose and plunged in the waves they thought the end had come. The hold was uncovered, and the occupants knew that if a bomb fell there they all would be killed, and if the ship sank they would be trapped and drowned. Only a single small ladder led to the deck. It was a terrifying experience. Eventually the ship arrived in Batavia and from there the evacuees sailed for Australia.

★   ★   ★   ★   ★

Miss Ettie Henderson (a native of Dunbeath and sister of the schoolmaster there) was for years a missionary teacher of the China Inland Mission. With 140 British and American children of the Mission School at Chefoo, she was interned in the notorious Weihsien Civilian Assembly Camp. It was there that Dr Eric Liddell (known familiarly as "Uncle Eric" among the children), the noted athlete and missionary, ended his young and active life. He was described as "the friend of everyone." His life story should go on as an example to all.

Working under tremendous difficulties, Miss Henderson kept the educational life of the children going, and, assisted by the boys and girls, managed, she said, to make life "fairly comfortable." The first news the internees had of the end of the hostilities was the arrival of an American 'plane which dropped seven parachutists. "You can imagine our delight," said Miss Henderson, "when the first soldier to enter the camp turned out to be one of my old pupils who had volunteered to parachute down on the camp, so anxious was he to bring us the great news."

Miss Barbara Doull, a native of Thrumster district, who had been in the Riviera for many years in the employ of Lady Hadfield, was compelled to remain in unoccupied France for two years after the capitulation of that country. For a twelvemonth her whereabouts were unknown to friends in the homeland because of an interrupted mail service. "It's months since I had news of anyone," said a postcard that broke her enforced silence.

Miss Doull (now Mrs H. Wood, Kelmscott Road, London) succeeded in returning to Britain via Spain and Portugal and by 'plane to Eire. Going through Spain was a tedious journey for several days, and there was one spell of 28 hours on an overcrowded train with neither food nor water available. The shortage of imported coal affected these two countries badly.

In Lisbon (where the party had to remain five weeks) Miss Doull enjoyed her first substantial meal for many months. In Southern France conditions had been really bad. Dry bread had had a big place on the everyday menu. To buy a new dress one had to surrender two old ones. Shoes had to be ordered months ahead, and when supplied were wooden. Even wine became scarce and was rationed. The Germans had commandeered huge supplies.

★　★　★　★　★

The black market flourished wherever commodities were scarce. That means that food and raiment illegally reached profiteering hands and were bought and resold at highly inflated prices. Southern France was no exception. Here is a tale from that countryside in its unhappy days. A live pig is a difficult thing to smuggle. Dead, it can still be a handful. This was the experience of two Frenchmen. They had killed an animal and arranged to get the carcase to a town some miles away. But how? The idea they used was unique. A taxi was hired. The dead pig was fully attired as a bride and placed upright on a rear seat in the car. The gentlemen also "dressed" for the occasion and the "bridegroom" sat beside the "bride" while the "best man" took up the position alongside the driver. All might have gone well had they resisted the temptation to enter an estaminet in an intervening village. While the men were indoors celebrating, the village constable happened to pass. He spotted the "bride" and good-naturedly put his hand through the open window to extend congratulations. He would! And thus a well-laid scheme once again went agley.

Nobler gift was never given.

Their Name Liveth for Evermore.

PEACE was "bought with a price." The price was widespread sacrifice, destruction, suffering, and death. We can count the dead, but who can calculate the agonies of war? Caithness shared in the cost of victory – shared in the agonies of war.

The agonies of war – spread over six long years. All were tragic years, relieved only by glorious chapters of courage and endurance. Everywhere reverses were Britain's portion in the early struggle, and the free world (what was left unenslaved of it) must have wondered at the pluck of the nation and the tenacity of its people.

Tragic years indeed. Think of 1940-41. Our Forces chased from France, Belgium, Norway, Greece, and across the desert to the gates of Egypt. Our great cities (especially London) bombed nightly without fail and without mercy. People moved in terror, and in the more dangerous areas slept underground or in shelters. Death and destruction were everywhere, and Rumour – ofttimes alarming – was a great ally of the enemy. It was all very disturbing and unsettling – nerve-wracking to all, even for those most remotely removed from the actual prosecution of the war.

Life was very uncertain in those days, and prayers became very earnest and very real. "God plucked us back," declared Rev. Prof. E. P. Dickie, M.C., B.D., whose words these are:– "Our fighting men were never more courageous – on the high seas, in the burning sands of the desert, in the skies above the city of London . . . Our people in their homes and in the war factories were more deeply devoted to their tasks than ever they had been before. . . . And from the very rim of the dark abyss, God plucked us back."

★　★　★　★

It was "men in the pride of their manhood days" who went forth to "battle for Britain"– to stem the tide – and it was mainly the young who were slain – mainly men who had been in their cradles when the Four Years' War was drawing to a close in 1918, or were not even born at that time. Life for them had but begun when they were tossed aside in its "fitful fever."

Caithness is a small and poorly populated county – its area 628 square miles and its population round about 30,000 – but it contributed handsomely to all the Services, and paid the price in the country's struggle for freedom and the future.

A glance at the saddening list of "killed" indicates sad homes and sad hearts in our little county – sorrows that will linger while life lasts. Our warrior sons rest in the soil of many foreign countries and in the seas of the whole world. There comes to mind the touching verse of one who is probably a Caithness poet:–

The Dead are marching past. . . .

The tramp of marching feet goes on;
I wait, I listen, wish them gone,

But four abreast, they're marching past,
With empty hands and eyes downcast.

They're tramping past to a silent drum,
No music beats to their footsteps' hum;
The names of men flow soundless on,
And each of them was a mother's son.

When Remembrance Day comes round – whatever the appointed day – Caithnessians can wear the blood-red poppy with a sense of pride and observe the Silence in humility and prayer. Be it ever a simple and a humble salute to "our heroes dead." The sacrifice of each and all deserves our veneration.

★ ★ ★ ★ ★

The list of Caithness casualties is indeed formidable – indeed the greatest catastrophe that could befall the district. Actual Caithnessians who were killed or died on service numbered 310, and an additional 120 who had close connections with the county. Two-thirds of our Naval casualties (100) were men under 30 years of age (average age $32\frac{1}{2}$); a boy of 17 was the youngest and the eldest a seaman of 57. Almost three-fourths of our Army casualties (211) were men under 30 (average age $25\frac{1}{2}$), the ages ranging from 18 to an officer of 54. The Air Force (killed 78) showed a still higher proportion of youth – more than 60 per cent of the Caithness casualties in this wing of the services being under 25 years of age (average age $23\frac{1}{4}$). Sixty-eight of our casualties held commissioned rank.

Fifteen remain posted as "missing."

Prisoners of war suffered much when in enemy hands and most of them attributed their survival to the fairly regular receipt of Red Cross parcels. Conditions were particularly bad in the Far East – inhuman would be a truer description. Men in Japanese hands just passed from ken, in some cases for long years – they had small chance (if indeed any) of communicating with home, and the Japanese authorities withheld information as to their fate. Prisoners were "dead" until the war was over, and when the war was over some of those believed prisoners were discovered actually to be dead. For instance, an obituary notice gave these condemning facts;– Taken prisoner by the Japanese at Singapore February 15, 1942; died in Thailand January 22, 1943; intimation of death received November 1, 1945. There were other cases equally distressing.

Caithness men in enemy hands numbered 93, and there were also 17 with county connections. Four at least of these prisoners escaped and returned safely to this country.

The wounded totalled approximately 150.

Civilians killed were:– Men 16, women 9, and children 15. Injured were – 6 men, 8 women, and three children; a number sustained minor injuries. Nine civilians were interned in enemy countries.

★ ★ ★ ★ ★

The county's total casualties may be summarised as under:–

Killed or died–	Caithness.	Caithness connection.
Navy	90	10
Army	148	64
Air Force	41	37
Civilians	31	9
	310	120
Missing	10	5
Prisoners of War	93	17
Do., Civilians	9	0
Wounded	128	7
Injured (civilians)	17	0
	257	29

In the Great War (1914-18) casualties were even much heavier and Caithness losses were deplorably high. Including those connected with the county, the Caithness losses in killed and missing (1914-18) reached the startling figure of 949 men. Fifty-nine of them were officers.

Thus in two great wars against Germany the little county of Caithness alone mourned the loss of 1379 of her stalwart sons. Well may we say with the poet:–

"Nobler gift was never given,
Richer blood was never shed;
So we hail our heroes living,
And salute our heroes dead."

Never a greater day than this.

The Coming of Peace.

PEACE came to tortured Europe on Tuesday, the eighth day of May, 1945 – fighting having ceased with the first minute of that day, after 2072 days of intensive warfare that in some measure affected every country in the world. Germany accepted the Allied terms of unconditional surrender.

Victory in Europe had cast a long shadow before it. Germany had been shorn in battle of all the territorial gains she had acquired in her years of opportunity – years of conquests through preparedness – and fighting had been carried to within her own borders. The shattering of her factories, the paralysing of her transport systems, and the demands of her armies were more than militaristic Germany could stand. Berlin fell to Russian armies that had recovered heroically from seeming rout. It was no pendulum swing from Stalingrad, Moscow, Petrograd – it was a one-way traffic for hundreds of miles and Berlin was the Russians' crowning triumph. The German armies in the East had for months retreated steadily and taken heavy punishment in the process, important sections of it frequently being shepherded into positions from which there was no escape from annihilation except by surrender in huge numbers.

★　★　★　★　★

June, 1944, will be a month remembered for all time. It was then the British Army returned to fight in Normandy. The Empire Forces had for many months been patiently rebuilding, training and equipping. And this was D-Day. The task of regaining a foothold for the Army in France was believed almost impossible, but the hazardous undertaking was accomplished with the aid of much ingenuity. Montgomery's men had to fight desperately for small gains, especially around Caen, but with the capture of this inland port and the sweeping moves of the American Armies, an immense stretch of French territory was quickly retaken. What was happening on the Eastern front began to happen also in France and the Low Countries, and Germany's "soft underbelly" had to be defended on Italian soil. Italy, Finland and Bulgaria had ceased as partners in the Axis. The once mighty German military machine began to creak under continued heavy pressure on all fronts. Indeed, months before the final surrender the position of the enemy as defenders of the Fatherland was recognised as hopeless. The Germans suffered colossal casualties in dead and wounded and those of them who found escape from the holocaust in prison cages were latterly numbered in millions.

★　★　★　★　★

The destruction of the enemy's war industries by consistent and persistent bombing by the American Air Force by day and the Royal Air Force by night on a gigantic scale had been a vital factor in the weakening process. Even an extensive U-boat warfare faded as regards successes against Allied shipping.

Behind the Royal Air Force as Secretary of State for Air for five years was Sir Archibald Sinclair, M.P. for Caithness. In his earlier days in office, a leading national periodical stated that "his bombing policy has its critics, but on the whole Sir Archibald has so far been one of the Cabinet's most consistently successful Ministers. . . .His job of work is terrific, and directed to one end: hammering the German military, naval and industrial machine out of shape until the Allied armies can land and finish the job. . . . Air Minister Sinclair believes in big-scale bombing, is sure it will eventually "turn the tide in Britain's favour." And he was right! There are those who may recall that after his appointment to the Air Ministry Sir Archibald aptly and meaningly used the quotation: We must "be copy now to men of grosser blood and teach them how to war." He developed and relentlessly pursued an all-out bombing policy that bewildered and blasted the enemy and hastened the day of defeat. The most significant tribute to the thoroughness of his policy came from the enemy when (in May, 1945) Field Marshall von Rundstedt attributed Germany's collapse "largely to the successful nature of Allied bombing."

Messages of congratulation were sent him (Sir Archibald) on Victory Day. Wick expressed her thanks for the important part he had played in achieving victory and was "proud that a Freeman of the burgh should so distinguish himself."

★　★　★　★　★

The official announcement of the cessation of hostilities was made by Mr Churchill at 3 p.m. on Tuesday, 8th May, and that evening H.M. the King broadcast to the nation and the Empire.

That Tuesday became known as VE Day (Victory in Europe Day) and the following day as VE 2 Day. Both were observed as general holidays throughout the country, and the people celebrated in a fashion commensurate with the historic event.

Immediately following the official announcement the town hall bell in Wick and church bells in Wick, Thurso, Halkirk, Latheron and other centres were rung. Thanksgiving services took place in the churches and were well attended.

The large cities of the country welcomed the coming of peace in Europe amid enthusiastic scenes, particularly in areas that had been badly *blitzed*. In the latter months of the war London and the south of England generally suffered much from rocket and V-bomb attacks. These inventions of the Germans carried no pilots. They were mighty missiles and were launched across the sea and arrived and exploded in England, causing widespread damage, although a degree of accuracy as to targets was never mastered.

Here in Caithness rejoicing was more modified and VE Day was more or less observed as a quiet public holiday. The town streets were gaily beflagged – few houses or buildings were without some decoration, and streamers stretched above the roadway at many points. Bonfires were lit in districts where permissible, and youth found outlets in fireworks and dancing.

Peace "bought with a price" had come and with it an indescribable feeling of relief. Calm after the storm – safety after a perilous voyage.

★ ★ ★ ★ ★

The surrender of Germany hastened the like doom of Japan. It meant that the whole invincible might of the Allies was available against the Far Eastern foe.

Japan had prospered on war and aggression from the beginning of this century and she had been fighting against an ill-armed China for years before Germany set Europe ablaze. America and Britain had vast interests in the Far East and with Germany battering Britain, Japan chose the moment to strike. Assuring America of her determination to maintain peace at almost any cost, that same day (December 7, 1941) the Japanese war-lords launched their attack – a treacherous attack by hundreds of aircraft on American naval forces and shipping in Pearl Harbour. It was a staggering blow to America, and will go down in history as unforgettable and unforgivable. The United States accepted the challenge and became an active and powerful Ally of Britain.

★ ★ ★ ★ ★

The course of the Pacific War was parallel to Germany's early exploits in Europe. Japan quickly overran thousands of square miles of territory and all valuable islands to the very gates of Australia. The swarming yellow race added victory to victory, taking Indo-China, Malaya, Burma, and on to within the borders of India. Recovery of ground and islands was an Herculean task.

The tide of battle turned, however, with the advance of time, and much was recaptured before Germany collapsed. The Japanese Navy and shipping suffered severely, and her air force was unequal to the task of matching the Allies' might in the air.

The coming of peace in Europe meant that great

land, sea and air forces were released for service in the Eastern theatre of war – forces against which no single Power could hope to stand.

Japan's homeland was seriously threatened and her surrender was hastened by the entry of Russia into the war against her and by the use of a new and fearful weapon of annihilation, the atomic bomb. Two only were dropped. The first fell on Hiroshima, a military stronghold, and was reckoned to have destroyed two-thirds of the city with an awful thoroughness. A Tokio broadcast said the bomb literally "seared to death all living things, human and animal, in Hiroshima. Those outdoors were burned to death and those indoors were killed by the indescribable pressure and heat ." The second atomic bomb fell on Nagasaki and again caused widespread devastation.

The use of such an inhuman weapon was questioned even by our own people, and in the House of Commons Mr Churchill made it clear that the use of the atomic bomb was fully justified. It saved, he estimated, a million and a quarter Anglo-American lives.

★ ★ ★ ★ ★

Sixty hours after the fall of the first atomic bomb Japan, fearful of a continuance of the war she had so brutally and exultantly embarked upon and pressed to the limit of her might, offered to surrender. It was the tale of the ages with the scientist still in the ascendancy.

The capitulation of Japan was announced to the British nation in a dramatic midnight broadcast on Tuesday, the 14th day of August, 1945. The announcement was made by Mr Attlee, leader of the Labour Party, who three weeks previously had succeeded Mr Churchill as Prime Minister as the result of a Labour victory at a general election. The next two days (Wednesday and Thursday) were appointed as national holidays in celebration of this turning-point in the world's history.

The greatest threat which civilisation had ever been called upon to face had been destroyed, and Peace, with all high hopes and great opportunities to which it gave rise, had been restored to suffering humanity. "Rejoice" was the order of the day – rejoice, and give thanks to God for our deliverance. Rejoice, although war would leave a legacy of problems – even grave problems. The day people had so long and so earnestly yearned and prayed and worked for had come at last. This was the real ending of hostilities and with it the ending of many anxieties for those on service or in enemy hands.

★ ★ ★ ★ ★

Caithness joined in the rejoicings by the ringing of bells, the lighting of bonfires (miniature ones were set ablaze on the main streets of Wick); buildings were floodlit when darkness fell, and there were coloured lights on the main streets; fireworks cracked all over the town, and bursting rockets sparkled in the misty air; there were sounds of music, song and laughter − merry-makers sang, they cheered and they danced; flags reappeared, and all was gay. Once again the beacon lights of Freedom gleamed brightly. From mournful black-out to scenes like these was a welcome change indeed.

On the Sunday there were church services to thank God for deliverance, and to pause in solemn remembrance of what a nation had gone through and from what we had been saved. These services of thanksgiving were attended by worshippers of all ages in every town and village.

★ ★ ★ ★ ★

Victory brought happiness, but it also brought responsibilities − a point made by H.M. the King in a broadcast to his people. He counselled them to "make sure by the actions of every man and woman throughout the Empire that the peace gained amid measureless hazards and suffering shall not be cast away."

The best that victory can give us is to banish from the earth the threat of war and the causes of war; to preserve mankind from fear and want, oppression and tyranny.

Peace was earned through sacrifice − sacrifice of blood, sweat, toil and tears − and so costly a gift must be carefully guarded. May it be an enduring peace − peace for all time, please God − bringing freedom and security with consequent prosperity to all peoples.

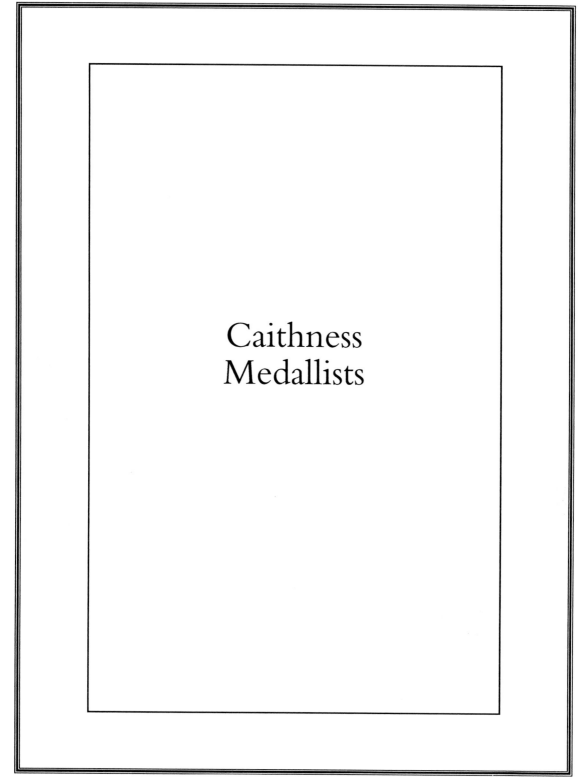

Caithness
Medallists

Honours from the field of battle.

Heroic Deeds by Caithnessmen Recalled.

"LOOK *Gazette,* February 3." That simple cable message from Libya was to reveal to his wife and daughters the heroic desert exploits of a Thurso officer. He was Brigadier Campbell – known as "Big Jock Campbell" (6ft 4in. tall and 48 years old). The message referred to the award of the Victoria Cross, the highest military honour a proud and grateful country can bestow.

Caithness was proud to claim as a son Brigadier John Charles Campbell, Royal Horse Artillery, an officer whose bravery and leadership on the battlefield were beyond all praise and of whom it was said, "He wins the V.C. all the time." Already he had earned the Distinguished Service Order and a Bar to that medal, as well as the Military Cross (won during the 1914-18 war).

Major-General Campbell

The official announcement in the *Gazette* stated that on November 21, 1941, Brigadier Campbell was commanding the troops, including one regiment of tanks, in the area of Sidi Rezegh Ridge and the aerodrome. His small force holding this important ground was repeatedly attacked by large numbers of tanks and infantry.

Wherever the situation was most difficult and the fighting hardest he was to be seen with his forward troops, either on his feet or in his open car. In this car he carried out several reconnaissances for counter-attacks by his tanks, whose senior officers had all become casualties earlier in the day.

Standing in his car with a blue flag Brigadier Campbell personally formed up tanks under close and intense fire from all forms of enemy weapons.

On the following day the enemy attacks were intensified and again Brigadier Campbell was always in the forefront of the heaviest fighting, encouraging his troops, staging counter-attacks with his remaining tanks, and personally controlling the fire of his guns. On two occasions he himself manned a gun to replace casualties.

During the final attack on November 22 he was wounded, but continued most actively in the foremost positions controlling the fire of batteries which inflicted heavy losses on enemy tanks at point-blank range, and finally acted as loader to one of the guns himself.

"Throughout these two days," the citation concluded, "his magnificent example and his utter disregard of personal danger were an inspiration to his men and to all who saw him. His brilliant leadership was the direct cause of the very heavy casualties inflicted on the enemy.

"In spite of his wound he refused to be evacuated and remained with his command, where his outstanding bravery and consistent determination had a marked effect in maintaining the splendid fighting spirit of those under him."

★ ★ ★ ★ ★

Brigadier Campbell was awarded the Distinguished Service Order on April 1, 1941, and the award of the Bar to it was announced less than a month later. In August and September, 1940, he commanded harassing parties of tanks and guns on five occasions and inflicted considerable loss on the enemy, particularly during the withdrawal from Buk Buk to Sidi Barrani. He won the Bar to the D.S.O. for gallant conduct during operations against the enemy lines of communication west of Bardia on December 14, 1940.

The Victoria Cross was pinned on his breast in Cairo by General Auchinleck. Within a month

Campbell was dead. He lost his life in a motoring accident. He was on his way back to the Libyan battle area to take over command of the 7th Armoured Division (he had been promoted Major-General) and while proceeding through a treacherous pass by night he misjudged a curve, and the car overturned. This was a lamentable end to a notable and fearless soldiering career, especially when it is added that all the other occupants of the car escaped uninjured.

Brigadier Campbell was born in 1894 in Traill Street, Thurso. He was educated at the Miller Institution (Thurso Academy) and later at St. Andrews and Sedbergh in Yorkshire. He went through the Royal Military Academy at Woolwich, and was commissioned in July, 1915. He originated the Rover tank columns which played such an active part in the fighting in Libya. These were promptly called "Jock's Columns."

★ ★ ★ ★ ★

Eighty-two other decorations for distinguished leadership and for bravery were awarded to Caithnessmen during the war years, and an additional 47 had the honour of being mentioned in despatches in recognition of outstanding services and devotion to duty. Quite a number of our lads received merit certificates, and six were commended for brave actions.

Thirty medals were awarded to sailors, soldiers and airmen connected with the county, and the services of another eleven were deemed worthy to be mentioned in despatches.

Here is a list of the awards:–

	Caithness	Caithness connection.
Victoria Cross	1	0
Commander of Order of British Empire	1	0
Distinguished Service Order	4	3
Bar to Distinguished Service Order	2	0
Distinguished Service Cross	2	1
Military Cross	3	1
Officer of the British Empire	9	4
Distinguished Service Medal	10	1
Military Medal	13	1
Distinguished Flying Cross	6	6
Distinguished Flying Medal	4	2
Air Force Cross	1	1
U.S. Air Medal	0	2
Legion of Merit	1	1
British Empire Medal	9	2
Member of the British Empire	9	3
Croix de Guerre	3	1
George Medal	5	0
Bronze Medal	2	0
Royal Red Cross Medal	1	0
American Star	2	1
Mentioned in Despatches	47	11
Commended for Bravery	6	1

Nineteen Caithnessians were among civilians honoured by the King.

Caithness Medallists.

D.S.O., Bar to D.S.O., C.B.E.

MURRAY, BRIGADIER GENERAL GEORGE, M.C., 2nd Seaforths, commanded 152nd Brigade in 51st (Highland) Division. Awarded D.S.O. in February, 1943 for gallant and distinguished services in the North African campaign; and Bar to that medal later in the same year for conducting in person front line operations and reconnaissances into no man's land.

Again mentioned in despatches (January, 1944) and awarded C.B.E. in Victory Honours List (June, 1945).

Won M.C. in 1914-18 war and was twice mentioned in despatches. Wounded three times.

Son of Colonel D. Keith Murray, solicitor, Thurso, Vice-Lieutenant of Caithness, and Mrs Murray, Springbank, Thurso. Wife and daughter.

Distinguished Service Order.

DAVIDSON, MAJOR JOHN H., 5th Seaforths. Awarded D.S.O. for gallantry in the last stages of the Tunisian battle – for the skill and daring with which he led his company, and dealt with many counter-attacks on a vital feature which he retained, although at one time the company was reduced to ten men.

Killed on active service (died of wounds) in Sicily on 4th August, 1943, aged 33 years.

Well-known farmer and a B.Sc. (Agr.) of Edinburgh. Husband of Isobel Stewart, Lower Dounreay, and only son of the late Mr and Mrs George Davidson, Oldhall, Watten. One daughter.

MACKENZIE, LIEUT. HUGH C. H., 2nd Monmouthshire Batt. (att. Border Regiment). Awarded D.S.O. after the fighting on the Rhine.

Wounded by sniper on 12th April, 1945.

Grandson of the late Mr Donald Mackenzie and of Mrs Mackenzie, 12 Vansittart Street, Wick.

An M.A. (Hons.) graduate of St. Andrews University, and former dux pupil of Wick High School.

The citation read:– On April 11, 1945, Lieut. Mackenzie's company was ordered to carry out an attack on a strongly held enemy position at Rethem, in Germany. This entailed moving over very open ground under intense fire from enemy small-arms weapons. After the leading platoon had been held up 300 yards short of the objective by heavy fire, it was decided to pass two platoons through, in an attempt to get them on to the objective under cover of smoke. When the smoke screen had been put down, Lieut. Mackenzie led his platoon forward, but owing to the inadequacy of the smoke, they were driven back by fire, suffering casualties, Lieut. Mackenzie himself receiving three bullets through his steel helmet, one of which grazed his head and knocked him unconscious.

It was then decided to make a second attempt and a further smoke screen was put down. Just as the two platoons were starting off, Lieut. Mackenzie recovered and reassumed command of his platoon. This time the attack met with more success and they advanced to within 50 yards of the objective, killing two enemy sections on the way. Further advance became impossible owing to the thinning of the smoke screen and most intense fire from very commanding positions. The two platoons went to ground in shallow shell holes and continued to engage the enemy at close range despite the lack of cover and the fact that the enemy were firing at every movement, even hitting the wounded again and again.

During this time Lieut. Mackenzie received five wounds – two in the arm, one in the back, one in the chest, and the other in the face. Despite this, he continued to encourage his men and refused to withdraw. Eventually, he was ordered to disengage and, on his return, had to be ordered to report to the R.A.P.

By his fine leadership and superb example, while seriously wounded and in great pain (concluded the citation) Lieut. Mackenzie inspired his platoon to efforts which eventually resulted in the capture of the objective.

D.S.C., M.B.E.

MACDONALD, LIEUT. WILLIAM S., R.N.V.R. Awarded Distinguished Service Cross for outstanding zeal, patience and cheerfulness, and for never failing to set an example of wholehearted devotion to duty without which the high traditions of the Royal Navy could not have been upheld. Mentioned in despatches.

Lieut. Wm. S. Macdonald.

Awarded M.B.E. (Military Division) in March, 1943, in recognition of outstanding courage and seamanship in trying to salvage a merchantman, and in rescu-ing survivors in heavy seas while serving in H.M.S. "Borage", and for cheerful and inspiring leadership.

Second in command H.M.S. "Marigold," a corvette believed to have destroyed the submarine that torpedoed the aircraft carrier "Ark Royal".

Teacher in Glasgow and married Wick girl, Miss Connie Shepherd.

Well-known football player with Wick Academy, Queen's Park, and Scottish amateur internationalist.

Youngest son of the late Mr and Mrs John R. Macdonald, Laurelia Cottage, Wick. Father lost his life in last war while serving in the Navy. A sister (Mrs Jack) resides in Bower.

Distinguished Service Cross.

CARMICHAEL, ACTING TEMP. LIEUT.-COMDR. JOHN, R.N.V.R. Awarded D.S.C. in February, 1944, for gallantry and devotion to duty. Later same year mentioned in despatches for gallantry and good service.

Before joining Navy was employed in a London bank. Son of the late Rev. D. Carmichael and of Mrs Carmichael, Reay.

Military Cross.

DELMEGE, MAJOR A. C. STUART, 1st King's Dragoon Guards, R.A.C. Awarded Military Cross (about October, 1943) for distinguished services in Middle East. Son of Major Delmege, Shurrery, Thurso.

GREEN, MAJOR G. H., 5th Seaforths. Awarded Military Cross for gallant and distinguished services in North-West Europe. Headmaster of Bilbster School, and son of Mr George Green, The Breck, John O'Groats.

MURRAY, CAPTAIN JAMES INNES, 1st Punjab Regiment, Indian Army. Awarded Military Cross for gallant and distinguished services in Burma.

Son of Dr and Mrs Murray, 13 Church Hill, Edinburgh, and grandson of the late Mr James Innes, North Calder, Thurso. Educated at Halkirk, Edinburgh Academy and Fettes College.

Distinguished Service Medal.

MACKINTOSH, PETTY OFFICER ANGUS, R.N.R. Awarded D.S.M. for gallant service in the Norwegian campaign (Narvik). Also received the Free French Croix de Geurre for gallantry and devotion to duty in the evacuation of Free French forces.

First Thurso man to win decoration in the war. Coxswain of Thurso lifeboat. Home address – Wilson Street, Thurso.

BAIN, — JOHN, Royal Navy. At Buckingham Palace on July, 1943, received D.S.M. for life-saving during the evacuation from Greece and Crete.

Resided at Liff, Dundee. Son of Mr and Mrs D. Bain, March Croft, Mavsey, Lybster, who had another son (Flt.-Lieut. Alex. Bain) also honoured.

BAIN, SEAMAN DONALD, R.N.R. Awarded D.S.M. for devotion to duty. He was wounded and burned at his gun-post on the "Jervis Bay" but he and another gunner continued in action even after seven of the gun crew had been killed. He recovered in a Canadian hospital.

This was the first decoration won in the war by a Wick man. Only son of the late Mr Sinclair Bain and of Mrs Bain, 136 Willowbank, Wick.

BREMNER, SEAMAN BENJAMIN G., R.N.R. Awarded D.S.M. in August, 1944, for great courage, determination and skill in operations in light coastal craft. Youngest son of Mr and Mrs Donald Bremner, 37 Cairndhuna Terrace, Wick.

CROWDEN, SEAMAN GEORGE B., R.N.R., of H.M.T. "St Kenan." Awarded D.S.M. for gallantry and devotion to duty while serving off Norwegian coast (Namsos) in 1940. Third son of Mr and Mrs J. H. Crowden, Dunnet. Three brothers were serving at sea.

FARMER, STOKER FRANK, R.N.R. Awarded D.S.M. and decorated by the King in May, 1944. Wife and family resided at 12 Cairndhuna Terrace, Wick, and widowed mother (Mrs T. Farmer) at 32 Cairndhuna Terrace. Her youngest son.

GUNN, PETTY OFFICER DAVID, R.N.R. H.M.S. "Prince Leopold." Awarded D.S.M. in November, 1944, for gallantry, skill, determination and undaunted devotion to duty during the landing of Allied forces on the coast of Normandy.

Much active service, and his ship had been twice torpedoed. Son of Mr and Mrs Alex. Gunn, West End, John O'Groats.

MACKAY, SEAMAN GEORGE R.N.R. Decorated at Buckingham Palace with D.S.M. for work in the minefields.

Stated to be "of Thurso". Parents resided at Bettyhill. Grandson of the late Mr Thos. Mackay, shepherd, Achlipster, Spittal.

MACKENZIE, LEADING SEAMAN ROBERT G., R.N.R. Awarded D.S.M. for bravery at the evacuation of British troops from Namsos (1940), during which operations he was slightly wounded.

Holder of the Palestine medal and Long Service medal, and first Caithnessman to win decoration in the war. Son of Mr George Mackenzie, The Willows, Lybster.

OAG, PETTY OFFICER HENRY G., Naval Commando. Awarded D.S.M. for gallantry on the beaches of Sicily. Seven years in Navy. Son of Mr James Oag, Gansclett Farm, Thrumster.

Military Medal.

BREMNER, PTE. DONALD J., 5th Seaforths. Awarded M.M. (posthumously). Killed in action in Sicily on 2nd August, 1943, aged 22 years. Youngest son of the late Mr Donald J. Bremner and of Mrs Bremner, 5 Murrayfield, Castletown.

Citation stated:– During the advance on Francofonte, on July 13, 1943, Pte Bremner was the driver of the leading carrier of a platoon. On two occasions when his carrier encountered strong enemy opposition he drove his carrier with such skill and daring and with such disregard for his own safety under fire that he enabled the carrier commander to put his plans into action as quickly as possible and so force the enemy to withdraw.

Again on 14th July he made four journeys with his carrier, conveying orders which were vital to the success of the battle, across a gap which was swept by machine-gun fire.

Throughout the battle Pte. Bremner was continually active and undertook duties which brought him under heavy fire with such coolness and presence of mind that his example was an inspiration to all who saw him.

CUSTER, CORPL. WILLIAM, So. African Forces. Awarded M.M. about September, 1942, for gallant conduct in Libya. Taken prisoner at Tobruk, 20th June, 1942. Son of the late Mr and Mrs William Custer, The Ha', Durran, Olrig.

DAVIDSON, SERGT. DONALD, Lovat Scouts. (Later C.S.M.) Awarded M.M. in January, 1945, for having led a patrol of two men through the enemy lines to a depth of over five miles to observe and report on a certain area, for a period of four and a half days. Son of Mr and Mrs Alex. Davidson, Helshedder, Reay.

DAVIDSON, SERGT. JOHN, 5th Seaforths. (Later C.S.M.) Awarded M.M. in October, 1943, for services in Italy, and again mentioned in despatches for services in Sicily. Brother of above. Mr and Mrs Davidson had five sons on service, the youngest of whom (Dugald) was killed. All five brothers were gamekeepers in various parts of the Highlands before the war.

FALCONER, DRIVER JOHN, Royal Corps of Signals. Awarded M.M. about April, 1944. Wife resided Bowertower, Bower; and eldest son of Mr and Mrs William Falconer, South Keiss.

FORBES, CORPL. ALEXR., 5th Seaforths. Posthumously awarded M.M. for gallant actions in Sicilian campaign. Killed on 2nd August, 1943, aged 25 years. Wife (Betty Macleod, of Wick) and infant daughter resided at 47 Lochalsh Road, Inverness. Youngest son of Mr and Mrs Donald Forbes, 11 Green Road, Wick, who held the proud distinction of having seven sons and a son-in-law on war service.

GUNN, PTE. DAVID, 5th Seaforths. Awarded M.M. for services in Middle East. Later posted missing. Youngest son of Mr and Mrs James Gunn, 18 Henrietta Street, Wick.

HARPER, SERGT. MURRAY, 2nd Seaforths. Awarded M.M. for gallantry in action about August, 1944. Wounded North Africa on October 22, 1942, and again in Tunisia in April, 1943. Youngest son of the late Mr George Harper and of Mrs Harper, 52 Willowbank, Wick.

MACLEOD, R.-Q.-M.-SERGT. ALEXR., R.A.C. (Glasgow). Awarded M.M. for conspicuous gallantry in North African campaign (July, 1943), and mentioned in despatches a second time for meritorious service. Son of Mrs D. Paul, Church Street, Halkirk.

MORE, SERGT. JOHN W., 5th Seaforths. Awarded M.M. for distinguished services. Mobilised with Battalion. Brother of L.-Corpl. Frank C. More, killed. Eldest son of Mr and Mrs Francis More, 24 Wellington Street, Wick.

SINCLAIR, CORPL. ALEXR., Camerons. Mentioned in despatches at El Alamein, and awarded M.M. for distinguished services in Sicily, October, 1943. Promoted sergeant. Son of Mr and Mrs James Sinclair, Carroy, Dunbeath.

SINCLAIR, SERGT. A. D., 5th Seaforths. Awarded M.M. for gallantry in Sicily. Youngest son of Mr and Mrs George Sinclair, Upper Geiselittle, Weydale, Thurso (late of Isauld Hill, Reay).

SUTHERLAND, COY.-SGT.-MAJOR DONALD, 5th Seaforths. Awarded M.M. (about October, 1944) for conspicuous bravery during operations in the Le Havre area of France.

The citation stated: This n.c.o. as a platoon sergeant showed the highest qualities of leadership and disregard for his own safety during the attack on the morning of July 18, 1944, at the triangle of roads just west of Bois de Bures.

On breaking cover on the start line the right hand section of the platoon came under intense machine-gun fire and were pinned to the ground. Sergt. Sutherland appreciating the situation immediately placed a light machine-gun into a position to give covering fire and went forward himself from a flank to mop up the opposition. He came under heavy fire and was grenaded. His sten gun jammed and he was forced to retire. Having called on another section to mop up other posts he then went forward again with a lance-corporal and though encountering grenades and fire he silenced the post. This having been completed he then rallied his men and pushed on to join his platoon commander and the remainder of his platoon.

It is probable that had it not been for his excellent work the whole company attack might have been held up, which would have seriously affected the battalion gaining their objective. His action and courage were of the highest order.

Wounded in September, 1944. Wife and family resided at 15 Braal Terrace, Halkirk. Only son of Mr and Mrs W. Sutherland, Braal, Halkirk.

Air Force Cross.

SINCLAIR, FLT.-LIEUT. W. C. Royal Air Force. Awarded Air Force Cross in New Year Honours List, 1946, for exceptional devotion to duty as a flying instructor. Joined R.A.F. on leaving school. Son of Mr and Mrs James Sinclair, Rose Cottage, Watten. His wife (Corpl. Sheila Brotchie, Edinburgh) was mentioned in despatches for services with the W.A.A.F.

Distinguished Flying Cross.

ANDERSON, PILOT OFFICER WILLIAM, Royal Air Force. Aged 33 years. Posthumously awarded D.F.C. after having completed 53 operational flights over enemy territory, some of them over heavily defended targets in Germany. The offical citation stated that "on one occasion, in June, 1943, while attacking Mulheim his aircraft was coned by searchlights for over 20 minutes and badly damaged by anti-aircraft fire. Despite all this, Pilot Officer Anderson managed to release his bombs manually, and by this prompt action probably saved the aircraft and crew from destruction. An efficient engineer, this officer has consistently displayed great courage and outstanding devotion to duty."

Pilot Officer Anderson was posted missing in November, 1943, and later presumed killed. He was the only son of Mr James M. Anderson, 3 Dempster Street, Wick. Married: wife and son in Glamorgan, South Wales.

MACKAY, FLYING OFFICER ALEXR. J., Royal Air Force. Awarded D.F.C. about Novr., 1944, for having completed numerous operations against the enemy, in the course of which he invariably displayed the utmost fortitude, courage, and devotion to duty.

Home in Edinburgh, but native of Wick, where he was born in 1912.

DOULL, PILOT OFFICER JACK W., Royal Air Force. Awarded D.F.C. in August, 1944. The official citation said he had completed many successful operations against the enemy, in which he had displayed high skill, fortitude and devotion to duty.

Pilot Officer Doull was in Malta during the siege, and saw service in Crete and North Africa. Son of Mr and Mrs Alex. G. Doull, Quatre Bras, Lybster.

MACKAY, FLYING OFFICER ALEXR. J., Royal Air

65

Force. Awarded D.F.C. for gallantry and devotion to duty on air operations over Europe (October, 1945). Youngest son of Mr and Mrs Sinclair Mackay, 52 High Street, Wick.

ROBERTSON, FLIGHT-LIEUT. ROBERT D., Royal Air Force. Awarded D.F.C. Citation stated he had a fine record of operational missions, and added:– "In the face of intense opposition from the enemy ground defences he has pressed home telling attacks against many troop concentrations in the vicinity of Deventer, Venlo, and Emmerich. This officer's outstanding qualities of leadership and his fine example of courage and devotion to duty have played a large part in the excellent results achieved throughout his tour of operations."

Flight-Lieut. Robertson previously served as a Lieutenant in the Seaforths. Only son of Col. J. J. Robertson, D.S.O., and Mrs Robertson, Thuster, Wick (formerly of "Norwood," Wick), whose daughter, Senior Comdr. Ann Robertson, A.T.S., was awarded the American Bronze Star.

SMITH, FLYING OFFICER JOHN W., Royal Air Force. Awarded D.F.C. in January, 1945, when an observer in a well-planned and brilliantly executed sortie deep into enemy territory in which two enemy aircraft were brought down and three others on the ground effectively attacked.

Flying Officer Smith was 29 years of age and a navigator in a Mosquito that took part in many daring raids. He was posted missing on 21st November, 1944, later as presumed to have lost his life on that date. Only son of Mrs M. Smith, Main Street, Castletown, and the late John R. Smith, Benshaw, Newcastle. Married: wife resident in Barry, Glamorgan.

Distinguished Flying Medal and George Medal.

FORBES, FLIGHT-SERGT. NEIL D., R.A.F. Awarded D.F.M. and George Medal for gallantry on two separate occasions. The 'plane on which he was engineer stalled on returning from an operational sortie and crash-landed. It was carrying bombs, and fire broke out. Although suffering from shock, bruises and cuts, Sergt. Forbes assisted his pilot to rescue other members of the crew. For this action he received the George Medal.

The D.F.M. was awarded for his part in a fight which occurred with seven Ju. 88's over the Bay of Biscay. The wireless operator was killed, Sergt. Forbes was wounded in both legs, and the Halifax bomber was badly damaged.

Flight-Sergt. Forbes was a motor mechanic in a Tain garage until 1940. He is the only son of Mrs Forbes, Stafford Street, Tain, and formerly of Wick, where this airman was born.

Family group outside Buckingham Palace: Sergt. A. G. Sinclair, M.M.; Sergt. Betty Sinclair, A.T.S. (his wife); Mr George Sinclair (father), and Guardsman Murdo Sinclair (brother), an ex-prisoner of war in Italy.

Distinguished Flying Medal.

GORDON, SGT.-PILOT ALEXANDER, Royal Air Force. Aged 24 years. Posthumously awarded D.F.M. He won this honour by his courage, determination, and devotion to duty, qualities which he constantly displayed over a long period of time, but the immediate occasion was the Battle of Cape Matapan, in which a bomb dropped by Sergt. Gordon's aircraft scored a direct hit on an Italian cruiser, crippling it to such an extent that the remainder of the fleet were forced to slow down in order to protect it thus enabling the British Fleet to overtake and join action.

Sergt. Gordon was reported missing in Middle East on 31st May, 1941, later as killed in action on that date. Served in R.A.F. for nine years. Second son of Mr and Mrs Alex. Gordon, Newton, Wick.

INNES, SERGT. JOHN A., Royal Air Force. Awarded D.F.M. (about Octr., 1944) in recognition of gallantry while serving as a flight engineer with No.408 (R.C.A.F.) Squadron. The official citation stated that he had participated in many sorties, displayed commendable skill and courage, and proved himself to be a worthy member of the aircraft crew. On his last sortie Sergt. Innes was wounded whilst over Hamburg. Although in much pain, he remained at his post until the mission was completed. Not until leaving the aircraft after it had landed in England did he mention his injuries. He set a fine example of fortitude and devotion to duty.

Son of the late Mr J. D. Innes, Blingery, and of Mrs Brims, Latheron Mains.

MACKINNON, SGT. ANDREW W., Royal Air Force. Awarded D.F.M. in March, 1945, in recognition of gallantry and devotion to duty on air operations. Reported missing from operational flight over Germany in summer of 1944, but later as safe and in hospital in England.

Citation stated that on June 12, 1944, Sergt. Mackinnon was rear gunner in a Halifax bomber detailed to attack Amiens. Over the target the aircraft was tackled by two enemy fighters. Sergt. Mackinnon returned the fire, destroying one aircraft and forcing the other to abandon the attack.

Later in the same month (June 28), Sergt. Mackinnon took part in an attack on Blainville when a Messerschmitt 109 came into battle. Sergt. Mackinnon fired into the Messerschmitt setting it on fire, and it was seen to crash in flames.

Three days later (July 1), Sergt. Mackinnon was in a Halifax bombing St. Martin-le-Hortier when the aircraft was set ablaze by anti-aircraft fire. An enemy fighter came into the attack, but Sergt. Mackinnon kept up a stream of fire which caused the fighter to abandon the fight and break away in flames. Sergt. Mackinnon's aircraft was so badly damaged that he had to abandon it by parachute.

Sergt. Mackinnon's devotion to duty and tenacity of purpose in the face of the enemy (the citation concluded) were an inspiration to his crew and members of his squadron, and worthy of the highest merit.

Son of Bombr. John Mackinnon, R.A. (on active service abroad) and of Mrs Mackinnon, Schoolhouse, Westerdale.

British Empire Medal.

ALLAN, MR HUGH R., Diver. Awarded B.E.M. for courageous devotion to duty as a diver while off the coast of Normandy. He went down from the salvage vessel "Uplift" in mined waters during the invasion of Europe. Home address – New Houses, Dunnet.

GUNN, WAR OFFICER ALEXANDER, Royal Army Service Corps. Awarded B.E.M. for meritorious war services. Called up with the 5th Seaforth Highlanders in August, 1939, he went overseas with the battalion and transferred in Decr., 1942, to the R.A.S.C., served in Persia and Iraq Command until demobilisation.

Youngest son of Mr and Mrs William Gunn, Mayfield, Hoy, Halkirk. On the staff of the Bank of Scotland at Halkirk and Thurso.

LYALL, MR ALEXANDER, Merchant Navy. Decorated by King with B.E.M. at Buckingham Palace, June, 1945. Son of the late Mr and Mrs Alexr. Lyall, Scarfskerry.

MACLEAN, AIRCRAFTMAN JAMES, R.A.F. Awarded B.E.M. for his share in the rescue work after the officers' mess of the 2nd Tactical Air Force, Base Censorship Unit, had been demolished by a long-range missile of the V2 type on December 17, 1944. Aircraftman Maclean immediately volunteered to assist the rescue party, trying to extricate survivors from the wreckage of the five-storey building. Soon after his arrival a volunteer was called for to support the roof of a tunnel that had been opened. Someone with a powerful back was needed, and Maclean undertook this arduous duty, although fully aware of the danger of being buried alive. His great effort was instrumental in the rescue of two officers.

A.C. Maclean was a gardener at Dunbeath Castle, and later in Torridon in Ross-shire: Only son of Mr Kenneth Maclean, retired estate joiner, Balnabruich, Dunbeath.

MALCOLM, SERGT. PAT, 6th Seaforths. Awarded B.E.M. in New Year Honours List, 1946. Called up with Militia before outbreak of war; served in France before capitulation, and later in various theatres of war. Assistant in County Library. Son of Mr J. G. Malcolm, joiner, Bower.

MUNRO, L.-CORPL. JAMES, Seaforths. Awarded B.E.M. in New Year Honours List, 1946. Third son of Mrs Munro, Rangag, Latheron, and of the late Mr James Munro, Lochdhu, Altnabreac.

ROSS, S/SERGT. DONALD B. Awarded B.E.M. (1946). Served in Army six years. Grandson of Donald Bethune, harbourmaster, Dunbeath.

SINCLAIR, JAMES, Merchant Navy. Awarded B.E.M. and decorated by the King, June, 1944. Resided in South Shields but native of Caithness, being son of the late Mr and Mrs William Sinclair, "Daisy Hill," Stroma.

SWANSON, CHIEF PETTY OFFICER CHARLES R., R.N.R. Mentioned in despatches March, 1942, for distinguished services at sea. Awarded B.E.M. in King's New Year Honours List, 1944. Served on a minesweeper, and his ship was one of the first British vessels which had on board a German magnetic mine taken from a captured enemy ship early in the war.

C.P.O. Swanson is son of Mrs Swanson and the late Mr John Swanson, Staxigoe. Home address – 48 Nicholson Street, Wick.

Officer of the British Empire and American Legion of Merit.

TAYLOR, LIEUT.-COLONEL H. BRIAN, Royal Armoured Corps. Awarded O.B.E. late 1944. Awarded the American Legion of Merit, degree of

Flt. Lieut. Alexr. Bain, O.B.E., and his brother, John Bain, Royal Navy, awarded D.S.M. Natives of Mavsey, Lybster.

Officer, in 1945.

Elder son of the late Captain H. A. Taylor of Sandside, Reay.

Officer of the British Empire.

BAIN, FLIGHT-LIEUT. ALEXR., R.A.A.F. Awarded O.B.E. for hazardous flying over desolate and dangerous ground with the Australian Exploration Expedition, having previously served in Egypt and Iraq, where he gained the Kurdistan medal.

Son of Mr and Mrs D. Bain, March Croft, Mavsey, Lybster, and brother of John Bain, D.S.M.

BEGG, CAPTAIN SINCLAIR, Merchant Navy. Awarded O.B.E. (September, 1941) for bravery, coolness, and devotion to duty shown in bringing his ship to port after she had been severely damaged by enemy action.

Capt. Begg comes of old seafaring stock, his late father and grandfather (maternal) belonging respectively to Nybster and Scarfskerry. He was a prisoner in Germany in 1914-18 war. Home address – Netherby Road, Leith.

LESLIE, LIEUT.-COLONEL NORMAN DAVID, Queen's Own Cameron Highlanders. Mentioned in despatches for services in North Africa ("London Gazette," Jany. 13, 1944). Awarded O.B.E. (Military Division) in recognition of gallant and distinguished service in North-West Europe ("Gazette," Octr. 9, 1945). Awards were gained whilst serving with the 51st (Highland) Division.

Lieut.- Colonel Leslie is a grandson of the late Colonel and Mrs E.W. Horne of Thuster.

LESLIE, LIEUTENANT GEORGE CUNNINGHAM, Royal Navy. (Brother of above.) Awarded O.B.E. (Military Division), gained whilst serving as First Lieutenant on H.M.S. "Cassandin" on Russian convoy routes.

MACADIE, CHIEF ENGINEER DONALD, Merchant Navy. Awarded O.B.E. (January, 1945) for meritorious conduct whilst on dangerous service duty. He was once torpedoed and was 12 hours in water before being rescued.

Home address – 25 Pitt Street, Edinburgh. Brother of Mr James Macadie, watchmaker, Wick.

SINCLAIR, CAPTAIN DAVID MURRAY, Merchant Navy. Awarded O.B.E. in King's New Year Honours List, 1943. Native of Castletown, and son of the late Captain Kenneth and Mrs Sinclair.

SWANSON, CHIEF ENGINEER JAMES MACKAY, of the Donaldson Line. Made Officer of the British Empire for distinguished services during the war years.

Home address – 40 Sunnyside Dr., Clarkston, Glasgow. Both C.E. Swanson and his wife are natives of Thurso.

WALLACE, COMMANDER ALLAN P., R.N.R. Awarded O.B.E. in King's Birthday Honours (June, 1945) for distinguished services in connection with the Ministry of War Transport. Son of the late Captain Wallace, Seaview, Mey, and brother of Mrs Finlayson, Barnyards, Wick.

Member of the British Empire.

ADAMSON, ACTING SKIPPER-LIEUT. ALEXR., R.N.R. Awarded M.B.E. in King's Birthday Honours (June, 1945). Home address – Vansittart Street, Wick (now Cairndhuna Terrace).

DUNDAS, CAPTAIN ALEXR. M., s.s. "St. Ninian." Awarded the M.B.E. decoration (probably in May, 1941). Second son of the late Mr Matthew Dundas, a former well-known Stroma pilot.

MACFARLANE, FLIGHT-LIEUT. JOHN S., R.A.F. Awarded M.B.E. decoration in New Year Honours List, 1946, for services on a Bomber Command Station in Scotland. Mentioned in despatches, 1943 and 1945. Native of Thurso. Second son of the late Mr James Macfarlane and of Mrs Macfarlane, 34 Princes Street, Thurso. Accountant Commercial Bank, Crieff.

MACKAY, CAPTAIN DONALD M., Merchant Navy. Awarded M.B.E. in King's Birthday Honours (June, 1943). Son of the late Mr and Mrs Angus Mackay, Shore Street, Thurso.

MACKENZIE, — DAVID M. Awarded M.B.E. for work as Camp Leader of Stalag 383 during his five years' capitivity in Germany. He was mentioned in despatches in July, 1940. Son of the late Mr Angus Mackenzie, Harland Gardens, Castletown, and of Mrs Mackenzie, Kirkcaldy.

MUNRO, CAPTAIN HENRY B. M., Royal Indian Army Service Corps. Awarded M.B.E. in recognition of gallant services on Eastern Frontier of India (1943). Son of the late Mr John Munro and Mrs Munro, 14 Princes Street, Thurso, and was a chemist with Messrs Cowan & Geddes, of that town.

SHEARER, CAPTAIN ROBERT, The Northamptonshire Regiment. Awarded M.B.E. in recognition of outstanding service in North-West Europe. Announcement of award published in "London Gazette" January 24, 1946. Youngest son of the late Major Robert Shearer and of Mrs Shearer, Janet Street, Thurso.

THOMSON, — CHARLES, Merchant Navy. Awarded M.B.E. in January, 1945, for "meritorious sea service." Home address – 33 Shore Street, Thurso.

Croix de Guerre.

MACLEOD, CORPL. JACK M., Royal Scots Fusiliers. Took part in heavy fighting at Walcheren and Flushing Islands and mentioned in despatches. Awarded Belgian Croix de Guerre (with Palm). Wounded in Germany in April, 1945. Home address – Borgie, Berriedale.

MILLER, PTE. WILLIAM, 5th Seaforths. Awarded Croix de Guerre about April, 1945. Wife and family resided at 52 Grant Street, Wick, and parents in Girnigoe Street, Wick.

American Star.

ROBERTSON, SENIOR COMDR. ANN, A.T.S. Awarded American Bronze Star (July, 1945) by U.S.A. for special services at Shaef. Comdr. Robertson took important part in the Normandy invasion plans.

Eldest daughter of Col. J. J. Robertson, D.S.O., and Mrs Robertson, Thuster House (formerly of "Norwood," Wick).

Royal Red Cross Medal.

KENNEDY, MATRON (Acting) ELIZABETH J., T.A. Nursing Service. Awarded the R.R.C. (Royal Red Cross) 2nd Class in the King's Birthday Honours List of June, 1946. Served in the Middle East and honour awarded for meritorious service while acting matron of a military hospital in Syria. Returned to civilian duties as a Queen's District Nurse in Brechin, Angus. Daughter of the late Mr John Kennedy and of Mrs Kennedy, Aukengill.

George Medal.

BREMNER, SURGEON LIEUT.-COMMANDER ROBERT M., Royal Navy, aged 37 years. George Medal posthumously awarded "for great bravery in going to the help of two of his fellow men who were in mortal danger."

Lost his life in an air raid in April, 1942 (south-west English coast) when the house in which he was residing received a direct hit. Three other occupants were also killed.

"During an air raid, a civilian was trapped by fallen concrete blocks, and unable to move, and it seemed probable that the building would collapse further before he could be rescued. Surgeon Lieut.-Comdr. Bremner crawled through a tunnel full of escaping steam until he reached the man and using his own strength he freed him, and drew him back to safety.

"In April, 1942, a soldier was badly hurt by an explosion of a mine, on the South Coast. The only approach to him was up an almost vertical cliff about 100 feet high. Surgeon Lieut.-Comdr. Bremner scaled the lower part of the cliff by using two ladders lashed together, and then climbed the rest of the way unaided. When he got to the top he saw the injured man trying to crawl towards him. He had been told not to go into the minefield, where there were hidden mines only a short distance apart, but he at once made his way through it to where the man was lying, picked him up, and carried him back to the edge of the cliff, whence he was lowered to safety. Unfortunately, the soldier died before he reached hospital, but Surgeon Lieut.-Comdr. Bremner had made a very gallant attempt to save his life."

Dr. Bremner was the elder son of the late Mr John Bremner, fishcurer, and of Mrs Bremner, 6 Upper Dunbar Street, Wick. He joined the Navy some years before the outbreak of war, after graduating in medicine at Edinburgh University. He was buried at Wick with military honours.

FORBES, MR JOHN (52), factory aircraft spotter, Fraserburgh. Awarded George Medal (September, 1942) for rescuing two girls who were running about frantically in a minefield after a mine had exploded and killed the sister of one of the girls. Mr Forbes entered the minefield and brought the girls to safety. Mr Forbes stated that an unknown soldier had shared the dangers in the rescue.

A native of Lybster, son of the late Mr and Mrs George Forbes, Shelligoe. He is a cooper to trade and was for some years employed in Wick.

MANSON, DR. MALCOLM, medical officer of Wood Green, London. Awarded George Medal in Civil Defence Honours List (February, 1941) for bravery during air raid on London. Official statement read:–

"A heavy high explosive bomb fell, causing a tunnel to collapse. A number of people were trapped under debris and clay. Dr. Manson arrived on the scene within a few minutes of the occurrence, and immediately assumed the direction and leadership of the rescue work. For nearly three hours he worked without intermission, releasing trapped people and giving medical aid where it was needed, and all the time keeping effective control. Throughout, he was in grave danger from frequent falls of clay. It seemed likely that a further portion of the tunnel would collapse. At one period he was lying full length on the heap endeavouring to release a man partially buried when there was a shout from the look-out man of 'run for it.' The doctor ignored the warning and continued his efforts for the trapped man. There was a large fall of clay and the doctor was struck by a large piece full on the back. He was partially buried and had to be dragged out feet foremost. He rested for a few minutes, and then, in spite of severe pain, carried on with the work. Dr. Manson's pertinacity, courage and disregard of personal safety set a wonderful example to the men, and was no doubt responsible for the saving of a number of lives which otherwise would have been lost. He sustained serious injuries during the rescue operations."

Dr. Manson is the fourth son of Mr Alexr. Manson (native of Gills, Canisbay) and Jacobina S. Green, Wick. He served with R.A.M.C. in last war and was awarded the M.C.

ROSIE, SERGT. GEORGE M., Metropolitan Police. Awarded George Medal for great courage and devotion to duty in face of extreme danger – August, 1941. He was on duty during an air raid when a high explosive bomb damaged a house, the two upper floors collapsed, and fire broke out at the back of the building. Sergeants Rosie and Cox climbed through a ground floor window and found a man pinned underneath a large boulder and considerable debris. The sergeants were well aware that any movement of the boulder would probably cause a complete collapse of the house, but they began to remove the rubble with their hands, and after half-an-hour were successful in liberating the victim. Owing to the confined space he could not be carried out, and the rescuers had to drag him to safety. The whole structure of the house collapsed shortly after the rescue had been effected.

Sergt. Rosie is the eldest son of ex-Constable Murdoch Rosie and Mrs Rosie, Ivybank, Castletown.

Bronze Medal.

MALCOLM, COASTGUARDSMAN JOHN, Gourdon, Kincardine. Awarded the Bronze Medal for gallantry in saving life at sea. During the height of a November (1941) storm a ship which had been bombed by enemy aircraft drifted helplessly ashore near the mouth of the North Esk. The sea was rough and the wind reached gale force. All night long efforts were made to reach the ship by rocket apparatus, and after nearly eleven hours' work rescue by the breeches buoy was begun. In the afternoon the rescue-line was fouled by an underwater obstruction half-way to the wreck (150 yards). Malcolm volunteered to "under-run" the line. Holding on to the line, he pulled himself through the sea. Three times terrific waves engulfed him. As he cleared the line at the third attempt he was catapulted in the air, but he held on grimly and was pulled ashore. Thanks to Malcolm's bravery all 43 members of the vessel's crew were saved.

Johnshaven life-saving crew were awarded the shield for the most meritorious rescue by rocket apparatus during 1941.

Coastguardsman Malcolm belongs to Wick, being son of the late Mr and Mrs William Malcolm (stevedore), Harbour Terrace. Before joining the coastguard service in 1939 he was in Navy for three years.

Two Snaps from Buckingham Palace.

Coastguard John Malcolm, Gourdon, with his wife and children.

Sergeant G. M. Rosie, Metropolitan Police, with his wife, parents and sister.

Mentioned in Despatches.
(Oak Leaf Emblem).
(Generally for devotion to duty and meritorious service.)

BAIN, CORPL. J. I. S., Royal Air Force. Mentioned in despatches during Burma campaign. Served apprenticeship as cabinet maker in Wick; now employed in Edinburgh (Civil Service). Married Halkirk girl. Son of the late David Bain (cooper), Argyle Square, Wick, and of Mrs Bain, Roselea, Castletown.

BAIN, L.A.C. GEORGE R., Royal Air Force. Mentioned in despatches (1942). Shop assistant. Fifth surviving son of Mr and Mrs Andrew Bain, 6 Ackergill Street, Wick, who had three other sons on service.

BANNERMAN. S/SERGT. GEORGE, 5th Seaforths. Mentioned in despatches Novr., 1945. Son of Mr and Mrs G. Bannerman, 7 Willowbank, Wick. Married, and wife (Ella Manson) resided at 21a Kinnaird Street, Wick.

BEGG, BOMBDR. ALEXR. S., Royal Artillery. Mentioned in despatches (Italy, 1945). Assistant with county sanitary inspector. Only son of Mr and Mrs Alexr. B. Begg, 15 Argyle Square, Wick.

BROTCHIE, CORPL. SHEILA (Mrs W. C. Sinclair), W.A.A.F. Mentioned in despatches. Husband, a native of Watten, was awarded Air Force Cross.

CAMPBELL, S/SERGT.-MAJOR JOHN, Royal Army Service Corps. Mentioned in despatches (August, 1946) for service on the Assam-Burma line of communication. Joined Seaforth Highlanders in 1945 and was on service in Hong Kong, Shanghai, Singapore, Panang and India. Transferred to Indian Army in 1941. Son of Mr James Campbell, 1 Smith Terrace, Thurso.

CHRISTIAN, SEAMAN ALEXR. G., Royal Navy. Mentioned in despatches (Novr., 1943). Electrician. Took part in the evacuation of Crete, and was aboard the "Kashmir" when she was sunk. Rescued after being five hours in water. Son of Mr and Mrs David Christian, 20a Girnigoe Street, Wick.

CLARK, CAPTAIN ARCHIBALD, 1st Seaforths. Mentioned in despatches for work in Burma with the Chindits. Son of Mr and Mrs Daniel Clark, 5 Argyle Square, Wick, who had two sons killed on service.

CLARKE, MAJOR LEONARD A., 14th Army. Mentioned in despatches for bomb disposal work in Burma in 1942. Son of Mrs Helen Clarke, late of "Seaview", Lybster and grandson of Mr and Mrs Francis Sinclair, Lybster.

CURTIS, S.Q.M.S. RONALD F., 5th Royal Tank Regiment. Mentioned in despatches (North-West Europe) and awarded Certificate of Merit. Native of Worksop, Notts. Wife and baby daughter resided at Smerlie, Lybster.

DURRAND, REGT.-SERGT.-MAJOR JOHN G., 5th Seaforths. Mentioned in despatches (North Africa, 1944). Postman in Wick. Wife resided 1 Macleay Terrace, Wick. Son of Mr and Mrs George Durrand, 4 Kirkhill, Wick.

FALCONER, CAPTAIN GEORGE, 14th Punjab Regiment, Indian Army. Mentioned in despatches "in recognition of gallant conduct in carrying out hazardous work" when a fire started on board an ammunition ship in Bombay harbour. Born in Wick. Son of the late Mr Donald Falconer and of Mrs C. F. Falconer (both natives of Wick), 16 Gosford Place, Edinburgh; and grandson of Mr George Falconer, who resided for many years at Janetstown, Wick, and later at Mybster.

FORBES, B.S.M. GEORGE S., Royal Artillery. Twice mentioned in despatches – Anzio, March, 1944, and again at the crossing of the Elbe, April, 1945. Home address – George Street, Halkirk. Formerly resided at Banniskirk.

GALLEITCH, SERGT. WILLIAM J. S., 5th Seaforths. Mentioned in despatches in recognition of gallant and distinguished services in the field (N.W. Europe). Holder of Efficiency Medal (Territorial). Mobilised with battalion and served in North Africa, Sicily and on Western Front. Student at Agricultural College, Aberdeen. Elder son of Mr and Mrs Robert Galleitch, Ballie, Westfield, Thurso. Married, and wife and son resided at Macduff, Banffshire.

GEDDES, SERGT. DAVID, 1st Seaforths. Mentioned in despatches for distinguished service in the Far East – India, Assam, Burma – where he served from 1942 until demobbed in Feby., 1946. Occupation, plasterer. Son of Mrs M. Geddes, 2 Cairndhuna Terrace, Wick. Married, and wife resided 76 Nicolson Street.

GEDDES, SERGT. DONALD ALEXR., Royal Engineers. Mentioned in despatches. Served in France, Africa and Italy. Son of Mr and Mrs D. M. Geddes, Toftingall, Watten.

GILBERTSON, MAJOR (later Lt.-Col) THOMAS W., Royal Artillery. Mentioned in despatches (Italy, 1945). In January, 1944, was appointed Chief Revenue Officer under the Allied Military Government in Sicily. Married – wife a daughter of Mr and Mrs Alex Stephen, Coach Road, Wick. Only son of the late Mr and Mrs C. J. Gilbertson, Moray Street, Wick.

GRANT, LIEUT. GEORGE, Pioneer Corps. Mentioned in despatches (1945). Before joining up was on the staff of Messrs Mackay, ironmongers, Thurso.

GUNN, SEAMAN GEORGE S., Royal Navy. Mentioned in despatches (1945) for his part in the sinking of an enemy submarine. Accountant in Bank of Scotland, Kirkwall. Eldest son of the late Mr and Mrs William A. Gunn, Rotterdam Street, Thurso.

GUNN, PTE. ROBERT, Australian I.F. Mentioned in despatches (Middle East, 1944). Son of Mr and Mrs John Gunn, Skaill, Lybster.

HARPER, SERGT. DAVID, Royal Air Force. Mentioned in despatches (Italy, 1945). A reservist – came through Dunkirk. Son of the late Mr and Mrs D. Harper, Dempster Street, Wick. Wife resided – 24 Malmesbury Place, Armley, Leeds.

HARPER, PTE. DONALD, 2nd Seaforths. Mentioned in despatches (N.W. Europe). Died of wounds 12th Septr., 1944. Wife (Elizabeth Forbes) resided at Larel, Halkirk.

HENDERSON, SERGT. COXSWAIN S. Mentioned in despatches. At Westward Ho', Devon, on Feby. 13, 1945, while in charge of a DUKW craft, went to the rescue of a Wellington aircraft which had crashed into the sea. The C-in-C stated: "The courage and determination of the above n.c.o. and crew in attempting rescue in seas which rendered the journey hazardous in an amphibian were most commendable." Home address – Juniper Bank, Thurso, where wife resided.

HYMERS, MAJOR JAMES, attached to India Tank Brigade, Signals Squadron. Mentioned in despatches in Spring of 1945 (Burma campaign), where he was still serving in Spring of 1947. Son of Mr and Mrs Robert Hymers, Achswinegar, Lybster.

LEITH, LEADING SEAMAN WILLIAM, R.N.R. Mentioned in despatches (1943) for good services aboard H.M.S. "Sotra", a vessel later reported lost. Second son of Mrs Leith, 7 Harbour Terrace, Wick, and of the late Captain William Leith.

MACKAY, PETTY OFFICER (later Lieut). WILLIAM S., R.N.V.R. Mentioned in despatches March, 1941, and again late 1944. Awarded Palestine Medal (1935-36) and Long Service Medal (R.N.R.) Native of Helmsdale. Home address – 9 New Houses, Lybster.

MACKENZIE, L-BDR. DAVID J. M., Royal Artillery. mentioned in despatches (N.W. Europe). Before joining up, was on the staff of Messrs Malcolm & Tait, booksellers, Thurso. Eldest son of Mr and Mrs Sinclair Mackenzie, 45 Olrig Street, Thurso.

MACLEOD, L-CPL, MARCUS, 6th Seaforths. Mentioned in despatches in recognition of outstanding conduct when he saved the life of a wounded comrade in an engagement during the Italian campaign. Bricklayer to trade. Son of Mr and Mrs Alex Macleod, 13 Ackergill Crescent, Wick.

McALLAN, COY.-QUARTERMASTER-SERGT. WILLIAM, 5th Seaforths. Mentioned in despatches (N. W. Europe). Draper with J. H. Miller, High Street, Wick. Youngest son of Mrs McAllan, Victoria Place, Wick, and of the late William McAllan.

MILLER, MAJOR JAMES, B.Sc. (Agr.), Royal Engineers. Mentioned in despatches (second time) for services in Burma campaign. His exploits in Burma, where he was largely responsible for blasting a way through the jungle, and the construction of roads, bridges and airfields in the forward areas during General Slim's victorious advance, earned for him the title of "The Bulldozer King." Son of Mr George Miller, J.P., and Mrs Miller, Old Stirkoke, Wick.

MILLER, TEMP. SKIPPER DONALD, R.N.R. Mentioned in despatches (1943). In charge of a minesweeper. Took part in the evacuation from Dunkirk. Home address – 35 Cairndhuna Terrace, Wick.

MOORE, CORPL, GORDON, 1st Highland Light Infantry. Mentioned in despatches (N.W. Europe). Youngest son of Rev. G. Moore and Mrs Moore, Old Parish Manse, Wick.

MOWAT, TY. LEADING WRITER ROBERT JOHN BAIN (later Petty Officer Writer), Royal Navy. Mentioned in despatches (June 8, 1944) for distinguished service. Son of Mr and Mrs William Mowat, Alterwall, Lyth. Married, and wife and family resided at "Mariviol," Tulloch Street, Dingwall.

MUNRO, LIEUT. (later Captain) A. ERIC, Pioneer Corps. Mentioned in despatches (Italy, 1945). Mobilised as sergeant with Seaforths on outbreak of war. Elder son of the late Mr G. D. Munro and of Mrs Munro, Ornum House, Lybster. Married, wife being a daughter of Mr and Mrs John Sutherland, Morven House, Lybster.

MUNRO, R.Q.M.S. A. H., 5th Seaforths. Mentioned in despatches (1944). Native of Caithness. Youngest son of the late Mr Hugh Munro (stationmaster at Hoy) and of Mrs Munro, Dornoch.

MUNRO, L.-CORPL. JOHN, Royal Army Medical Corps. Mentioned in despatches (N.W. Europe). Second son of Mrs Munro, Younger's Buildings, Castletown.

PATERSON, S./SERGT. W. F., Royal Army Medical Corps. Mentioned in despatches (1944). Youngest son of the late Mr and Mrs John Paterson, Princes Street, Thurso. Wife resided in Inverness where, before the war, he was a hospital orderly.

REID, LEADING SEAMAN GILBERT M., R.N.P.S. Mentioned in despatches (1942). Son of Mrs Keena Reid, Marine Terrace, Thurso.

STEPHEN, S.Q.M.S. ROBERT P., Royal Army Ordnance Corps. Mentioned in despatches (Middle East, 1942). Joined Army ten years previously. Son of Mr and Mrs Alex. Stephen, 6 Coach Road, Wick.

STEPHEN, L.A.C. ROBERT, Royal Air Force. Mentioned in despatches (Western Front, 1945). A despatch rider who saw much service. Son of Mr Thomas Stephen and the late Mrs Stephen, Reay.

SUTHERLAND, SERGT. J., Royal Artillery. Mentioned in despatches (N.W. Europe). Son of Mr Sinclair Sutherland and the late Mrs Sutherland, who resided at Oalstone, Lyth.

TAIT, SUB-LIEUT. JOHN B., R.N.V.R. Mentioned in despatches for "gallantry and leadership when in command of H.M. L.C.T. 980 during the landing of Allied Forces on the coast of Normandy. Throughout the operations until he was killed, Sub.-Lieut. Tait's courage and resource while under heavy fire were an inspiration to his men, and made it possible for the tanks to be landed in the shortest possible time."

Eldest son of the late Mr Robert Tait, fishcurer, and of Mrs Tait, 15 Brown Place, Wick.

SUTHERLAND, LIEUT. PETER, Royal Army Service Corps. Mentioned in despatches (April 4, 1944) for "gallant and distinguished service in the Middle East" (1943). Served from Septr., 1939, until the end of hostilities in various roles, including the dropping of supplies by parachute to partisans and our own forward troops. Son of the late Mr A. B. Sutherland and of Mrs Sutherland, Rangag, Latheron; married Cecilia, youngest daughter of Dr and the late Mrs Kennedy, Dunbeath. Employed by the Commercial Bank of Scotland at Lybster and later at Irvine.

WARES, FLIGHT-SERGT. DONALD, Royal Air Force. Mentioned in despatches. Had war service in Egypt, The Sudan and Cyprus. Holder of Africa Star and long service and good conduct medal (18 years). Son of Mr D. Wares, 50 Henrietta Street, Wick.

WARES, CORPL. DONALD A., Royal Air Force. Mentioned in despatches (March, 1945). Joined Air Force in May, 1939. Eldest son of Mr and Mrs D. A. Wares, 42 Vansittart Street, Wick.

WORK, SEAMAN JAMES, R.N.R. Mentioned in despatches (May, 1945). Eldest son of Mr and Mrs James Work, Durness Street, Thurso.

Certificate of Merit.
(Awarded in recognition of outstanding good service and devotion to duty.)

COGHILL. SERGT. WILLIAM, Royal Army Service Corps. (France – 1945.) Was at Dunkirk, through African campaign, and on Western Front since D-Day. Home address – 27 Sinclair Street, Thurso.

DOULL, COY.-SERGT.-MAJOR ALASTAIR, 5th Seaforths. (Western Front.) Killed 28th October, 1944. Only son of Mr John G. C. Doull, flesher, Lybster. Wife and infant son resided at West Manse, Latheron.

DURRAND, T.-SERGT.-MAJOR DAVID R., Royal Artillery (Anti-Aircraft Command). Awarded Certificate of Merit January 1, 1943. Home address – 28 Bank Row, Wick.

GUNN, PTE. JOHN M., 5th Seaforths. Home address – Achswinegar, Lybster.

HENDERSON, CORPL. DAVID, Royal Air Force. A grocer in Wick before joining in 1940. Wife resided at Scouthal, Watten. Youngest son of Mr and Mrs Wm. Henderson, 33 Kennedy Terrace, Wick.

MACLEOD, COY.-SERGT.-MAJOR DONALD, 5th Seaforths. (Western Front.) Killed in action 21st August, 1944. Eldest son of Mr and Mrs John Macleod, Quarryside, Murkle, Castletown.

MILLER, PTE. WILLIAM, 5th Seaforths. (Awarded two Certificates – one for North African campaign and the other for the Western Front.) Son of Mr William Miller, Girnigoe Street, Wick. Home address – 52 Grant Street, Wick.

PAUL, CORPL. A., 5th Seaforths. Third son of Mr and Mrs James Paul, Rowan Tree House, Forsinard.

REID, C.Q.M.S. WILLIAM, 5th Seaforths. Before mobilisation was in Commercial Bank, Thurso. Son of Mr and Mrs James Reid, "Deskford," Thurso.

SINCLAIR, SERGT. DAVID H. K., 5th Seaforths. Son of Mr Donald Sinclair, retired bank agent, "St. Duthus," Halkirk.

SUTHERLAND, SERGT. W. A., Royal Artillery. (May, 1944.) With A.A. Battery as a gun-fitter since 1939. Home address – Dunbeath Hotel.

SUTHERLAND, PTE. A., 5th Seaforths. (Western Front – 1945.) Home address – Greenland, Castletown.

SUTHERLAND, PTE. JACK, 5th Seaforths. Mobilised with battalion. Son of Mr and Mrs J. G. Sutherland, Scrabster, Thurso.

SUTHERLAND, COY.-SERGT.-MAJOR DONALD, 5th Seaforths. Awarded Certificate in recognition of outstanding devotion to duty and courage while serving with the Battalion. Sixth son of Mr and Mrs William Sutherland, Smithy House, Haster.

ADAMS, MISS J., Dunnet Head, Thurso. Awarded special Naafi Certificate (September, 1945) as testimony to the endurance, courage and devotion displayed in helping to maintain canteen service under shellfire in the Dover area.

Commended for Bravery.

CUMMINGS, ENGINEER WILLIAM W., Merchant Navy. Commended (24th Novr., 1942) for good service aboard s.s. "Destro" when the vessel was attacked by enemy aircraft in the Mediterranean. Native of Edinburgh and regular member of the Merchant Navy. Took part in the dangerous work of evacuating troops at Greece and Crete. Home address – Seater House, Huna. Wife a daughter of the late Coxswain John Dunnett, Seater.

MACGREGOR, CHIEF RADIO OFFICER JAMES (Hamish), Merchant Navy. Commended for bravery at sea, 1943. Home address – 133 Craigleith Hill Avenue, Edinburgh. Son of Mrs MacGregor (formerly of Co-operative Buildings, Wick) and of the late James Macgregor, who was lost on H.M.S. "Invincible" at the Battle of Jutland, 1915.

MACKAY, ABLE-SEAMAN DAVID ROSS, H.M.S. "Rosario". Commended in a Special Order of the Day by Commander-in-Chief, Devonport, for prompt and courageous action. The order stated that on July 12, 1946, two ratings (one of them A.B.

Mackay) dived into the water and rescued an injured man who had fallen between H.M.S. "Rosario" and the tug "Camel" as the latter was coming alongside. The water between the ships was confused and dangerous, due to the movement of the tug's paddles.

Able-Seaman Mackay was the youngest of five sons of Mr Donald Mackay, mason, and Mrs Mackay, 4 West End, Lybster, who served in the Forces. Before joining the "Rosario" he was gunner of M.T.B. 703 for two years in the Mediterranean.

MACKENZIE, CAPTAIN MAXWELL D., Merchant Navy. Commended for courage and devotion to duty when cargo ship s.s. "Primrose Hill" was torpedoed by enemy submarine (U-Boat 28) and set on fire while proceeding to Takoradi, West Africa (Decr., 1943). In lifeboats for nine days with practically no water and very little food. Picked up by m.v. "Sanan" and landed in Freetown.

Second son of Mr and Mrs Wm. J. Mackenzie, "Acairseid," Dunnet, by Thurso, who had four sons in the Merchant Navy. Son-in-law of Mr and Mrs John Sutherland, 21 Moray Street, Wick, where wife and three of a family resided.

SINCLAIR, S.Q.M.S. DONALD, R.A.O.C. Commended for good services in the Middle East. Promoted Warrant Officer. Served in France before capitulation, and was evacuated from St. Nazaire. He was previously employed in Wick Branch of the British Linen Bank. Only son of Mr James Sinclair, Willowbank, Wick, former skipper of the "Millrock" and other coastal vessels.

STEVEN, CHIEF OFFICER DONALD M., Merchant Navy. Commended for brave conduct against the enemy at sea (1942). Home address – 7 Clarence Drive, Glasgow. Only surviving son of Captain and Mrs Walter Steven, Rowena House, Mey. Elder brother, Captain Walter Steven, was killed when his ship was attacked and sunk by German raider in the South Atlantic (1941).

Decorations Awarded Men of Caithness Connection.

D.S.O., A.F.C., D.F.C.

MACKENZIE, ACTING WING-COMDR. RUSSELL M., Royal Air Force. Awarded A.F.C. in 1942 for meritorious service in England; D.F.C. for Middle East services early 1944; D.S.O. in May, 1944.

Wing-Comdr. Mackenzie was an "excellent operational leader" who administered his squadron in exemplary manner, and "led many strikes against the enemy." "His many meritorious feats of flying include sharing in the destruction of a JU88, and a one-engine flight from the Aegean to Cyprus," stated the citation. "In July, 1943, in face of intense anti-aircraft fire from the shore and ships in the harbour, Wing-Comdr. Mackenzie shared in the destruction of a large armed enemy merchant ship. His personal courage and devotion to duty have always been of the highest order, and it is due to his inspiration that his squadron has contributed successfully towards upsetting the flow of German supplies to the Dodecanese Islands."

Wing-Comdr. Mackenzie is a grand-nephew of Mr John Macbeath, Knockally, Dunbeath, whom he has visited.

Distinguished Service Order.

HORNE, LT.-COLONEL RODERICK D., Seaforths. Awarded D.S.O. in Tunisian campaign. He gallantly led three counter-attacks under heavy fire. Resided in London. Grandson of the late Major J. Horne of Stirkoke.

WASHBOURN, LIEUT. RICHARD, of H.M.S. "Achilles". Awarded Distinguished Service Order for gallantry in the River Plate battle with the German battleship "Graf Spee." Lieut. Washbourn was wounded in the head early in the action, but (said the official report) "in spite of his wounds he continued to control the main armament with the utmost coolness. He set a magnificent example .... and thus the primary control kept working and secured throughout the action a high rate of hits on the enemy."

Lieut. Washbourn is a grandson of the late Mrs Sinclair, Manystones, Mid-Clyth.

Distinguished Service Cross.

M'ASKILL, CHIEF ENGINEER NORMAN, Merchant Navy. Awarded D.S.C. in January, 1943. After his ship was torpedoed off Malta he was confined in a prison camp in North Africa for more than a year, and escaped along with 300 others. Parents for a time resided at Willowbank, Wick.

Military Cross.

ANSTRUTHER, SIR RALPH, Bart., Coldstream Guards. Awarded Military Cross, September, 1943. Wounded North Africa in March, 1943. Baronet (seventh) of Balcaskie and Watten. His late father, Major Robert Anstruther, Black Watch, won M.C. in last war.

O.B.E. and Legion of Merit.

MACDONALD, LT.-COLONEL ROBERT E. Awarded O.B.E. in September, 1945, for services in the Mediterranean theatre of war; also awarded American Legion of Merit. Son of Mr William

Field-Marshall Sir H. Alexander congratulates Lt.-Col. Robert E. Macdonald, O.B.E., and Legion of Merit.

Macdonald, St. Louis, and grandson of the late Mr and Mrs Robert Macdonald, The Smithy, Swiney, Lybster.

Officer of the British Empire.

GUNN, WING-COMDR. G. R., M.B., Ch.B., Royal Air Force. Awarded O.B.E. Three years' service in India. Son of the late Mr Donald Gunn and of Mrs J. H. Gunn, 48 Blacket Place, Edinburgh, and grandson of the late Mr and Mrs William Gunn, Camilla Street, Halkirk.

KEIR, SQN.-LEADER RONALD J., Royal Air Force. Awarded O.B.E. in New Year Honours List, 1946. Younger son of Mr William Keir, I.S.O., M.B.E., late general inspector of sea fisheries in Scotland, and grandson of the late Mr John Tait, fishcurer, Wick.

NORRISH, LT.-COLONEL T. W., Royal Corps of Signals. Awarded O.B.E. for distinguished services in North-West Europe. (In 1914-18 war served in the Navy and was awarded the Greek Medal of Merit for special services with the Greek Navy.) Native of Birmingham, and married Barbara Steven, daughter of the late Mr Thomas Steven and of Mrs Steven, 5 Harbour Terrace, Wick.

Distinguished Service Medal.

RANKIN, CHIEF MOTOR MECHANIC PERCIVAL, R.N. Awarded D.S.M. "for leadership and skill shown in a motor torpedo boat in an action during

75

the night of July 17-18 (1944) with enemy coastal forces." Eldest son of Rev. Wm. P. and Mrs Rankin, Bracknell, Berkshire, and formerly of Keiss Baptist Church.

Military Medal.

CROSS, LIEUT. JOHN D., Seaforths. Awarded M.M. Taken prisoner at St. Valery and escaped. Killed in action at Anzio Beach Head, Italy, on 19th March, 1944. Son of Mr and Mrs F. Cross, Murray Road, Invergordon, and married Miss Vera Harper, Wick.

Distinguished Flying Cross.

FINLAYSON, LIEUT. ROBERT M., U.S. Army Air Corps. Awarded D.F.C. Although on the day he was shot down his aircraft sustained severe damage, and two of its crew were killed by flak, he remained at his bomb sight and released his bombs exactly over the target, destroying an enemy airfield. Medal awarded for his steadfast determination and devotion to duty.

Lieut. Finlayson is a son of Mr and Mrs H. G. Finlayson, Peoria, Illinois, and grandson of the late Mr and Mrs D. Finlayson, Castletown. He was made prisoner in Germany about April, 1945.

GRAHAM, SQDN.-LEADER JOHN C., R.A.F. Awarded D.F.C. in March, 1945, for operations against submarines. This officer, stated the citation, "has a long record of outstanding courage, determination, and devotion to duty. Both in the air and on the ground he has set a magnificent example to all." A Canadian, he joined the R.A.F. in peace time, and had the honour of being mentioned in despatches (1943). Married Doreen Bremner, youngest daughter of Mr and Mrs D. Bremner, 22 West Banks Terrace, Wick.

KRUGER, FLYING OFFICER WILLIAM S., R.A.A.F. Awarded D.F.C., 1945. Married Barbara, daughter of Mr and Mrs William Calder, Eastside, Dunnet.

MAITLAND, FLIGHT-LIEUT. IAN, R.A.F. The official citation stated that this officer had participated in many sorties against targets deep in enemy territory, taking part in repeated attacks on Rostock and such heavily defended areas as Kiel, Hamburg, Essen, Huls, and other targets in the Ruhr. As wireless operator, he has rendered valuable service in assisting in the safe return of his aircraft in bad weather. During an attack on Huls in October, 1941, his aircraft was attacked by three enemy fighters, but Flying Officer (as he then was) Maitland's vigilance and skilful directions enabled his captain to out-manoeuvre the attackers. On a number of occasions he has extinguished, by machine-gun fire, concentrations of searchlights. Twice at Rostock, from a height of a few hundred feet, he shot up the airfield adjoining the Heinkel works and set a number of buildings on fire. "His

courage and efficiency as gunnery officer," the statement concluded, "have had a beneficial effect upon the standard of gunnery in the squadron."

Flight-Lieut. Maitland was killed in action over Flanders in August, 1942, aged 37 years. Eldest son of Mr and Mrs John Maitland, Fasnacloich, Appin, Argyll and grand-nephew of Mrs Barnie, Boultach, Latheron.

SMITH, CAPTAIN GEORGE S., Eighth American Air Force. Awarded D.F.C. and Oak Leaf Clusters on two later occasions (in 1944) for extraordinary achievements while serving as Air Commander of A.A.F. heavy bomber formations in aerial assaults on Nazi military and industrial installations.

Captain Smith "demonstrated outstanding qualities of leadership" and "marked professional aptitude and skill in combat . . . under hazardous and dangerous circumstances."

Son of Mr and Mrs Thomas Smith, Grosse Pointe, Michigan, U.S.A., and grandson of the late Mr David Cormack and of Mrs Cormack, Leens, Alterwall, Lyth.

Distinguished Flying Medal.

FAIRWEATHER, SERGT. STANLEY J., R.A.F. Awarded D.F.M. in May, 1941, for shooting down two enemy aircraft. He is well known in Wick and Keiss. Youngest son of Mr and Mrs J. Fairweather, 55 Ferry Road, Leith (who are natives of Caithness).

STEVEN, SERGT.-OBSR. (Later Squadron Leader). ALASTAIR W., R.A.F. Awarded D.F.M. for displaying exceptional ability and devotion to duty during a daylight attack on Kiel on June, 1941. Youngest son of Mr and Mrs George Steven, 2 Roull Road, Corstorphine, Edinburgh (and formerly of Wick), who had another son – Pilot Officer Douglas M. Steven – killed in a flying accident in 1941.

British Empire Medal.

CAMPBELL, CHIEF ENGINEER JAMES, Merchant Navy. Awarded B.E.M. for saving the minesweeping trawler in which he was serving and the lives of the crew. Ship was drifting helplessly in a gale when, although scalded by escaping steam, Campbell repaired damaged boiler tubes and got the ship under control. This was in the winter of 1942.

Campbell is married man with six children whose home is in Grimsby. He is grandson of Mr and Mrs James Oag, 31 Smith Terrace, Wick.

MOWAT, MR DONALD, Ship's Electrician. Awarded B.E.M. for gallantry at sea. In September, 1941, he and the captain, chief engineer and doctor stayed aboard their torpedoed ship and kept her afloat for 17 hours until she sank when in tow.

Donald Mowat (6ft tall and weighing 16 stones) was formerly a traffic policeman in Edinburgh. He is son of Lieut. Gavin Mowat, Edinburgh City Police (retired) who, as well as his wife, is native of Scarfskerry.

Member of the British Empire.

BADENOCH, SURGEON-LIEUT. FRANCIS R., M.B., Ch.B., R.N.V.R. Awarded M.B.E. in September, 1941, for "courage in rescue work during enemy air raids on Portsmouth." Grandson of the late Mr and Mrs Francis Reid, North Keiss. Parents resided in Dollar.

DAVIDSON, MAJOR A. H., Royal Engineers. Awarded M.B.E. in New Year Honours List, 1946; in 1943 awarded Certificate of Commendation. Former science teacher in Wick High School, late of Oban. Native of Tobermory.

INGLIS, RADIO OFFICER ALEXANDER, Merchant Navy. Awarded M.B.E. in September, 1943. One of three members of a ship's crew decorated for courage and devotion to duty at sea. Married and home in Edinburgh. Grandson of the late Mr Robert Mowat, Rockhill, Aukengill.

Croix de Guerre.

WHEATLEY-SMITH, SQDN.-LEADER THOMAS R., R.A.F. Awarded Croix de Guerre and recommended for decoration for his part in the Normandy and Arnhem airborne operations. He was mentioned in despatches. Later on active service in Burma. Native of Tunbridge Wells, Kent. Wife (Anne Budge) and two children resided 18 Bexley Terrace, Wick.

American Decorations.

CLYNE, FLYING OFFICER H. W. Awarded U.S. Air Medal. Son of the late Mr Daniel Clyne, headmaster of Gorgie School, Edinburgh, and of Mrs Clyne, 40 Saughtonhall Avenue. Father belonged to Watten.

MALCOLM, LIEUT. GEORGE S., U.S. Air Force. Awarded Air Medal with two Oak Leaf Clusters in November, 1944. He was a navigator on a B-17, and the awards were given for "exceptionally meritorious achievement while participating in fifteen separate bombing combat missions over enemy-occupied Continental Europe." The citation added: "The courage, coolness and skill displayed by this officer reflect great credit upon himself and the armed forces of the United States."

Lieut. Malcolm was made a prisoner of war in Germany in March, 1944. Son of Mr George W. Malcolm, Sturgis, South Dakota, U.S.A. whose late parents (Mr and Mrs John Malcolm) resided 25 Brown Place, Wick.

SUTHERLAND, STAFF-SERGT. THOMAS M., American Infantry. Awarded Bronze Star Medal for initiative and courage in action on February 23, 1945, when he risked his life in support of his company's operations. Holder of the Purple Heart. Son of Mr and Mrs T. Sutherland, 2904 Walnut Street, Erie, P.A., and grandson of the late Mr Tom L. Sutherland, of Stemster, Bower, and later of 8 Girnigoe Street, Wick.

Mentioned in Despatches.

APPLEGATE, SERGT. ROY G., Seaforths. (Middle East – January, 1944). Native of Evanton. When in Wick was goalkeeper for Thistle F.C.

GASS, CAPTAIN THOMAS, R.A.M.C. (N.W. Europe – 1945.) Elder son of Mr and Mrs Gass, "Olrig", Carluke, and grandson of the late Mr and Mrs J. J. Murray, Gladstone Cottage, Castletown.

GUNN, FLIGHT-LIEUT. ALASTAIR D.M., Royal Air Force. Twice mentioned in despatches. Taken prisoner in Norway after flying from Wick Aerodrome and was one of 50 R.A.F. officers shot after recapture by the Germans following an attempt to escape. Younger son of Dr J. T. Gunn and of Mrs Gunn, Deansland, Auchterarder.

MORRISON, MAJOR R., Royal Army Intelligence Corps. Mentioned in despatches in recognition of gallant and distinguished services in North-West Europe. (Early in 1941 he was attached to the Intelligence staff at Wick Aerodrome.) Eldest son of Mr and Mrs D. Morrison, 22 Commiston Terrace, Edinburgh, and grandson of the late Mr T. L. Sutherland, 8 Girnigoe Street, Wick.

MURRAY, STAFF-SERGT. JOSEPH F., Australian I.F. Mentioned in despatches in recognition of distinguished services in the Middle East (including Egypt, East Africa, The Western Desert, Sudan, Greece, Crete, Syria, and Tobruk) during the period February to July, 1941. Third son of Mrs Murray and the late Mr John Murray, Melbourne, Australia. and grandson of the late Robert Morris, Reiss Lodge, Wick.

SIMPSON, CORPL. W., Royal Army Medical Corps. Twice mentioned in despatches. Was prisoner of war in Germany for four years. Second son of Police Constable J.M. Simpson, 3 Malvern Road, Hampton, Middlesex, who is a native of Stroma.

SMITH, SERGT. JAMES G., R.A.F. (N.W. Europe – March, 1945.) Wife (née Chattie Budge) and two young children resided at 23 Green Road, Wick. Parents (Mr and Mrs Charles Smith) at St. Catherine's Place, Kirkwall.

TAIT, LT.-COLONEL ALISTAIR M., R.A.M.C., 10th Indian Division. Mentioned in despatches for gallant and distinguished services. Overseas since 1940. Eldest son of Mr A. J. Tait, rector of Stirling High School, and of Mrs Tait, Glenlora, Bridge of Allan (both of whom were formerly on Miller Academy teaching staff), and grandson of Mrs Morrison, 3 Durness Street, Thurso.

WARNETT, CORPL. WALTER G., Royal Marines. (Mentioned July, 1943.) Holder of Long Service and Good Conduct Medal after 15 years' service. Elder son of ex-Section Officer William Warnett, coastguard, late of Barrogill Street, Wick, and brother of Mrs R. Finch, 40 Burn Street, Wick.

WATSON, LIEUT. ROY, Australians. (Mentioned June, 1944.) Served in Middle East and New Guinea. Eldest son of Mr and Mrs J. Watson, North Geelong, Australia, and grandson of the late Mr and Mrs Henry Lyall, Henrietta Street, Wick.

Commended for Bravery.

COOK, CAPTAIN JOHN E., Merchant Navy. 31st August, 1943 – Received from the King expression of commendation for brave conduct when his ship encountered enemy ships, submarines and aircraft. Awarded Order of the Red Star by the Presidium of the Supreme Council of the Union of Soviet Socialist Republics for courageous services in the carriage of armaments to the Soviet Union. Son of Rev. Matthew and Mrs Cook, Baptist Manse, Falkirk, who had seven sons (born in Keiss) with 51st Division in France, and one of them was made prisoner of war in Germany.

Civilians Honoured During the War Years.

SINCLAIR, SIR ARCHIBALD, M.P., Baronet of Ulbster, Secretary of State for Air – Created Knight of the Thistle in King's Birthday Honours List, 1941.

SINCLAIR, MR GEORGE FLETT, deputy general manager (Road Services), London Transport – Made Knight of the Order of the British Empire (K.B.E.) in King's Birthday Honours List, 1945, for special services rendered to his country during the war. Also received Order of the Patriotic War (First Class) from Supreme Soviet of the U.S.S.R. for the successful fulfilment of assignments in transporting war supplies and foodstuffs across Iran to the Soviet Union. Son of the late Mr and Mrs G. F. Sinclair, Sinclair Terrace, Wick.

ALEXANDER, MR JAMES T., secretary and treasurer Imperial Bank of India, Madras, gazetted Companion of the Indian Empire (C.I.E.) in New Year Honours List, 1943. At the outbreak of war he was appointed Deputy Controller of enemy firms in Bombay. Youngest son of the late Mr and Mrs George Alexander, Thurso.

KENNEDY, DR JOHN R., Dunbeath. Made Member of the Royal Victorian Order (M.V.O.) in October, 1942, for his services following the air crash in which the Duke of Kent was killed. Doctor in Dunbeath for more than 40 years.

BREMNER, MR WILLIAM ALEX., Glencairn House, Stroma. Awarded British Empire Medal (Civil Division) in New Year Honours List, 1946, in recognition of valuable service to the Admiralty as auxiliary coastguard, H.M. Coastguard Service. Well-known Stroma fisherman. Served in 1914-18 war and was coxswain of the leading vessel when the attack was made on Zeebrugge on St. George's Day, 1918.

BUDGE, SKIPPER THOMAS, fisherman, 11 Argyle Square, Wick. Awarded British Empire Medal (Civil Division) in King's Birthday Honours List, 1943. A leader in Caithness fishing affairs since the last war, in which he served in the Navy. Had two sons on service.

MUNRO, MR JOHN, temporary postman, Thurso. Awarded British Empire Medal (Civil Division) in New Year Honours List, 1946.

COUPER, MR JAMES, hon. secretary of Shetland Local Savings Committee. Made Member of the British Empire in New Year Honours List, 1946. Native of Wick, and brother of Police Constable Couper, Watten.

MACLEOD, MR JOHN B., acting coxswain of Thurso lifeboat. Made Member of the British Empire in King's New Year Honours List, 1945. Home address – 41 Shore Street, Thurso. Skipper of local motorboat "Learig".

MACLEOD, MR JOHN A., manager of the Calgary District of the Metropolitan Life Insurance Company; president of the Alberta Division of the Canadian Red Cross Society, and actively associated with numerous patriotic campaigns. Made Officer of the British Empire in King's Honours List announced on Dominion Day, 1946. Native of Caithness, and son of the late Mr and Mrs James Macleod, Roster, Clyth.

MATHESON, MR EDWARD. Made Member of the British Empire in King's New Year Honours List, 1945. Seventeen years with Imperial Bank of Iran. Son of the late Rev. and Mrs Matheson, Lybster.

MOORE, MR JOHN A., town clerk, Wick. Made member of the British Empire in King's Birthday Honours List, 1942.

OLSON, MR JAMES W., M.A., headmaster of Findochty junior secondary school. Made Member of the British Empire in King's Birthday Honours List, 1945. Officer in Seaforths last war. Former dux pupil of Castletown H.G. School. Son of Mr Hugh Olson, Aberdeen, formerly a merchant in Castletown.

ROSIE, MR PETER, Civil Defence Controller for the Borough of Epsom and Ewell (Surrey). Made Member of the British Empire in King's Birthday Honours List, 1945. Native of Keiss, where mother resided. Had a long and distinguished police career, serving for 27 years and retiring as a Chief Inspector of the C.I.D. at Scotland Yard.

SUTHERLAND, CAPTAIN CHARLES, Dundee Home Guard. Decorated by the King with the M.B.E. in the summer of 1941. "Charlie" lost both legs in the last war. An expert rifleman and Bisley prizeman. Son of the late Mr Peter Sutherland, formerly headmaster of Watten School.

WATERS, DR GEORGE A., Editor of "The Scotsman". Knighthood conferred on him in King's Honours List – June, 1944. Native of Thurso.

ANGUS, FIREMASTER CHARLES, late of Renfrewshire Brigade. Awarded King's Police and Fire Services Medal in New Year Honours List, 1942. Holder of O.B.E. and various other medals. Native of Castletown, and brother of Mr George Angus, Breadalbane Terrace, Wick.

CORMACK, MR WILLIAM K., Chief Constable of Caithness. Awarded King's Police Medal in King's Birthday Honours List, 1941. A.R.P. Controller for county of Caithness.

SUTHERLAND, LIEUT. WILLIAM S., Glasgow Police. Awarded "King Christianden Tiendes Fribendsmedaille" in recognition of valuable assistance given to the Danish Government during the war years. This medal was struck by the King of Denmark to commemorate the liberation of his country from Nazi oppression. Lieut. Sutherland was officer in charge of the aliens' registration department in Glasgow. He is son of the late Constable Donald Sutherland and of Mrs Sutherland, Moray Street, Wick. Had son killed in South Africa (August, 1943).

Civilians of Caithness Connection.

CUNNISON, MR ALEXANDER, C.B., J.P., Permanent Secretary, Ministry of Pensions. Created a Knight Commander of the Bath (K.C.B.). Grandson of the late Mr David Keith, Castletown.

MACDOUGALL, REV. JOHN, St Michael's Church, Edinburgh (formerly of Wick). Made Officer of the Order of the British Empire (O.B.E.) in King's Birthday Honours, 1945 for work as secretary, Church of Scotland Committee on Huts and Canteen Work for H.M. Forces for four years.

NAESMITH, MR ANDREW, J.P. of Accrington. Made Officer of the Order of the British Empire in King's Birthday Honours, 1944. Grandson of the late Mr and Mrs John Sinclair, Lhaid, Occumster, and nephew of the late Mrs Harvey, The Bungalow, Newton Road, Wick.

WARNOCK, MR JOHN CARSWELL, B.Sc. Made Officer of the Order of the British Empire in King's New Year Honours, 1943. Agricultural organiser for Caithness. Probably the youngest member in the agricultural world to have received this honour.

THAIN, MR ALEXANDER, 14 Eltringham Gardens, Edinburgh. Awarded M.B.E. (Civil Divison) in King's New Year Honours, 1946. Civil Defence Worker, and later appointed chairman of the Civil Defence Welfare Council for the City of Edinburgh. Nephew of the late Mr A. Thain, J.P., M.B.E., 1 Breadalbane Crescent, Wick.

Caithnessia's
Roll of Honour

YOUR PAGE.
for insertion of photo, or particulars
of any relative or friend

KILLED, OR DIED ON SERVICE.

ADAMSON, PTE. MURDO C., Gordon Highdrs. Killed at the Mareth Line – March 28, 1943. Draper to trade; later insurance agent. Youngest son of Mr and Mrs M. Adamson, Hill of Mid-Clyth.

ALEXANDER, SEAMAN WILLIAM G., Royal Navy Patrol Service. Aged 30 years. Drowned in the course of his duties at St. Mary's Holm, Kirkwall – March 19, 1942. Native of Wick (home address – 39 Kinnaird Street) and painter to trade. Married, and at the time of his death wife and family resided at 1 Terrace Street, Embo, Dornoch. Buried at Dornoch.

ALLAN, PTE. ALEXANDER. Aged 22 years. Killed in action (probably at Tobruk) – January, 1943. Employed in B.L. Bank, Thurso. Only son of Mrs Allan, George Street, Thurso, and of the late Alexr. Allan, farmer.

ANDERSON, PILOT OFFICER WILLIAM, Royal Air Force. Awarded D.F.C. Reported missing over Germany in Novr., 1943; later presumed killed. Completed 53 operational flights over enemy territory. Joiner to trade. Only son of James M. Anderson, 3 Dempster Street, Wick. Wife and child resided in Glamorgan, South Wales.

Let the zephyrs sigh o'er their watery graves,

Let the rain clouds weep whilst the sea winds moan!

Let the sea-birds cry 'midst the wailing waves,

Whilst the sea doth keep what it claims for its own.

– H. HENDERSON

ANDERSON, SEAMAN JAMES, H.M.S. "Jervis Bay." Lost his life in the sinking of the ship – Novr. 6, 1940. Motor driver. Married. Home address – Old Schoolhouse, Thrumster.

BAIKIE, CAPTAIN WILLIAM COGHILL, Merchant Navy. Presumed killed when his ship s.s. "British Viscount" (British Tanker Co.) was torpedoed on April 3, 1941. Wife (Euphemia Cheyne, daughter of the late Mr and Mrs Cheyne, Mey and Melvich) and son resided at 4 Sinclair Terrace, Wick. Captain Baikie was a son of the late Mr James Baikie, Mey, and of Mrs Baikie, 4 Sinclair Tce.

BAIKIE, SEAMAN DONALD J., Royal Navy Patrol Service. Aged 21 years. Lost at sea on June 16, 1942, on H.M.S. "Tranquil", and seven weeks later his body was found at Deal. Buried in St. James Cemetery, Dover. Second son of Mr and Mrs James Baikie, West End, Lybster.

BAIN, SEAMAN JAMES, Royal Navy Reserve. Aged 27 years. Lost with the "Jervis Bay" on Novr. 6, 1940. Married. Home address – 18 Wellington Street, Wick. Second son of Mr and Mrs James S. Bain, 74 Nicholson Street, Wick.

BAIN, SPR. WILLIAM J. C., Royal Engineers. Aged 23 years. Killed at Salerno, Italy – Septr. 16, 1943. Joiner to trade. Youngest son of Mr and Mrs David Bain, 14 Wilson Street, Thurso.

BAIN, PETTY OFFICER DONALD, Royal Navy. Aged 29 years. Posted missing, presumed killed, in the loss of H.M.S. "Repulse" – Decr. 10, 1941. Joined Navy 10 years previously. Married. Home address – 5 New Houses, Papigoe. Second son of the late James Bain and of Mrs Bain, 5 Henrietta Street, Wick.

BAIN, SEAMAN JOHN M., Royal Naval Reserve. Aged 27 years. Lost with the "Jervis Bay" on Novr. 6, 1940. Youngest son of the late Mrs Bain, and of William Bain, 24 Kinnaird Street, Wick.

BAIN, GNR. GEORGE, Royal Artillery. Aged 35 years. Killed at Marsa Brega – Decr. 14, 1942. (Buried in Benghazi.) Timber merchant's lorry man. Married. Home address – 75 Henrietta Street, Wick. Eldest son of Mr and Mrs Alexr. Bain, 11 Henrietta Street.

BAIN, PTE. DAVID, Highland Light Infantry. Aged 32 years. Killed in Western Europe – May 2, 1945. Cooper to trade. Youngest son of the late William Bain, fisherman, and Mrs Bain, 29 Vansittart Street, Wick.

BANKS, PTE. WILLIAM, 140th Pioneer Corps. Contracted serious illness while on service and discharged March, 1944. Died at Scarmclett, Bower – Jany. 28, 1945. Formerly farmworker at Murza, Bower. Eldest son of Mr and Mrs William Banks, 15 Boathaven Road, Wick. (Father served six years in R.A. and in Seaforths 1914-18).

BOOTH, PTE. GEORGE A., 2nd Seaforth Highdrs. Aged 22 years. Killed in action June 12, 1940, and buried at Commiere of Veulettes. Served apprenticeship as a grocer with Mr D. Shearer, Thurso, and joined Supplementary Reservists prior to outbreak of war. Parents resided at 2 Durness Street, Thurso.

Details of parentage, home address etc. in these lists are given as at time casualty was announced.

BREMNER, SURGEON LIEUT.-COMDR. ROBERT M., M.B., Ch.B., Royal Navy. Aged 37 years. Killed during air raid on English south-east town – April 3, 1942. (Buried at Wick.) Joined Navy, 1932. Honoured posthumously. Elder son of the late John Bremner, fishcurer, and of Mrs Bremner, 6 Upper Dunbar Street, Wick.

BREMNER, SEAMAN DAVID R., Royal Naval Reserve. Aged 29 years. Lost with the "Jervis Bay" – Novr. 6, 1940. Fisherman. Married. Home address – 31 Smith Terrace, Wick. Third son of Mr and Mrs Donald Bremner, 37 Cairndhuna Terrace, Wick.

BREMNER, SEAMAN WILLIAM, Royal Naval Reserve. Aged 32 years. Lost with the "Jervis Bay" – Novr. 6, 1940, Fisherman. Youngest son of Mr and Mrs John Bremner, 5 Macarthur Street, Wick.

BREMNER, L.-CPL. ALEXR., 5th Seaforth Highdrs. Aged 22 years. Killed in Middle East on April 6, 1943. Only son of Mr and Mrs Bremner, Haster Farm, Wick. (Best known in Shebster and Forss districts).

BREMNER, GNR. WILLIAM, Royal Artillery. Aged 26 years. Posted missing in Far East in Jany., 1941; six months later as prisoner in Hong-Kong. Posted missing second time (Octr. 2, 1942) and presumed lost at sea in the sinking of the ship "Lisbon Maru". Grandson of the late Mr William Bremner, shoemaker, Janetstown, Wick.

BREMNER, PTE. DONALD J., 5th Seaforth Highdrs. Aged 22 years. Awarded Military Medal. Killed in Sicily – August 2, 1943. Son of the late Donald John Bremner and of Mrs Bremner, 5 Murrayfield, Castletown.

BREMNER, PTE JAMES (Hamish), 2nd Cambs. Regiment. Aged 34 years. Died in Thailand – Jany 22, 1943, while prisoner of war in Japanese hands. Captured at fall of Singapore – Feb., 1942. Intimation of death received Novr. 1, 1945. Youngest son of James Bremner (late P.O. Official) and Mrs Bremner, 96 Douglas Ave., Walthamstow, London, E.17 (formerly of Wick), and husband of Marie Thurston, Cambridge.

BREMNER, PTE. DAVID M., 6th Seaforth Highdrs. Aged 21 years. Reported missing at Dunkirk, later as killed on May 28, 1940. Called up with Militia. Youngest son of the late William Bremner and of Mrs Bremner, 29 Huddart Street, Wick.

BREMNER, FLT.-SERGT. W. S., Royal Air Force. Posted missing March 22, 1944, later as presumed killed on that date. Joined R.A.F. in 1939 and took part in numerous operational flights over enemy territory. Eldest son of Mrs A. Bremner, Mid-Clyth.

BROWN, PTE. JOHN M., 5th Seaforth Highdrs. Aged 31 years. Killed at El Alamein on Novr. 2, 1942. Grocer to trade. Son of Mr and Mrs Brown, 58 Duncan Street, Thurso, and husband of Marjory Brown, Seaton Cottage, Pitmedden.

BRUCE, PETTY OFFICER JAMES R., Royal Naval Reserve. Aged 33 years. Died in Berwick Infirmary on 3rd April, 1941, through wounds received in action on board H.M.T. "Cramond Island." Seine-net fisherman. Married. Wife resided 72 Kinnaird Street, Wick. (Interred at Wick.)

BRUCE, LEADING STOKER WILLIAM, Royal Navy. H.M.S. "Punjabi." Aged 25 years. Posted missing, presumed killed at sea, while on convoy going to Russia – May 1, 1942. Five years in Navy. Married. Home Address – Baillie's Buildings, Castletown. Son of Mrs Paterson, Shebster, Reay.

BRUCE, L-SERGT. JAMES J. (Hamish), 7th Seaforth Highdrs. Aged 21 years. Killed in action near Horst, Holland – November 22, 1944. Interred in Venray British Cemetery. Only son of the late William Bruce (railway guard) and of Mrs Bruce, 3 Miller Avenue, Wick.

BRUCE, CORPL. ALEXANDER (Sandy), 5th Seaforth Highdrs. Aged 24 years. Died of wounds in France, August 15, 1944. Employed on Scrabster Farm. Youngest son of Mr and Mrs Alex. Bruce, Scrabster.

BUDGE, BOSUN JAMES ALEXANDER. Lost at sea through enemy action in January, 1942. Fourth son of the late Mr and Mrs William Budge, Co-operative Buildings, Wick.

BUDGE, BOY JOHN, Royal Navy. Aged 17 years. Reported missing, believed lost, when H.M.S. "Royal Oak" was torpedoed at Scapa on 14th October, 1939. Joined Navy two years previously. Youngest son of the late Mr and Mrs D. Budge, Louisburgh Street, Wick.

BUDGE, SERGT. WILLIAM B., 5th Seaforth Highdrs. Aged 26 years. Died in Haymeads Hospital, Hertfordshire, on 8th February, 1944 (result of road accident). Took part in campaign from El Alamein to Sicily and was twice wounded. Second son of Mr and Mrs John A. Budge, 31 High Street, Wick. Interred at Wick..

BUDGE, GUARDSMAN WILLIAM, Scots Guards. Aged 20 years. Killed in Italy on 13th Novr., 1943. Only son of Mr and Mrs William Budge, Greystones, Stirkoke.

BUDGE, DRIVER WILLIAM C., Royal Army

Service Corps. Aged 25 years. Posted missing in Middle East on 28th April, 1941, later presumed killed at sea off coast of Greece on April 26-27, 1941. Joined Army in 1937. Youngest son of the late Angus Budge and of Mrs Budge, 1 Baron's Well, Wick.

CALDER, CHIEF OFFICER WILLIAM, s.s. "Arabistan." Aged 38 years. Ship posted missing on August 14, 1942; later as sunk by enemy action in So. Pacific when homeward bound. Believed to be only one survivor (the chief engineer) of crew of 60. He was taken prisoner by Japanese but not allowed to give information until released in autumn of 1945. C.O. Calder was only son of the late Captain Charles Calder, Dunnet, who for many years was chief pilot on the Suez Canal. Home is in Dunnet where wife and young daughter (whom he never saw) resided.

CALDER, SGT. PILOT GEORGE S., Royal Air Force. Aged 21 years. Killed in a flying accident on 15th October, 1942. Before the war entered the Forestry Commission. Elder son of Mr and Mrs K. Calder, Barrock, Dunnet. Buried in Corsback Cemetery.

CAMERON, ALEXANDER M., A/Riggers Mate, H.M.S. "Foss". Aged 32 years. Died suddenly at Aultbea, Ross-shire, on June 9, 1942. Wife and family resided at 6 Bayview Terrace, Thurso.

CAMPBELL, MAJOR-GENERAL JOHN CHARLES, V.C., D.S.O., M.C. Aged 48 years. Killed in a motoring accident in Middle East – February 10, 1942. Born in Thurso, and was son of the late Mr D. A. Campbell, formerly of Ulbster Estates Office. Mother was sister of the late Provost W. Mackay, Thurso. Wife and daughters resided Flore Fields, Flore, Northants.

CAMPBELL, FLIGHT-LIEUT. ALASTAIR WILLIAM, Royal Air Force. Aged 25 years. Missing on meteorological air operations on Octr. 28, 1944, later presumed to have lost his life on that date. Husband of Janet A. Paterson, and only son of Mr and Mrs D. G. Campbell, 48 Princes Street, Thurso.

CAMPBELL, LEADING-SEAMAN DONALD. Aged 29 years. Died in Mount Vernon Hospital, Northwood, Middlesex – November 27, 1943. Husband of Eileen Fakay and youngest son of the late John Campbell and Mrs Campbell, 29 Cairndhuna Terrace, Wick. (Interred in Wick Cemetery.)

CAMPBELL, SERGT. ALEX. HENRY, Calgary Highlanders. Killed in Holland Decr. 10, 1944. Home address – 2127 16th Street, West Calgary, Alberta, Canada. His father (Angus Campbell) was a native of Thurso and his mother belonged

to Reay. Nephew of Mrs E. M. Sinclair, "Craigview," Portskerra, Melvich.

CAMPBELL, GNR, DONALD G., ——. Aged 35 years. Died in Stannington Military Hospital, Northumberland – Decr. 27, 1943. Husband of Margaret Henderson, and elder son of Mrs Campbell and the late William Campbell, Upper Smerral, Latheronwheel.

CAMPBELL, SPR. JOHN WILLIAM, Royal Engineers. Aged 27 years. Died in Forse Military Hospital, Latheron (after a long illness) on January 3, 1944. Formerly of Braehour, Scotscalder.

CAMPBELL, SGLN. SINCLAIR, Royal Corps of Signals. Aged 31 years. Drowned off India – Novr. 9, 1942. Well-known in Watten and Lyth districts where he had been a farm-servant. Youngest son of the late Alexander Campbell of Upper Achow, Lybster and of Mrs Campbell. Wife resided East Ham, London.

CAMPBELL, PTE. WILLIAM, Scottish Commando Battalion. Fell in action in Syria – June 9, 1941. Parents resided at Janetstown, Thurso.

CAMPBELL, GEORGE, Thurso. Aged 34 years. Died in Dunbar Hospital – Novr. 13, 1945. Ex-Sergeant of 1st Seaforths – a regular. Invalided out of Army in 1942 as a result of a serious accident in Shanghai in 1940. Motor hirer. Married. Home address – Sinclair Street, Thurso.

CLARK, SERGT. DONALD G., Royal Air Force. Flight Engineer. Aged 24 years. Reported missing, later as killed in action over Berlin _ June 3rd, 1941. Four years in R.A.F. Fourth son of Mr and Mrs Daniel Clark, 5 Argyle Square, Wick.

CLARK, CORPL. TEMPLE F.S., Royal Air Force. Wireless operator-air gunner. Aged 21 years, and brother of above. Killed in action over Holland – May 10, 1940. Joined Air Force four years previously and was with first squadron to go to France (1939).

CLARK, L/SERGT. JAMES, 5th Seaforth Highdrs. Aged 28 years. Killed at Tripoli – Jany. 21, 1943. Employed at Watten Mains and later at Isauld, Reay. Second son of Mr and Mrs Henry Clark, Watten Mains, and husband of Christina Miller, Quoybrae, Watten.

COGHILL, SECOND-HAND GEORGE G., Royal Navy. R.N. Patrol Service. Served on M.B. "Matoya". Aged 45 years. Killed on active service – January, 1941. Buried at Shotley. Husband of Elizabeth Petrie, 40 Albion Road, Edinburgh, and eldest son of the late William Coghill and of Mrs Coghill, Roadside, Reiss, Wick.

COGHILL, SERGT. WILLIAM, 5th Seaforth Highdrs. Aged 31 years. Killed at El Alamein – Novr. 2, 1942. Prior to the war was employed at Nottingham Mains, Lybster. Eldest son of Mr and Mrs William Coghill, Lochside, Castletown, and husband of Jessie Cooper, Haimer, Thurso.

COGHILL, PTE. JAMES, Seaforth Highdrs. Posted missing, later as killed in France on June 4, 1940. Son of Mr William Coghill, Phillips Mains, Mey.

COOPER, MARINE JAMES W. A. Aged 24 years. Reported missing, presumed lost on board H.M.S. "Hermes" – April 9, 1942. Third son of Mr and Mrs J. Cooper, Geise Farm, Thurso.

CORMACK, ABLE-SEAMAN ANGUS. Aged 21 years. Reported missing, presumed drowned on active service in April, 1942. Son of Mrs Christina Cormack, Ben Bhraggie, Lybster.

COWAN, PTE. WILLIAM G., ——. Aged 28 years. Killed in Middle East in April, 1943. Third son of Mr and Mrs Cowan, Victoria Cottage, Janetstown, Thurso.

CUMMING, SERGT. HUNTLY GORDON, M.P.S., Royal Army Medical Corps. Accidently killed in Middle East on September 20, 1942. Youngest son of Mr and Mrs Cumming, 3 Traill Street, Thurso.

The moment's gloom will pass,
  The sun again will shine,
The flowers begem the grass
  Around thy hallowed shrine.
And in the days ahead
Our footsteps shall be led
Where lies our noble dead,
  Both yours and mine.

– WM. CORMACK.

CUNNINGHAM, SERGT. ROBERT, Royal Air Force. Died July 1, 1942, following an aircraft accident. Crashed near Fowey, Cornwall. Had been many times over enemy territory. Joined R.A.F. before the war. Youngest son of Mr and Mrs George Cunningham, Village, Dunbeath (late of Knockglass).

DAVIDSON, MAJOR JOHN HENRY, D.S.O., 5th Seaforth Highdrs. Aged 33 years. Died of wounds in Sicily – August 4, 1943. Well-known farmer and a B.Sc. (Agr.) of Edinburgh. Husband of Isobel Stewart, Lower Dounreay, and only son of the late Mr and Mrs George Davidson, Oldhall, Watten.

DAVIDSON, QMR. JAMES R., Royal Naval Reserve. Aged 20 years and 11 months. Lost at sea through enemy action from H.M.S. "Patroclus" (an armed merchant cruiser) on Novr. 3, 1940. Second son of Mr and Mrs James Davidson, 18 Argyle Square, Wick.

DAVIDSON, PTE. DUGALD C., 6th Seaforth Highdrs. Aged 24 years. Wounded in France and died in an emergency hospital in England – May 30, 1940. County's first military casualty to be reported. (Buried in Reay Churchyard.) Son of Mr and Mrs Alexr. Davidson, Helshedder, Reay, whose five sons served with Territorial battalions.

DOULL, COY.-SERGT.-MAJOR ALASTAIR W., 5th Seaforth Highdrs. Aged 29 years. Killed on Western Front – October 28, 1944. Fought throughout the North African campaign and was wounded at El Alamein (Octr. 1942) and again in Sicily. Only son of Mr John G.C. Doull, flesher, Lybster. Wife (Bunty Sutherland) and infant son resided at West Manse, Latheron.

DOULL, SERGT. ALEXANDER S., Royal Air Force. Aged 22 years. Killed in flying accident in South of England – January 24, 1943. Clerk with L.M.S. at Watten and Wick. Youngest son of Mr and Mrs Peter Doull, Gowrie Place, Wick. (Interred at Wick.)

DUFF-DUNBAR, CAPTAIN KENNETH J., 7th Seaforth Highdrs. Aged 27 years. Killed in Normandy on August 6, 1944. Served in North African campaign with 5th Seaforths. Only child of the late Lieut.-Commander K. J. Duff-Dunbar, D.S.O., R.N. (lost in 1914-18 war) and of Mrs K. J. Duff-Dunbar, Hempriggs House, Wick.

DUNBAR, PTE. ROBERT S., 5th Seaforth Highdrs. Aged 23 years. Killed at Wadi-el-Akarit, Tunisia – April 6, 1943. Was in Glasgow before the war. Belonged to Boultach, Latheronwheel, and son of Mr and Mrs B. Dunbar, Cogle, Watten.

DUNDAS, LIEUT. COMMANDER GEORGE C., United States Navy. Died in St. Alban's Naval Hospital, New York – December 14, 1945. Son of the late Mr and Mrs A. C. Dundas, Dunnet.

DUNDAS, SEAMAN JAMES, R.N. Patrol Service. Reported missing on war service during operations connected with the liberation of Europe on July 5, 1944, later as presumed killed. Metropolitan policeman for eight years. Wife resided at 37 Holborn Avenue, Thurso. Son of Mr and Mrs James Dundas, Achscrabster.

DUNDAS, THIRD OFFICER CECIL, Merchant Navy. Killed on s.s "Jumna" (1941 or before). Native of Stroma.

DUNNETT, THOMAS, Merchant Navy. Reported missing in the Atlantic and later presumed lost "with all his gallant crew" on October 13, 1942. Son of Mr and Mrs Thomas Dunnett, Mill of Mey, Scarfskerry.

DUNNETT, SERGT. ALEXR. J., Seaforth Highdrs. Aged 35 years. Died in Leeds Military Hospital on Novr. 22, 1943. Married (address – Aston View, Leeds), and son of Mrs Dunnett, Heatherdeep, Watten, and the late Alexr. Dunnett, joiner, Bowermadden. Brother (P.C. William Dunnett) was killed in air raid on London.

DUNNETT, CORPL. JOHN, Royal Army Ordnance Corps. Aged 32 years. Reported missing, and 18 months later as prisoner in Japanese hands and interned in Borneo. Died there on June, 7, 1945. Draper, later traveller for London firm. Brother was also a prisoner (in Italy). Second son of Mr and Mrs David Dunnett, 24 Louisburgh Street, Wick. Married, and wife resided in London.

DUNNETT, —— ALEXANDER, Seaforth Highdrs. Aged 28 years. died of wounds at a mobile casualty clearing station at Tunisia on April 8, 1943. Youngest son of the late John Dunnett and of Mrs Dunnett, Bowermadden, Bower.

DUNNETT, SERGT. DAVID, Royal Air Force. Wireless operator and air gunner. Aged 20 years. Lost his life on air operations in Middle East – Feby. 17, 1943. Younger son of Mr and Mrs Tom Dunnett, Shore, Dunbeath (formerly of Wick). (His brother Tom was prisoner of war.)

DURRAND, L.-CPL JAMES B., 5th Seaforth Highdrs. Aged 22 years. Killed in Tunisia on April 6, 1943. Assistant with Sloans Ltd., Wick. Only son of Mrs Durrand and of the late Robert Durrand, 44 Laurelbank, Wick.

ELDER, L.A.C. ALASTAIR J. B., Royal Air Force. Aged 23 years. Reported missing at sea through enemy action on Novr. 7, 1944; later presumed to have lost his life on that date. Eldest son of Mr M. A. Elder, 2 Wilson Street, Thurso, and grandson of Mr and Mrs John Black, 12 Duncan Street, Thurso (with whom he resided).

FALCONER, PTE. DAVID T., 5th Seaforth Highdrs. Aged 25 years. Killed in Tunisia on March 23, 1943. Son of Jessie Cormack, and grandson of the late David Cormack and of Mrs Cormack, Alterwall, Lyth.

FARQUHAR, SEAMAN DONALD, Merchant Navy. Aged 42 years. Lost at sea (within sight of land) when s.s. "Giralda" was bombed – Jany. 30, 1940. Wife and family resided at Sandwick; parents (Mr and Mrs James Farquhar) at 4 Argyle Square, Wick.

FERGUSON, L.-CPL. JOHN B., 5th Seaforth Highdrs. Aged 22 years. Posted wounded and missing in Middle East – January 21, 1943; later presumed to have died of wounds on or shortly after that date. Butcher's assistant, and mobilised with Territorials. Grandson of the late Hugh Mackay, Thurso, and nephew of Mrs Munro, 7 Couper Street, Thurso.

FORBES, AB.-SEAMAN JAMES WILLIAM, Merchant Navy. Aged 41 years. Lost at sea on s.s "Granta" (as result of mine explosion) – January 12, 1940. Husband of Florence Albertson, South Shields, and eldest son of Mr William Forbes, Larel, Bower.

FORBES, SERGT. JOHN H., Australian Imperial Forces. Served in Middle East, later in Java where he was taken prisoner when the island was occupied by the Japs. Worked on Burma-Thailand railway, later at Singapore, and transferred from there to Japan. The "Montevidio-Maru" (the ship carrying the prisoners) was torpedoed by an American submarine in the China Sea (Septr. 12, 1944) and Sergt. Forbes was among those lost. Second son of Mr and Mrs William Forbes, Portland Terrace, Berriedale. Married – wife and daughter resided in Melbourne, Australia.

FORBES, CORPL. ALEXANDER, M.M., 5th Seaforth Highdrs. Aged 25 years. Killed in Sicily on August 2, 1943. Posthumously awarded Military Medal. Youngest son of Mr and Mrs Donald Forbes, 11 Green Road, Wick, who held the proud distinction of having seven sons and one son-in-law on war service. Wife (Betty Macleod) and infant daughter resided at 47 Lochalsh Road, Inverness.

FORRESTER, SPR. JAMES, Royal Engineers. Aged 26 years. Died in Military Hospital. (No details – probably 1941.) Only son of James Forrester, Hillside, Gills, Canisbay, and the late Mrs Forrester.

FRASER, W. M. ALISTAIR, Royal Navy. Aged 19 years. Reported missing, presumed lost at sea – October 18, 1944. Only child of Mr and Mrs Alexr. Fraser, 22 Stratford Ave., Rochdale (formerly of Wick) and grandson of Mr and Mrs Andrew Dunnett, Mounthooly House, Wick.

FYFE, LEADING SEAMAN PETER. Aged 21 years. Lost at sea in vicinity of Algiers on February 7, 1943, when ship (H.M.T. "Tervani") was torpedoed. Only son of the late Jack Fyfe, Lorraine Cottage, Reay, and of Mrs P. G. Dalby, 16 Villette Place, Waite Street, London.

GEDDES, CHIEF PETTY OFFICER ROBERT. Died in a Military Hospital, Kirkwall, on May 12, 1944. Husband of the late Elizabeth Green, of 3 Coghill Square, Wick.

GLASS, PTE PETER M., 6th Seaforth Highdrs. Aged 20 years. Wounded in Italy on January 23, 1944, and died in Bignold Hospital, Lybster – January 17, 1945. Laundry employee. (Buried in Wick Cemetery.) Eldest son of Mr and Mrs John M. Glass, 54 Dempster Street, Wick.

GORDON, FLT.-SERGT. ALEXANDER, D.F.M., Royal Air Force. Aged 24 years. Reported missing in Middle East, on May 31, 1941, later as killed in action on that date. Joined R.A.F. nine years previously. Second son of Mr and Mrs Alex Gordon, Newton, Wick.

GRANT, SPR. ROBERT, Royal Engineers. Died in Doncaster Royal Infirmary (military wing) on March 19, 1942. Youngest son of Mr and Mrs William Grant, George Street, Halkirk.

GRANT, PTE. ROBERT T., 5th Seaforth Highdrs. Aged 21 years. Killed in Middle East on Novr. 2, 1942. Employed on Thurso East Farm. Son of Mr and Mrs William Grant, Tower Hill, Thurso.

GROAT, TPR. GEORGE, Royal Armoured Corps. Aged 23 years. Reported missing, presumed killed, in Burma on Feby. 27, 1945. Mason to trade. Fourth son of the late Neil Groat, and of Mrs Groat, Heather Inn, Thrumster, who had four other sons on service.

GUNN, LIEUT. WILLIAM A., Seaforth Highdrs. Aged 28 years. Killed in Western Europe on Octr. 26, 1944. Was on staff of Bank of Scotland at head office in Edinburgh. Third son of the late Mr and Mrs Wm. A. Gunn, 16 Rotterdam Street, Thurso, and husband of Jeanne Barry.

GUNN, LIEUT. DAVID, Royal Engineers. Aged 25 years. Killed in Italy on July 28, 1944. Joined Army a few days before outbreak of war. Became a Commando and took part in daring raids on the Continent after capitulation of France. Also saw service in India, Persia, Iraq and Sicily. Attached Indian Army. Third surviving son of Mr and Mrs John Gunn, Cairnroich, Lybster.

GUNN, CORPL. WILLIAM S., Reconnaissance Corps. Aged 27 years. Killed in N.W. Europe – Sept. 7, 1944. Brother of above. Member of London Police Force and served throughout the worst of the blitzes.

GUNN, ABLE-SEAMAN ALEXANDER, Merchant Navy. Aged 26 years. Died at sea (of pneumonia) Novr. 8, 1940. Second son of Edward Gunn and the late Mrs Gunn, 33 Cairndhuna Terrace, Wick. Survived by wife and infant son.

GUNN, CORPL. GEORGE, Canadian Army. Aged 37 years. Died in hospital in London, Ontario – August 24, 1943. Vanman, but emigrated to Canada 17 years previously. Survived by wife (native of Canada) and two daughters. Third son of Mr and Mrs John Gunn, 42 Huddart Street, Wick, who had other four sons on service.

GUNN, GNR. JOHN A., Royal Artillery (attached M.N.) Aged 26 years. Killed at sea about Octr., 1941. Employed in sawmill previous to war. Husband of Catherine Manson, 5 Miller Square, Wick, and fourth son of Mr and Mrs James Gunn, 18 Henrietta Street, Wick.

GUNN, SPR, ALASTAIR, Royal Engineers. Aged 28 years. Killed in Normandy on July 5, 1944. Youngest son of the late Donald Gunn, Brabster, Canisbay, and of Mrs Gunn, 2 Macgregor Avenue, Mosspark, Renfrew.

GUNN, PTE JOHN G. C., 5th Seaforth Highdrs. Aged 31 years. Killed in Normandy on June 29, 1944. Farm-servant at Stemster, Huna. Third son of Mr and Mrs William Gunn, Humberston Farm, Dingwall (formerly of Strath, Watten).

GUNN, PTE. WILLIAM, Anti-Tank Corps (attached 5th Seaforths). Aged 19 years. Died on way to hospital from injuries sustained while driving north in army vehicle which failed to take hair-pin bend at Balnabruich, Dunbeath, and somersaulted over steep brae – Septr. 3, 1940 (Buried at Thurso.) Son of Mr and Mrs Alex H. Gunn, Grove Lane, Thurso.

GUNN, SERGT.-NAVIGATOR JOHN F. M., Royal Air Force. Aged 27 years. Killed on air operations – Septr. 22, 1943. M.A. of Edinburgh University. Joined Metropolitan Police. Youngest son of John Gunn and the late Mrs Gunn, Barrock, Lyth.

GUNN, CORPL. DONALD BEGG, Royal Air Force. Aged 40 years. Died in Larbert Hospital – Septr. 5, 1944. (Buried at Wick.) Husband of Minnie Miller, 6 Barbara Place, Wick, and son of the late Mr and Mrs Robert Gunn, 5 Sinclair Terrace, Wick.

GUNN, L.A.C. HUGH, Royal Air Force. Aged 23 years. Died at No. 14 India General Hospital, Leimakhong, Imphal, Assam, on Octr. 16, 1944. Some time a porter at Lybster Railway Station. Youngest son of Mr and Mrs Donald Gunn, 8 Jeffrey Street, Lybster.

HARPER, LEADING SEAMAN GNR. JOHN, Royal Naval Reserve (in which he had 20 years' service). Reported missing, presumed killed – May, 1941. Rent collector with Wick Town Council. Home address – Cairndhuna Terrace, Wick. Son of Mr D. Harper and the late Mrs Harper, 15 Breadalbane Terrace, Wick.

HARPER, PTE. JAMES M., 5th Seaforth Highdrs. Aged 38 years. Died in County Hospital, Inverurie – May 1, 1941. Second son of the late John Harper, Sibster, Halkirk, and of Mrs Macdonald, The Hillocks, Altnabreac, and husband of Isabella Cormack, Milton, Wick. (Buried in Halkirk Cemetery.)

HARPER, PTE. DONALD, 2nd Seaforth Highdrs. Aged 27 years. Died of wounds in N.W. Europe – Septr. 12, 1944. (Posthumously mentioned in despatches.) Husband of Elizabeth Forbes, Larel, Bower, and third son of Mr and Mrs Harper, Carsgoe, Halkirk.

HARRIS, PTE. JAMES, 5th Seaforth Highdrs. Aged 21 years. Reported missing Novr. 2, 1942, later as killed at El Alamein on that date. Grandson of Mr and Mrs A. Banks, Hall Cottage, Mey.

HARROLD, CHIEF PETTY OFFICER JOHN M., E.R.A., H.M.S. "Penelope." Aged 23 years. Died of wounds in hospital at Naples in February, 1944. Only son of Mr and Mrs William Harrold, "Hildersay," Coulter, Aberdeen, and formerly of 32 Girnigoe Street, Wick.

HARROW, CHIEF ENGINEER WALTER, Australian Merchant Navy. Presumed lost on August 20, 1944, when his ship (a Shire liner) met with an accident. Engineer to trade, and emigrated to Australia. Son of the late Donald Harrow, Macrae Street, Wick, where sister resided.

HEDDLE, SERGT. JOHN D. R., Wireless Operator and Air Gunner. Aged 18 years. Reported missing July 7, 1942, later as killed through enemy action when on flight over Germany. This was the third massed raid in which he had taken part. Born in Caithness and employed in wireless work in Thurso. Only son of Mr and Mrs Heddle, Ham Cottage, Brough, Dunnet.

HENDRY, CHIEF ENGINEER DONALD, H.M.S. "Avanturine." Aged 49 years. Died suddenly journeying by rail to Glasgow – Feby. 19, 1943. Son of Donald Hendry, Castletown, and of the late Mrs Hendry. Husband of Alice Davidson, New York City.

HENDERSON, CHIEF PETTY OFFICER ALEXANDER, Royal Naval Reserve. Aged 36 years. Reported missing July 29, 1944, later as presumed killed through enemy action on minesweeper "Lord Wakefield," lost off Normandy. Skipper of seine-net boat "Sprig." Held R.N.R. medal for 20 years' service. Husband of Isobel B. Gunn, 18 Henrietta Street, Wick. Grandson of the late Alex. Henderson, 12 Argyle Square, Wick.

HENDERSON, GEORGE ALLAN. Aged 28 years. Died in Town and County Hospital, Wick – Decr. 26, 1946. Joined the Navy along with his twin brother early after the outbreak of war. Seriously wounded in an important naval engagement in the Mediterranean, and was long in hospital in England. Youngest son of the late James Henderson and of Mrs Henderson, "Heather Bell," Brough, Dunnet.

HUMPHREY, FLT. SERGT. JACK C.L., Royal Air Force. Aged 24 years. Posted missing on June 12, 1944, later presumed to have lost his life on that date. Member of crew of a Sunderland 'plane that was damaged and came down in the sea 40 miles off the coast of France after attacking a U-boat, believed destroyed. Joined R.A.F. Boys' Service at age of 16. Youngest son of Mr and Mrs J. G. Humphrey, Kenneth Street, Wick.

INNES, SEAMAN JOHN, Royal Naval Reserve. Aged 33 years. Lost with H.M.S. "Jervis Bay" – Novr. 6, 1940. Painter to trade. Elder son of Mr and Mrs William Innes, 8 Kinnaird Street, Wick. Married. Wife and family resided Burnside, Oldwick, Wick.

KEITH, PTE JACK, Seaforth Highdrs. Aged 27 years. Reported missing Jany. 11, 1944, in Italy; later as prisoner of war in Germany. Died at Stalag B4, Germany – June 18, 1944. Police Constable at Halifax. Husband of Catherine Pow, Edinburgh, and grandson of Mrs E. Macleod, West Banks, Wick.

KENNEDY, CHIEF RADIO OFFICER CHARLES, Merchant Navy. Aged 32 years. Lost at sea through enemy action, February 22, 1944, while serving on an oil tanker. Stated to have been killed by machine-gun fire from enemy submarine, which fired on the crew after they had taken to the ship's boats. The survivors were 37 days adrift before being picked up. Husband of Mary Watson, 4 New Houses, Dunbeath, and youngest son of John R. Kennedy, M.V.O., M.B., C.M. and the late Mrs Kennedy, Castleview, Dunbeath.

KENNEDY, RADIO OFFICER JOHN. Posted lost at sea on May 5, 1943. Only son of Mr and Mrs William Kennedy, Schoolhouse, John O'Groats, late of South Craig, Craigmillar, and husband of Isobel Sloane, Kilve, Somerset.

LEITCH, SERGT. SINCLAIR, 2nd Scots Guards. Aged 25 years. Killed at Salerno, Italy – Septr. 11, 1943. Ploughman in Lyth district. Eldest son of Mr and Mrs John Leitch, Howe, Lyth.

LEITH, PTE. ALEXANDER, Pioneer Corps. Aged 44 years. Died suddenly at Nymegan, Holland –

Novr. 25, 1945. Wife (Maudie Davidson) and family resided 33 Nicholson Street, Wick. Eldest son of the late William Leith and of Mrs Leith, 7 Harbour Terrace, Wick.

LESLIE, PTE. JOHN, Australian Imperial Forces. Aged 44 years. Died in a Japanese prisoner of war camp at Ambon – March 16, 1945. Third son of the late Robert Leslie and of Mrs Leslie, 61 Willowbank, Wick.

LEVACK, —— ALEXANDER. Lost his life at sea through enemy action – February 10, 1941. Only son of the late Alex. Levack and of Mrs Levack, Park Cottage, Brough.

LINDSAY, SEAMAN ANDREW R., Royal Navy. Aged 19 years. Killed in action March 20, 1944. Associated with the family business of Lindsay & Co., Ironmongers, Thurso. Second son of the late Bailie James Lindsay and of Mrs Elizabeth Lindsay, Olrig Street, Thurso.

LYALL, ABLE-SEAMAN ALEXANDER S., Royal Navy. Aged 19 years. Reported missing at sea March 9, 1943, and later presumed to have died. Youngest son of Mrs R. Durrand, 80 Willowbank, Wick.

LYALL, DVR. ANGUS, Royal Army Service Corps. Aged 34 years. Died in City Hospital, Edinburgh – Jany. 12, 1941. (Buried in Edinburgh.) Husband of Bella Sutherland, 6 Bonnington Road, Leith, and of Windy House, Berriedale. Youngest son of the late Mr and Mrs H. Lyall, 17 Henrietta Street, Wick.

LYALL, SGN. JOHN, Royal Corps of Signals. Aged 32 years. Died in General Hospital, Middle East – March 28, 1943. Farm-servant. Third son of Mr and Mrs David Lyall, Whitefield, Watten.

MACADAM, SERGT. JOHN S., Royal Air Force. Navigator. Aged 20 years. Reported missing on his first operational flight over enemy territory in May, 1943. Younger son of Mrs Macadam, Angle Park, Wick, and the late David Macadam, Watten Mills.

MACADIE, SERGT. WILLIAM, Royal Air Force. Air gunner. Aged 23 years. Posted missing on flying operations – Decr. 20, 1943, later presumed lost. Son of Mr and Mrs R. Macadie, Field House, Staxigoe, Wick (formerly of Skelbo).

MACADIE, PTE. THOMAS J., Sherwood Foresters. Aged 22 years. Killed in Italy in May, 1944. Called up with the Territorials when 17, and was in R.A. before transfer to Sherwood Foresters. Second son of Mr and Mrs James T. Macadie, 4 Robert Street, Wick.

MACBEATH, PTE. ARCHIBALD S., Seaforth Highdrs. Aged 19 years. Killed in Normandy –

June 28, 1944. Both parents deceased and brought up by his grandfather, Francis Macbeath, Achorn Road, Dunbeath.

MACDONALD, SEAMAN HUGH K., Merchant Navy. Aged 21 years. Killed through enemy action in summer of 1940. Only son of Mr and Mrs James Macdonald, 30 Durham Avenue, Portobello, and now of Lybster.

MACDONALD, CORPL. JOHN R., 7th Seaforth Highdrs. Aged 24 years. Killed near Moyland – Feby. 18, 1945. Previously wounded in June, 1944. Monumental mason in peace-time. Only son of Mr and Mrs Robert Macdonald, 63 Argyle Square, Wick.

MACDONALD, GUARDSMAN DONALD, 2nd Scots Guards. Died of wounds in Middle East – Septr. 25, 1943. Husband of Margaret Oag, Sarclet Village, Thrumster. Mother resided 26 Broadhaven, Wick.

MACDONALD, PIPER WILLIAM, 5th Seaforth Highdrs. Aged 28 years. Killed in Middle East – Jany. 21, 1943. Foreman on farm of Thurso-East, and member of Thurso Pipe Band. Only son of Mr and Mrs Donald Macdonald, Thurso East, Thurso.

MACDONALD, PTE. MACKINTOSH S., Pioneer Corps. Aged 36 years. Killed in France in May, 1940. Eldest son of the late Mr and Mrs Macdonald, 13 Argyle Square, Wick.

MACDONALD, FLT.-SERGT. WILLIAM L., Royal Air Force. Flight Engineer. Aged 20 years. Killed in flying accident in India – May 25, 1945. Only son of Mr and Mrs W. L. Macdonald, 22 Polwarth Crescent, Edinburgh and grandson of Mr and Mrs R. Macdonald, 16 Kinnaird Street, Wick.

MACGREGOR, FLT.-SERGT. JAMES H., Royal Air Force. Aged 29 years. Died as a result of flying accident in Oxfordshire – May 31, 1944. (Buried at Wick.) Had completed 32 operational fights over enemy territory. Was in Pulteney P.O. before enlisting. Only son of the late Seaman Thomas Macgregor, R.N.R. (lost on H.M.S. "Laurentic" in 1914-18 war) and of Mrs Macgregor, 14 Telford Street, Wick.

MACKAY, FLYING OFFICER ALEXANDER, Royal Air Force. Reported missing in June, 1943, later as missing, believed killed, as result of air operations over enemy country. Held post under the Forestry Commission in Fifeshire. Son of Adam Mackay, 11 Davidson's Lane, Thurso.

MACKAY, FLYING OFFICER NEIL, Royal Air Force. Navigator. Aged 35 years. Reported missing, later officially notified as having lost his life on air operations at Arnhem – Septr. 21,

1944. Had been on many operational flights. A chemist. Son of Mr and Mrs Tom Mackay, 3 Bank Street, Thurso.

MACKAY, PILOT OFFICER JOHN G., Royal Air Force. Aged 43 years. Died at Radclyffe General Hospital, London – Jany 26, 1941. Came safely through the retreat at Dunkirk. Wife and family of seven resided at "Errolbank," Perth Road, Scone. Fourth son of Mr and Mrs Donald Mackay, "The Bungalow", Halkirk.

MACKAY, PETTY OFFICER ROBERT, Royal Naval Reserve. Accidentally drowned – Decr. 21, 1940. Married. Home address – Maclean's Cottages, Thurso.

MACKAY, LEADING STOKER DENNIS L, Royal Navy. Lost aboard H.M.S. "Fiji" at Crete – May, 1941. Served in Navy for six years. Son of Mr and Mrs Adam Mackay (resident in Edinburgh), and grandson of Mr and Mrs Neil Mackay, Post Office, Dunbeath.

MACKAY, JOHN ALEXANDER, Radio Operator. Aged 25 years. Injured on board R.M.S. "Ceramic" en route to Australia, and died from his injury in the Royal Northern Infirmary, Inverness, on Septr. 23, 1940. Younger son of Mr and Mrs G. W. Mackay, 9 Smith Terrace, Wick.

MACKAY, SERGT. THOMAS, Australian Imperial Forces. Died June 2, 1945, while a prisoner of war at Sandakan, Borneo. Eldest son of Mr and Mrs T. Mackay, Knockglass, Westfield, Thurso.

MACKAY, CORPL. ALEXANDER, South African E.C. Reported missing in Abyssinian campaign in October, 1941, later presumed dead. Lorry driver in Dunbeath before emigrating. Son of the late John Mackay and of Mrs Mackay, Torbeg, Dunbeath.

MACKAY, PTE. ALEXANDER B., 5th Seaforth Highdrs. Aged 31 years. Killed at the Mareth Line – Feby. 27, 1943. Husband of Deborah Davidson, Guidebest, Latheron, and younger son of Mr and Mrs Adam Mackay, Leodibest, Latheron.

MACKAY, PTE. ANGUS, 5th Seaforth Highdrs. Aged 24 years. Killed at Tilly, France – August 8, 1944. Farm-servant. Seventh son of the late David R. Mackay, Assery, Westfield, and of Mrs Mackay, 4 New Houses, Thrumster. Two brothers were prisoners of war.

MACKAY, PTE ANGUS, 5th Seaforth Highdrs. Aged 22 years. Killed at Wadi-el-Akarit – April 6, 1943. Son of Angus Mackay, shepherd, and of Mrs Mackay, Golsary, Rumster, Lybster.

MACKAY, PTE. ROBERT, 5th Seaforth Highdrs.

Aged 28 years. Died of wounds on Western Front – Feby. 23, 1945. Mobilised with Territorials and was wounded in October, 1944. Before war was employed in Dornoch as a butcher. Husband of Jessie Miller, 4 Baron's Well, Wick, and fourth son of Mrs Mackay, 13 Kennedy Terrace, Wick, and the late Mr Mackay, Dornoch.

MACKAY, PTE GEORGE D., Seaforth Highlanders. Accidentally killed while on duty at the coast near a town in the North – May 2, 1941. (Buried in Halkirk Churchyard.) Husband of Elizabeth D. Campbell, Sordale, Halkirk, and second son of Mr and Mrs Andrew Mackay, Blackburn, Dunbeath.

MACKAY, JOHN H., late of Pioneer Corps. Aged 27 years. Died in Bangor Military Hospital – June 20, 1943. Invalided out of Army some time previously. (Buried at Berriedale.) Twin son of Mr and Mrs James Mackay, New Borgue, Dunbeath.

MACKAY, FLT. SERGT. JOHN, Royal Air Force. Observer and Wireless Operator. Aged 21 years. Reported missing on operational flight – Feby. 9, 1942, later presumed to have lost his life on that date. Only son of Mr and Mrs John Mackay, Spittal.

MACKENZIE, L.-CORPL. WILLIAM, C.M. Police. Aged 34 years. Died in Tambaya Hospital – Septr. 1, 1943, while a prisoner of war in Japanese hands. Belonged to Keiss. Wife (Margaret Donaldson), also a native of Caithness (Clyth), and three children resided at 6 Livingstone Place, Edinburgh.

MACKENZIE, PTE. JAMES M., 5th Seaforth Highdrs. Aged 25 years. Killed on Western Front – March 25, 1945. Joined Army 1937 and had been on foreign service for six years. Third son of the late Donald Mackenzie and of Mrs Mackenzie, 5 Oldwick Road, Wick.

MACKENZIE, PTE. ROBERT, Seaforth Highdrs. Aged 30 years. Killed in enemy air raid on Wick – July 1, 1940. Son of Robert Mackenzie, tailor (killed by the same bomb) and of Mrs Mackenzie, 49 Argyle Square, Wick. Married. Home address – Cliff Cottages, Shore Lane.

MACKENZIE, SGN. JAMES A., Royal Electrical Mechanical Engineers (Signals Section). Aged 37 years. Killed in Italy in April, 1944. Employed by British Linen Bank. Eldest son of Robert Mackenzie, fishsalesman, and the late Mrs Mackenzie, 35 Kinnaird Street, Wick. Married and wife resided in Forfar.

MACKENZIE, SERGT. DAVID G., Royal Air Force. Aged 20 years. Lost his life Decr. 7, 1944, as the result of an aircraft accident "somewhere in England." (Buried in Berriedale Churchyard.) A gardener at Dunbeath Castle in peace-time. Younger son of Mr and Mrs William Mackenzie, The Cottage, Brough, Dunnet (late of Knockally, Dunbeath).

MACKIE, PTE. ALFRED, 5th Seaforth Highdrs. Aged 20 years. Killed at the Mareth Line – March 18, 1943. Assistant grocer before the war. Fifth son of Mrs B. Gunn, 128 Willowbank, Wick. (Pte Mackie had five brothers on service.)

MACLEOD, PILOT OFFICER WILLIAM R., Royal Air Force. Reported missing after operational flight over enemy territory on December 26, 1944, later presumed to have lost his life on that date. Educated at Castletown and Thurso, and Arts Student at Edinburgh University before joining Air Force. Youngest son of Mr and Mrs Alexr. Macleod, Bogbain Farm, Ross-shire (late of Granton Mains, Bower).

MACLEOD, RADIO OFFICER NORMAN A. Aged 30 years. Reported missing, later officially notified as lost at sea through enemy action on February 24, 1945. (Interred in Calais Military Cemetery.) Husband of Myra S. Edwards, 44 High Street, Wick. Parents resided in Stornoway. R.O. Macleod was on the staff at Wick Radio Station for eight years.

MACLEOD, DONALD M. (Doyle), Able Seaman, S.T. Aged 21 years. Died at sea – December 21, 1942. (Interred in Latheron Churchyard.) By the time he was $16\frac{1}{2}$ years this seaman had served two years with the 5th Seaforths. Joined Navy in 1937, and later volunteered for submarine service. Parents (Mr and Mrs Edward Macleod) resided at Castle Heather, Smerlie, Lybster. Five weeks before his death married Corpl. Isobel Omand, W.A.A.F., Lybster.

MACLEOD, ABLE SEAMAN GEORGE F. Aged 24 years. Lost at sea in September, 1942. Eldest son of Mr and Mrs Alexr. Macleod, Baligill, Strathy, Thurso.

MACLEOD, ABLE SEAMAN HUGH, Royal Naval Reserve. Lost with the armed cruiser "Rawalpindi" – Novr. 23, 1939. Belonged to Helmsdale but resided in Wick. Carter before the war. Wife and family resided 15 Ackergill Crescent, Wick. Awarded posthumously the R.N.R. long service and good conduct medal.

MACLEOD, ERNEST R., Merchant Navy. Aged 29 years. Lost at sea on board s.s. "Sirikishna" (as result of enemy action) – Feb. 24, 1941. Passed all his working life at sea. Son of Mr and Mrs Donald Macleod, Seafield Cottage, Cairnroich, Lybster.

MACLEOD, COY.-SGT.-MAJOR DONALD, 5th Seaforth Highdrs. Aged 37 years. Killed in N.W. Europe – August 21, 1944. Served in North Africa and Sicily. Elder son of Mr and Mrs John Macleod, Quarryside, Murkle, Castletown.

MACLEOD, BOMBDR. ALEXANDER, Royal Artillery. Aged 30 years. Died overseas. Husband of Elizabeth G. Ross, 20 Rose Street, Thurso, and eldest son of the late Pte. Allan Macleod and of Mrs Macleod, 4 Durness Street, Thurso.

MACLEOD, TROOPER ALEXANDER, 1st Special Air Service. Aged 26 years. Reported missing, believed prisoner; later as killed in N.W. Europe on July 14, 1944. Grave identified in March, 1945. Called up with Territorials, and later volunteered as a Paratrooper. Carter in peacetime. Only son of Mr and Mrs Alex Macleod, 29 Grant Street, Wick.

MACLEOD, GUARDSMAN WILLIAM S., Scots Guards. Aged 20 years. Killed in N.W. Europe – Septr. 9, 1944. Second son of Mr and Mrs Donald Macleod, Ivy Cottage, Reay.

There Comes No Returning

I am weary and sad, in sorrow I'm mourning,
For my love went away and there comes no returning;
He left me in sorrow when war was a-calling,
At the fall of the year, when leaves were a-falling.

And now, at the last, has come the sad ending,
Life's thread has snap'd fast, and for it comes no mending;
It was best to have lived and died in the noon-day
Than wait till old age came, and came in its doom-day.

The flowers, the sweet roses, 'twas better to free them
To memory wreathed, than withering see them;
To ever remember, to ever remember,
The roses in June, than the snows of December.

The young heroes who died, Fame can never forsake them,
And the sorrows of age can never o'ertake them;
They shall ever be young in the land where no tear flows,
In the halls of Valhalla, the home of the Heroes.

– "JENNY HORNE" (Shebster).

MACLEOD, PTE DONALD G., Royal Army Service Corps. Aged 21 years. Killed at sea by enemy action (probably in sinking of "Laurentic") – June 17, 1940. Draper. Youngest son of the late Donald G. Macleod and of Mrs Macleod, 44 Henrietta Street, Wick.

MACLEOD, PTE. JOHN, 5th Seaforth Highdrs. In early twenties. Killed in Middle East – Novr. 2, 1942. Elder son of Mr and Mrs William Macleod, New Road, Westerdale, Halkirk, and husband of Jeanette Bain, Bullechach, Harpsdale.

MACLEOD, SERGT. BENJAMIN SUTHER-LAND, Royal Air Force. Air gunner. Aged 22 years. Killed when Lancaster bombers collided over a village in France early in the morning of May 8, 1944. Buried with 13 other airmen in St. Donlchard cemetery, Bontges. Formerly of Wick. Wife and two young sons resided at 178 East Surrey Grove, Peckham, London.

MACNICOL, SERGT. RICHARD S., Green Howards. Taken prisoner June 1942. Died in an Italian prisoner of war camp – Feby. 4, 1943. A forester before the war. Eldest son of Mr and Mrs MacNicol, Shurrery Lodge, Reay, and husband of Hannah Bremner, Halkirk (later Fort-William).

MACNICOL, SERGT. DONALD, 5th Seaforth Highdrs. Aged 23 years. Killed in Sicily – July 14, 1943. Third son of Mr and Mrs Nicol MacNicol, and husband of Winifred Fraser, Dalnawillan, Altnabreac.

MACPHEE, PTE. DUNCAN, Seaforth Highdrs. Aged 30 years. Killed in Middle East about Novr., 1942. Wife resided at 12 Macrae Street, Wick; and third son of James Macphee, Harpsdale, Halkirk.

MACPHERSON, PTE. WILLIAM J. S., 5th Seaforth Highdrs. Aged 25 years. Killed in Middle East in April, 1943. He was slightly wounded early in the action in which he subsequently lost his life, but declined advice to proceed to a dressing station. Before the war he was in bakery and confectionery business. Youngest son of the late Mr and Mrs W. J. S. Macpherson, "Tighnamara," Olrig Street, Thurso.

McALLAN, PTE. JOHN, Gordon Highdrs. Aged 30 years. Killed at the Mareth Line – March 28, 1943. Baker to trade. Eldest son of the late William McAllan and of Mrs McAllan, 3 Victoria Place, Wick, and husband of Mary Webster, 2 Ackergill Street, Wick.

McIVOR, WILLIAM J. D., R.N. Patrol Service. Aged 34 years. Killed by enemy action at Portland – April 12, 1941, while ashore during an air raid. Buried at Dorset. Fourth son of Mr and Mrs Alexander McIvor, Tighnamara, Latheronwheel.

McIVOR, AB-SEAMAN WILLIAM A. Aged 19 years. Lost off H.M.S. "Gloworm" in the Battle of Narvik – April 8, 1940. Grandson of Mr and Mrs Alexander McIvor, Tighnamara, Latheronwheel.

McKAIN, AB-SEAMAN FRANCIS, Royal Naval Reserve. Aged 29 years. Reported missing, presumed killed, on Aircraft Carrier H.M.S "Avenger" – November 15, 1942, Cooper to trade. Wife (Mary Sutherland) resided at 11 Vansittart Street, Wick, and parents (Mr and Mrs John McKain) at 23 Oldwick Road, Wick.

McKINNON, CRAFTSMAN JAMES W., Royal Electrical and Mechanical Engineers. Aged 28 years. Accidentally killed in Normandy – June 28, 1944. Crossed to France on D-Day. Elder surviving son of Mrs McKinnon, Stempster, Bower, and the late John McKinnon, Shielton, Watten.

McVICAR, FLIGHT-ENGR. ANGUS, Royal Air Force. Killed while on a flight to attack target in Germany. Buried at Florennes, 14 miles from Charleroi, Belgium – 1943. Eldest son of Mr and Mrs McVicar, Free Church Manse, Dunbeath.

MALCOLM, L.-BOMBDR. JOHN, Anti-Tank Regt., R.A. Aged 22 years. Killed in action – October 3, 1944. Plasterer to trade. Only son of Mr and Mrs Benj. Malcolm, Thurso.

MATHESON, HUGO S., Wireless Operator on s.s. "Highlander." Lost at sea (result of enemy action) in Novr., 1940. The "Highlander" had previously been engaged in an epic fight at sea with enemy aircraft. Eldest son of the late Rev. Hugh Matheson and of Mrs Matheson, Buchollie, Lybster.

MATHESON, SERGT. WILLIAM, Royal Air Force. Killed in action in July, 1942. Only son of the late John Matheson, Ackergill Street, Wick, and of Mrs James Thomson, 2 Auckenleck Terrace, Port-Glasgow.

MATHIESON, PTE. JOHN D., 5th Seaforth Highdrs. Aged 24 years. Killed in the Middle East – Jany. 22, 1943. Only son of Margaret Mathieson, Greenvale, Dunnet.

MIDDLETON, FLYING OFFICER ANGUS S., Royal Air Force. Posted missing, believed killed, following an operational flight over enemy territory – July 22-23, 1944. Later stated to be buried with other members of aircraft crew near village of Brillac, France. Joined Air Force in peacetime. Son of George C. Middleton, 4 County Houses, Watten.

MILLAR, RENWICK D. F., Radio Officer, Merchant Navy. Aged 19 years. Killed or drowned in the sinking by enemy action of the s.s. "Port Hunter" in the South Atlantic – July 11, 1942. His first voyage. Elder son of Mr and Mrs D. Mackay Millar, 16 Duddingston Square East, Portobello, and grandson of Mr and Mrs R. J. G. Millar, "Woodstock," Wick.

MILLER, CHIEF ENGINEER WILLIAM, s.s. "Clan Maciver." Died at Cape Town on June 12, 1941. Husband of Catherine S. Payne, "Cairndhuna," Lennox Avenue, Gravesend, Kent, and eldest son of the late Mr and Mrs William Miller, 22 Wellington Street, Wick.

MILLER, SECOND OFFICER TEMPLE F., s.s. "Empire Spring." Reported missing, presumed lost at sea – February 14-15, 1942. Husband of Helen Wares Bruce, 116 Killoch Dr., Knightswood, Glasgow, and elder son of William Miller, "Ben Morven," Lybster.

MILLER, RADIO OFFICER ANDREW, Merchant Navy. Presumed lost when ship torpedoed in the Atlantic – February 7, 1942. Joined M.N. before the war. Wife (Margaret Kennedy) resided at Schoolhouse, John O'Groats; only son of the late John Miller, Maligoe, Mey and of Mrs Miller, Brough, Dunnet.

MILLER, ABLE-SEAMAN FRANCIS, Royal Navy. Aged 20 years. Died in the Town and County Hospital, Wick, as the result of wounds – January 17, 1945. Second son of Mr and Mrs John Miller, Ulbster.

MILLER, SEAMAN JAMES, Royal Naval Reserve. Aged 36 years. Died in Liberton Hospital, Edinburgh – June 16, 1942. Buried at Wick. Held medal for 20 years' service. Younger son of the late Alexr. Miller and of Mrs Miller, 8 Kinnaird Street, Wick.

MILLER, SEAMAN WILLIAM B., Royal Naval Reserve. Aged 27 years. Lost with the "Jervis Bay" – Novr. 6, 1940. Third son of Mr and Mrs William Miller, 31 Smith Terrace, Wick, who had five sons on service.

MILLER, SEAMAN PETER, Royal Naval Reserve. Youngest brother of above. Aged 23 years. Reported missing April 13, 1942, later presumed lost at Singapore – Feby. 16, 1942. Was a survivor from the cruiser "Laurentic" which was torpedoed and sunk towards the end of 1940.

MILLER, SERGT. WILLIAM, 6th Seaforth Highdrs. Aged 32 years. Killed in the crossing of Garigliano River, Italy – January 18, 1944. Mobilised with Territorials and awarded Territorial Efficiency Medal. Served in France, Madagascar, India, Iraq and Sicily before going to Italy. Only son of Mr and Mrs George Miller, Nybster, Aukengill (late of Calder and Sortat, Lyth).

MILLER, SERGT. WILLIAM J., Cameron Highdrs. Aged 28 years. Killed on the Rhine in March, 1945. Husband of Christine Gray, and eldest son of Mr and Mrs William Miller, The Lodge, Dalblair Road, Nairn, and formerly of Dalnaglaton, Westerdale.

MILLER, CORPL. CURTIS B., Seaforth Highdrs. Aged 31 years. Posted missing in Italy in March, 1944; later as presumed killed. Wife (Euphemia Gunn) and family resided at 35 Huddart Street, Wick. Son of the late Mr and Mrs Benjamin Miller, Roadside, Spittal.

MILLER, SUB-CDR. JOHN R., Indian Army Corps. Aged 30 years. Died in hospital at Jubbalpore, India – Feby. 1, 1945. Enlisted Seaforths in 1936. Husband of Ada Moir (Sergt., W.A.C.) and only son of the late Mr and Mrs John Miller, Wick. Sometime resided with his uncle, the late John Christie, 8 Louisburgh Street.

MORE, L.-CORPL. FRANK C., 5th Seaforth Highdrs. Aged 22 years. Died of wounds at Tripoli – Jany. 23, 1943. Plumber to trade. Second son of Mr and Mrs Francis More, 24 Wellington Street, Wick.

MORRISON, CORPL. GEORGE C. P. (Charlie), 2nd Seaforth Highdrs. Aged 27 years. Died of wounds at Wadi-el-Akarit – April 7, 1943. Dairy roundsman. Only son of the late William Morrison and of Mrs Morrison, Kirkhill Cottage, Wick, and husband of Lilian Steven, 7 Willowbank, Wick.

MOWAT, ABLE-SEAMAN GEORGE, Merchant Navy. Aged 57 years. Presumed lost at sea when ship on which he was serving was sunk by enemy action on January 31, 1942. Had been deep sea sailor for 40 years. Unmarried. Eldest son of the late Mr and Mrs Neil Mowat, Sinclair Street, Thurso.

MUIR, SERGT. JOHN S., 5th Seaforth Highdrs. Aged 37 years. Died of wounds near Bremen, Germany, on April 13, 1945. Was previously wounded at Antwerp. Baker to trade. Left family of eight children. Husband of Alexandrina D. Mackay, 51 Henrietta Street, Wick, and only surviving son of Mrs J. Muir, 2 West Banks Terrace, Wick.

MUNRO, SEAMAN JOHN, Royal Naval Reserve. Aged 28 years. Posted missing, presumed lost, from H.M.S. "Jervis Bay" – Novr. 6, 1940. Fisherman. Younger son of the late John Munro and of Mrs Munro, New Houses, Keiss.

MUNRO, CORPL. KENNETH, Scots Guards. Aged 28 years. Reported missing in Tunisia – April 29, 1943; later as killed on that date. Was in police service. Eldest son of Mrs Munro and of the late Angus Munro, Newlands, Occumster.

MUNRO, FLT. SERGT. MURRAY S., Royal Air Force. Wireless Operator. Aged 22 years. Officially presumed to have lost his life while on air operations over Germany on night of April 10-11, 1945. Husband of Margaret Mackay, Achiesgill, Lairg, and younger son of Mr and Mrs David Munro, Roadside, Tannach, Wick.

MUNRO, TROOPER WILLIAM, Royal Armoured Corps. Brother of above. Died in Southfield Hospital, Liberton, Edinburgh, as result of war service, on Novr. 12, 1946, aged 31 years. Saw service in the Middle East and in Tunisia until the landing in Sicily. Home address, 39 Cairndhuna Terrace, Wick.

MURRAY, LIEUT. JAMES, Royal Artillery. Aged 29 years. Killed in Italy in May, 1944. Received his commission in Tunisia. Youngest son of the late Mr and Mrs James Murray, late of 14 Kinnaird Street, Wick. (Father was lost at sea in 1914-18 war.)

NEWLANDS, PTE. THOMAS ———. Aged 34 years. Died of wounds in France – June 7, 1940. Wife resided in Castletown.

PAUL, PTE. DAVID J., 6th Batt. Green Howards. Aged 31 years. Reported missing August 9, 1944, later as having died of wounds on the 14th of that month while a prisoner of war. Vanman in Halkirk. Husband of Eliza Munro, 15 Wellington Street, Wick, and son of Mrs D. Paul, Church Street, Halkirk.

RICHARD, ENGINEER OFFICER DAVID F., Merchant Navy. Aged 26 years. Posted missing, presumed lost through enemy action, while serving on an oil tanker in January, 1945. Was on torpedoed ship in 1940. Brought up in Wick – address: 13a Willowbank. Son of Mr and Mrs Louis Richard, 53 Gairn Crescent, Aberdeen. Married. Wife resided 58 Newlands Crescent, Aberdeen.

RITCHIE, SERGT. WILLIAM M., No. 99 Squadron, Royal Air Force. Aged 22 years. Posted missing on June 12, 1941, after raid over Germany (at Buer, Westphalia) from which his 'plane did not return. Had taken part in several flights over enemy territory and in the chase of the battleship "Bismarck". Educated at Lybster and Wick. Employed Commercial Bank at Turriff. Youngest son of Mr and Mrs David Ritchie, Commercial Bank House, Lybster.

ROBERTSON, MARINE MALCOLM, Royal Marines. Aged 23 years. Lost his life in the battle for Crete – May 23, 1941. Before the war was employed in London. Son of the late Mr and Mrs John Robertson, Bellevue Cottage, Stroma, and brother of P.C. John Robertson, Wick (now of Mey).

ROSS, GUARDSMAN DAVID, Scots Guards. Aged 26½ years. Killed in the Middle East – June 16, 1941. Twin son of the late David Ross and of Mrs Ross, Gillock, Bower.

ROSS, PTE. JOHN M., Gordon Highdrs. Aged 20 years. Killed in action in Holland on Novr. 20, 1944. Third son of Mr and Mrs John Ross, Strathy Point, by Thurso, and brother of Mrs Thomas Alexander, Stirkoke Mains, Wick.

ROSS, PTE. ROBERT, Paratroops. Aged 22 years. Elder brother of above. Died of wounds in Italy – January 8, 1944.

RYRIE, DONALD BREMNER, Senior Radio Officer, s.s. "Southern Empress". Posted missing, presumed lost at sea during October, 1942. Second son of the late Mr and Mrs Donald Ryrie, Keiss, and husband of Jean Ferris, Tilliefoure, Monymusk, Aberdeenshire.

SANDISON, SERGT. PETER, Royal Air Force. Flight Engineer. Reported missing, presumed killed – September 16, 1942. Body recovered from sea by Germans four days later. Fifth operational flight. Ten years in R.A.F. Youngest son of the late Donald Sandison and of Mrs Sandison, Framside, Thurso. Married five days prior to the raid on Essen from which he did not return. Wife belongs to Barrow.

SHEARER, TELEGRAPHIST JAMES, Royal Navy. Aged 22 years. Reported missing, later presumed killed, through enemy action in the sinking of H.M.S. "Barham" off the coast of Sollum – Novr. 25, 1941. Telegraphist in Wick Post Office. Second son of Mr and Mrs William Shearer, 32 Girnigoe Street, Wick.

SHEARER, FLT.-SERGT. JAMES, Royal Air Force. Aged 22 years. Killed on flying operations in Sicily – Septr. 29, 1943. Eldest son of Mr and Mrs D. M. Shearer, Pentland View, Brough, Dunnet.

SIMPSON, ABLE-SEAMAN JOHN. W., Aged 21 years. Posted missing from H.M. Trawler "Medoc" – Novr. 6, 1940; later presumed to have lost his life through enemy action on that date while on patrol duty in the English Channel. Only son of Mr and Mrs Donald Simpson, Mossview, Brough, Dunnet.

SINCLAIR, LIEUT. KENNETH, Royal Naval Reserve. Lost at sea through enemy action probably in April, 1941. Wife (Eleanor Webb) and family resided at Liss, Hants. Youngest son of the late Captain and Mrs Kenneth Sinclair, Clairmount, Castletown.

SINCLAIR, WILLIAM, Second Engineer Officer, M.V. "Stork." Aged 22 years. Accidentally drowned at Rouen, France – Octr. 7, 1945. Only son of Mr and Mrs George W. Sinclair, 54 Easter Road, Edinburgh (late mail bus driver, Mey and Thurso).

SINCLAIR, BOSUN JAMES G., Merchant Navy. Aged 29 years. Reported missing, later as killed at sea by enemy action on July 5, 1940. Bosun on s.s. "Hartleford" (torpedoed). Third son of Mr and Mrs James Sinclair, 17 Lower Dunbar Street, Wick. Married: wife resided in Blyth.

SINCLAIR, SEAMAN DAVID, Royal Naval Reserve. Lost on armed merchant cruiser "Rawalpindi" – Novr. 23, 1939. Served in Navy previous war and then transferred to the merchant service. Youngest son of the late Peter Sinclair, The Cairn, Stroma.

SINCLAIR, ALEXANDER S., Mercantile Marine. Aged 49 years. Lost at sea as a result of enemy action on June 20, 1940. Son of the late Captain and Mrs David Sinclair, Scrabster. Two of his brothers lost their lives on service in 1914-18 war.

SINCLAIR, SEAMAN DONALD, Merchant Navy. Aged 20 years. Lost at sea through enemy action – February 14, 1940, when s.s. "Gretafield" was torpedoed off Wick. Third son of Mr and Mrs James Sinclair, 49 Kennedy Terrace, Wick.

SINCLAIR, GUNNER WILLIAM, Royal Artillery. Aged 21 years. Died in a Military Hospital at Oxford – July 20, 1944, from wounds received in Normandy. (Buried in Halkirk Churchyard.) Third son of the late Mrs Isabella Sinclair and of William Sinclair, 2 New Houses, Spittal, Watten.

SINCLAIR, PTE. ALEXANDER, Australian Imperial Forces. Aged 39 years. Died of illness whilst a prisoner of war at Ambon on Novr. 6, 1944. Second son of John Sinclair and of the late Mrs Sinclair, Firth View, Mid-Clyth (late of Clyth Mains).

SINCLAIR, PTE. LAUCHLAN S., Seaforth Highdrs. Aged 25 years. Killed in action in Sicily – July 14, 1943. Fifth son of Mr and Mrs G. Sinclair, Rattar Mains, Scarfskerry.

SINCLAIR, FLT.-SERGT. JOHN M., Royal Air Force. Reported missing on operational flight over Norway about March, 1945. 'Plane of which he was one of the crew of seven later found wrecked near Assgarstand. Six bodies were found and only two identified. Only son of Mr

and Mrs Sinclair, Station House, Bonar-Bridge, who were long stationed in Caithness.

SINCLAIR, SERGT. WILLIAM A. R., Royal Air Force. Air gunner. Aged 22 years. Reported missing after operational flight over Hamburg – July 28, 1943, later presumed killed on that date. Joined R.A.F. year before outbreak of war. Youngest son of Mr and Mrs John Sinclair, 20 Louisburgh Street, Wick.

SLATER, SEAMAN JAMES, Royal Navy. Reported missing, presumed killed on active service, about Septr., 1941. Member of crew of corvette H.M.S. "Fleur de Lys" which was sunk. Native of Buckie and in Fishery Office here. Wife and children resided in Willowbank, Wick.

SMITH, FLYING OFFICER JOHN WILLIAM, Royal Air Force. Aged 29 years. Reported missing 21st Novr., 1944; later presumed to have lost his life on that date. Navigator in a Mosquito, and took part in many raids over sea and land targets. Awarded D.F.C. in January, 1945. Joined R.A.F. shortly after leaving school. Only son of Mrs M. Smith, Main Street, Castletown, and the late John R. Smith, Benshaw, Newcastle. Married: wife resided in Barry, Glamorgan.

SMITH, ABLE-SEAMAN JAMES, Royal Navy. Aged 23 years. Gunner and diver. Killed in action on H.M.S. "Arethusa," in Eastern Mediterranean – Novr. 18, 1942. Joined Navy in 1936. Son of Mrs Smith, 42 High Street, Thurso, and of the late Steele Smith.

SMITH, ABLE-SEAMAN DONALD, Merchant Navy. Lost at sea while serving with the Rescue Ship "Stockport" in the Atlantic – February 25, 1943. Native of Stroma. Wife and family resided at 27 Vansittart Street, Wick.

SMITH, SEAMAN NICOL, Royal Navy. Went down with the submarine "Grampus" about June, 1940. Two years in submarine service. Third son of Mr and Mrs Donald Smith, Newton Cottage, Stroma. Married in London.

SMITH, PTE. WILLIAM, 1st Airborne Division. Reported missing following operations at Arnhem, later as killed on September 19, 1944. Youngest son of Mr and Mrs James Smith, The Haven, Stroma.

SMITH, PTE. PETER J. G., 5th Seaforth Highdrs. Aged 24 years. Died of wounds received in the later stages of the fighting in Sicily – August 4, 1943. Second son of Donald S. Smith, motor bus proprietor, Brims' Buildings, Castletown.

SPENCE, BOMBDR. DAVID, Tank Corps. Aged 30 years. Killed as result of a tank accident – Octr. 19, 1945. Interred at Canisbay. Husband of Elizabeth Banks, New Houses, Canisbay, and eldest son of Mr and Mrs David Spence, Newton, Wick.

STEVEN, CAPTAIN WALTER J., Merchant Navy. Aged 31 years. Killed by enemy action in the Pacific – August 19, 1941. Ship sunk by enemy raider when on homeward voyage. It was his first trip as captain. Elder son of Captain and Mrs Walter Steven, Rowena House, Mey.

STEVEN, SEAMAN GEORGE, Merchant Navy. Died in hospital at Bombay on Decr. 10, 1944. Son of Donald Steven, coastguard, Keiss, and husband of Margaret Macleod, Halkirk.

STEWART, INSTR.-LIEUT. HUGH, Royal Navy. Aged 24 years. Lost on H.M.S. "Royal Oak" when torpedoed at Scapa Flow on October 14, 1939. Had distinguished scholastic career at Wick and St. Andrews. Youngest son of Mr and Mrs Neil Stewart, 2 Smith Terrace (now of West Banks Terrace), Wick.

STEWART, PTE. ROBERT, Royal Welsh Fusiliers. Aged 22 years. Died of wounds in North West Europe – October 1, 1944. Mobilised with the Territorials. Eldest son of the late Mr and Mrs James Stewart, 1 Harrow Hill, Wick.

STEWART, SERGT.-PILOT WILLIAM A., Royal Air Force. Aged 27 years. Killed in a flying accident at Misurata, North Africa – May 22, 1943. An M.A. graduate and member of the teaching profession. Was at Blairgowrie before enlisting. Only son of Mr and Mrs William Stewart, Lanergill, Watten.

SUTHERLAND, CAPTAIN DUNCAN B., The York and Lancaster Regiment. Aged 30 years. Died at No. 2 British General Hospital, C.M.F. (Italy) – Novr. 22, 1944 (as result of an accident – overturning of a military car). Student at Aberdeen College of Agriculture. Youngest son of James A. Sutherland, shoemaker, and the late Mrs Sutherland, Lower Village, Latheronwheel. (His eldest brother, Alexander, who was a student in Arts in Edinburgh, joined Royal Scots in 1914-18 war and was killed in action.)

SUTHERLAND, LIEUT. WILLIAM M., Army Pay Corps, Glasgow. Died after having ten days' leave at his home in Halkirk, early in 1946. Late proprietor of Ulbster Arms Hotel, Halkirk.

SUTHERLAND, FLIGHT-LIEUT. HAMISH, Fleet Air Arm. Aged 20 years. Lost his life (probably July, 1945) when the 'plane of which he was one of the crew of three crashed at sea. Celebrated 20th birthday day before his death. Before volunteering for service with the Fleet Air Arm in May, 1943, was in employment of Messrs Keith & Murray, solicitors, and was a

sergeant of Thurso Squadron Air Training Corps. Son of Mr and Mrs Donald Sutherland, Smith Terrace, Thurso.

SUTHERLAND, SERGT.-PILOT IAN ST. CLAIR, Royal Air Force. Killed in flying accident – Novr. 30, 1943. (Interred in Tomb of Dunn.) Banker – Thurso and Kirkwall. Married. Elder son of the late John A. M. Sutherland, teacher, Lanergill, and of Mrs Sutherland, Harpsdale Schoolhouse, Halkirk.

SUTHERLAND, SERGT. PETER, Royal Canadian Air Force. Observer. Aged 21 years. Reported missing following a flight over enemy territory on Septr. 13, 1942, on his first operational task. Later presumed killed on that date. Son of Mr and Mrs William Sutherland, James Street, Winnipeg, Manitoba. Father belongs to Lybster and mother (Maudie Shearer) to Wick. Was three years of age when parents emigrated. Married Canadian girl two weeks before leaving Canada to come to Britain.

SUTHERLAND, RADIO OFFICER DOUGLAS S. Aged 21 years. Lost with H.M.S. "Rawalpindi" – Novr. 23, 1939. Younger son of Mr and Mrs J. W. Sutherland, 3 Murrayfield, Castletown.

SUTHERLAND, COY.-SERGT.-MAJOR ALEXANDER. Reported as prisoner of war after the fall of Singapore; died in a prisoner of war camp in Thailand on June 8, 1944. Son of Mr and Mrs A. Cormack, Sinclair Street, Halkirk.

SUTHERLAND, SERGT. ROBERT ALEXR., Seaforth Highdrs. Aged 31 years. Died in Lawson Memorial Hospital, Golspie, on Septr. 10, 1942 (result of accident). Was a well-known local athlete. Third son of Mr and Mrs J. G. Sutherland, Scrabster Farm, Thurso.

SUTHERLAND, L.-CORPL. HARRY, 5th Seaforth Highdrs. Died of wounds in North Africa – Jany. 21, 1943. Mother resided at Gerston, Halkirk.

SUTHERLAND, L.-CORPL. CHARLES G. R., 7th Seaforth Highdrs. Aged 25 years. Died of wounds in Western Europe on March 28, 1945. Previously wounded in Normandy – June, 1944. Employed on Berriedale estate. Fifth son of John Sutherland and the late Mrs Sutherland, New Borgue, Berriedale.

SUTHERLAND, SPR. HENRY B., Royal Engineers. Aged 24 years. Died of wounds in North West Europe on July 4, 1944. Transferred to R.E.'s from 5th Seaforths. Joiner to trade. Wife (Jessie Bremner) resided at 21 Kennedy Terrace, Wick. Son of Mr and Mrs William Sutherland, Smithy House, Haster.

SUTHERLAND, PTE. JOHN D. M., 5th Seaforth Highdrs. Aged 24 years. Reported missing (after Mareth Line battle) – March 19, 1943; later (by Vatican Radio) as prisoner in Italian hands. Died in prisoner of war camp, Germany – December 12, 1944, from effects of meningitis. A bricklayer before the war. Younger son of David Sutherland, Burnside, Thrumster.

SUTHERLAND, PTE. CLARENCE, 1st Airborne Division. Aged 18 years, 9 months. Killed on 10th May, 1945, as result of aircraft accident 10 miles north of Oslo, Norway. Formerly resided at 25 Saltoun Street, Wick, and was employed with Messrs D. R. Simpson, ironmongers.

SUTHERLAND, PTE. ADAM M., London Scottish (att. Gordon Highdrs.) Aged 20 years. Posted missing January 23, 1944, in Anzio landings; later presumed to have died of wounds in enemy hands on that date. Second son of John Sutherland, shepherd, and Mrs Sutherland, Gordonbush, Brora; and grandson of Mr and Mrs John Macbeath, Knockally, Dunbeath, and of the late Mr and Mrs John Sutherland, Houstry, Dunbeath.

SUTHERLAND, SGMN. JAMES BLACK-STOCK, Royal Corps of Signals. Aged 25 years. Killed in motoring accident, January 19, 1946, while on leave from Palestine. Served more than three years in Africa, Egypt and Palestine and held the Africa Star. Eldest son of Mr and Mrs R. Sutherland, 5 Harbour Quay, Wick.

SUTHERLAND, JOSEPH A. Died in Cambridge Military Hospital, Aldershot, on December 15, 1941. Parents resided at Newlands, Forse, Lybster.

SUTHERLAND, ALEXANDER JOHN, Home Guard. Aged 23 years. Fatally injured as result of an accident during an exercise – April 22, 1942. Second son of Mrs Sutherland and of the late Donald Sutherland, farmer, Middleton, Thurso.

SUTHERLAND, PTE. ANGUS. Aged 20 years. Invalided from the Army and died at home – Octr. 3, 1944. Given military funeral at Latheron, when Home Guard formed guard of honour. Enlisted Seaforths when 15 as a boy recruit. Fourth son of Mr and Mrs Andrew C. Sutherland, Latheronwheel.

SWANSON, CAPTAIN MURDOCH M., 5th Seaforth Highdrs. Aged 33 years. Died of wounds in Middle East in Novr., 1942. Farmed Watten Mains. Family, business, social and sporting associations made him well known throughout the county. Youngest son of Captain and Mrs James Swanson, Ormlie Hall, Thurso.

SWANSON, PETTY OFFICER JOHN, Royal Navy. Aged 34 years. Died in a Naval Hospital, Invergordon – June 9, 1944. Fisherman and skipper of the "Stack Rock." Husband of Robertina Harper, and third son of Mr and Mrs George Swanson, No. 5 New Houses, Papigoe, Wick.

SWANSON, SEAMAN WALTER, H.M.S. "Hood". Lost when that well-known battleship blew up at sea when engaged in battle – May 30, 1941. Son of the late Walter Swanson, High Street, and of Mrs B. Murray, Holborn Avenue, Thurso.

SWANSON, GNR. CLARENCE M., Royal Artillery. Aged 30 years. Died in Germany on 1st August, 1945. Youngest son of Mrs Swanson, Lower Gillock, Wick.

SWANSON, PTE. DONALD, 5th Seaforth Highdrs. Aged 28 years. Killed in Germany – March 26, 1945. Two brothers (John and Alexr.) attended his funeral. Was engaged on farm work before the war. Third son of Donald Swanson and the late Mrs Swanson, East Watten, Watten, who had four sons in the Army.

TAIT, SUB.-LIEUT. JOHN B., Royal Navy. Aged 29 years. Killed in action in June, 1944. (Mentioned in despatches.) Served in Metropolitan Police for eight years. Eldest son of the late Robert B. Tait, fishcurer, and of Mrs Tait, 15 Brown Place, Wick.

TAIT, JOHN CORMACK, Merchant Navy. Aged 37 years. Died at 36 Percy Street, Blyth – Septr. 27, 1945. Third son of the late Mr and Mrs James Tait, 5 Cairndhuna Terrace, Wick.

TAIT, L.-CORPL. DONALD, 1st Gordon Highdrs. Aged 27 years. Killed in Normandy – July 3, 1944. Transferred from London Scottish. Employed in hotel. Husband of Melba Stewart, and only son of the late John M. Tait and of Mrs D. Durrand, 28 Bank Row, Wick.

TAYLOR, GNR, DAVID, A., Royal Artillery. Died on active service in Italy – October 25, 1943. Husband of Margaret Morrison, Nairn. Parents resided in Halkirk.

TAYLOR, JOHN. Aged 17 years. Canteen assistant with N.A.A.F.I. Reported missing, presumed killed, on war service in Mediterranean – Novr. 10, 1942. Only son of John Taylor, 6 Market Street, Wick.

THOMSON, GNR. ALEX, Royal Artillery. Aged 33 years. Died at Hull (result of an accident) – Octr. 13, 1943. (Interred in Wick Cemetery.) Eldest son of the late Mr and Mrs Alex. Thomson, late of 4 Coghill Square, Wick.

WALLACE, SERGT. WILLIAM, 5th Seaforth Highdrs. Killed in a railway smash at Bourne End, Herts., on Sunday, Septr. 20, 1945. Home address – 21 Wilson Street, Thurso.

WARES, L.-CORPL. CHARLES, 5th Seaforth Highdrs. Aged 25 years. Killed at Tripoli – Jany 21, 1943. Wife (Helen Gunn) and family resided at Lower Dounreay, Reay; and youngest son of Mr and Mrs John Wares, Lower Dounreay.

WARES, SERGT. ALASTAIR J. D., Royal Air Force. Aged 19 years. Reported missing from operation over Germany on March 8, 1945, later believed lost (killed) on that date. Second son of Mr and Mrs D. A. Wares, 42 Vansittart Street, Wick.

WATT, LEADING-STOKER DAVID A., Royal Navy. Aged 31 years. Lost through enemy action – March 15, 1942. Enlisted nine years previously. Wife resided in Dunfermline. Son of Mr and Mrs Peter Watt, High Street, Thurso, who had other five sons serving in H.M. Forces.

WEBSTER, SEAMAN-GUNNER ALEXANDER, Royal Naval Reserve. Aged 32 years. Lost with the "Jervis Bay – Novr. 6, 1940. Carter in peace-time. Wife resided 41 Argyle Square, Wick. Second son of Mr and Mrs A. Webster, 31 Cairndhuna Terrace, Wick.

WEIR, SERGT. DENNIS, Tank Corps. Aged 31 years. Killed in a road accident near Madgeburg, Germany – June 27, 1945. Joined Royal Scots in 1935 and did much soldiering abroad. He was a member of a Chindit force that penetrated deep into Japanese occupied Burma with tanks. Husband of Isabella Sinclair, Lybster and elder son of Mr and Mrs Wilfred Weir, Kyleakin, and formerly of Wick.

THE LADS WHO WILL MARCH TO THE PIPES NO MORE.

The dawnlight jokes with the morning hills,
And filters the gloom from the sleepy rills;
And the sun's bright smile flits mile on mile
To moor and glen and dark defile;–
 But the heart of the Land is sore, is sore,
 For the lads who will march to the pipes no more!

The Empire broadens its noble sway,
And fashions its sons for the future day;
And its flag flies wide, in freedom's pride,
O'er peak and scarp and sounding tide;–
 But the heart of the Land is sore, is sore,
 For the lads who will march to the pipes no more!

The dewfall crystals the field and lawn,
And glitters as clear as the first bright dawn;
And the skylarks sing, on festal wing,
To boy and knight and jewelled king;–
 But the heart of the Land is sore, is sore,
 For the lads who will march to the pipes no more!

The furnace throbs and the hammers pelt,
And labour is hot in its urgent welt;
And children play, in their care-light way,
By path and stream and woodland gay;–
 But the heart of the Land is sore, is sore,
 For the lads who will march to the pipes no more!

– John Horne (in "Mid-way Tracks")

MEN OF CAITHNESS CONNECTION.

ADAMS, PILOT OFFICER ROBERT M., Royal Canadian Air Force. Aged 20 years. Killed on active service in the North of Ireland in March, 1943. Buried in county Fermanagh. Son of Mr and Mrs R. M. Adams (Seaborn Robertson, late of Keiss Castle), 350 Inglewood Drive, Toronto.

AGNEW, CAPTAIN PATRICK ALEXR., 5th Seaforth Highdrs. Killed in Sicily in July, 1943. Took over estate of Navidale, Sutherland, and was well known in Caithness, being first secretary of the County Egg Marketing Society.

ANDERSON, SERGT. BENJAMIN, 5th Royal Inniskillin Dragoon Guards. Aged 28 years. Killed near Dunkirk about June, 1940. Trained for Army in Queen Victoria School, Dunblane. Youngest son of the late Corpl. Ben. Anderson, Papigoe (killed in 1914-18 war) and of Mrs Anderson, 19 Polwarth Crescent, Edinburgh.

BAIN, CAPTAIN (AND QMR.) ALEXANDER, 10th Highland Light Infantry. Aged 54 years. Reported missing, later as presumed killed while in charge of a lorry party which ran into a German ambush in Normandy on June 28, 1944. Thirty-two years' service in H.L.I. Second son of the late Mr and Mrs Robert R. Bain, formerly of 20 Breadalbane Terrace, Wick. Wife and son resided 16 Dalhousie Street, Glasgow.

BAIN, L.-CORPL. KENNETH G., Lothians and Border Yeomanry. Aged 19½ years. Died at Langenbielan Hospital, Silesia, Germany – September 27, 1940. Younger son of Mr and Mrs Alexr. Bain, 108 Easter Road, Edinburgh and grandson of the late Robert Bain, sailmaker, Wick.

BAIN, RIFLEMAN DAVID S. M., Royal Ulster Rifles. Aged 25 years. Killed in Western Europe – March 24, 1945. Third son of Mr and Mrs Alexr. Bain, 48 Fortress Road, Kentish Town, London, N.W.5, and formerly of Hempriggs, Wick.

BREMNER, ENGINEER DONALD, Merchant Navy. Aged 49 years. Killed in 1943 when the vessel on which he was serving was torpedoed near Algiers. Twice previously he was on torpedoed ships. Father resided Croy, Inverness-shire, and was a native of Stemster, Bower. Engr. Bremner left wife and five children.

BREMNER, PTE. JAMES, 1st Gordon Highdrs. Posted missing. Taken prisoner in June, 1940, and died on 24th of that month in a prisoner of war camp at Tourni, Belgium. Son of Mr and Mrs James Bremner, 2 Edwin Street, Glasgow, and formerly of Wick.

BROKENSHA, LIEUT. GUY W., Fleet Air Arm. Reported missing, presumed killed – August 11, 1942. Belonged to Durban, So. Africa. Wife and young daughter resided at Old Manse, Watten, wife being daughter (Margaret) of Colonel J. J. and Mrs Robertson, late of "Norwood," Wick.

BURT, CAPTAIN ARTHUR S., O.B.E., Royal Navy. Died at Wick – April 18, 1944. Collapsed in Naval Office in Harbour Terrace. Native of Ealing, London and for almost four years resident naval officer at Wick.

BUDGE, LIEUT. DONALD, 7th Seaforth Highdrs. Aged 26 years. Killed in Normandy – July 11, 1944. Architect in Inverness. Only son of Mrs Budge, 6 Charles Street, Inverness.

BUDGE, PILOT OFFICER WILLIAM F., Royal New Zealand Air Force. Aged 24 years. Died (or killed) on service, 1942. Second son of Mr and Mrs John Budge, Auckland, and grandson of the late Mr and Mrs Donald Budge, Roadside, Keiss.

CALDER, CAPTAIN ROBERT J., United States Army. Aged 27 years. Killed in France, probably towards end of August, 1944. Grandson of the late Mr and Mrs Robert Calder, Lochside, Dunnet, and of the late Mr and Mrs Thomas Allan, West Dunnet. Parents resided in Yakima, Washington.

CAMERON, SERGT. DONALD R., Toronto Scottish. Killed in Italy – August 28, 1944. Son of William and Amy Cameron, of Toronto (late of Portskerra), and nephew of Mrs Angus Cameron, 21 Halmyre Street, Leith.

CAMPBELL, DVR. CHARLES D., Royal Army Service Corps. Aged 22 years. Died in Highgate Hospital, London – Octr. 24, 1945, as result of war injuries received in Italy. Third son of Mr and Mrs D. Campbell, 15 Alma Street, Kentish Town, London.

CAMPBELL, MORVIN A., Technician, Royal Tank Regiment. Aged 22 years. Killed in Middle East about Christmas, 1942. Born in Wick but went to London with parents. Second son of Mr and Mrs Donald Campbell, 15 Alma Street, London.

CHRISTIE, GNR, GEORGE, Royal Artillery. Aged 38 years. Died in Bridge of Earn Hospital – April 29, 1942, as result of injuries received in a motoring accident. (Buried at Wick.) Native of Lowestoft but resided in Wick for several years working at kippering trade. Wife belongs to Wick and home address was 11 Kennedy Terrace.

COWAN, ANDREW L., late Flight-Sergeant, Royal Air Force. Aged 32 years. Died at "St Roman," George Street, Peebles – Jany. 21, 1946. Husband of Peggy Robertson, Wick, and youngest son of Mr and Mrs Robert Cowan.

CROSS, LIEUT. JOHN D., M.M., Seaforth Highdrs. Killed at Anzio Beach Head, Italy – March 19, 1944. Mobilised as a private and was with 51st Division in France and taken prisoner at St. Valery, but later escaped and reached this country after many thrilling experiences. Awarded M.M. Son of Mr and Mrs F. Cross, Murray Road, Invergordon, and married Vera Harper, Wick.

CROSS, FLT.-LIEUT. WILLIAM M., M.B., Ch.B., Royal Air Force. Died on war service – July 17, 1941. Late of Armadale, and husband of Eileen Watson, Robroyston, Glasgow.

DIXON, RFN. BRYAN D., 1st Batt. The Rifle Brigade. Aged 28 years. Reported missing, later as presumed died of wounds in the heroic defence of Calais – May 24, 1940. Husband of Jean M'Menamin.

DUNNETT, PTE DAVID, W., Essex Scottish Regiment, Canadians. Aged 20 years. Killed in Normandy – July 11, 1944. Only son of the late David Dunnett and of Mrs Margaret Dunnet, Winnipeg, Canada – both of whom belonged to Thurso and emigrated about 20 years ago.

ELDER, PTE. FINLAY, Australian Imperial Forces. No details given, but name on Reay War Memorial.

ELRICK, SERGT. GEORGE (Dodo), Royal Air Force. Aged 29 years. Killed on Decr. 3, 1942, in a level crossing car-train crash near Windsor, Ontario. Enlisted in Gordons in Aberdeen prior to the war, and transferred to R.A.F. Was at Dunkirk. Twice injured. Sergt. Elrick was born in Wick, and son of Mr and Mrs David Elrick. Wife and family resided at 25 Errol Street, Aberdeen.

FAIRWEATHER, MAJOR ALEXANDER, Regiment President Steyn, South Africa. Aged 26 years. Killed in Egypt – July 3, 1942. Son of Mr and Mrs A. Fairweather, Kroonstad, O.F.S., South Africa. Father left Wick in 1899 for the South African War. He belonged to Halkirk and settled in South Africa.

FAIRWEATHER, SERGT. GEORGE, Canadians. Killed in Italy – October 6, 1943. Eldest son of Mr and Mrs W. M. Fairweather, Port Hammond, B.C., Canada, and grandson of the late Mr and Mrs George Fairweather, Quoynee, Bower. Father a veteran of South African War, and was awarded O.B.E. in 1914-18 war.

FIELDSENDS, PTE. JAMES, Canadian Black Watch. Aged 23 years. Killed in France in July, 1944. Born in Caithness. Eldest son of Mr and Mrs James Fieldsends, Drummondville, Quebec, Canada, and grandson of Mrs Alexr. Gunn, Ernan Cottage, Castletown.

FINNEY, 2nd LIEUT. JOHN H., Royal Army Service Corps, attached Airborne Coy. Aged 31 years. Died (as the result of an accident) – February 8, 1944. Husband of Charlotte Ramsay, Reay, Thurso, and Dounans, Aberfoyle.

FLEMING, SEAMAN JOHN, H.M. Trawler "Oswaldian." Aged 26 years. Lost at sea through enemy action – August 12, 1940. Son of Mr and Mrs John Fleming, Grimsby, and grandson of Mr A. Fleming, Papigoe, Wick. Left wife and child.

FORBES, SQUADRON-LEADER J. W. S., Royal Air Force. Reported missing, later as believed killed in action (1942). Only son of the late Rev. J. R. Forbes of Canisbay, and of Logie Easter, and of Mrs Forbes, Ardmore House, Edderton.

GEATER, 2nd LIEUT. J. STANLEY, Pioneer Corps. Died December 17, 1943, near Stratford-on-Avon, as the result of an accident. Husband of Mona Nicol, Wick, and younger son of Mr and Mrs Geater, Aberdeen.

GEDDES, CORPL. JAMES, Seaforth Highdrs. Aged 29 years. Killed in September, 1944, in North West Europe. Husband of Hetta Hudson, 96 Downey Road, Bradford, and only brother of Isabel, Kirn.

GERRY, PILOT OFFICER REGINALD T., Royal Air Force. Bomber Command. Killed in action about September, 1940. Son of Mr and Mrs H. D. Gerry, Alberta, Canada – both of whom belong to Thurso.

GILCHRIST, SERGT. JOHN, Royal Artillery. Killed in North Africa, early in 1943. Son-in-law of Mrs Donald Mackenzie, Oldwick Road, Wick, where his youngest son resided. Native of Rothesay.

GRAHAM, COY.-SGT.-MAJOR DONALD, 5th Seaforth Highdrs. Killed in a road accident at Lubeck, Germany, in June, 1945. Appointed Sgt.-Instructor to Thurso Territorials after nine years' service with 2nd Batt. Seaforths.

GRIEVE, FLIGHT-SERGT. ALEXANDER, Royal Air Force. Killed in March, 1943. Interred Ardrossan, Ayrshire. Second son of the late James Grieve, diecutter, and of Mrs Grieve, 14 Nelson Street, Edinburgh.

GULLOCH, LIEUT. WILLIAM DUNCAN, Black

Watch (attached K.O.S.B.) Aged 19½ years. Reported missing, believed killed in Burma – Feby. 13, 1944. Attended St. Andrews University. Only son of Colonel W. S. Gulloch and Mrs Dora Gulloch, Nairobi – natives of Freswick and Wick respectively.

GUNN, FLIGHT-LIEUT. ALASTAIR DONALD MACKINTOSH, Royal Air Force. Aged 25 years. Shot down near Trondheim, Norway – March 5, 1942, when on operational flight from Wick R.A.F. Station. Was in the big break of prisoners from Stalag Luft III. in March, 1944, and was one of the 50 R.A.F. officers shot after recapture by the Germans about April 6 of that year. Twice mentioned in despatches. Educated at Fettes and Pembroke College, Cambridge. Younger son of the proprietor of Latheron, Dr J. T. Gunn, and of Mrs Gunn, Deansland, Auchterarder.

GUNN, COLOUR.-SERGT. DONALD ALEXR. (Allie), The Queen's Royal Regiment. Killed in Italy in April, 1945. Third son of the late Donald Gunn and of Mrs Gunn, 48 Blacket Place, Edinburgh.

HARMSWORTH, CAPTAIN PETER, Welsh Guards. Aged 28 years. Killed in Tunisia in April, 1943. Wife and young daughter resided at Tweedleham Grove, near Canterbury. Second son of Mr and Mrs Vyvyan G. Harmsworth of Thrumster.

HAWKEN, PILOT OFFICER IAN D., Royal Air Force. Reported missing on 3rd June, 1940; later presumed killed in air combat near Paris on that date. Second son of Mr and Mrs Sydney C. Hawken, Highgate, London, and grandson of the late Mr and Mrs John Munro, Achlibster, Halkirk.

HENDERSON, ––– JAMES CORMACK (Hamish). Aged 31 years. Killed by enemy action – Novr. 6, 1940. Address given as 11 Buccleuch Street, Glasgow, and of Aberdeen.

HENDRY, ALEXANDER LILLIE –––. Aged 29 years. Died of wounds in Italy – June 28, 1944. Elder son of Mr and Mrs John Hendry, Stag River, Argentina, and grandson of the late Mr and Mrs James Hendry, Parkside, Lybster.

HOGG. ––– T. CAMPBELL, Scots Guards. Aged 21 years. Died of wounds – April 20, 1945. Only son of Mr and Mrs R. N. Hogg, Oxenfoord Mains, Dalkeith, and nephew of

He is not dead,
Though flesh of him be lying
Lashed by the winds that blow, fitful and free,
Where sad the sound of hungry sea-birds crying
And the boom of an angry sea.

He is not dead,
The soul of him undying
But going forth now at the break o' day,
With eager eyes to new adventures hieing,
Irradiant, young and gay!

– ELLA R. C. MACONALD

Major and Mrs Campbell, Stanstill.

HORNE, PTE. IAN, Carleton and York Regiment, Canadian Army. Aged 21 years. Reported missing in Italy – May 23, 1944; later as killed on that date. Son of Mr and Mrs John Horne, South Devon, Canada, and grandson of the late John Horne, Weydale, Thurso.

JAPPIE, PTE DAVID A., Seaforth Highdrs. Killed in Normandy about July 1944. Twelve years' service in the Army, 10 abroad. He was in Burma campaign for twelve months, was wounded and sent back to England. Son of the late Mrs John Clyne, who resided in Coach Road, Wick. Wife resided in Halifax, Yorkshire.

KERR, FLIGHT-SERGT. T. A., Royal Air Force. Reported missing January, 1940; later presumed lost on 'plane which came down in the sea off the Isle of Man. Belonged to Cambuslang. Married, and wife resided at West Park, Wick. For a time he was employed as a road engineer with Caithness County Council.

LAUGHLIN, SERGT. GEORGE C., Ayrshire Yeomanry. Aged 26 years. Killed in Italy – April 20, 1945. Husband of Dell Mackenzie, Melbourne House, Halkirk. Parents resided in Paisley.

MACDEVITT, PTE JOHN J., Cameron Highdrs. Killed in Italy in March 1944. Husband of Ethel Bruce, 20 Kennedy Terrace, Wick.

MACDONALD, GNR., DUNCAN G., LL.B., –––. Aged 26 years. Taken prisoner in June, 1942. Died in hospital in Italy in Novr. 1942. Only son of Mr D. Macdonald and the late Mrs Macdonald, 20 Sherbrooke Avenue, Pollokshields, Glasgow.

MACKAY, 2nd LIEUT. FINLAY MILLER, B.L., Royal Corps of Signals. Died in India in Novr., 1942. Husband of Eileen S. Lindsay, and younger son of Mr and Mrs James Mackay, 25 Hillview Terrace, Blackhall, Edinburgh. Grandson of the late Mr and Mrs Finlay Miller, 43 Durness Street, Thurso.

MACKAY, ––– DONALD STEWART, 8th Black Watch. Killed at El Alamein – October 24, 1942. Grandson of the late Mr and Mrs Donald Mackay, 18 Durness Street, Thurso.

MACKAY, FLYING OFFICER JAMES, Royal Canadian Air Force. Killed in aircraft crash –

Decr. 16, 1943, when returning from raid on Germany. (Buried at Harrogate, Yorkshire.) Only son of Mr and Mrs James Mackay, Dodsland, Saskatchewan, Canada, who are natives of Thrumster.

MACKAY, C.Q.M.-SERGT. ANGUS M., Black Watch. Aged 29 years. Killed in Normandy – July 1, 1944. Teacher in Edinburgh. Husband of Violet Tynan, and eldest son of Captain and Mrs D. M. Mackay, Edinburgh.

MACKAY, ELIZABETH TAYLOR (Betty), A.T.S. Killed when on service in an East Anglian town – May 11, 1945 (result of enemy air raid action). One of 26 A.T.S. killed by direct hit on hostel. Eldest daughter of Mr and Mrs Donald Mackay, Easter Rarichie, Nigg, and granddaughter of Mr and Mrs Donald Mackay, The Bungalow, Halkirk.

MACKENZIE, SERGT.-OBSERVER COLIN J. H., Royal Air Force. Coastal Command. Aged 20 years. Reported missing March 26, 1943, later presumed killed on that date. Son of Mr and Mrs John R. Mackenzie, Chalfont St. Peter, Bucks., and grandson of Mrs Sutherland, 11 Brown Place, Wick.

MACKENZIE, A.C. FRANCIS RAYMOND, Royal Air Force. Accidentally drowned about September, 1942. Parents deceased. Grandson of the late Mr and Mrs George Budge, Burn of Rattar, Dunnet.

MACLEAN, GUNNER BYRON FITZROY, Australian Imperial Forces. Served in Malaya. Captured in Feby., 1942. Died later in a Japanese prisoner of war camp. Only son of Mrs Maclean and of the late Murdoch Maclean, Coogee, Sydney, Australia, a native of Whitebridge, Scarfskerry. Gunner Maclean was a grandnephew of the late George Banks, Rattar, Scarfskerry.

M'CORQUODALE, CAPT. ANGUS, Coldstream Guards. Aged 30 years. Killed in retreat to Dunkirk (1940). Nephew of The Lady Horne of Stirkoke.

McGREGOR, SGT. PILOT DAVID B., Royal Canadian Air Force. Killed in air operations in summer of 1942. Younger son of Mr and Mrs Aleck McGregor, Regina, and nephew of James Macadie, watchmaker, Wick.

McHARDY, SERGT. JAMES, Seaforth Highdrs. Aged 24 years. Killed in Sicily in July, 1943. Youngest son of Mr and Mrs McHardy, Easter Moy, Urray, Muir of Ord.

MALONE, SERGT.-GNR. THOMAS J., Royal Air Force. Killed in a flying accident – July 9, 1944. Son of the late Mr and Mrs T. J. Malone,

and grandson of the late Hector Macadie, shoemaker, 19 Wilson Street, Thurso.

MAITLAND, FLIGHT-LIEUT. IAN, D.F.C., Royal Air Force. Aged 37 years. Notified missing and later officially reported as killed in action over Flanders – August 28, 1942. Buried in Bonsou-les-Walcourt Cemetery, 27 miles southwest of Namur. Eldest son of Mr and Mrs John Maitland, Fasnacloich, Appin, Argyll and grandnephew of Mrs Barnie, Boultach, Latheron.

M'LAUCHLAN, ABLE-SEAMAN JOHN. Reported missing, presumed drowned on convoy to Russia, about September, 1942. Grandnephew of Mrs A. Gunn, Earnan Cottage, Castletown.

MANSON, CAPTAIN JAMES S., Royal Army Medical Corps. Reported missing, later as presumed killed in action in France between May 29 and June 2, 1940. Graduate in medicine of St. Andrews University. Belonged to Arbroath, father being the late D. L. Manson, and was grandson of the late Mr and Mrs George Manson, Kirklea, Dempster Street, Wick.

MANSON, CORPL. MERLIN J., Canadians. Aged 21 years. Died of wounds in Italy in July, 1944. Grandson of the late Mr and Mrs Donald Manson, Hill of Calder, Scotscalder. Parents in Saskatchewan, Canada.

MARTIN, CPL. INSTR. GRAHAM, Royal New Zealand Air Force. Lost on coastal patrol at New Zealand – October 23, 1942. Youngest son of Mr and Mrs John Martin, 62 Fitzgerald Avenue, Christchurch, N.Z., and grandson of the late Mr and Mrs John Martin, Oldwick Farm, Wick.

MATHIESON, FLT.-SERGT. ALISTAIR J., Royal Air Force. Killed in action – May 25, 1942. (No details.)

MELVILLE, L.-SERGT. CATHEL S., Scots Guards. Aged 30 years. Killed in action in Germany – April 6, 1945. Butcher to trade. Belonged Golspie, but wife (Joey Angus) and child resided at 12 Murrayfield, Castletown.

MOGGACH, SERGT. ALEXANDER S., Royal Air Force. Aged 25 years. Died on active service in April, 1942. Native of Banff. Husband of Margaret Napier.

MORE, PILOT OFFICER DONALD, Royal Canadian Air Force. Aged 19 years. Presumed lost on flying operations over Western Europe – July 6, 1944. Eldest son of Mr and Mrs T. More, 203 Atlas Ave., Toronto, Canada, and grandson of the late Mr and Mrs John Bremner, 4 Harbour Terrace, Wick.

MOORE, FUSILIER JAMES MACFARLANE, ———. Aged 25 years. Killed by a shell splinter five miles south of Cassino in May, 1944. Husband of Renee Sinclair, 39 Main Street, Uddingston (his home town).

MUNRO, CAPTAIN A. D. (Donald), 5th Seaforth Highdrs. Aged 26 years. Killed on Western Front in Feby., 1945. A Territorial. Severely wounded in right shoulder at El Alamein. Graduate (M.A.) of Aberdeen University. Eldest son of Mr and Mrs A. J. M. Munro, "Morven," Alness, and grandson of the late Mr and Mrs J. G. Duncan, "Rosemount", Wick.

MUNRO, CORPL. THOMAS H., 1st Herfordshire Regiment. Aged 26 years. Killed in Italy – Decr. 9, 1944. Husband of Gladys Munro, and only son of Mr and Mrs Donald Munro, 69 Stanley Street, Bedford; and grandson of Mrs Page, 24 Kennedy Terrace, Wick.

MUNRO, SPR. D. M., Royal Engineers. Reported missing, later as killed in action in the Middle East – Decr. 4, 1942. Nephew of Mrs Angus Munro, 5 Davidson's Lane, Thurso.

NICOLL, L.-BOMBDR. R. G. (Robbie), Canadian Army. Aged 23 years. Killed in Sicily – July 26, 1943. Youngest son of Mr and Mrs William Nicoll, Waskatenau, Alberta, Canada – both of whom are natives of Caithness.

PELLING, L.A.C.W. DOROTHY, Women's Auxilliary Air Force. Aged 20 years. Killed through enemy action – June 23, 1944. Grandmother (Mrs Robertson) resided Upper Lybster.

PERRY, CORPL. JAMES, Cameron Highdrs. Aged 21 years. Killed on Western Front in March, 1945. Joined Hampshire Regiment when 16, but transferred to London Scottish, Lovat Scouts, and then Camerons. Born in Wick. Elder son of Mr and Mrs J. Perry, 57 Talke Road, Fullbrook, Walsall, Staffordshire, and grandson of Mr and Mrs D. Oag, 45 Cairndhuna Terrace, Wick.

PLOWMAN, FLT.-SERGT. ARTHUR, Royal Australian Air Force. Aged 27 years. Killed on air operations during November, 1944. Youngest son of Mrs Plowman and the late Donald Plowman, Orange, N.S.W., Australia, and nephew of the late John Mill, Tain, Olrig.

RANSON, CAPTAIN ROBERT, Merchant Navy. Reported missing December 20, 1942, later presumed lost at sea through enemy action. Husband of Grace Cumming, 46 Craigmount View, Edinburgh, and 3 Traill Street, Thurso.

ROBERTSON, ABLE-SEAMAN JOHN W., Royal Navy. Died October 11, 1940, in R.N. Hospital, Grimsby. Nephew of Mrs R. Campbell, Hill of Forss, Thurso.

ROBERTSON, FLT. SERGT. ALAN W. S., Royal Air Force. Aged 21 years. Reported missing from a flight over Germany on the night of March 23, 1944. Grandson of John Weir, for long headmaster of Murkle School, near Thurso.

SCANLON, SERGT. MICHAEL G. C., Royal Air Force. Air gunner. Aged 21 years. Killed on active service in April, 1942. Only child of Mr and Mrs Scanlon, 14 Crarae Avenue, Edinburgh 4.

SHEARER, CORPL. WILLIAM, Toronto Scottish. Killed in France – August 1, 1944. Only son of Mr and Mrs Alexander Shearer, St. Clair Avenue, Toronto, and grandson of the late Mr and Mrs William Shearer, Girnigoe Street, Wick and nephew of William Shearer, Girnigoe Street.

SHEARER, LANCE-CORPL. EDWARD J, (Sonny), 5th Seaforth Highdrs. (Intelligence section). Aged 22 years. Severely wounded at Tripoli – January 21, 1943, and died in Cairo on May 25, 1943. Brought up in Thurso. Only son of Mr and Mrs Edward Shearer, Old Schoolhouse, Avoch, who are natives of Thurso.

SINCLAIR, LIEUT. IAN H., Paratroop Battalion. Aged 21 years. Killed in North Africa in March, 1943. Elder son of Dr G. H. Sinclair and Mrs Sinclair, the Green, Lockerbie, and grandson of Mr and Mrs Sinclair, Latheron, West Latheron.

SINCLAIR, CORPL. WILLIAM, 4th Cameron Highdrs. Aged 26 years. Died of wounds in France. Had the distinction of shooting down a German aeroplane with a Bren gun. Cabinetmaker to trade. Only son of Mr and Mrs William Sinclair, Balnafettack, Inverness, both of whom belong to Bowermadden.

SINCLAIR, PTE. DONALD IAN, 6th Airborne Division, King's Own Scottish Borderers. Aged 19 years. Killed while crossing the Rhine – March 24, 1945, when glider shot down at 2000 feet. Buried at Haminkelin, 36 miles n.n.w. of Dusseldorf. Elder son of Nicol S. Sinclair and Mrs Sinclair, Gargrave, Yorks., and grandson of the late Donald and Mrs Sinclair, North End, Stroma.

SINCLAIR, SEAMAN ROBERT MACKENZIE, Royal Navy. Aged 26 years. Member of the R.C.N.V.R., he was among those selected to take a course in England leading to a commission, and left Edmonton in August, 1940. Three months later he was posted "believed killed in action overseas" when ship was torpedoed off the south coast of England. Son of Mr and Mrs Charles Sinclair (née Lalla Mackenzie), Edmonton, Canada, both of whom were well known in Mey and Thurso. Nephew of Robert Mackenzie, Co-operative Buildings, Wick.

SINCLAIR, SERGT. GEORGE G., Royal Air Force. Observer. Aged 23 years. Killed in action in January, 1942. Youngest son of the late George G. Sinclair, Shanghai, and of Mrs M. Jones, Sydney, Australia, and grandson of Mrs Catherine Coghill, Nottingham Mains, Forse.

SMEED, TROOPER EDWIN J., 7th Hussars. Reported as missing in Burma, and later officially intimated killed in action on March 30, 1942. Younger son of the late Mr and Mrs George H. Smeed, High Barnet, and grandson of the late James Sinclair, watchmaker, Wick.

SMITH, FLIGHT-LIEUT. ALEXANDER G., Royal Air Force. Aged 24 years. Killed in a flying accident in February, 1945. Only son of the late Frederick S. Smith, of "Thurso," Reigate, and of Mrs Smith, Stafford House, Beaufort Road, Reigate. Grandson of the late Mr and Mrs Alexr. Begg, East Banks, Wick.

SMITH, FLT.-SERGT. DONALD SINCLAIR, Royal Air Force. Aged 23 years. Killed in action over France – Novr. 18, 1943. Only son of Mr and Mrs Smith, Martin Drive, Blackpool and grandson of the late Mr and Mrs Stewart Sinclair, Lybster.

SMITH, PETTY OFFICER WILLIAM C., Royal Naval Reserve. Died in a Naval Hospital – April 18, 1943. Husband of Margaret M. Mowat, 28 Barrock Street, Thurso, and son of the late James Smith and of Mrs Smith, 11 Stuart Street, Portessie, Buckie.

SMITH, CORPL. WILLIAM JAMES, Royal Air Force. Aged 23 years. Died at New Manse, Bower – May 16, 1944. Enlisted at outbreak of war. Contracted illness in 1943. Eldest son of Rev. William C. Smith and Mrs Smith (Bower), now of The Manse, Lochluichart, Ross-shire.

SMITH, PTE. LACHLAN, Lovat Scouts. Aged 29 years. Died of wounds in Italy – Novr. 19, 1944. Husband of Isabella Harper, Carsgoe, Halkirk, and third son of the late Andrew Smith and of Mrs Smith, Dunlichty Farm, by Inverness.

STEVEN, PILOT OFFICER DOUGLAS M., Royal Air Force. Killed in 1941 (probably July) as result of a flying accident. Son of Mr and Mrs George Steven, 2 Roull Road, Corstorphine, Edinburgh, and formerly of Wick.

STEVEN, SAPPER JAMES, Royal Engineers (South Africa). Killed in action in Italy in April, 1945. Third son of Mr and Mrs William Steven, well-known Edinburgh Caithnessians, who had four sons on service.

STEVEN, FLT.-SERGT. D. M., Royal Air Force. Killed in air operations over N. W. Europe in June, 1944. Fourth son of Mr and Mrs William Steven, Edinburgh, and brother of Spr. James above.

STEVENSON, CAPTAIN WILLIAM R., Cameron Highdrs. Killed in N.W. Europe about October, 1944. Son of Lord and Lady Stevenson, Heriot Row, Edinburgh, and brother of Mrs G. H. B. Henderson, Reaster.

STEWART, L.A.C. JOHN A., Royal Air Force. Killed on air operations in Burma – April 5, 1944. Only son of the late J. A. Stewart and of Mrs Stewart, Forres, and nephew of George S. Henderson, The Schoolhouse, Dunbeath.

STEWART, JAMES J., ex-Seaforth Highdrs. Aged 44 years. Died Septr. 20, 1945. Mobilised with 5th Seaforths at the outbreak of war; served later with the Camerons, and was discharged in Octr., 1944, on account of ill-health. Died at home. Wife (Isabella Webster) and five of a family resided at 26 Cairndhuna Terrace, Wick. (Belonged to Inverness.)

STODDART, CORPL. HARRY M., Cameron Highdrs. Aged 28 years. Died of wounds in Normandy – July 21, 1944. Served in North Africa and Sicily. Bricklayer in Wick with Messrs Watson. Belonged to Alness. Wife (Mary Page) and young son resided at 43 Nicholson Street, Wick.

STRACHAN, CORPL. JOHN P. H., Royal Air Force. Killed in a flying accident near Keiss, Wick – August 31, 1944. Husband of Johan Harper, 1 Lower Dunbar Street, Wick, and younger son of Mr and Mrs A. Strachan, 242 Clipington Road, Dundee.

SUTHERLAND, L.A.C. DONALD, Royal Air Force. Aged 26 years. Lost his life in air accident on August, 20, 1943, while training off East London, South Africa. Member of Lanarkshire Constabulary. Only son of Lieut. W. S. Sutherland, Glasgow Police, and of Mrs Sutherland, 62 Wedderlea Drive, Glasgow. Grandson of the late Constable Donald Sutherland, and of Mrs Sutherland, 26 Moray Street, Wick.

SUTHERLAND, JAMES KENNETH, M.B., Ch.B., M.R.C.P., M.R.C.O.G. Died on active service – May, 1940. Youngest son of the late James Sutherland and of Mrs Sutherland, Glencairn, Gilwern, near Abergavenny, South Wales.

SUTHERLAND, FLT. SERGT. JOHN SINCLAIR, Royal Air Force. Bomber Command. Aged 21 years. Killed on operational flight over Germany – Feby. 20, 1943. Son of Lieut.-Commander William Sutherland, R.N. (retired), a native of East Clyth.

SUTHERLAND, PTE. JOHN, 4th Seaforth Highdrs. Reported missing at St. Valery, later to have been killed on June 4, 1940. Farm-servant. Son of Mrs J. Bain, Clashnabuiac Farm, Alness, and grandson of the late Mr and Mrs James M'Kain, 27 Vansittart Street, Wick.

SWAINSON, LIEUT. JOHN, Canadians. Aged 23 years. Accidentally killed in Holland – May 31, 1945. Younger son of Mr and Mrs A. Swainson, 3082 Washington Avenue, Victoria, B.C., and grandson of the late Mr and Mrs John Adamson, Ingimster, Wick.

WALLACE, ABLE-SEAMAN DANIEL M., Quartermaster. Aged 30 years. Reported missing, presumed lost with H.M.S. "Egret" – August 27, 1943. Husband of Margaret Miller, Old Schoolhouse, Bower, and son of Mr and Mrs Murray, Tradespark Road, Nairn. (Native of Nairn.)

WATSON, SERGT. IAN REAY, Royal Canadian Air Force. Reported missing after operations early in 1943, and later presumed killed. Mother, Mrs J. R. Watson (née Jean Sutherland) native of Isauld, Reay, and resident 1640 Sherbrooke Street, West Montreal. Only son.

WATT, PTE. GEORGE L. M., 4th Seaforth Highdrs. Aged 23 years. Died in a prison camp in Germany – June 24, 1943. Only son of Mr and Mrs James Watt, The Bungalow, Evanton, Ross-shire.

WHITELAW, ABLE-SEAMAN WILLIAM. Aged 18½ years. Killed by enemy action in January, 1944. Youngest son of Mr and Mrs James Whitelaw, Garden City, East Calder, and grandson of the late William Macleod, Castletown.

NEW LEAVES COME AGAIN

Softly the leaves are falling,
Falling, but not in vain;
They're a moving pageant calling
To new leaves come again.

Bare forest trees are humming
A mournful, sad refrain;
But a day is always coming
When new leaves come again.

So each year hath its winter,
And most days have their rain;
The poplars stand and shiver,
But new leaves come again.

And each heart hath its sorrow,
And each life hath its pain;
But sun shines on the morrow,
And new hope comes again.

–C. L. BAIN.

MISSING.

ANDERSON, ABLE-SEAMAN GEORGE, Royal Navy. Aged 24 years. Reported missing at sea about September, 1940. Anderson had previously earned recognition of his services when a ship on which he was serving was attacked by an enemy 'plane. Wife (Susan Watt) and his mother belong to Wick. Young couple resided in Wick before going to 2 Bridge Street, Leith.

ANGUS, SEAMAN CHARLES, Royal Navy. Aged 21 years. Posted missing about May, 1940. Son of Mr and Mrs Donald Angus, Shore Street, Thurso (Name appears on Thurso War Memorial.)

BRIMS, CAPTAIN ANDREW, Merchant Navy (Liverpool). Reported missing, presumed lost at sea through enemy action (probably July) 1943. Fourth son of Mr and Mrs Andrew Brims, 4 Shore Street, Thurso.

CARTER, SEAMAN JAMES. Aged 20 years. Reported missing at sea – December, 1943. Notice received on his twentieth birthday. Son of Mr and Mrs Hugh Carter, Inver House, Lybster. (Name on Lybster War Memorial.)

DUNDAS, PTE. WILLIAM ALEXR., Royal Artillery. Posted missing in Middle East on May 31, 1942. Son of Mr and Mrs David Dundas, Ormlie, Thurso. (Name on Thurso War Memorial.)

GUNN, PTE DAVID, M.M., 5th Seaforth Highlanders. Reported missing in Middle East in October, 1943. Was prisoner of war. Youngest son of Mr and Mrs James Gunn, 18 Henrietta Street, Wick.

MACPHEE, PTE. GEORGE. Reported missing while serving with Central Mediterranean Forces about June, 1944. Wife resided 40 Cairndhuna Terrace, Wick, and second son of Mr and Mrs Isaac Macphee of same address.

NICOL, SPR. WILLIAM, Royal Engineers. Reported missing after the fall of Singapore. Postcard received from him 17 months later (in July, 1943) stating that he was taken prisoner in Malaya. Reported missing again early in 1945, this time at sea as the result of the sinking of a ship transporting prisoners of war from Thailand to Japan. Fourth son of the late John Nicol (who lost his life serving with the Navy in 1914-18 war) and of Mrs Nicol, 8 Tolbooth Lane, Wick. Wife (Annie Bruce) and daughter resided at 20 Kennedy Tce., Wick. (Home address – 12 Barrogill Street.) Before the war he was employed as a joiner.

STEWART, SEAMAN WILLIAM, Royal Navy. Posted missing – June, 1944. Brother of Mrs W. Mackay, Jeffrey Street, Lybster. (Name on Lybster War Memorial.)

TAYLOR, TROOPER JAMES (8th Hussars), Royal Armoured Corps. Reported missing, believed prisoner of war, as from 27th May, 1942, during operations in Libya. Son of Mrs Taylor, Sinclair Street, Halkirk. Previously in employ of Mr Cairnie, chemist, Thurso.

Men of Caithness Connection.

BOAK, DAVID BARCLAY, Scots Guards. Reported missing in Middle East – June 13, 1942. Son of Mrs J. Boak, 2 East Cottages, Granton, and grandson of Mr and Mrs Alexander Miller, 43 Nicholson Street, Wick.

BROWN, SEAMAN DAVID, H.M. Canadian Navy. Posted missing – May 9, 1944. His late mother (Nicolson to name) was brought up in Shore Lane, Wick, and her brother is R. A. Nicolson, hairdresser, Basingstoke.

SIMPSON, SUB.-LIEUT. J., Pilot Officer in Fleet Air Arm. Aged 21 years. Posted missing from a night flying operation off the west coast of Scotland – September 27, 1943. Joined services May 24, 1941. Brother a prisoner of war in Germany. Third son of Police Constable J. M. Simpson, 3 Malvern Road, Hampton, Middlesex, who belongs to Stroma.

THYNE, LIEUT. J. P., Royal Army Medical Corps. Reported missing in 1940. A doctor in London, but known in Mid-Clyth, where his wife (Mackenzie to name) belongs.

TUCK, GUNNER FRANK R., Royal Artillery. Aged 23 years. Posted missing, probably June, 1940. Parents' address – Strath House, Watten.

Names of fallen not on our list but taken from war memorials:–

MACKAY, HUGH, Merchant Navy (Thurso).

ROBERTSON, JOHN, Merchant Navy (Lybster).

PRISONERS OF WAR.

ANGUS, DRIVER ALISTER, Royal Army Service Corps. Reported missing after fall of Singapore; postcard received from him 17 months later (July, 1943) stating he was a prisoner of war. Wife resided at 28 Holborn Avenue, Thurso, and parents (Mr and Mrs Alexr. Angus) at Rose Street, Thurso.

BAIN, PTE. DONALD, Seaforth Highlanders. Posted missing January 18, 1944, while serving with Central Med. Forces; later as wounded prisoner of war in Germany. In civil life a mason in Wick. Son of Mr and Mrs David Bain, 14 Wilson Street, Thurso. (Brother killed.)

BAIN, PTE ROBERT, Seaforth Highlanders. Posted missing October 5, 1943, in North Africa; later as prisoner of war in Italian hands. Wife resided at Black Isle, Watten.

BANKS, PTE. WILLIAM, 4th Seaforth Highlanders. Taken prisoner of war by Germans in June, 1940. Cooper to trade. Wife resided at 52 Willowbank, Wick, and son of Mr and Mrs D. Banks, Henrietta Street, Wick.

BUDGE, TPR. WILLIAM S., Royal Tank Regiment. Reported missing in Middle East (Tobruk) on June 20, 1942; later as prisoner of war. Son of Mr and Mrs George Budge, 22 Green Road, Wick.

CAMERON, PTE. JAMES, Seaforth Highdrs. Taken prisoner at St. Valery in 1940. Home address – 7 Holborn Avenue, Thurso. Repatriated October, 1944.

CAMPBELL, CORPL. W. J., Royal Tank Regiment. Posted missing in Middle East (probably Tobruk) June 20, 1942; later as prisoner in Italian hands. Prior to serving in M.E. was in India with the Tank Corps. Son of Mrs Campbell, Crescent Street, Halkirk.

CAMPBELL, SERGT. (later W.O.) GEORGE MORVEN, Royal Air Force. Air gunner. Reported missing as result of air operations in July, 1943. Younger son of Mr and Mrs Campbell, The Manse, Shurrery, Reay.

CARTER, ABLE-SEAMAN JACK, Merchant Navy. Taken prisoner and interned in France. Ship was sunk in Indian Ocean some months before May, 1941. Son of Mrs Carter, Lybster, and the late John Carter, late of Castlehill, Dunbeath. Married, and wife living in Glasgow.

CORMACK, DRIVER JOHN, Royal Army Service Corps. Posted missing June 20, 1942 (Tobruk); later as prisoner in Italy. Escaped from Italian prison camp to Switzerland, and came home on leave in November, 1944. Husband of Mrs Cormack, 33 Girnigoe Street, Wick.

CROWE, PTE. ALEXANDER, Royal Army Service Corps. Taken prisoner in the fall of France in June, 1940, and escaped with three companions three months later, reaching Britain again in March 1941. Employed as a baker. Elder son of Mr and Mrs John Crowe, 23 Cairndhuna Terrace, Wick. Married, and wife resided in Willowbank.

CUSTER, CORPL, WILLIAM, M.M., R.E., South African Forces. Reported missing after the fall of Tobruk (June 20, 1942); later as prisoner of war in Italy. Son of the late Mr and Mrs William Custer, The Ha', Durran, Olrig.

DAVIDSON, L.-SERGT. THOMAS, Seaforth Highdrs. Reported missing June 29, 1940; later as prisoner of war in Germany. Regular soldier – joined some time before the war. Was at Dunkirk. Son of Mr and Mrs John Davidson, Ashley House, Wick. Married: wife resided 9 Back Shore Street, Thurso.

DAVIDSON, PTE. WILLIAM, Royal Army Medical Corps. Reported missing in France in June, 1940; later as a prisoner of war in Germany. Grocer's assistant. Only son of Mr and Mrs William Davidson, Willowbank, Wick.

DONN, AIRCRAFTMAN JAMES, Royal Air Force. Posted missing in December, 1941, after fall of Singapore, and 18 months after (July, 1943) intimated he was prisoner in Japanese hands. Captured in Java. Son of Mrs M. M. Donn, Bayview Hotel, Lybster. Native of Thurso.

DOUGLAS, PTE. JAMES, Cameron Highdrs. Prisoner in Germany – probably June, 1940. Home address – Stemster, Halkirk.

DUNBAR, PTE. JOHN G. W., 4th Seaforth Highdrs. Posted missing June, 1940; later as a prisoner of war in Germany. Employed with L.M.S. Coy. at Dornoch. Son of Mrs Dunbar, Station Cottage, Bilbster.

DUNNETT, SERGT. WILLIAM, Royal Army Service Corps. Prisoner of war in Italian hands June 20, 1942 (Tobruk); later in Germany. Eldest son of David Dunnett, school attendance officer, and of Mrs Dunnett, 24 Louisburgh Street, Wick. Wife (Dorothy Gibson) resided in Tain. (Brother also a prisoner, and died in Borneo.)

DUNNETT, PTE. THOMAS, Argyll and Sutherland Highdrs. Posted missing June 5,

1940; later as prisoner of war in Germany. Eldest son of Mr and Mrs Tom Dunnett, Dunbeath. Wife resided at Latheronwheel.

DUNNETT, PTE. ALEXANDER, 2nd Royal Scots. Prisoner of war in Japanese hands after Hong-Kong battle. Regular soldier – six years in army. Son of Mr and Mrs Donald Dunnett, Achcastle, Lybster.

ELDER, CORPL. GEORGE, 2nd Seaforth Highlanders. Reported missing in July, 1940; later as prisoner of war. Enlisted six years previously. Second son of Mr and Mrs John Elder, 9 Macarthur Street, Wick. Married – wife resided in Rosemarkie.

FLETT, SERGT.-OBSERVER GEORGE, Royal Air Force. Ship sunk by enemy action in Mediterranean when coming on leave but was rescued and landed in French Morocco where he was interned in September, 1941. Son of George Flett, fishsalesman, Pittenweem (formerly of Wick) and of the late Mrs Flett. Grandson of the late John Bain, bookseller, and of Mrs Bain, Breadalbane Crescent, Wick.

FORBES, GNR. DAVID, New Zealand Expeditionary Force. Wounded in Crete and taken prisoner of war. Son of Mr and Mrs Donald Forbes, 11 Green Road, Wick. (Brother killed).

GRANT, SPR. JOE, Royal Engineers, South African Forces. Reported missing in Middle East – June, 1942; later as prisoner in Italian hands. Mason to trade. Elder surviving son of Mr and Mrs R. Grant, 7 Alexandra Place, Wick.

GUNN, PTE. GEORGE ——. Reported missing in the Middle East about April, 1941, and in October of same year as a prisoner of war in Germany. Wounded and captured in Crete. A shepherd. Third son of Mr and Mrs Adam Gunn, Knockally, Dunbeath.

GUNN, PTE. ALEXANDER, 4th Seaforth Highdrs. Mobilised with Territorials. Prisoner of war in Germany for five years. Younger son of Mrs Gunn and of the late Alexander Gunn, Gothiegill, Castletown.

GUNN, PTE. ALEXANDER, Cameron Highlanders. Wounded and prisoner of war in Germany for five years. Now postman at Brough, Dunnet. Younger son of William Gunn, West End, Castletown.

HAMILTON, PTE. ANDREW, 4th Seaforth Highdrs. Posted missing about June, 1940; later as prisoner of war in Germany. Farm-servant in Ross-shire for three years before war. Son of Mrs William Miller, Bridge-end, Westerdale, Halkirk.

HARCUS, —— R. Address – Thurso East. Returned home in May, 1945, after being prisoner of war.

HARROLD, PTE. GEORGE, 5th Seaforth Highlanders. Taken prisoner of war by Italians in closing stages of Tunisian campaign (March, 1943); transferred to Germany as prisoner when Italy collapsed. Compositor to trade. Elder son of the late William Harrold and Mrs Harrold, 33 High Street, Wick.

HENDERSON, CORPL. JOHN, Royal Corps of Signals. Posted missing in Middle East 20th June, 1942; and later as prisoner in Italian hands. Joined army in 1936. Son of James Henderson, 7 Riverside, Thurso; wife resided at 4 Kirkhill, Wick.

JOHNS, —— M. Home address – Campbell Street, Thurso. Returned home May, 1945, after being a prisoner of war.

KEITH, CORPL. ANGUS, Royal Army Service Corps. Reported missing April 28, 1941; later as a prisoner of war in Germany. Joined regular army on leaving school. Eldest son of Mr and Mrs Angus Keith, Achavrole, Dunbeath.

KEITH, PTE PETER, 4th Seaforth Highdrs. Posted missing in June, 1940; later as a prisoner of war in German hands. Repatriated among the wounded, 1943. Fourth son of Mrs Robert Keith, Hoy, Olrig.

KENNEDY, SERGT. WILLIAM, 5th Seaforth Highdrs. Posted missing, later as prisoner. Son of the late William Kennedy, and of Mrs Kennedy, Hoy Farm, Halkirk. Baker in Wick, and wife resided Northfield, Hempriggs.

KENNEDY, GNR. DAVID, Royal Artillery (Searchlight Corps). Brother of above. Was prisoner of war in Germany.

LAMOND, GNR. WILLIAM, Royal Artillery. Posted missing on June, 2, 1941, while serving in Middle East; later as prisoner of war in Germany. Wife resided in Latheronwheel.

LAWSON, PTE. WILLIAM A, ——. Reported missing about June, 1940; later as prisoner of war in Germany. Gamekeeper with Mr A. D. Pilkington. Son of Mr and Mrs Lawson, Brubster Cottage, Reay.

LEGGATT, C. —— Returned home May, 1945, after being a prisoner of war in Germany. Son of Mr and Mrs Wm. C. Leggatt, Station House, Thurso.

MACDONALD, DVR. NEIL G., Royal Corps of Signals. Reported missing in Malaya at fall of Singapore; postcard received from him 18 months later stated he was a prisoner of war. Eldest son of Mr and Mrs Alexander Macdonald,

36 Holborn Avenue, Thurso. Wife resided in Fraserburgh.

MACDONALD, PTE. NEIL, 4th Cameron Highlanders. Posted missing in June, 1940; later as a prisoner of war in Germany. Painter to trade. Called up with Militia. Younger son of Mr and Mrs Malcolm Macdonald, 72 Louisburgh Street, Wick.

MACDONALD, PTE. JAMES, Seaforth Highlanders. Taken prisoner by Germans about June, 1940. Son of George Macdonald, Milton, Reay.

MACDONALD, DVR. ANGUS, Royal Army Service Corps. Posted missing about June, 1940; later as a prisoner of war in Germany. Son of John Macdonald, Ousdale.

MACDONALD, LAWRENCE, ——. Taken prisoner by Germans about June, 1940. Called up with Militia six months before war. Youngest son of Mrs Macdonald, Inver, Dunbeath, and of the late Hugh Macdonald.

MACGREGOR, PTE. WILLIAM, 4th Seaforth Highdrs. Reported missing in France in June, 1940; later as a prisoner of war in Germany. Employed in Francis Street Garage until he enlisted before the war. Son of Mr and Mrs John Macgregor, 11 Telford Street, Wick.

MACGREGOR, PTE. JAMES, Seaforth Highlanders. Reported missing on June 7, 1940; later as prisoner of war in Germany. Son of Mr and Mrs Alexander Macgregor, Murkle, Thurso.

MACIVOR, PTE. ARCHIBALD, Seaforth Highlanders. Reported missing January, 1943, and later as prisoner of war in Italian hands. Wife resided at No. 1 New Houses, Keiss. Third son of Mr and Mrs James Macivor, Drymount, Latheron.

MACKAY, TPR. HUGH, Royal Tank Brigade. Posted missing June 20, 1942 (Tobruk); later as prisoner of war in Italian hands. Eldest son of Mr and Mrs Tom Mackay, Camster Cottage, Occumster. Married: wife resided in Dorking, Surrey.

MACKAY, PTE. JOHN, 5th Seaforth Highdrs. Reported missing in Middle East in Novr., 1943; later as a prisoner of war. Son of Mr and Mrs Mackay, Shurrery Manse, Reay.

MACKAY PTE. GEORGE (No. 2816319). A Caithness soldier who was prisoner of war in Italy and sent a greetings message from the Vatican Radio on Decr., 24, 1941. No address given. Believed to belong to Scotscalder and to have relatives in Wick

MACKAY, PTE. ALEXANDER, 4th Seaforth Highdrs. Posted missing about June, 1940; later

as a prisoner of war in Germany. Belongs to Stirkoke and gardener to trade. Wife resided in Lower Dunbar Street, Wick.

MACKAY, PTE. COLIN, Gordon Highlanders. Posted missing in France, probably June, 1940; later as prisoner in Germany. In peace-time a farm-servant in Aberdeenshire. Fourth son of the late David R. Mackay, farmer, Assery, Westfield, and of Mrs Mackay, 4 New Houses, Thrumster.

MACKAY, PIPER JOHN, Gordon Highdrs. Brother of above. Posted missing – probably June, 1940. Among first wounded repatriated. Joined army in peace-time. Married and resided in Aberdeen.

MACKENZIE, DAVID M., ——. Was camp leader of Stalag 383 during his five years' captivity in Germany. Was mentioned in despatches and awarded M.B.E. Son of the late Angus Mackenzie, Harland Gardens, Castletown, and of Mrs Mackenzie, Kirkcaldy.

MACLEOD, SERGT. ALAN, Scots Guards. Prisoner in Italian hands – November 1941. Grandson of Mrs R. Mackenzie, 49 Argyle Square, Wick.

MACLEOD, SERGT. KENNETH M., Scots Guards. Brother of above. Posted missing in Middle East, June 13, 1942, and later as prisoner of war in German hands.

MACLEOD, PTE. JOHN G., 4th Seaforth Highdrs. Reported missing in June, 1940; later as prisoner in Germany. Eldest son of Mr and Mrs John Macleod, Myrelandhorn, Wick.

MACLEOD, PTE. WILLIAM, 2nd New Zealand Expeditionary Force. Taken prisoner by Italians in Western Desert – July 13, 1942. Brother of Miss E. Macleod, Camilla Street, Halkirk.

MACPHERSON, GUNNER GEORGE, Royal Artillery. Reported missing in Middle East on January 29, 1942; later as prisoner in Italian hands. Son of Mrs Macpherson, 55 Kennedy Terrace, Wick, and of the late John Macpherson, Gordon Highlanders.

McCARTHY, PTE WILLIAM, 2nd Cameron Highdrs. Served in North Africa from March, 1941. Wounded in chest on December 4 of that year and was four months in hospital. Taken prisoner at Tobruk (June, 1942) and after the fall of Italy was three months "at liberty" in that country before recapture by the Germans. Was in a working camp in Germany from December, 1943, until end of war. Eldest son of the late James McCarthy and of Mrs McCarthy, Thrumster (now at Skinnet Farm, Halkirk). Had two brothers in the Forces.

McNAB, PTE. EDWARD, Seaforth Highdrs.

Prisoner of war in Germany. A native of Wick. Wife and family resident in Thurso.

MILLER, PTE. WILLIAM, 4th Seaforth Highlanders. Posted missing in June, 1940; later as prisoner of war in Germany. Son of Mr and Mrs William Miller, Albion Cottage, Lybster.

MILLER, PTE. DONALD, Seaforth Highdrs. Posted missing in Sicily; later as prisoner of war. Son of Mr and Mrs James Miller, Backlass, Watten.

MOORE, 2nd LIEUT. WILLIAM, 4th Seaforth Highdrs. Reported missing June, 1940; later as prisoner of war in Germany. A student at St. Andrews, Son of Rev. G. Moore and Mrs Moore, The Manse, Wick.

MOWAT, FLIGHT-SERGT. JACK, Glider Pilot. Posted missing in Septr., 1944, following operations at Arnhem; later as prisoner of war in Germany. Wife resided in Main Street, Lybster. Only son of William Mowat, Main Street, Lybster.

MOWAT, GUNNER DAVID, Royal Artillery. Taken prisoner by Japanese in Malaya, and later reported missing, presumed killed, in sinking of ship conveying prisoners of war to Japan. Son of George Mowat, Roadside, Ulbster.

MOWAT, PTE. JAMES ALEXR., Royal Army Ordnance Corps. Posted missing in France – May 16, 1940; letter received from him dated March 30, 1941, bearing French postmark stated that he was "now getting well." Escaped and arrived in Britain after months of adventure. Son of Mr and Mrs John A. Mowat, Portland Arms Hotel, Lybster.

MUNRO, LEADING SEAMAN GEORGE, Royal Navy, V.R. Picked up off Tunisia from torpedoed vessel and interned in Algiers for ten months. Released when British occupied North Africa towards end of 1942. Resided at 57 Henrietta Street, Wick, and son of Mr and Mrs Donald Munro, 1 Bayview Terrace, Thurso.

NORRIS, FLIGHT-SERGT. FRANK, Royal Air Force. Taken prisoner in 1944 when his 'plane came down at Leghorn, in Italy. Son of Mr and Mrs Norris, of Lybster and Thurso.

OLIPHANT, PTE. GEORGE, Sherwood Foresters. Posted missing in Malaya in February, 1942; 16 months later known to be prisoner of war. Eldest son of Mr and Mrs G. Oliphant, Elzy Farm, Staxigoe.

ROBERTSON, PTE. WILLIAM, Seaforth Highlanders. Reported missing in North Africa – April 6, 1943; later as a prisoner in Italian hands. Was on staff at Pentland Hotel, Thurso. Son of Mr and Mrs James Robertson, 31 Grove Lane, Thurso.

ROSS, PTE. WILLIAM, 1st Airborne Division. Posted missing at Arnhem in Septr., 1944; later as a prisoner of war in Germany. A regular soldier – served five years in India. Son of Mrs Young, 10 Robert Street, Wick, and grandson of Mr and Mrs David Ross, North Keiss.

SANDISON, CORPL. DAVID, South African Forces. Reported missing, later as prisoner of war in Benghazi about Septr., 1942. Served in 1914-18 war. Son of the late Isaac Sandison, baker and grocer, Wick, and of Mrs Sandison, Johannesburg. Family emigrated about 20 years ago.

SHEARER, LIEUT. JAMES W., Anti-Tank Corps. Reported missing about June, 1940; later as prisoner of war. Teller in British Linen Bank. Son of Mrs Robert Shearer, Rose Street, Thurso.

SHEARER, PTE. HUGH S., Seaforth Highdrs. Posted missing in June, 1940; later as war in Germany. Son of Mrs Shearer; Balblair House, Lybster.

SINCLAIR, GUARDSMAN MURDO, Scots Guards. Reported missing in Middle East – June, 1942; later as prisoner (German broadcast, Septr. 1942). Was employed by A. D. Pilkington, Esq. of Achvarasdal. Son of Mr and Mrs George Sinclair, Upper Geiselittle, Weydale, Thurso (late of Isauld Hill, Reay).

SINCLAIR, SERGT. DONALD, 1st Airborne Division. Reported missing from the operations at Arnhem in Septr., 1944; later as prisoner of war. Was on staff of North of Scotland Bank at Strichen, and formerly at Wick. Second son of Donald Sinclair, J.P., retired bank agent, "St. Duthus," Halkirk, and of the late Mrs Sinclair.

SINCLAIR, SERGT. DAVID D., Seaforth Highlanders. Reported missing in Italy – May 31, 1944; and later as prisoner of war in Germany. Mobilised with Territorials and saw service in Madagascar, India, Persia and Iraq, Syria and Italy. Youngest son of the late James Sinclair and of Mrs Sinclair, Mains of Forse, Latheron.

SINCLAIR, GUNNER ADAM, Royal Artillery. Posted missing in Middle East – June 20, 1942; later as prisoner of war in Italy. Son of Mrs James Sinclair, Upper Latheron.

SINCLAIR, DVR. JOHN, Royal Army Service Corps. Brother of above. Posted missing in Middle East – June 20, 1942; later as prisoner of war in Italy.

SINCLAIR, —— DONNIE, Cameron Highdrs. Reported missing in France about June, 1940; later as prisoner of war in Germany. Mother, Mrs Sinclair (late of Berriedale) resided in Newtonmore.

111

SKENE, L.-SERGT. JOHN, 1st Lothian and Border Yeomanry. Posted missing in France in June, 1940; later as prisoner in Germany. Son of John Skene, engine-driver, and Mrs Skene, Main Street, Lybster. Married, and wife resided in Edinburgh.

SMITH, GUNNER STEEL, Anti-Tank Corps. Reported missing in France about June, 1940; later as prisoner in Germany. Regular soldier. Wife resided 4 Wilson Street, Thurso.

SMITH, PTE. WILLIAM, Cameron Highdrs. Prisoner of war in Germany (probably 1940). Wife resided at 35 Holborn Avenue, Thurso.

STEWART, SERGT. BEN. G., Royal Air Force. Air gunner. Reported missing on Feby. 25. 1944; later as a prisoner of war in Germany suffering from concussion. Son of Mr and Mrs Alexander Stewart, Hempriggs, Wick.

STODDART, LIEUT. J. B., Royal Corps of Signals. Reported prisoner in Japanese hands in Malaya. Wife (née J. Macpherson) resided at 59 Princes Street, Thurso.

SUTHERLAND, SERGT. HARRY, 1st Worcestershire Regiment. In May, 1941, reported missing in Greece, but later rejoined his regiment. During first Abyssinian campaign (when with Seaforths) was missing for six weeks but got back after spending that period in Arab hands. Posted missing in Middle East, probably in June, 1942 (Tobruk); later announced as prisoner in Italian hands, and afterwards in Germany. Fifteen years in the Services, first 10 years with the Seaforths. Wife resided at 7 Whitehouse Lane, Wick.

SUTHERLAND, PTE. ALEXANDER, Royal Army Ordnance Corps. Reported missing after fall of Singapore early in 1942; postcard (dated June 20, 1942) received from him saying he was prisoner in Japanese hands. Son of Mr and Mrs Allan Cormack, Sinclair Street, Halkirk.

SUTHERLAND, PTE. JOHN D., Cameron Highlanders. Taken prisoner by Italians in Middle East – June 21, 1942. Escaped when Italy capitulated, and reached home July 9, 1944. Later joined R.E.'s. He had four brothers in the Services, three of whom – William, Don and George – met in Burma. A fifth brother (James) was in the Navy. Son of Mr and Mrs James Sutherland, 1 Freswick Gardens, Thurso.

SUTHERLAND, DVR. WILLIAM, Royal Army Service Corps. Was prisoner of war, returning home in May, 1945. Native of Forse, Latheron.

SWANSON, CORPL. JOHN, Royal Army Service Corps. Reported missing in Italy on Octr. 3, 1943; later as prisoner of war in Germany. Before joining up was employed as a sorting clerk in post office at Wick and Leeds. Third son of Mr and Mrs John Swanson, Kirkhill, Wick.

MEN OF CAITHNESS CONNECTION.

ANDERSON, PTE. JOHN, Royal Army Medical Corps, 1st Airborne Division. Reported wounded and missing at Arnhem; later as prisoner of war in Germany. Son of Mr and Mrs Alexr. Anderson, Police Station, Coulter, and grandson of the late Mr and Mrs John Manson, Reiss.

BREMNER, CORPL. RODERICK S., New Zealand Forces. Served in Greece and Crete, where taken prisoner. Had three brothers on service. Son of Mr and Mrs Alexander M. Bremner, New Zealand (natives of Wick).

FINLAYSON, LIEUT. ROBERT M., U.S.A. Army Air Corps. Reported missing from an operational flight over Germany (probably April, 1945); later as prisoner. Medical student at Michigan. Only son of Mr and Mrs H. G. Finlayson, of Peoria, Illinois, and grandson of the late Mr and Mrs D. Finlayson, Castletown.

GOODMAN, PTE. R., King's Own Scottish Borderers, 1st Airborne Division. Posted missing at Arnhem in September, 1944; later as prisoner of war in Germany. Native of Dalbeattie. Wife (formerly Betty Macdonald) resided at 114 Willowbank, Wick.

HENDERSON, SPR. DONALD, F., Royal Engineers. Reported prisoner of war in Italy, 1942. Parents – Mr and Mrs David Henderson, 10 Rossie Place, Edinburgh, both of whom belong to Caithness; Canisbay and Mey respectively.

LEITH, PTE. JOHN B., Australian Imperial Forces. Posted missing in February, 1942; later as a prisoner in Malaya Camp. Son of Mr and Mrs John Leith, Delny Farm, Delny.

MACDONALD, CORPL. ROBERT M., 1st Regina Rifle Regiment. Reported missing on Western Front (Holland) on October 17, 1944; and later as prisoner of war in Germany. Son and only child of Mrs Mary J. Macdonald and of the late Robert Macdonald, confectioner, Vancouver, and grandson of the late John Mackay and of Mrs Mackay, Torbeg, Dunbeath.

MACGRUER, FLIGHT-SERGT. D., Royal Air Force. Prisoner of war in Japanese hands for $3\frac{1}{2}$ years. Son of Mr and Mrs F. MacGruer, Edinburgh, and grandson of the late George Malcolm, joiner, and the late Mrs Malcolm, Castletown. Married Isobel, daughter of Mr and Mrs Alexander Stephen, Coach Road, Wick.

MATHESON, REV. JAMES G., B.D., Chaplain to the Forces. Reported missing in Libya – June 29, 1942; later as prisoner. Escaped 1943, and rejoined British Forces. His youngest brother (Norman) was also a prisoner (taken 1940). Belongs to Beauly, and was Free Church minister at Castletown.

MATHESON, PTE. GEORGE G., Seaforth Highdrs. Posted missing probably June, 1940; later as prisoner in Germany. Home address given as 3 Glebe Terrace, Helmsdale, and West Banks, Wick. Wife and child resided New Borgue, Dunbeath.

MALCOLM, LIEUT. GEORGE S., United States Air Force. Reported missing in March, 1944; later as prisoner of war in Germany. Son of George W. Malcolm, Sturgis, South Dakota, U.S.A., whose parents (the late Mr and Mrs John Malcolm) resided at 25 Brown Place, Wick.

M'ASKILL, CHIEF ENGINEER NORMAN, Merchant Navy. After his ship was torpedoed off Malta he was confined in a prison camp in North Africa for more than a year, and escaped along with 300 others. Parents resided for a time at Willowbank, Wick.

M'BAY, GUNNER ROBERT. Reported lost with merchant cruiser "Rawalpindi" on Novr. 23, 1939; later as prisoner of war. Son of Mr and Mrs M'Bay, Johnshaven. Resident in Castletown.

SIMPSON, CORPL. W., Royal Army Medical Corps. Taken prisoner in May, 1940, and repatriated in May, 1944. Son of Police Constable J. M. Simpson, 3 Malvern Road, Hampton, Middlesex, who is a native of Stroma. (Brother "missing.")

SINCLAIR, LIEUT. JAMES D., Fleet Air Arm. Reported missing after flying operations off Sicilian coast; later as prisoner in Italian hands. Son of Mr and Mrs William Sinclair, "Morven," Pollokshields, Glasgow, and nephew of Rev. R. R. Sinclair, Wick.

STALKER, PTE. DAVID, Seaforth Highdrs. Taken prisoner about June, 1940, in France. Son of Mr Stalker, stationmaster, Tain (formerly of Lybster).

STEWART, MAJOR KENNEDY, Royal Army Service Corps. Prisoner of war in Germany – taken at St. Valery in 1940. Formerly county librarian of Caithness.

WOUNDED.

ALLAN, PIPER ALISTAIR, 5th Seaforth Highdrs. Wounded in Middle East – Novr., 1942. Captured by enemy, escaped and was later wounded. Was employed in Wick Post Office before the war. Son of Mr and Mrs William Allan, 23 Henrietta Street, Wick. Wife resided Ashley House.

Piper Allan was one of a party of four men, which included the M.O. of the battalion, his sergeant and two stretcher-bearers. While being driven into the enemy lines they escaped, after being in the hands of the Germans for less than three-quarters of an hour.

ANDERSON, PTE. NEIL M., Argyll and Sutherland Highdrs. Wounded in Western Europe in Feby., 1945. Hit by shrapnel on left thigh and foot and taken by air to hospital in Swansea. Second son of Mrs Anderson, South Keiss, and of the late Andrew Anderson.

ANDERSON, PTE. ROBERT, Paratroops. Wounded in action in Normandy – June, 1944. Youngest son of Mrs Anderson (and late George Anderson), 34a Vansittart Street, Wick. Wife resided at 7 Moray Terrace, Brora.

ANDERSON, CORPL. GEORGE, New Zealand Forces. Wounded in North Africa campaign and discharged. Brother of above. Met another brother (James) out East and had happy re-union after 19 years.

ANGUS, CORPL. WILLIAM, 5th Seaforth Highdrs. Wounded in right arm in N.W. Europe about August, 1944, and taken to hospital in England. Employed as hairdresser in Thurso. Wife resided 2 Grove Lane, Thurso.

BAIN, SEAMAN DONALD, Royal Naval Reserve. Wounded and burnt in the "Jervis Bay" action on November 6, 1940. Now burgh officer at Wick. Wife belongs to Castletown. Mother – Mrs S. Bain, 136 Willowbank, Wick.

BAIN, PTE ROBERT, 5th Seaforth Highdrs. Wounded in Sicily – July, 1943; again in N.W. Europe in Septr., 1944, and taken to hospital in Leamington. Hairdresser to trade. Son of Mr and Mrs Andrew Bain, 6 Ackergill Street, Wick, who had six sons in the Services.

BAIN, PTE. (later A/Sergt.) JOHN, 5th Seaforth Highdrs. Wounded in head and chest in Normandy about July, 1944, and taken to hospital in Scotland. Served in Africa and Sicily. Co-op. assistant before mobilisation. Son of Mr and Mrs John Bain, 15 Davidson's Lane, Thurso.

BANKS, TPR. DENNIS, attached Canadian Tank Corps. Wounded in Normandy about July, 1944, and taken to hospital in England. Youngest son of Mr and Mrs Alexander Banks, 50 Louisburgh Street, Wick. Married: wife in Surrey.

BANNERMAN, CORPL. GEORGE, 5th Seaforth Hdrs. Wounded in shoulder by shrapnel in the Middle East – January, 1943. Reporter. Wife (Ella Manson) resided 21a Kinnaird Street, Wick. Son of Mr and Mrs G. Bannerman, 7 Willowbank, Wick.

BOWLES, PTE. JAMES T., Gordon Highdrs. Wounded in arm while on service in Italy – March, 1944. Was with Forestry Commission. Youngest son of Mrs Bowles, High Street, Wick, and the late James T. Bowles.

BREMNER, SEAMAN WILLIAM, Royal Navy. Injured on service and discharged. Son of Mrs Bremner, 29 Huddart Street, Wick, whose youngest son (David) was killed at Dunkirk. Married: wife and family resided Vansittart Street, Wick.

BREMNER, PTE. GEORGE, 8th Seaforth Highdrs. Brother of above. Contracted illness on service and discharged 1945. Married: wife and family resided 14 Bexley Terrace, Wick.

BREMNER, CORPL. DAVID, 5th Seaforth Highdrs. Wounded in Normandy about August, 1944, and taken to England suffering from a double fracture of the elbow and dislocation of the arm. Served in North Africa and Sicily. Youngest son of Peter Bremner and the late Mrs Bremner, 10 Vansittart Street, Wick.

BREMNER, PTE. JOHN, 5th Seaforth Highlanders. Wounded in North Africa – July, 1943; again on Western Front in March, 1945 (head and leg). Compositor in peace-time. Younger son of Mr and Mrs Francis Bremner, Sheriff Court Buildings, Wick.

BRUCE, PTE. BENJAMIN, ——. Home on leave early in May, 1945, after having been wounded in the foot in the fighting in Germany. Son of Mr and Mrs Tom Bruce, Ulbster Place, Thurso.

BRUCE, PTE. DAVID, 5th Seaforth Highdrs. Wounded in the thigh in the Middle East (probably Tripoli) about January, 1943. Formerly employed by Messrs Hepworth, Thurso. Son of Mr and Mrs Alexander Bruce, The Cottage, Scrabster.

BRYSON, PTE. ANDREW, Paratroops. Wounded in Normandy about July, 1944, and taken to hospital in this country. Mobilised with

Territorials. Butcher's assistant. Son of Mrs Bryson, Swanson Street, Thurso.

BUCHANAN, CORPL. JAMES, 5th Seaforth Highdrs. Wounded in Tunisia in April, 1943. Cabinetmaker. Wife resided at 1 Coghill Square, Wick; and son of the late T. Buchanan, cooper.

BUDGE, PTE. JAMES, Royal Army Ordnance Corps. Wounded in France (probably May, 1940). Wife resided 53 High Street, Thurso.

CALDER, PTE. COLIN, Black Watch. Wounded in Normandy about July, 1944, and taken to hospital in this country. Called up with Militia previous to war. Son of Alexander Calder, 16 Wilson Street, Thurso.

CAMERON, SPR. DONALD, Royal Engineers. Wounded in chest and leg in Western Europe on Septr. 20, 1944. Brother of James Cameron, a repatriated prisoner, and of Mrs John Maclean, 7 Holborn Avenue, Thurso.

CAMPBELL, PTE. UISDEAN, Seaforth Highlanders. Wounded in action in Middle East on Novr. 2, 1942. Eldest son of Mr and Mrs Campbell, Shurrery, Reay.

CAMPBELL, —— ROBERT, Royal Air Force. Wounded in the Middle East about January, 1943. Youngest son of Mr and Mrs William Campbell, Ramscraigs, Dunbeath.

CANOP, SPR. JAMES W., Royal Engineers. Wounded in action on Western Front (leg injury) in Jany., 1945, and taken to this country. Wife resided at 4 Holborn Avenue, Thurso.

CLARK, PTE. DAVID, ——. Wounded in left shoulder in Normandy – July, 1944, and taken to England. Son of Mr and Mrs Henry Clark, Watten Mains.

CORMACK, PTE. J., Seaforth Highdrs. Wounded at Lanciano – Decr. 16, 1943, and again at Anyso – March 12, 1944. Son of Mr and Mrs Cormack, Northfield, Hempriggs, Wick.

CORMACK, PTE. D., Seaforth Highdrs. Brother of above. Wounded at the Garigliano – January 23, 1944.

DAVIDSON, PTE. JOHN, 6th Seaforth Highlanders. Wounded at Dunkirk in Spring of 1940. Transferred later to 5th Seaforths and became C.S.M. Won M.M. Son of Mr and Mrs Alexr. Davidson, Helshedder, Reay.

DOULL, PTE. JOHN, 4th Seaforth Highdrs. Wounded in Middle East – March, 1943 (left arm injury) on his 23rd birthday. Second time wounded: on his 20th birthday (1940) received injuries in France. Joined army before the war. Stepson of Mr and Mrs John Henderson, 24 Willowbank, Wick.

ELDER, —— JOHN, Royal Air Force. Served in Russia and injured when 'plane crashed (1942). Home address – Inver, Dunbeath.

FLETT, SERGT.-OBSERVER GEORGE, Royal Air Force. Sustained severe eye injury when 'plane crashed into the sea while on operational flight. With the exception of the pilot and Sergt. Flett, the crew were lost. Son of George Flett, fishsalesman, Pittenweem (formerly of Wick) and of the late Mrs Flett.

FRASER, AB.-SEAMAN HUGH, Royal Naval Reserve, H.M.S. "Danube" (H.M. Examination Service). Severely injured through enemy aircraft action in Thames Estuary on morning of Octr. 13, 1940, and discharged as medically unfit for further service, July 18, 1941. Home address – 45 Eastcourt Lane, Gillingham, Kent. Elder son of James Fraser, 13 Breadalbane Terrace, Wick.

FRASER, PTE. WALTER, 5th Seaforth Highlanders. Wounded in Normandy about July, 1944, and taken to hospital in England; wounded again severely (necessitating amputation of right arm) on Western Front in April, 1945. Employed in Orkney before enlisting. Youngest son of the late Walter Fraser and of Mrs Fraser, Thurso East Farm, Thurso.

FORBES, FLIGHT.-SERGT. NEIL D., Royal Air Force. Injured in a 'plane crash day he won D.F.M. Only son of Mrs Forbes, Stafford Street, Tain, and formerly of Wick (where he was born).

GRANT, SERGT. ALEXANDER, Seaforth Highlanders. Wounded in the wrist on July 14, 1944, while serving in N.W. Europe, and taken to this country. Married, and wife resided at Hillcrest, East Mey. Third son of Mr and Mrs William Grant, Burn of Rattar, Scarfskerry.

GROAT, PTE. BENJAMIN, 5th Seaforth Highlanders. Wounded in Sicily in August, 1943 – gun-shot wound in right leg. Youngest son of Mrs Neil Groat, Heather Inn, Thrumster.

GUNN, SERGT. HAMISH, Seaforth Highdrs. Wounded on Western Front in Feby., 1945, and taken to this country. Served throughout North African campaign and was wounded at El Alamein. Wife resided 23 Grove Lane, Thurso.

GUNN, SERGT. DON., Ulster Rifles. Wounded in Normandy about July, 1944, and brought to hospital in England. Foot amputated. Son of the late James Gunn and of Mrs Gunn, Bardnaclavan, Thurso.

GUNN, SPR. WILLIAM, Royal Engineers. Wounded in N.W. Europe about July, 1944, and taken to hospital in Ayrshire. Was at Dunkirk, and later with Commandos at

Madagascar and elsewhere. A painter to trade. Wife resided at 60 Kinnaird Street, Wick. Son of Mr and Mrs John Gunn, Huddart Street, Wick.

GUNN, PTE. ALEXANDER, 2nd Seaforth Highdrs. (later Gordons). Wounded while serving with Seaforths in France in 1940. Son of Mr and Mrs John Gunn, 42 Huddart Street, Wick.

GUNN, PTE. DAVID, Seaforth Highdrs. Wounded in Egyptian campaign – Novr., 1942; wounded again in March, 1943. Farm-servant. Third son of Mr and Mrs George Gunn, 17 Wellington Street, Wick.

GUNN, PTE. DAVID, Seaforth Highdrs. Wounded in the Middle East on January 11, 1943. Son of Mr Alexander Gunn, Lochside, Calder.

GUNN, PTE. JOHN, M.M., Seaforth Highlanders. Wounded in Middle East – Novr., 1942. Mother resided at Achswinegar, Lybster.

HARPER, CORPL. MURRAY, 2nd Seaforth Highdrs. Wounded in North Africa – Octr. 22, 1942, and again in Tunisia in April, 1943. Compositor to trade. Younger son of the late George Harper and of Mrs Harper, 52 Willowbank, Wick.

INNES, SERGT. JOHN A., Royal Air Force. Wounded in flying operation over Hamburg in autumn of 1944. Son of the late J. D. Innes, Blingery, and of Mrs Brims, Latheron Mains.

JAMES, SEAMAN JOHN F., Royal Navy. Injured in engagement while serving on a minesweeper in June, 1940. Son of Mr and Mrs J. James, 82 Nicholson Street, Wick.

KEITH, PTE. WILLIAM, 5th Seaforth Highlanders. Wounded in right arm and leg about August, 1943. His brother Angus was a prisoner of war in Germany. Younger son of Mr and Mrs Angus Keith, Roadside, Forse, Latheron.

KEITH, PTE. GEORGE, 5th Seaforth Highlanders. Wounded in Europe – August 21, 1944. Brother was a prisoner of war. Son of the late Robert Keith, Haimer, and of Mrs Keith, Hoy.

LEITH, LEADING-SEAMAN WILLIAM, Royal Naval Reserve. Injured in action on board H.M.S. "Sotra" – a vessel later reported lost. Second son of Mrs Leith, 7 Harbour Terrace, Wick, and of the late Captain William Leith. Married: wife belongs to Northern Ireland.

MACBEATH, CORPORAL JOHN, Royal Air Force. Sustained leg wound, 1942. Only son of Mr and Mrs Macbeath, Seaview, Inver, Dunbeath.

MACDONALD, CORPL. ALEXANDER, 5th Seaforth Highdrs. Wounded in leg and thigh in Normandy about July, 1944, and taken to hospital in Scotland. Served in Africa and Sicily. A compositor. Son of the late James Macdonald, joiner, and of Mrs Macdonald, Durness Street, Thurso.

MACDONALD, GUARDSMAN ROBERT, Scots Guards. Wounded in Central Mediterranean and placed on dangerously ill list with gun-shot wounds in the leg in Feby., 1944. Brother of Miss Netta Macdonald, Macgregor's Buildings, Lybster.

MACDONALD, PTE. JOHN, 5th Seaforth Highlanders. Shrapnel wound in right leg and both hands in Normandy about July, 1944, and taken to hospital in England. Served in African and Sicilian campaigns. Merchant's assistant. Son of Mr W. Macdonald, 56 Rose Street, Thurso.

MACDONALD, ———— JAMES, 2nd Seaforth Highdrs. Wounded in action in Normandy – June, 1944. Son of Mr and Mrs D. Macdonald, Braeval, Lybster.

MACKAY, SEAMAN MERYN, Royal Navy. Injured on service. Served in Navy prior to war. Son of Mr and Mrs Adam Mackay (resident in Edinburgh), and grandson of Mr and Mrs Neil Mackay, Post Office, Dunbeath.

MACKAY, PTE. NEIL, New Zealand Forces. Wounded in North Africa and discharged. Married: home in N.Z. Brother of Seaman Meryn Mackay (above). (A third brother, L. Stoker Dennis Mackay, was killed.)

MACKAY, CORPL. ANDREW, Gordon Highlanders. Severely wounded. Home address – Blackburn, Dunbeath.

MACKAY, SERGT.-MAJOR ALEXANDER, 5th Seaforth Highdrs. Wounded in Middle East – March, 1943. Wife resided at 25 Cairndhuna Terrace, Wick. Son of Mr and Mrs A. Mackay, 96 Willowbank, Wick.

MACKAY, L.-BOMBDR. WILLIAM, Royal Artillery. Wounded in Normandy – June, 1944. Served in North Africa and Italy. Wife resided Burnside Cottage, Papigoe; mother at 62 Argyle Square, Wick – father lost his life (in the Navy) in 1914-18 war.

MACKAY, L.-CORPL. DAVID, Black Watch. Wounded in Italy about Novr. 1944. Called up with Seaforths, and served in North Africa and Sicily. Wife resided at Shebster. Youngest son of Mr and Mrs David Mackay, Sandside, Reay (formerly of Isauld).

MACKAY, PTE. PETER, 5th Seaforth Highlanders. Wounded in Tunisia in April, 1943. Son of Mrs Annie Mackay, 5 New Houses, Roadside, Lybster.

MACKAY, PTE. JAMES, Gordon Highdrs. Wounded in France about May, 1940. Soldier in peacetime. Son of Donald Mackay, 53 Kennedy Terrace, Wick.

MACKAY, PTE. DAVID, 1st Cameron Highlanders. Received shrapnel wound in arm at Dunkirk. Son of Mr and Mrs D. Mackay, 65 Nicholson Street, Wick.

MACKAY, PTE. JOHN D. B., 5th Seaforth Highdrs. Wounded on Western Front in March, 1945. Previous to mobilisation in 1939 was valet in London. Youngest son of Mrs Mackay, 30 Moray Street, Wick, and of the late Archibald Mackay, painter.

MACKENZIE, LIEUT, HUGH C., Border Regiment. Wounded in N.W. Europe on April 12, 1945 – shot in left shoulder by a sniper. An M.A. (Hons.) of St. Andrews University. Grandson of the late Mr and Mrs Donald Mackenzie, 12 Vansittart Street, Wick.

MACKENZIE, SECOND-HAND ROBERT G., Royal Naval Reserve. Slightly wounded at Namsos (1940). Son of George Mackenzie, The Willows, Lybster.

MACKENZIE, CADET WILLIAM, Royal Air Force. Injured in air crash while training in South Africa (1944). Elder son of Mr and Mrs William Mackenzie, 26 Nicholson Street, Wick.

MACKENZIE, CORPL. ERIC, 5th Seaforth Highdrs. Wounded in N.W. Europe about August, 1944. Served in African and Sicilian campaigns. A coachbuilder. Son of Mrs Mackenzie, 8 Grove Lane, Thurso.

MACKENZIE, GUNNER GEORGE, Field Artillery. Wounded on Western Front in Feby., 1945. Through African and Sicilian campaigns and with B.L.A. since D-Day. Only surviving son of Mr and Mrs William Mackenzie, The Cottage, Brough, Dunnet (formerly of Knockally, Dunbeath).

MACKENZIE, PTE. WILLIAM, Seaforth Highlanders. Wounded in Normandy on July 2, 1944, and taken to this country. Second son of the late Sinclair Mackenzie, road surfaceman, Latheron.

MACKENZIE, PTE. MARCUS, 5th Seaforth Highdrs. Wounded in France about June, 1944 (right leg) and taken to England. Served N. Africa and elsewhere. Farm worker. Wife resided with mother-in-law at Smithy House, Scrabster.

MACKIE, PTE. ALBERT, ——. Wounded in right leg in Normandy – June, 1944, and taken to hospital in England. Grocer's assistant. Youngest son of Mrs B. Gunn, 128 Willowbank, Wick. Had five brothers serving, one of whom was killed.

MACKINNON, SERGT. ANDREW W., Royal Air Force. Reported missing from operational flight over Germany about July, 1944; later as injured and in hospital in England. (See Honours.) Father, Bombdr. John Mackinnon, R.A., was on active service in Italy. Mother resided at Schoolhouse, Westerdale.

MACLEOD, CORPL. JACK, M., Royal Scots Fusiliers. Wounded in Germany – April, 1945. Home address – Borgie, Berriedale.

MACLEOD, SPR. DONALD, G. C., Royal Engineers. Wounded in Middle East about October, 1942. Only son of the late Mr and Mrs D. Macleod, Upper Gardens, Thurso East.

MACLEOD, PTE. JOHN, Seaforth Highdrs. Wounded in the foot in the Middle East about April, 1943. Son of Alexr. Macleod, Thurdistoft, Castletown.

MACLEOD, PTE. JAMES, Argyll and Sutherland Highdrs. Wounded in the foot in Italy – July, 1944. Son of Mrs Allan Macleod, Pentland Crescent, Thurso. (Father killed in 1914-18 war and brother died on service in this one.)

MACLEOD, PTE. WILLIAM, 5th Seaforth Highdrs. Wounded in arm and leg in Normandy in July, 1944, and taken to this country. Severely wounded in March, 1945, on Western Front. Served in North Africa and Sicily. Son of the late Alexr. Macleod, carter, and of Mrs Macleod, Janetstown, Thurso.

MACLEOD, —— DAVID, Scottish Regiment. Wounded at Normandy – June, 1944. Wife resided at Huna with Angus Macleod, father-in-law.

MACNICOL, SERGT. DONALD S., 5th Seaforth Hdrs. Wounded in Normandy – July 26, 1944, and taken to hospital in England. Served previously in North African campaign. Son of Mr and Mrs John A. Macnicol, Shurrery, Shebster.

MACPHERSON, SERGT. ——, Seaforth Highlanders. Wounded in both legs in Normandy about August, 1944, and transferred to hospital in South Wales. Was employed with a building contractor in Halkirk. Married, and home address given as late of Braal Terrace, Halkirk.

McALLAN, SERGT. WILLIAM, 5th Seaforth Highdrs. Wounded in right armpit in N.W. Europe – June, 1944. Son of Mrs McAllan, Victoria Place, Wick, and of the late William McAllan.

McALLAN, PTE. CHARLES, 2nd Cameron Highdrs. Wounded in Italy – June, 1944. Brother of above. (A third brother, Driver John McAllan was killed.)

McADIE, TPR. A. M., 2nd Lothians and Border Regiment. Wounded (stomach) in North Africa – April, 1943. Discharged May, 1944. Home address – County Houses, Watten. Son of the late Mr and Mrs Peter McAdie, Newton Road, Wick.

MANSON, CAPTAIN BENJAMIN, Seaforth Highdrs. Wounded in Burma, late 1943. Headmaster of Staxigoe School. Son of Mr and Mrs William Manson, Coolhill, Keiss.

MARTIN, GNR. JOHN, R.A. Field, West Somerset Yeomanry. Wounded in both feet in Germany – April 20, 1945. Son of Mr and Mrs Martin, Seaview Farm, Oldwick, Wick.

MILLER, SEAMAN JOHN, Royal Naval Reserve. Wounded 1940. Wife (Ina Stewart) and family resided in Sarclet Village, Thrumster.

MILLER, CORPL. JACK, Royal Engineers. Wounded in N.W. Europe about August, 1944, and taken to hospital in England. Son of John Miller, Roadside, Killimster. Married, and wife and children resided at Killimster.

MILLER, PTE. WILLIAM P., Durham Light Infantry. Received multiple wounds in both legs while serving in Italy about August, 1944. Called up with Militia in 1939, and saw much active service, including Greece and Crete campaigns. Was employed by Messrs Ronaldson, Westerseat. Son of Mr and Mrs William Dallas, 43 Dempster Street, Wick.

MILLER, PTE. JOHN, Hampshire Regiment. Wounded in Italy about October, 1944. Previously wounded in Sicilian campaign. Painter before the war. Son of the late Mr and Mrs William Miller, 43 Dempster Street, Wick. Wife (belonging to Wick) resided in Edinburgh.

MILLER, PTE. MARCUS, Glasgow Highdrs. Wounded (neck) in Normandy and taken to England. Wounded again (right leg and ankle) and taken to Britain about Decr., 1944. Wife resided at 10 Harbour Place, Wick. Brother of Pte. John above. There were five brothers on service.

MORE, CORPL. (later Sergt.) JOHN, 5th Seaforth Highdrs. Wounded in N.W. Europe about October, 1944. Served throughout North African and Sicilian campaigns. Baker before the war. Son of Mr and Mrs Francis More, 24 Wellington Street, Wick. (Brother of Corpl. F. More, killed.)

MUNRO, SERGT. JAMES, Paratroops. Wounded in leg on Western Front in Feby., 1945, and taken to England. A regular soldier and saw service in Burma. Grandson of Mrs James Munro, Post Office, Weydale, Thurso.

MUNRO, PTE. D. S., Royal Corps of Signals. Contracted illness abroad and was convalescent patient at Forse Hospital (1943). Son of Mrs Munro, 14 Barrogill Street, Wick.

MURRISON, PTE. IAN, Highland Light Infantry. Took part in heavy fighting in Belgium and became a casualty through shell-shock in Septr., 1944. Flown to hospital in England. Elder son of Mr and Mrs H. Murrison, New Houses, Latheron.

OAG, PTE. ALEXANDER S., Seaforth Highlanders. Wounded in Normandy – June, 1944. Joined army before war, called up as reservist, and came through Dunkirk. Second son of Mrs Oag, 19 Kennedy Terrace, Wick. (There were five brothers on service.)

PATERSON, GUARDSMAN JAMES, Scots Guards. Wounded in Norway (at Narvik) about June, 1940 – and discharged. The hospital ship he was on was sunk, but he was rescued (how, he did not know) but suffered from exposure. Soldier in peace-time. Second son of Mr Paterson, Borgue, Dunbeath.

REID, SERGT. DONALD, Seaforth Highdrs. Wounded in Middle East – Novr., 1942. Son of Mr and Mrs George Reid, 6 Marine Terrace, Thurso.

RENDALL, PTE. GEORGE, King's Own Scottish Borderers. Wounded in Burma, early 1944. Eldest son of Mrs Rendall, Reiss.

RENDALL, PTE. T., Gordon Highdrs. Wounded on Western Front (bullet wounds in left thigh and arm) in January, 1945. Brother of above. (Mrs Rendall's third son, Sergt. Alexander, was home on leave in January, 1945, after four years' service in Far East.)

ROBERTSON, TPR. JAMES, Royal Tank Regiment. Wounded in the Middle East – late 1942. Eldest son of Mr and Mrs James Robertson, 31 Grove Lane, Thurso. (Brother missing.)

RONALDSON, PTE. D., ——. Wounded (right arm) in Italy – June, 1944. First joined London Scottish but was transferred to Seaforths. Son of Mrs Ronaldson, Westerseat, Wick.

ROSS, PTE. GEORGE, Glasgow Highdrs. Wounded in Normandy about August, 1944. Eldest son of Jessan Ross and the late Mrs Ross, 27 Oldwick Road, Wick.

SHEARER, SEAMAN DONALD M., Royal Navy. H.M.S. "Eskimo." Injured on service and discharged 1945. Son of Mr and Mrs D. Shearer, 27 Vansittart Street, Wick.

SHEARER, SEAMAN JAMES, Royal Navy. Elder brother of above. Discharged on account of illness contracted on service.

SHEPHERD, TELEGRAPHIST LANCE P., Royal Navy. Wounded (badly injured arm) about May, 1944. Employed in post office. Son of Mrs Shepherd, 19 Castle Street, Thurso. Wife and infant son resided South of England.

SIMPSON, PTE. JOHN, Commandos. Wounded about January, 1944. Cooper to trade. Youngest son of Donald Simpson, 5 Macleay Terrace, Wick. Wife resided at Allanton, Shotts.

SINCLAIR, SERGT. ALEXANDER, Cameron Highdrs. Wounded at El Alamein – Novr., 1942; wounded again (arm and leg) in Normandy – June, 1944. Youngest son of Mr and Mrs James Sinclair, Carroy House, Dunbeath.

SINCLAIR, PTE. R., 5th Seaforth Highdrs. Wounded at El Alamein. Son of Mr and Mrs H. Sinclair, 43 Telford Street, Wick.

SINCLAIR, JAMES, ——. Wounded in Normandy – June, 1944. Son of Mrs Bain, Jeffrey Street, Lybster.

SMITH, SEAMAN DONALD, Merchant Navy. Injured while at work aboard ship – August, 1945. Native of Stroma.

STEPHEN, PTE. SINCLAIR P., Seaforth Highlanders. Wounded in Normandy – July, 1944, and taken to Stobhill, Glasgow. Was on Employment Exchange staff. Second son of Mr and Mrs Alexr. Stephen, 6 Coach Road, Wick. Married, and wife resided at 4 West Banks Terrace, Wick.

STEVEN, PTE. STANLEY, Seaforth Highdrs. Wounded in the leg in the fighting in Italy – April, 1944. Called up with the Militia and served in France (Dunkirk). Clerk in law office. Youngest son of the late Thomas Steven and of Mrs Steven, 5 Harbour Terrace, Wick, who had three other sons serving.

STEVEN, PTE. JAMES, Royal Army Service Corps. Wounded in right arm and shoulder in Belgium in January, 1945. Brother of Pte. Stanley (above).

STEWART, GNR. DONALD, Royal Artillery. Wounded in Italy on 17th June, 1944. Elder son of Major D. Stewart, M.C., and of Mrs Stewart, "Stemor," Bexley Terrace, Wick.

SUTHERLAND, LIEUT. ROBERT, Cameron Highdrs. Wounded (head and thigh) in Italy about June, 1944. County's leading runner and Powderhall competitor in pre-war days. Then widely known as "R. Sutherland, Halkirk."

SUTHERLAND, LIEUT. JOHN, 49th Reconnaissance Regiment. Wounded in both legs at Stapleheide, Holland. Octr. 24, 1944, and conveyed by 'plane from Canadian hospital in Antwerp to Swindon. Remained six months in hospital. Served with 2nd Bn. London Scottish until March, 1943. Son of Mrs S. Sutherland, Post Office, Ulbster.

SUTHERLAND, ENGINE-ROOM ARTIFICER MAGNUS, Royal Navy. Wounded – no details. Brother of Lieut. John (above).

SUTHERLAND, CORPL. DAVID B., Royal Marines. Brother of above. Served on H.M.S. "Norfolk" until May, 1943; then with Combined Operations as instructor until discharged in January, 1946, on account of ear trouble caused by blast.

SUTHERLAND, COY.-SGT. MAJOR DONALD, Seaforth Highdrs. Wounded in N.W. Europe on Septr. 11, 1944, and taken to hospital at Bridge of Earn. Wife and family resided at 15 Braal Terrace, Halkirk, and parents at Braal Holdings.

SUTHERLAND, L.-CORPL. WILLIAM, 5th Seaforth Highdrs. Wounded in Middle East about Novr., 1942. Son of Mr and Mrs Sutherland (Clyne), 18 Braal Terrace, Halkirk.

SUTHERLAND, L.-CORPL. D. G. M., 6th Seaforth Highdrs. Wounded in Italy on April 1, 1944. Son of Mr and Mrs D. Sutherland, West End, Castletown. Married. Home address – 1 Monktonhall Terrace, Musselburgh, Midlothian.

SUTHERLAND, PTE. PETER, Seaforth Highlanders. Wounded in April, 1944, while serving in Italy. Was first with the Camerons. Draper's assistant. Son of Mr and Mrs Peter Sutherland, 41 Cairndhuna Terrace, Wick.

SUTHERLAND, PTE. ROBERT, 5th Seaforth Highdrs. Wounded in Middle East – Novr., 1942. Husband of Mrs Georgina Sutherland, Reay.

SUTHERLAND, PTE. ANDREW R., Black Watch. Wounded in Normandy about July, 1944, and taken to hospital in Liverpool. Wounded again on Western Front in March, 1945. A mason in peacetime. Son of Mr and Mrs Andrew Sutherland, 43 Green Road, Wick.

SUTHERLAND, PTE. DONALD, 2nd New Zealand Expeditionary Force. Wounded in foot and knee at El Alamein, and again in leg – April 20, 1943, in Tunisia. Brother of William and Thomas Sutherland, Dalnaglatan, Altnabreac, and son of the late Mr and Mrs Thomas Sutherland, Dirlot, Westerdale.

SUTHERLAND, GEORGE, ——. Wounded in

Normandy – June, 1944. Son of Mr and Mrs Sutherland, Limekilns, Lybster.

SUTHERLAND, PTE. ANDREW, 5th Seaforth Highdrs. Wounded in thigh and leg at Tripoli – Jany. 21, 1943; wounded in chest in Germany – March, 1945. Home address – Lyth, by Castletown.

SWANSON, L.-CORPL. ALEXANDER G., 5th Seaforth Highdrs. Wounded at El Alamein – Novr., 1942. Married: wife resided at Netherside, Castletown.

SWANSON, STAFF-SERGT. PILOT WILLIAM C., "E" Squadron, Glider Pilot Regiment, Army Air Corps, 1st Allied Airborne Army. Touched down at Arnhem, first lift, Septr. 17, 1944; evacuated to Nijmegan Septr. 25; flown to England from Brussels, Septr. 28. Wounded in left shoulder by sniper's bullet., Septr. 20, 1944; wounded in back by shellfire two days later. S.-S. Pilot Swanson joined Caithness Constabulary and was stationed at Wick where he resided at 13 Girnigoe Street.

THAIN, PTE. JAMES, 5th Seaforth Highlanders. Wounded in Middle East in Novr., 1942. Third son of Mr and Mrs James Thain, Dingwall, and grandson of the late William Thain, Ackergill.

THOMSON, CORPL. DAN, Lovat Scouts. Wounded in Italy about August, 1944, and in C.M.F. hospital. Shop assistant before the war. Younger son of the late William Thomson and of Mrs Thomson, 10 Girnigoe Street, Wick.

WATERS, GNR. FINLAY, Royal Artillery. Wounded in the right leg on service in the Middle East (1941). Farm-servant at Barnyards, Wick. Son of William Waters, Charity Farm, Wick.

WORK, PTE. HUGH, 5th Seaforth Highdrs. Wounded in Sicily in July, 1943 – gunshot wound in the head. Apprentice compositor. Son of Mr and Mrs G. Work, 8 Durness Street, Thurso.

MEN OF CAITHNESS CONNECTION.

ANSTRUTHER, SIR RALPH, BART., M.C., Coldstream Guards. Proprietor of Watten Estates. Wounded in North Africa in Spring of 1943.

BARNETT, MTR. PETER, Lovat Scouts. Seriously wounded in both legs in Italy – Feby., 1945. Wife resided at 7 Braal Terrace, Halkirk.

BETHUNE, SERGT. WILLIAM, ——. Wounded in Normandy – July, 1944, and taken to England. Wife resided at Shurrery Manse, Reay; parents at Invershin. Previously mentioned in despatches for prompt and gallant action in saving the life of a comrade.

FORREST, L.-BOMBDR., Ayrshire Yeomanry. Wounded in Italy about August, 1944. Native of Edinburgh. Wife (Macdonald to name) resided at 10 Campbell Street, Thurso.

INRIG, PTE. GEORGE W., Canadian H.L.I. Wounded while serving in N.W. Europe about Septr., 1944, and in hospital in France. Son of Mr and Mrs George Inrig, 11 Mountain Ave., Hamilton, Ontario, and grandson of the late Mr and Mrs D. Farquhar, 33 Williamson Street, Wick, and of the late Mr and Mrs James Inrig, Keiss.

MAINS, FLR. JOHN, Royal Fusiliers. Wounded in Italian campaign about Decr., 1943. Native of Glasgow. Wife (belonging to Watten) resided at Watten Mains.

McINTOSH, MAJOR ALASTAIR W., Gordon Highdrs. Severely wounded at Dunkirk whilst liaison officer with the French Force. Afterwards Adjutant with Home Guard at Aberdeen, and Staff Officer on Amgot in N.W. Germany. A nephew of the late A. G. McIntosh, schoolmaster, Spittal.

CIVILIAN CASUALTIES.

KILLED OR DIED.

Killed in an enemy air raid on Wick, July 1, 1940:–

MACKENZIE, ROBERT (aged 71 years), master tailor, Bank Row. Died in Bignold Hospital on July 3, 1940. Home address – 49 Argyle Square, Wick.

MACKENZIE, PTE. ROBERT, Seaforth Highdrs., aged 30 years. Son of Mr Mackenzie (above) and of Mrs Mackenzie, 49 Argyle Square. (See Service casualties.)

McTAVISH, MRS P. P., aged 44 years. Sister of Pte. Robert Mackenzie (above).

MACKENZIE, MRS ISOBEL MACKAY (aged 25 years). Daughter-in-law of Mr and Mrs R. Mackenzie (above), and daughter of Mr Alexander Henderson, Willowbank.

STEVEN, MRS MARY (aged 44 years). Home address – 43 Argyle Square.

SMITH, WILLIAM (aged 63 years), merchant, 2 Bank Row.

WATERS, DONALD (aged 50 years), fishcurer. Home address – Woodville, South Road.

BLACKSTOCK, FREDERICK (aged 5 years). Son of Mr and Mrs Blackstock, 10 Bank Row.

BRUCE, ISOBEL (aged 7 years). Youngest daughter of Mr and Mrs George O. Bruce, 18 Bank Row.

FLETT, JAMES BRUCE (aged 7 years). Died in Bignold Hospital – July 2, 1940. Son of Mr and Mrs James Flett, 2 Williamson Street.

MACGREGOR, KENNETH (aged $8\frac{1}{2}$ years). Died in Bignold Hospital – July 3, 1940. Youngest son of Mr and Mrs John Macgregor, 11 Telford Street.

MILLER, ELIZABETH B. (Bertha), (aged $5\frac{1}{2}$ years). Daughter of Mr and Mrs John Miller, 10 Harbour Place.

MILLER, AMELIA (AMY) S. (aged $9\frac{1}{2}$ years). Died in Bignold Hospital – July 2, 1940. Sister of Elizabeth (above).

THOMSON, DONALD WARES (aged 16 years 8 mths.) Apprentice shipwright. Killed while at work in the vicinity of explosion. Younger son of Mr and Mrs William Thomson, 49 Willowbank.

WARES, JOHN C. (aged 5 years). Son of Mr and Mrs D. M. Wares, 6 Saltoun Street.

Killed in an enemy air raid on Wick, 26th October, 1940:–

CAMERON, ELIZABETH B. (Betty), aged 10 years and 9 months. Only daughter of Mr and Mrs John A. Cameron, 6 Hill Avenue, Wick.

CAMERON, JOHN HORNE, aged 6 years and 8 mths. Younger brother of Betty (above).

DYER, MRS DAPHNE, aged 20 years. Wife of Flight-Sergeant Dyer, R.A.F.

BANKS, WILLIAM S. Accidentally killed at Saltness, Orkney, on June 1, 1943. Native of Gills, Canisbay.

BLACK, GEORGE TAYLOR (aged 20 years). Killed in a bombing raid on London – Septr. 28, 1940. Employed in a bank. Third son of Mr and Mrs William Black, "Scouthal", Halkirk.

DUNNETT, WILLIAM J. F. (aged 28 years). Died through enemy action over London on March 8, 1941. Interred in Bower Churchyard. Was policeman in London. Husband of Margaret Macdonald (he married five weeks before his death), and second son of Mrs Dunnett, Heatherdeep, Watten, and the late Alexander Dunnett, joiner, Bowermadden, who died of wounds received in 1914-18 war. Brother (Sergt. A. J. Dunnett) died on service.

GUNN, ADAM MACKAY, Radio Engineer (G.P.O.) Aged 22 years. Died in Darlington Memorial Hospital, Co. Durham, on June 14, 1940 (result of an accident "while on duty for his country"). Son of Mrs Gunn, Smerral, Latheronwheel, and of the late Adam Gunn (mason), Braehungie, Latheron.

MACKAY, ALEXANDER (30 years), labourer, 12 Mill Road, Thurso – fatally injured at work on a national service construction scheme in Orkney – Feby. 24, 1942. Husband of Barbara Thomson.

MACLEOD, MACKAY S. G. (aged 58 years). Fought with Canadians in 1914-18 war and married French girl. Lived at Dunbeath, where two daughters and a son were born. Returned to reside in France and after capitulation of that country was sentenced to death by the Germans for having helped British soldiers to escape, but later reprieved and sentenced to life imprisonment. Died in August, 1944, in a concentration camp. Only son of Mr and Mrs Mackay Macleod, Bayview, Latheronwheel.

MALCOLM, JAMES S., Inspector of Transport. Died in a prisoner of war camp at Sumatra. Brother of Mrs Mackenzie, Bulno, Dunbeath.

MEIKLEJOHN, DONALD (62), a machinist in the employment of the War Department, killed at a military establishment in the North of Scotland when testing a target trolley – September, 1944. Native of Janetstown, Thurso, who then resided at Moss Street, Elgin.

MUNRO, MISS MARGARET E. (aged 37 years). Died in Hampstead General Hospital through injuries sustained in a bombing raid on London – Septr. 20, 1940. Was in domestic service in London, and was first Caithness victim in that city. Daughter of Mrs A. Munro, Younger's Buildings, Castletown.

OAG, DONALD. Died on H.M.S. "Amarapoora" at Lyness on March 24, 1940. Wife and family resided at 1 Huddart Street, Wick.

RUSTILL, JANET BAIN (aged 44 years), and her two children – BRENDA, aged 11 years; PATRICIA, aged 18 months. Killed through enemy action over Hull – May 8, 1941. Wife and children of George Rustill, Hull, and daughter and grandchildren of Mr and Mrs D. Bain, 27 Nicholson Street, Wick.

SANDISON, NEIL (38 years); his wife (DORIS) and three children – JEAN (8 years), CAROLYN (4 years), SHEILA (15 months). All five killed by blast while taking refuge in a Morrison shelter in the hall of their home during an air raid on London in March, 1944. Elder son of Mr and Mrs Neil Sandison, 25 High Street, Banff, and formerly of Gladstone Place, Wick.

SINCLAIR, ROBERT FINLAYSON (aged 47 years), of the Sarawak Government Service. Died at Long Nawang, Borneo, in 1942. Second son of Mrs Sinclair, Latheron West, Latheron, and of the late John Sinclair, Quoys of Forse.

MRS SMITH and her daughter, MARGARET (Gretta), aged 10 years. Lost their lives as a result of bombing raid on one of the Shetland islands – Decr., 1941. Natives of Orkney but were resident in John O'Groats for six years, leaving there shortly before their death.

SUTHERLAND, JAMES W. R., of City of London Police. Died (aged 25 years) as result of injuries received during the blitz on London. Elder son of Mr and Mrs J. W. Sutherland, 3 Murrayfield, Castletown, and brother of Radio Officer Douglas S. Sutherland, lost with armed merchant cruiser "Rawalpindi", Novr. 23, 1939.

SUTHERLAND, HELEN GUNN, 7 Airlie Gardens, Glasgow. Killed in enemy air raid over Glasgow in March, 1941. Widow of David Sutherland, Wick.

TAYLOR, ROBERT. Accidentally killed at Wick Aerodrome on May 13, 1940. Wife and sons resided at 34 Oldwick Road, Wick.

INJURED.

Injured in enemy air raid on Wick – July 1, 1940:–

MRS BLACKSTOCK, Bank Row. Husband slightly injured. Son (Eric) killed.

P.C. D. BEATON CORMACK. (Now Inspector at Thurso.)

MRS D. GUNN, Bank Row; MRS G. HEPPLE (daughter), and MRS A. GUNN (daughter-in-law). Home destroyed.

MRS WILLIAM SHEARER, Rose Street and her youngest son GEORGE, then aged 14. (Now a Corporal in the army and on service at Rangoon.) Eldest brother lost on the "Barham." Home address now 32 Girnigoe Street.

MRS B. M. SINCLAIR, Union Street.

MRS WILLIAM SMITH, Bank Row. Home wrecked. Husband killed.

JENNY WARES, daughter of Mr and Mrs D. M. Wares, 6 Saltoun Street. (Brother killed.)

STEPHEN, ALEXR., tailor, Coach Road. Had remarkable escape when (working one storey up) building collapsed beneath him. Suffered from shock.

SWANSON, DAVID, shopkeeper, Bank Row. Shop property destroyed. Injured and suffered from shock. Since passed away at home in Breadalbane Terrace.

CAMERON, MRS JOHN A., 6 Hill Avenue, Wick. Badly injured through enemy air action on October 26, 1940. Bungalow destroyed. New address – Moray Street.

CAMERON, GEORGE (aged 14 years). Son of above. Badly injured in same air raid. Now student in Glasgow.

IN ENEMY HANDS.

FARQUHARSON, ARCHIBALD N., Stockbroker, Kuala Lumpur. Interned at Singapore. Wife resided – Fernlea, Wick.

GUNN, DONALD O. Interned at Manila, Philippine Islands – Jany., 1942. Native of Olrig, Caithness.

HENDERSON, MISS H. G. Church missionary in China for 22 years. Interned by the Japanese after outbreak of war in the Far East. Native of Dunbeath, and sister of G. S. Henderson, schoolmaster.

KENNEDY, LEWIS D., Commissioner of Customs for the Sarawak Government. Interned in Singapore. Eldest son of Dr J. R. Kennedy, M.V.O., Dunbeath.

MACKAY, STEWART, electrical engineer. Interned at the fall of Hong Kong. Wife (Minnie Miller of Halcro, Bower) and their young boy escaped to Australia.

MACLEOD, JOHN J., prison officer at Taiping. Interned at Singapore. Wife (Emma Bain) and two children escaped and reached South Africa. Son of Mr and Mrs J. Macleod, Ballachly, Dunbeath.

MACPHERSON, FINLAY C., Customs officer. Interned by Japanese for two years and seven months. Son of Mr and Mrs F. C. Macpherson, Sandside, Reay, and brother of G. Macpherson, merchant, Reay.

MORRISON, LEONARD. Had post in China before the war and was interned by the Japanese. Son of the late Mr and Mrs P. L. Morrison, Richmond House, Wick.

SINCLAIR, MRS JAMES, Australia. Mrs Sinclair was on a visit to Caithness when war broke out (she is a daughter of the late Mr and Mrs Donald Steven, Keiss) and was returning to Australia when the ship she sailed in was sunk by the enemy and she was among the survivors made prisoner. Released after about a year. James Sinclair, Australia (her husband) is the youngest son of the late William Sinclair, Stroma Island.

With Our Folks
At Home

It ain't the individual, nor the army as a whole,
But the everlasting teamwork of every blooming soul.

–Kipling.

Getting ready for the emergency of war.

Citizens had Much to do – And Much to Learn.

JOHN CITIZEN had much to learn and much to do "if war should come," judging from a series of leaflets issued from the Lord Privy Seal's Office in the months of July and August, 1939. In each instance he was advised to read the leaflet and "Keep it carefully – *you may need it.*"

The citizen was told he had to be "ready for the emergency of war" and the first leaflet dealt with (1) air raid warnings, (2) gas-masks, (3) lighting restrictions, (4) fire precautions, (5) evacuation, (6) identity labels, (7) food, and (8) instructions to the public in case of emergency.

(1) "Stay under cover" after the siren or hooter sounded was the chief advice under air raids. The police and air raid wardens would be on duty – outside; a system that was scrapped after experience, probably on account of casualties in areas attacked.

(2) Keep your gas mask safely and in good condition, and take it with you if going away for any length of time.

(3) All windows, skylights, glazed doors or other openings which showed a light, required to be screened in wartime with dark blinds or blankets, or brown paper pasted on the glass, so that no light was visible from outside. Shops everywhere were besieged for dark-coloured paper, and generally the supply was insufficient to meet the demand. All street lighting was to be discontinued and lights on vehicles dimmed.

(4) Large numbers of small incendiary bombs might start so many fires that the fire brigades could not be expected to deal with them all. Everyone should be prepared to tackle a fire started in his own home, and , taking precautions, should have the top floor cleared of all inflammable materials, lumber, etc.; have some buckets handy, along with sand or dry earth.

(5) Try to decide now (the leaflet read) whether you wish your children to go under the Government evacuation scheme and let your local authority know.

(6) In war you should carry about with you your name and address clearly written; in the case of children a label should be sewn to their clothes in such a way that it would not readily become detached.

(7) It was very important that at the outset of an emergency people should not buy larger quantities of foodstuffs than they normally bought and normally required. If you wished and were able to lay in a small extra store of non-perishable foodstuffs, there was no

reason why this should not be done. They would be an additional insurance.

(8) Arrangements would be made for information and instructions to be issued to the public in case of emergency, both through the Press and by means of broadcast announcements.

The receiving and reading of such official leaflets, ominous shadows of gathering war-clouds, was unsettling for many – prospects of war were anything but pleasant; prospects of bombing attacks were horrifying. There were those who felt that some things vital were being taken from their lives. The less serious-minded treated the leaflet contents much more lightly.

★　★　★　★

Public information leaflet No. 2 was entitled, "Your gas-mask – how to keep it and how to use it." Take care of your gas-mask, it advised, and your gas-mask will take care of you. It was possible that in war your life might depend on your gas-mask and the condition in which it had been kept . . . The official respirator had been most carefully designed and fully tested, and would give adequate protection against breathing any of the known war gases. Instructions followed: How to store it, how to put it on and take it off, how to put it away – ensuring that it was always ready for your protection.

The second portion of the leaflet dealt with the masking of windows, giving the motto for safety as "Keep it dark!" – one of the great protections against the dangers of air attack after nightfall being the "black-out." Hostile aircraft would get no indication as to their whereabouts, but this would not be fully effective "unless *you* do your part." No light must be visible outside. Most important – do not forget your skylight, or glazed doors, or even fan-lights; make sure that no light showed when your front door or back door was open.

Do not leave things until the last, but get together the materials needed. But with the coming of war the supply of suitable dark-coloured material for black-out purposes would not meet the demand. Black paper was used as a substitute, and dark blue or black or dark green glazed cloth.

★　★　★　★

The third leaflet dealt with evacuation – the removal of children, mothers, expectant mothers and blind persons from crowded or dangerous areas – areas likely to be attacked – to prevent the creation of anything like panic or the crippling dislocation of civil life.

The safer areas became known as "reception"

areas and Caithness was registered as a reserve reception area. In April, 1939, arrangements were made for the reception and billeting of children and teachers in the landward area of the county in the event of war. The persons for whom accommodation was available were returned as 3081, including a maximum number of 1961 children. The numbers of persons to be taken by each parish were:– Reay 154; Thurso, 128; Halkirk, 390; Olrig, 325; Dunnet, 152; Bower, 151; Canisbay, 267; Wick, 414; Watten, 130; Latheron, 970 = 3081. Mr James Robertson, county clerk, was appointed reception officer, and the district clerks were to be assistant officers in connection with this evacuation scheme.

Caithness was not officially used as a reception area, though many children from vulnerable districts came north to reside with friends in the county, and when Servicemen were stationed here their wives and offspring began to follow them until the influx was so great that housing accommodation was taxed beyond all reason. Servicemen came and went (as did hundreds of workers), but many of the wives stayed on for the duration, finding conditions here as regards food and safety better than where they belonged.

★ ★ ★ ★ ★

Children were also evacuated to Ireland and the Colonies – away from the danger zone. Not many went from Caithness but two were aboard an evacuee ship (s.s. *Volendam)* carrying 320 children and other passengers to Canada when the vessel was torpedoed in the Atlantic by a U-boat in August, 1940. Happily, not a single child was lost: there was only one casualty, the purser of the vessel. The children had previously been trained by experts in lifeboat drill, and to this was attributed their remarkable escape. It was wonderful work on the part of the ship's crew and those in charge of the evacuees. The children sang popular songs – most of them regarded the incident as "one more drill" – as they took to the lifeboats in the darkness of the night. Most of them returned to Scottish ports clad in little more than pyjamas. They were wrapped in coats of all kinds and in blankets, but not more than a dozen had stockings.

The Wick children aboard the sunken ship were two little girls – Mamie and Gracie Bremner, daughters of Mr Robert Bremner, post-office telegraph inspector, and Mrs Bremner, West Banks Terrace. All their personal belongings were lost, and their only "luggage" when they arrived home was a toothbrush and comb they had procured on the return journey.

Describing on arrival home what had occurred after the attack on the steamer, Mamie said: "There were four of us in one cabin. When the torpedo struck I didn't hear the explosion, but I felt the ship giving a lurch. I knew something was wrong. I had not been sleeping, and was only dozing at the time. The alarm bell went, and we all hurried out. We had had regular lifeboat drill and knew what had to be done.

"There was no panic. We were put into a lifeboat, which was lowered into the water, and then the lifeboat made off towards a light. This was a rescue ship, on which we were taken aboard an hour after leaving the liner. The seas were heavy, and some of the children were a bit sick, but most of us were singing. Several other lifeboats came to the rescue ship, and soon there was a large number aboard. We returned to Britain in this vessel."

Gracie said she had been carried on deck by a sailor "and she didn't have to walk at all."

Both girls were proud of the souvenir with which each child had been presented – a small card with a piece of white heather attached, and a message inscribed – "Heartiest congratulations. We are proud of your bravery. Good luck."

Plans for national housekeeping.

Our Food in War-Time.

PUBLIC information leaflet No. 4 (issued in July, 1939) explained that our country was dependent to a very large extent on supplies of food from overseas. More than 20 million tons were brought into our ports from all parts of the world in the course of a year. Our defence plans had therefore to provide for the protection of our trade routes, for reserves of food, and for the fair distribution of supplies. The Government had over a period of 18 months purchased considerable reserves of essential foodstuffs as one of the precautionary measures taken to build up our resources to meet the conditions of war, and prepared a measure of rationing such as might be required.

Foreseeing that the amount of stocks in any area might be affected by air raid damage or flow of supplies might be interrupted temporarily by transport difficulties, traders and householders were asked to store extra foodstuffs of the non-perishable type as a stand-by against an emergency. Articles of food suggested for household storage included meat and fish in cans or glass jars, flour, suet, canned or dried milk, sugar, tea, cocoa, plain biscuits. Such a store could be drawn upon regularly for day to day use and replaced by new purchases. The point was emphasised that such reserves should be bought *before an emergency arises;* to buy extra quantities later would be unfair to others.

★ ★ ★ ★ ★

A Ministry of Food was to be set up in the event of war, and in each area food control would be in the hands of a local committee whose principal duty would be to safeguard the interests of consumers, be responsible for supervising retail distribution, and license shopkeepers to trade. The prices of food were to be controlled and supplies directed wherever needed. The object of the scheme was to make certain that foodstuffs were distributed fairly and equally and to ensure everyone of a proper share.

The scheme for rationing affected five articles of food in the first instance – butcher meat, bacon and ham, sugar, butter and margarine, and cooking fats. The first rationing cards were issued in November, 1939 – 28,000 of them from the Food Control Office in Wick for the people of Caithness.

★ ★ ★ ★ ★

That leaflet gave a pretty accurate forecast of events to follow. The chief point that may be made was that other foods were also affected including, milk, cheese, jam and tea; other articles, principally tinned foods and dried fruits, were placed on points (each individual was given a maximum number of points per month); there were tokens for soap, and personal points had to be surrendered for sweets, of which the allowance was approximately 3ozs. per week (if obtainable). These "points" for food and sweets were on a four-week period basis, and did the period close with points unused – these were then valueless; only the new period points were acceptable. There were hard and disappointing days for the housewife between 1940 and the end of the war. The last date given (the end of the war) causes doubt in the writer's mind, for the same coupons and points system is yet in vogue, and this week (February, 1946) the Government says the country has to go back to war-time bread (much darker in colour owing to a greater extraction from the wheat). Thus we will be deprived of white bread, the only noticeable concession gained by victory over our enemies.

★ ★ ★ ★ ★

Clothing coupons were introduced and applied to old and young, male and female, and all garments and boots and shoes had a coupon as well as a money value. Certain household goods (towels and curtain materials for instance) required coupons (generally mother's) at time of purchase.

Coal, too, was rationed. The country was to learn (owing to the ultimate shortage of coal and inferior quality of supplies) the truth of the old saying that it's easier to build lums than to keep them reeking.

What to do with money. Ah, what money? Wages were good, particularly for those employed on what was described as "work of national importance,' but prices, too, were high; indeed, generally speaking, wages were increased only to catch up with the inflated valuation of goods. Income-tax, too, became a serious business. The tax net mesh became exceedingly small, and few escaped.

What everyone should do with their money was, the Government insisted, invest it in war savings. Well, many did – there wasn't much else to do! – hoping probably to live long enough to enjoy the use of it when controls vanished.

★ ★ ★ ★ ★

Public information leaflet No. 5 (August, 1939) advised concerning fire precautions in wartime. The enemy would probably make use of fire bombs (he did!) – the object being not only to destroy property but also to create panic. Some would fall on the roofs of houses – one of these houses might be *yours,* said the leaflet thoughtfully. The householder and his family would require to take the first steps in defending their home. Instructions followed for dealing with the bomb itself, and the fire or fires it started. Act quickly, was the advice – every minute lost would make the job more difficult.

For the purpose of spraying water around a burning bomb stirrup handpumps were issued to all streets. These pumps had a special nozzle, producing spray or jet according to requirements. Small bags of sand were also distributed – two to each household and business premises.

Street fire-fighting teams were later formed, all equipped with stirrup pumps and steel helmets. These teams were composed mainly· of females, but in this area their efficiency was never tested. Each sector had a leader. There were three to every hand-pump – one to direct the spray, another to pump, and the third to bring supplies of water. These teams were trained until they were prepared to meet any situation "calmly and with confidence," judging from performances at demonstrations and tests. No matter the duty undertaken, it was always beneficial to know something of the problem to be tackled – experience in actual practice gave an added confidence.

* * * * *

Air raid precautions instructions were also issued by the county of Caithness authorities, giving air raid wardens' posts and names and addresses of the wardens in separate sectors. ("Get to know your wardens *now* and consult them on any matters which are not perfectly clear to you.") The leaflet advised concerning incendiary bombs, gas-masks, ear plugs (to reduce the crash and concussion of explosion), treatment for the injured and gas contaminated casualties.

What to do if you are bombed out of your house – Where to go (the Wick centre was the High School, unless arrangements had been made previously with friends or relatives in other parts of the town); What to take with you (take your gas-mask, identity card, and any perishable food. Have a suitcase ready packed with necessary clothing in case you have to leave in a hurry.) At the end of September, 1939, each member of the civil population was given a National Registration number and issued with a card (known as identity card).

* * * * *

Fire-watching arrangements came into force in the summer of 1941, and in September of that year men born between 1881 and 1923 were required to register for Civil Defence duties – for fire service; except those already in certain stated services. One thousand one hundred registered at Wick, where the Town Council had a three-hour Sunday meeting (October, 1941) to deal with 300 applications for exemption from fire-watching. One hundred were granted exemption, 50 applications were deferred, and 150 refused. Numbers available must have been disappointing generally because in June, 1942, women aged 20 to 45 were called upon to register for fire prevention duty. Many were "called" but few were chosen. Thirteen hundred women registered at Wick but the number melted to 350 when exemptions were made. For instance, there were 550 mothers with children under 14 years, and an additional 350 were exempted on grounds of hardship.

Three fire-watching posts were established in Wick where those on duty from dusk till dawn passed the time in whatever fashion they cared. Tea was made available for the watchers, as also were sleeping quarters. The idea was that one would be on duty while other members of the team slept. The watchers discovered that outside it was pretty dreary; inside it was kind of cheery. Fire-watching was the youngest of the protective services, and maybe a pampered child. There was a fee of 3/- for each

duty, indoor accommodation, refreshments available, and sleeping quarters – comforts and facilities unknown to other services.

* * * * *

Wick was the only town in the North of Scotland (apart from Invergordon) compelled by the Government to adopt this fire - watching scheme. The idea was that if incendiary bombs were dropped during the hours of darkness the danger would be timeously tackled and huge conflagrations prevented. Everyone saw that the compulsory services of the watchers were unnecessary – the police, for instance, were ever on the move at night and could always spot anything unusual and give the alarm – and it was probably this feeling of needlessness that weighed heaviest in what spirit of unwillingness existed.

The scheme was under the control of the Town Council who appointed Mr Peter Mackenzie to the post of Chief Fire Guard Officer, and he was responsible for the organisation and maintenance of the service.

Fire Guard personnel was reported as insufficient in April, 1944, owing to the call-up for the Forces and the direction of men into the Home Guard. The Council then decided to modify the scheme and agreed to bring four business premises posts under the street party scheme.

The National Fire Service was stationed in strength at Wick and maintained a 24-hour service in premises acquired near The Camps. These brigades were well equipped, carefully and capably trained, and ready for any emergency. This is the kind of service that profitably could be merged into our everyday public services.

* * * * *

Under Defence Regulations, a large area in the North of Scotland became a Protected Area on March 11, 1940. The area affected embraced practically all the Highlands and Islands northwest of the Caledonian canal, and travellers by road, rail, sea and air had to satisfy the authorities before admittance. This meant that the area was safeguarded from enemy espionage or other subversive activities, and the close censorship of mail was an additional precautionary measure.

The effect of the 1940 Order was briefly that "on and after that date no person will be allowed to remain in or leave the area without a permit except those who, not being enemy aliens, are resident, that is to say those whose homes are in the area on the date in question," and those who belonged to certain exempted classes such as the Services and police, those with official duties permits, and those in essential services, all of whom were warned "that they may be called upon to produce evidence that they are entitled to the exemption claimed and therefore should carry with them official documents establishing the fact."

A Certificate of Residence was authorised and was obtainable through the police, and had to be presented on leaving or re-entering the area. The certificate had to bear a police stamp and among other details gave age, height, colour of hair and eyes, complexion and build of holder. It had to be produced along with identity card. Inspection of these documents caused travellers by rail much delay at Inverness.

★ ★ ★ ★ ★

Changes were made in the Order in March, 1942, by which the areas were reconstituted and new areas (the West of Scotland, for instance) were included. The extreme North of Scotland was declared a "Regulated Area." Restrictions continued in accordance with military exigencies as a Regulated Area was described as one in which it was necessary to empower naval, military or air force authorities to impose from time to time "restrictions upon the movements of persons within that area for purposes connected with training or other naval, military or air force operations." The rules included registration of visitors to hotels, boarding houses or lodging houses, and also a ban on the possession of telescopes or binoculars, except by permit from the military authorities. There was also a ban on cameras. No. 1 Area consisted roughly of the area along the north of Scotland and the north of Caithness within five miles of the coast, and part of the east of Caithness.

The Restricted Areas were again revised in April, 1944, when the War Secretary framed two by-laws, one of which applied to "a coastal strip from Caithness to East Lothian." The regulations required that all persons over 16 years carry identity cards and produce them on demand. Special permission was required for use of binoculars and telescopes and for the carrying of cameras. No person or party could camp out or sleep in any hut or vehicle without permission from the military authorities; and the right was held to debar visitors to stay overnight in private premises or hotels. Further power given the military authorities provided that they "could place special restrictions on access to particular places within the area on short notice." Nevertheless the lifting of the more severe restric-

tions was welcomed by our people.

The birth of an Organisation.

The Beginnings of Civil Defence.

(By Police Sergeant N. D. Sutherland, Wick.)

TO the average British citizen the letters "A.R.P." (or "R.A.P.," as they were often misquoted) had a sort of mysterious and far-away atmosphere about them when first introduced. Mussolini's attack on Abyssinia aroused only a passing uneasiness and even the ruthless attacks on Spanish civilians during the civil war in that country did not bring home "the shape of things to come." It was not until the 1938 crisis, which preceded the Munich agreement, that the country as a whole began to realize in earnest that the danger was perhaps greater than could be imagined and that measures for protecting the civilian required some serious attention. Caithness had a draft scheme of organisation prepared in the late Spring of 1938, when an Emergency Committee was formed, and at the same time the clerks to the District Councils were asked to begin enrolling volunteers. Results were more or less disappointing – it could hardly have been otherwise, for who (it was asked) would think of attacking Caithness? The county had no military objective worthy of the name and it was so far away from "anywhere" that a potential enemy could hardly reach it, were arguments advanced. This attitude of mind persisted until it was rudely altered. Thus, about the time of Munich, the county had a scheme in outline, a few untrained volunteers, some equipment, and one qualified instructor (Mr James Elliot, chief sanitary inspector, having passed through one of the Home Office Anti-gas Schools in March, 1938).

But despite scepticism, Munich did give a real scare. Thereafter things began to look more healthy as regards the strength of the new organisation. The local police took an active part in recruiting and their persuasive charms were, in large measure, successful in bringing the A.R.P. services and the Special Constabulary well up to strength. Buildings throughout the county were tentatively earmarked for Wardens' Posts, First-aid Posts, etc. At Wick the Old North School, condemned for educational purposes, was an invaluable acquisition. It was given a new lease of life as an Instructional Centre and it is true to say that, like many a human being who was no longer young, it filled admirably the breach in the hour of need. With some alterations the old building soon had a Wardens' Post, a First-Aid Post, a Lecture Room, a Rescue Depot, a Cleansing Depot, a Gas-proof Room and an Assembly Hall. The Hall later became a hive of industry as large numbers of volunteers worked at the assembly of the since familiar gas-masks.

★ ★ ★ ★ ★

But the first real step towards putting the wheels of A.R.P. in motion was the training of local Anti-Gas Instructors. Fourteen men were nominated for this course, which commenced under Mr Elliot's tuition on 26th October, 1938. Those early instructors deserve to be mentioned individually – firstly, because of their public-spiritedness in submitting themselves voluntarily to a fairly intensive study and stiff examinations in something which was entirely new; and secondly, because of the excellent work which they subsequently did in training the rank and file of A.R.P. The class was made up as follows:

A. T. BOYD, assistant sanitary inspector, Wick (now county sanitary inspector).

A. G. BRUCE, teacher, Thurso (later Officer in Charge Decontamination Service, Thurso).

D. CAMPBELL, headmaster, Lybster (later Head Warden Southern District).

J. N. CONNON, teacher, Wick (later Assistant G.I.O., now in Harris Academy, Dundee).

N. D. CAMERON, minister of religion, Canisbay.

G. S. HENDERSON, headmaster, Thrumster (now headmaster, Dunbeath).

J. MACDONALD, headmaster, Wick (later Head Warden Eastern District, now at Perth).

J. MACLEOD, headmaster, Latheron.

J. MILLER, Department of Agriculture, Thurso (later a major in the Army).

P. MILLER, Civil servant, Wick (later County Chief Warden and Training Officer) now in Dunnet.

W. REID, headmaster, Halkirk (later a major in the Home Guard).

J. G. SCOLLAY, headmaster, Dunbeath (now in Wick).

G. STEVEN, headmaster, Lyth (later Chief Warden for the County).

N. D. SUTHERLAND, Police Constable (later Sergeant).

The writer (whose name appears at the end of the list) will no doubt be pardoned for having felt at the beginning a certain sense of inferiority complex on finding himself in such distinguished company. This was quickly dispelled, however, by the splended *cameraderie* which grew up in the class and by the great helpfulness of the instructor. Gradually we

were initiated into the mysteries of A.R.P. – or perhaps, I should say, of gas, for poison gas formed the bedrock of all training in those days. We learned to distinguish the smell of B.B.C. from that of K.S.K. (or did we?), the colour of chlorine from that of phosgene, that there might be danger in a "smell like fresh mustard," and so on. There has been, and likely will be, much controversy over the wisdom of this early stress on gas to the almost exclusion of other forms of attack, but I have always maintained that it was a really fine piece of genius. Gas was the one potential weapon which could be negatived in a reasonable space of time by simple instruction and by the issue of gas-masks to all civilians. The government decided it was worth it as a form of insurance, and I am prepared to go the length of saying that our early preparations in this direction saved the British public from the added horrors of chemical warfare.

To return to our class: our examinations (written, practical and oral) came in December, and most of the candidates were thereafter able to boast of a new certificate, to write the letters L.A.R.P. after their names, and to start the job of passing on their accumulated knowledge to personnel in their districts. The great system of A.R.P. had started to function.

From then until the outbreak of war in September, 1939, the big task of initial instruction was in full swing. From Dunbeath to John O'Groats, and from Wick to Reay, the crofter, the mason, the fisherman, the teacher, the housewife – men and women from every occupation and of all ages – walked or cycled, often over very long distances, and in all kinds of weather, to attend the lectures and demonstrations. All were volunteers; all were keen; most of them maintained their keenness over the long weary years of war. The county owes a big debt to those people who served the homeland so quietly and yet so faithfully and so well.

★ ★ ★ ★ ★

My own first assignment as an Instructor was rather a peculiar and amusing one, and may be worth while recording. I had just been married and had resumed duty for only one day after my honeymoon when I was ordered to "go overseas" – at least that is what it looked like to me at the time. I was to instruct the wardens and special constables on the Island of Stroma. Several boxes of equipment were prepared for me and I crossed to the "Sable Isle" in the little boat which plies between there and the mainland two or three times per week. My instructional work was not to commence until the evening of the following day but I thought it advisable to open out my equipment shortly after arrival. Imagine my consternation when I discovered that every box, every gas-mask, every hole and corner that could be discovered was packed full with confetti! I had been the victim of a practical joke which to some extent had misfired – the jokers, no doubt, hoping that the boxes would be opened in front of the class! My week's stay on Stroma was most interesting despite the influenza epidemic which was raging there. I kept the germs at bay by saturating my handkerchiefs with powerful gasmask disinfectant and I was able to draw some useful topical analogies between the 'flu germs and certain forms of aerial attack when I addressed a well-attended public meeting!

While on the subject of early instruction, I must record the most excellent work performed by doctors and other First-aid instructors throughout the county in passing on their knowledge to the personnel of the Casualty Services; they spared no effort in fitting out this branch of the Organisation for the tasks that might lie ahead. Later on many of the doctors were attached to First-Aid Posts or Points where they were a tower of strength to their First-aiders during big exercises and when the real thing came.

* * * * *

Perhaps the only outstanding local event in A.R.P. immediately prior to the outbreak of war and deserving of special recognition was a big display organised as part of the Herring Queen festivities at Wick in July, 1939. By this time initial training was fairly well advanced and the display came as a sort of co-ordinated try-out of the services, as well as an indication to the public of what reasonably might be expected to happen. The show was put on in Smith Terrace and Huddart Street and it involved rescue work from smoke-filled buildings, fire-fighting, and decontamination work. The officer in charge of the display was Mr Elliot, who made a first-class job of it; a running commentary was given by Mr Pat Miller; rescue work was in charge of Mr A. T. Boyd; fire-fighting in charge of Mr G. Henderson (Thrumster), and decontamination (with a mixed team partly composed of special constables) under my own charge. From what I could gather, the public, although still a little sceptical about the need for A.R.P., were favourably impressed by the first display given in the county. It was A.R.P. in action and that was something which everybody could understand.

It would be impossible here to describe adequately the vast amount of administrative work which the creation of the new organisation involved; suffice it to say that it ran into many bulging files. The burden of the work fell on the County Clerk's Department, the Police Department, and the Public Health Department. It was done quietly and without any fuss – very often when the average citizen had long since retired to rest. More need not be said.

Proud of their own Service.

The Duties of Civil Defence.
(By Police Sergeant N. D. Sutherland, Wick.)

IT is only fitting that a chapter of this publication should be devoted to a brief general description of the various services which composed the local A.R.P. Organisation. Admittedly every county, town and city of Britain had much the same kind of organisation, with much the same services, and with the personnel doing much the same kind of routine work as Caithness, but this is essentially a county survey, dealing with county people, and it seems only right and proper that the local services should be described. Under the following headings, then, I will try to show what part the respective services had to perform.

POLICE. – The local Police Service is not, and never has been, a large one, but it was a nucleus of disciplined men round which a new organisation could be built. The first step taken in 1939 was to augment the service by the recruitment of Special Constables up to a strength of approximately 150 men, and there is no gainsaying the fact that this body performed unique local service during the years of war. Routine police duty does not come within the ambit of this review, but apart altogether from that aspect (and it is an important one) the police and "specials" were the backbone of outstanding service in the community. I need mention only the raids on Wick in 1940, when they worked for long hours after their usual employment was finished; the many prolonged searches for unexploded bombs and missing aircraft; the responsibility for giving air raid warnings to the public, and frequent emergency billeting. During the war the police indeed became more of a great social service than ever before, and it is perhaps true to say that they formed the corner-stone of Civil Defence.

WARDENS. – Unlike the Special

CAITHNESS – AND THE WAR.

Constabulary, the air raid Wardens' service was something entirely new and without any tradition. But the war years altered all that and the wardens came to stand high in the record of services rendered. Caithness was given an allocation of 200 part-time wardens, many of these being enrolled and initially trained in the spring and summer of 1939. During enemy activity the main job of the warden was to report to Control on incidents arising out of the fall of bombs or other weapons – the lives of his friends depended on the quickness and accuracy with which this was done. But there was more than that, for he (or she) was expected to render first-aid to the injured, do light rescue work, and attend to the homeless until the specially trained services arrived in response to the first message. Fortunately, there were few occasions when this was necessary in Caithness but when the raids did come the wardens contributed more than their share to the good work of making life normal again. In quiet periods there were other jobs to be done – all too often thankless jobs, such as inspections of, and repairs to, gas-masks; the keeping of household registers, and so on. The warden was indeed the good everyday war-time friend of his fellow-house-holders. For that alone he deserves to be thanked and remembered.

RESCUE. – Of all the A.R.P. Service, Rescue was perhaps the most dangerous. It had the responsibility of getting people out, alive if possible, from what might well seem to be a hopeless heap of rubble or from a near tottering wall which would make the onlooker hold his breath in anguished suspense. Obviously the men for a job like that were the tradesmen – the masons, the joiners, the plumbers – the men who could weigh up a building (or what was left of it) and set to work on sound principles. But even a trade knowledge was not enough; special training, based on experience elsewhere, had to be taken by selected men and passed on to others before the service could become really skilled. The various trades did supply many of the Rescue men in the county, which, in the original scheme, was allowed only two teams – one based on Wick and the other on Thurso. In the light of events this was later reviewed and the number increased to five – a much more sensible arrangement. Rescue played a

Wick and district Special Constables, 1938. In centre front row are W. K. Cormack, chief constable; Brig.-General Dudgeon, H.M. Inspector of Constabulary for Scotland and Inspector A. F. Allan. Caithness "Specials" gave 60,000 hours of voluntary service in the first year of war.

valuable part in both the raids on Wick in 1940. It may be recorded that this service received, in its more recent days, some welcomed assistance from the fishermen of the burgh of Wick who, previously bound by another scheme, were until then unable to help with Air Raid Precautions.

CASUALTY SERVICES. – The First-Aid Parties, the First-Aid Post Service (including the mobile units), and the Ambulance Service may for convenience be included under this heading. Up to 1943, when they were absorbed in the Rescue Service, the First-Aid Parties each consisted of five men with special training in rendering initial aid to the injured; it is worthy of note that many of them were ex-R.A.M.C. men who willingly came forward to place their Great War experience at the service of the local authority. The Post Service was largely composed of ladies (with nursing or V.A.D. experience) who waited in the Posts to deal skilfully with the injured when the party men or the sitting case cars brought them in. The casualty services in the county performed some very good work, not only in connection with raid casualties but on occasion among survivors from ships which, as a result of enemy action, went down near the coast of Caithness.

THE REPORT AND CONTROL SERVICE. – It has often been said that the Control Room was the "brains of the A.R.P. Organisation," but it is doubtful if many realised just how true that was. This service, composed of a mixed team of ladies and gentlemen, had two distinct functions – (1) it was responsible for the receipt of all messages from the wardens or police, and acting on these, for the subsequent deployment of the mobile services (which could not take any initial action until directed by Control); and (2) it had to keep District Headquarters at Inverness fully informed of the progress of events from the very commencment of a raid (or other occurrence) until it was finally cleared up. Those who have seen a Centre in operation will have appreciated the intricacy of such a job – the need there was for extreme care in seeing that there were no mistakes; for one can well imagine what serious results a slip could cause. Wick had, of course, the main Report and Control Centre; it was, first of all, housed in the Public Health Offices and later in the building specially put up for the purpose in the Police station yard. Thurso had a sub-area Report Centre situated in the Town Hall, and it was more or less responsible for the Western districts of the county. I cannot think of the Report and Control Service without looking back to the dark days of 1940-41, when the county had frequently its two or three warnings per night and its fair share of actual visits from the *Luftwaffe*. There was little use going home to bed in those days – particularly if you were a member of the Report Control Centre; perhaps "Wailing Winnie" might allow you an odd hour's sleep on one of the bunks in the premises but she was then so capricious a lady that one could not even depend on that. The Report and Control Service accomplished a grand job, and it can boast of something that no other service can – it has had its romances! Perhaps, of course, the nature of the duty it involved gave it an unfair advantage over its sister and brother services in this respect.

THE MESSENGER SERVICE. – Closely identified with the Control Service were the Messengers – the life-blood of A.R.P. communications. Wick had one of the finest teams of messengers in the county – youthful, keen, well-trained, and ready for action at any time. True, many of them came too late to see actual service, but they nevertheless proved their worth. These lads were a shining example of what enthusiasm and good leadership and training can do.

THE DECONTAMINATION SERVICE. – As time went on, the country did not expect gas – neither did the Decontamination Service. But they were always ready – those men and women with the bleach powder – to deal with it if Hitler, with his warped outlook, ever gave the order to his airmen to use the stuff. Theirs was an unspectacular and exacting although highly skilled job; no laurels from actual service came their way but they deserve the thanks of the community for doing a first-class preventive job.

THE GAS IDENTIFICATION SERVICE. – Like the Decontamination Service, the G.I.O. was never required in actual practice. He was the one who, with his specialised knowledge of chemistry, was selected to take samples of gas and identify them. No need here to stress the importance of this man's key position had the "Jerries" used gas bombs among the high explosive weapons they dropped so frequently. Caithness was allowed two gas identification officers – the senior one being stationed at Wick and the other at Thurso. In normal circumstances a county of similar size would have only one G.I.O. but Caithness, with its three or four active R.A.F. stations, was considered of sufficient importance to merit special consideration. Both the

G.I.O.s and their assistants may feel that their part in Civil Defence was, as things turned out, a comparatively small one. But it might have been otherwise.

OTHER SERVICES. – It is not intended that the heading "other services" should convey the impression that the ones included are slumped together in the same way as "sums under 1/-" in a subscription list. Far from it. But there were certain services which did not strictly come within the scope of the A.R.P. Organisation, and they should not be confused with it. The most important of these were the Rest Centre Service, the Information Service, and the Emergency Mortuary Service. All had to deal with the aftermath of raiding and in the hands of their personnel lay the great responsibility of upholding morale. The Rest Centres were ready to provide emergency feeding and shelter; the Information Centres, immediate information and monetary assistance; and the Mortuary Service – well, it had a gruesome but a necessary job, and quite a lot depended on how it was handled. With the exception of the Information Centres, which did not come into being until later in the war, these services had their share of actual operations and very well did they tackle their job; indeed it was stated on more than one occasion that the organisation of the County Rest Centres was second to none in Scotland. On the Mortuary Service there fell a heavy burden – not so much as a result of air raids as from the tragic harvest which the sea produced in the earlier days of the war. These were grim and gloomy days but it is consoling to think that the brave lads who died round our coasts did not give their lives in vain.

Very little attempt has been made here to describe the combined functioning of the A.R.P. Organisation in detail, to record the special efforts of individuals or to reflect the steadfastness of Civil Defence which carried it through long periods of inactivity with unabated enthusiasm. But it gives an outline of the build-up of an Organisation which was planned to meet as far as possible any eventuality that might occur. We must, I think, hand it to the "architects" for producing something which stood the test of time, of action and of inaction, so well. And every volunteer can feel proud that he or she belonged to such an organisation.

* * * * *

Thoroughness was the keynote of all preparations. This can be gathered from circulars issued to Supervisors of Wick Burgh Rest Centres, giving opening arrangements and all necessary information, including names and addresses of all superintendents and deputies with office and home telephone numbers. There were five Rest Centres in Wick:– High School (staff 64, accommodation for 250); Barrogill Hall (staff 12, accommodation for 66); British Legion Club (staff 9, accommodation for 36); St. John's Church Hall (staff 9, accommodation for 18); Women's Club, Vansittart Street (staff 8, accommodation for 15). These five centres were equipped to accommodate 385 people and in the landward area provision was made for an additional 210:– Thrumster School (45), Whaligoe School (25), Mid-Clyth School (13), Mid-Clyth Hall (27), Lybster Old School (70), and Lybster British Legion (30). Supervisor of Rest Centres, M. Mackenzie, High School (deputy, H. B. Reid); catering supervisor Miss N. Harper (deputy, Mrs Fred. Harper); personal supervisor, Mrs Brown (deputy, Mrs M'Hardy).

Public shelters in the town were:– Basement shelters – W. & A. Geddes, High Street; Sinclair Brothers, Market Sq.; Bon-Accord Restaurant, High Street; surface shelters – Bignold Park, Station Road, Riverside and Kirkhill. The latter type of shelter became much more plentiful later on, but were never actually required.

The information leaflet (undated) gives the following list of supervisors, etc. at an advanced stage in A.R.P. organisation:–

County Executive Officer for A.R.P. and Executive Food Officer – James Robertson, County Clerk.

Controller A.R.P. and Chief Constable – W. K. Cormack, Police Station.

Casualty and Hospital Service – Dr Dick, Public Health Buildings; Deputy – Dr Leask, High Street.

Chief Billeting Officer and Emergency Information Officer – Provost Sutherland, town clerk's office.

Deputy Food Officer and National Registration Officer – T. W. Anderson, Parish Church Hall.

Training Officer, A.R.P. – W. Cruickshank, West Banks Avenue.

Fire Guard Staff Officer – P. Mackenzie, Back Bridge Street.

Emergency Relief Officer – John Gowans, County Offices.

Assistance Board – Sinclair Lyall, County Buildings.

Bomb Reconnaissance Officers – W. Black, West Banks Terrace, and Sergeant Carter, Police Station.

Casualty – 1st F.A.P. – J. Duncan, Old North School; 2nd F.A.P. – W. Sutherland, Brown Place,; Mobile Unit – Rev. G. Moore, Parish Manse.

Decontamination (Food) – James Elliot, Public Health Buildings; Decontamination Squad – J. G. Scollay, Old North School.

Fire – N.F.S. – S./Ldr. Meldrum, Scalesburn; Fireguards – D. Cormack, Back Bridge Street.

Gas Identification Officer – R. Scott, Polwarth, Francis Street.

Information Centre – W. W. Beveridge, Town Hall.

Officer of Bakeries – Provost Sutherland, Town Hall.

Mortuary – F. W. Robertson, Ph.D.

Report Centre – W. Robison, Public Health Buildings.

Rescue Squad – D. Harper, Old North School

Rest Centres – M. Mackenzie, High School; J. Stewart, Barrogill Hall; C. Ball, British Legion Club; Mrs Jenkins, St. John's Hall; Mrs E. Angus, Women's Club.

Salvage (a) Food Stores – T. W. Anderson, Parish Church Hall; (b) Household Goods – A. Finlayson, Town Hall. Utility Services – Burgh Surveyor – Mr Coutts, Town Hall; County Surveyor – C. K. Fraser, County Buildings; County Sanitary Inspector – Mr Elliot, Public Health Officer; Gas Company – S. Manson, Gas Works; Electricity – A. More, Town Hall; Telephones – Post Office; Water – D. Bruce, Town Hall.

Wardens – Chief Warden of County – G. Steven, Schoolhouse, Lyth; Head Warden of Wick – A. B. Henderson, Breadalbane Crescent; Deputy Head Wardens – A. Bruce, Barbara Place; D. Cormack, High Street; J. A. Budge, West Banks Avenue.

W.V.S. Secretary – Miss Elspeth Miller, Woolworth Buildings.

Home Guards – Lieut.-Col. Ian M'Hardy, County Buildings; Captain Harper, Bank of Scotland Buildings.

Posts – Casualty Posts – Bignold Hospital; 1st F.A.P. – Old North School; 2nd F.A.P. – Brown Place. Decontamination Posts – (a) Casualties – Bignold Hospital and Brown Place; (b) Personnel – Old North School; (c) Public – Henderson Home. Wardens' Posts – Headquarters – Cliff, Albert Street, Bank Row, Breadalbane Terrace, Brown Place, I.L.P. Hall, Kirkhill, Old North School, Vansittart Street, Wick High School.

First bomb on the mainland of Britain.

The Luftwaffe's Early Visits.

(By Police Sergeant N. D. Sutherland, Wick.)

THERE was still a considerable amount of initial emergency work to be done when the war broke out in September, 1939. Training in anti-gas measures were well forward (although not complete) but there were very few of the personnel who had had the opportunity of attending a course in elementary precautions against high explosives and incendiary weapons; many civilians in the country were still without gas-masks; air-raid shelters were almost unknown; and the arrangements for warning the public of the approach of hostile aircraft were merely an improvisation. But the hour had struck and effort was redoubled, with the result that, in a month or two, some of the deficiencies were made good. The Wick Autumn Holiday became, by order of the Town Council, an "Emergency Day" on which many people did their utmost to assist in every way possible to bring precautions up to scratch. The Caithness housewives struggled with their black-outs – results were in some cases good, in others not so good, but the law was lenient for a time.

The first air raid warning came about the middle of October. When the whistle at the John O'Groat Laundry started to screech out its steady note (there was no siren then) Wick people looked at one another in amazement. Was this really it? Or did the laundry people forget about the ban on hooters? Or were the police indulging in some sort of leg-pull? The appearance on the streets of policemen complete with steel helmets and gas-masks at the "alert" seemed to indicate that something serious might be afoot, and yet the men in blue were the subject of a good deal of chaff as they patrolled up and down advising a sceptical public to take cover. The first "alert" lasted for about 50 minutes. It was to be the first of many but it was a novelty then and it resulted in a great number of inevitable rumours about the location and number of the 'planes which had approached the county. It was preceded, too, by a rather curious incident – one that has never been explained to the full satisfaction of those involved.

Just before mid-day a Mrs Cormack, living at Nypster, Bower, went to her local warden (William Henderson) and told him that her brother-in-law, Alexander Cormack, had fallen ill from supposed effects of gas. The warden proceeded post-haste to the scene of the "incident" but was unable to detect anything that would point towards gas having been dropped by the enemy; there was no visible sign and no unusual smell.

Still the symptoms described by the sick man seemed to indicate most unusual circumstances; he had felt a choking sensation in throat and chest and at the time there was a disagreeably sulphurous smell in the area, so much so indeed that he went to the length of unyoking his horses. His brother and sister-in-law also noticed the unusual smell, but they had no after-effects. It was established that an unidentified 'plane had passed over the district shortly before.

The warden informed his headquarters at Wick, and the county sanitary inspector made full investigation into the whole incident, without, however, being able to throw much light on the cause of the trouble. It was generally accepted by the authorities that no actual gas had been dropped, but there is no reason to doubt that an aircraft had "got rid of something" over the district and that it had had an effect similar to what certain war gases might have been expected to produce. The "casualty" was able to return to work two or three hours after the symptoms appeared, and did not feel any the worse for his unusual experience.

Orkney received its first bombing on the same date and (whether or not there was anything in the Bower "incident") the fact that one district in the North of Scotland had been attacked made us realize that those fond hopes of our geographical position making us secure had been rudely disillusioned.

It was in March and April, 1940, that Orkney had its real baptism of fire, and the flashes of bursting bombs and anti-aircraft shells could be seen clearly from vantage points in Caithness while the piercing searchlights out-stripped the aurora borealis as they skipped across the sky.

No "alert" was sounded in the county during the March and early April raids on Orkney despite the fact that on 2nd April, Duncansby Head Lighthouse was *strafed* by machine-gun fire, and that a "Heinkel" aircraft made a forced landing near Wick a few evenings later. (Two of the crew of this 'plane were dead and the other two were made prisoners.) This lack of warning was a little perturbing and occasioned no small criticism of the system in operation; but the fault, if fault there was, did not lie with the local officials and representation was made to higher authority.

The evening of 10th April was a busy one. The siren sounded at approximately 9 o'clock and shortly afterwards enemy machines could be seen and heard flying overhead and there were sounds of loud explosions in the direction of Orkney. This date deserves to be specially remembered because it was shortly after 9 p.m. that the first bomb (a 500 pounder) fell on the county; but it was more than the first bomb on Caithness it was the FIRST ONE OF THE WAR on the mainland of Britain. Two or three days passed before the crater was found and little wonder, too, for the bomb had fallen away out in uninhabited moorland at Achavrole, Watten. No injury was done and no material damage sustained by anybody although the shock of the explosion had been felt for miles around. The cause of this incident was traceable to a night heath fire and it came as warning to those people whose blackouts were still faulty.

Two Wick men standing in the bomb crater (15ft deep by 40ft wide) at Achavrole.

From April to the end of June numerous warnings of the approach of hostile 'planes were received and on more than one occasion dog-fights could be seen over the sea near the county. During the afternoon of the 9th May the dead body of a German and parts of a wrecked aircraft were brought into Wick to confirm the good work of our fighters.

Early in June a bomb was dropped in a field at Limekilns, Upper Lybster, and a little later on the same night there was a loud explosion in the hills near Strathmore Lodge. It was concluded that in this instance an attempt had been made to blow up the weir of a nearby loch and no doubt that particular

"Jerry" returned to his base with a glowing account of his success as a dam-buster! And so Caithness was initiated into the ways of the *Luftwaffe*.

Civil Defence tested.

Wick Became Cynosure of Many Eyes.

(By Police Sergeant N. D. Sutherland, Wick.)

A ring and fragment of the bomb dropped at Achavrole.

The "victory" at Achavrole. The explosion split the wall of an outhouse about half-a-mile away.

JULY the first, 1940, was a melancholy day for Wick. About 4.30 o'clock in the afternoon, while the townspeople were going about their usual jobs and the children were playing happily in the summer sunshine with no thought or suspicion of what was coming their way, an enemy 'plane flew over the town and released two bombs against the harbour area. The missiles never reached their probable objective – they fell short by a matter of yards – and exploded within a few feet of each other near the south end of Bank Row. No warning siren preceded the attack – not even a preliminary message of the approach of hostile aircraft reached the police. So the public and the services, through no fault of their own, were caught completely off their guard. Even when the explosions took place, except at the actual locus and in the near vicinity, few people realized what had happened.

But urgent calls for assistance were soon coming in and the police and Civil Defence organised themselves as well as was possible in the circumstances. Bank Row presented a sorry scene of devastation and of desolation – the dead and dying and injured were lying about everywhere; some were trapped in rubble, others were underneath motor vehicles which had been stranded in the street. All the buildings from the middle of Bank Row to the south end were wrecked and there were signs of considerable blast damage over a wide area of Lower

Pulteneytown, and even "above the brae." Police, Wardens, First-Aid and Rescue personnel, assisted by members of the public, threw themselves into the work of rescuing the trapped, of tending to the injured, and of transporting the serious casualties to hospital. They did a good job of work, but there was little that could be done for many of the victims; eleven had already succumbed and four others passed away in hospital very soon afterwards. In addition to those who died, a further three people were seriously injured, twelve were slightly injured, and several others received minor cuts and bruises. One or two families were particularly hard hit – in one case a father, his son, his daughter, and his daughter-in-law were fatally injured, while in another two little sisters, both under 10 years of age, paid the full penalty of bombing. Perhaps the most poignant feature of the tragedy was the number of little innocents whose lives were so suddenly and so violently cut short in the midst of their happiness.

Many families had to leave their homes, which were rendered unfit and unsafe for habitation, and they were sympathetically cared for by willing friends throughout the burgh until emergency repairs or more permanent billets could be secured.

There were some miraculous escapes in the raid: one well-known Wick tailor (Alexander Stephen, Coach Road) picked himself unscathed out of what had become a heap of rubble and in which lay the bodies of two or three of his co-workers; a police officer (Sergeant, now Inspector, Cormack) was within a few yards of the bursting bombs and escaped with a minor shrapnel injury; and John Sinclair, the then popular courthouse-keeper, who was with him, was uninjured.

★　★　★　★　★

In comparison with the subsequent *blitzes* which fell on many Southern cities, the first raid on Wick many now seem a small affair. But it was almost the first of its kind on Britain and it was a sharp and unexpected blow for a small town far removed from a big centre from which ready assistance might be expected. When thinking of the part played by Civil Defence in this incident, one must keep in mind that all the services were untried – the experience which only big raiding could give was at this stage non-existent, proper and scientific incident control was unknown, and the finer parts of rescue work had yet to be discovered. When one adds to this the fact that personnel were working under the belief that an unexploded bomb lay buried somewhere in the vicinity (this was later disproved), we must hand it unstintingly to all those who unselfishly shouldered the burden of succouring the injured, calming the bereaved, and generally clearing up the incident. Little wonder that "a small town on the North East

of Scotland" became the cynosure of many eyes throughout Britain for a brief spell.

Bombing was something new to Britain in this war and it fell on Wick to provide something in the nature of an early test case for the organisation which had been built up to meet it; more than that, it was a test case for the morale of the civilian population – surely a vital factor in what was becoming a total war. And the good people of Wick stood up gallantly in their hour of trial, just as the people in southern towns and cities were to pass heroically through their trial by explosive and fire in the days that lay ahead. Many letters and tangible proofs of sympathy came from all quarters, among them a letter of sympathy to each bereaved household from Sir Archibald Sinclair, the newly appointed Air Minister.

Wick gradually returned to the normal tenor of its ways, but the memory of that first sharp attack will remain for ever imprinted on the minds of all those who passed through it.

★　★　★　★　★

Between the first and second serious attacks on Wick, there was a comparatively uneventful period in Caithness; the wailing of the siren became a common enough sound in both Wick and Thurso, but the activity had shifted from the North to the South as the epic battle of Britain was fought out in the sky over England. There was a small incident at East Clyth on the night of 22nd August when an enemy 'plane dropped three H.E. bombs in open country about 30 yards from a dwelling-house. The windows and door of the house were blown in and the roof damaged, but the householder with his wife and five children escaped injury.

And so to the evening of October 26, when Wick had, in point of view of missiles dropped, its heaviest raid of the war. At 6.20 p.m. three enemy aircraft, after first bombing the Thrumster area, flew very low and at great speed over the town and dropped their combined load partly on the north side of the town and partly within the grounds of the R.A.F. Station; one or two of the 'planes raked the streets with machine-gun fire as they snored towards their objective. Once again the warning system had been caught on the wrong foot, for it was not until 17 minutes after the attack that the message came through to sound the "alert"! Thereafter it became an excusable (but dangerous) joke that the sounding of the siren was an indication that no raid would take place.

From the sound of rapidly exploding bombs it became clear that Henrietta Street, Hill Avenue, and George Street had had a hot time of it. These streets

A CORNER OF BANK ROW – JULY 2, 1940.

ONE OF THE WRECKED HOMES IN BANK ROW.

did, in fact, suffer most, and some 140 dwelling-houses over the area were damaged. One bungalow in Hill Avenue, occupied by John Cameron, grocer, received a direct hit and the five occupants at the time all became serious casualties, three of which were fatal.

Although Hill Avenue had the worst incident of the raid, there were others almost as bad except for the fact that all the casualties, ten in number, were only minor.

★   ★   ★   ★   ★

A freak incident occurred in Rosebery Terrace where a bomb struck the gable of a municipal house, knocked a huge hole in the wall, and then ricochetted across the street into the garden of D.A. Sinclair's house, where it exploded and wrecked the front of the building. The Bignold Hospital was seriously damaged and the Medical Officer of Health had to order the evacuation of the patients. This was carried out smoothly and without panic before morning. Among the narrowest escapes was perhaps the one which occurred in Bridge Street (about 500 yards from the nearest incident), where a piece of red hot metal weighing about 6 or 7 pounds from one of the bombs penetrated the roof of Lipton's shop and landed a few feet away from the manager.

In all, twenty high explosive bombs were dropped during the attack, but, of that number, seven failed to explode on impact, and they had later to be dealt with by a bomb disposal unit. This high proportion of unexploded bombs, coupled with extensive damage to private houses, resulted in there being a large number of homeless persons on the north side of the town. As a temporary measure the Rest Centre at the High School very successfully accommodated and catered for most of these, while a few found refuge with friends inside and outside the town.

Despite the lack of warning, the conduct both of the A.R.P. Services and the public in general was very praiseworthy, all branches of the Services working efficiently and well and the morale of civilians remaining high throughout. The quick fall of darkness handicapped the work of repair parties, but, even so, most of the damaged public utilities were in working order by the following day and first repairs to housing were well under way in a comparatively short time.

Two as against twenty-two. That was the difference between the first and second raids on Wick in so far as bombs were concerned. But there was no comparison between the disastrous effect of those two July bombs and the much larger number of October ones, simply because the former fell togeth-

Snaps taken on October 27, 1940.

Rubble of the bungalow that vanished in Hill Avenue.

A damaged bungalow in Hill Avenue.

Where a bomb exploded in Rosebery Terrace.
View of damaged property.

er at a busy corner and at a busy hour of the day, while the latter were scattered from low flying aircraft over a wider and more "rural" area, when fewer people were about. Wick may indeed look back with gratitude on its escape in the second raid, for, had the bombs been released a few seconds earlier, they would have straddled the town. In that unhappy event this review would, I am afraid, be a much more tragic tale.

Scattered Raids.

If any man had had the temerity to prophesy in pre-war days that the rural area of Thrumster would have saved Wick from serious bombing, he would have been the laughing-stock of the community, or, more likely, be regarded (to put it in local parlance) as being "a fit subject for Montrose!" Looking back on the year 1941, however, one may justifiably say that the Royal Burgh does owe a great deal to Thrumster, or, more correctly, to official ingenuity in that area. It is needless to go into detail on what was done there, although the reader will probably read between the lines that a decoy system was practised with considerable success. Thrumster came first into the picture on the evening when Wick received its second air raid, and thereafter it absorbed most of the bombs which fell on the mainland of Caithness. It was constantly attacked in March, April, May, June and July of 1941, generally during the night or early morning hours. Well on for 50 bombs were showered down on a small area; and all this time Wick, although subjected to an unprecedented number of siren warnings and distant "shocks," escaped with little damage.

★ ★ ★ ★ ★

In the early Spring of 1941, there was considerable enemy activity, mostly by aircraft flying singly, or in pairs, just off the coast line of the county. In February, there were two or three attacks on coastal vessels, and on the 22nd of the month Stroma Lighthouse was attacked by machine-gun fire; windows were damaged at the Lighthouse, but fortunately there were no casualties. Two days later a single bomb fell harmlessly on waste ground near Noss Head. On March 17 the R.A.F. Station at Wick was raided twice within a few hours by a single 'plane, but there was very little damage and few casualties, and the town escaped almost entirely.

During the first two years of the war surprise was often expressed at the apparent immunity from attack enjoyed by the town of Thurso and, more particularly, by the nearby port of Scrabster, which handled much of the cargoes and thousands of the passengers going to and fro between the all-important Orkney Islands and the mainland. The reason may have been that the enemy did not realize its importance, or more likely that his airmen found it difficult to locate in darkness; in any case this lovely little town way up on the shores of the Pentland came through the war unscathed. On two or three occasions only did its inhabitants receive a scare. The first one was on the night of the 7th April, 1941, when a large bomb was dropped near the town refuse dump, which is about a mile west of the burgh; and a second was on the 23rd of June in the same year, when at 2.30 o'clock in the morning German aircraft attacked shipping in Thurso Bay and a minesweeper (H.M.S. *Beach*) was sunk with the loss of 12 of her crew.

★ ★ ★ ★ ★

The village of Castletown, which assumed some importance as a result of its close proximity to the R.A.F. Station at Thurdistoft, also had its share of luck. Only once, on 18th April, 1941, were bombs dropped by an enemy 'plane, and these fell on Burkle Hill, south of the village, where they all exploded in open country and no casualties or damage were caused. This incident gave rise to a rather amusing story. The local policeman at once cycled to the area where the bombs had exploded, and on arriving there he found that the nearest occupied dwelling was a tinkers' encampment. Having succeeded in gaining an entrance to the rather crazy tent, he found that the whole family had disappeared, and, fearing the worst, he shouted the question: "Is there anybody here?" The reply came from below a bed: "Ay, we're all in here!" "Is there anybody hurt?" asked the officer. "Oh ma goad," came the answer, "it nearly knocked us all into maternity."

And so went on the scattered raiding, which made the Caithness coast one of the most harassed (although, of course, not the most heavily bombed) in Scotland during the first six months of 1941. Two further incidents (to complete this phase) may be mentioned. On 18th April, four high explosives were dropped in a field at Smerral, Latheron, and house windows in the vicinity were blown in, but nobody was hurt. It is rather interesting to look back on the fact that quite a number of isolated attacks were made on the general Lybster-Latheron area, and one cannot help wondering what the enemy was in search of. Was he dropping his bombs aimlessly in the hope of hitting something worthwhile? Or did he imagine that the main railway line ran somewhere in the area? In any case almost all the bombs dropped on rural Caithness were utterly fruitless from the attackers' point of view. The second incident mentioned above occurred on 4th June, when at 7.25 p.m. a single aircraft circled twice over Wick and machine-gunned the streets. Bullets penetrated the roofs and windows of a few houses in the town and one passed clean through the bonnet of a local doctor's car, but there were no civilian casualties. Before leaving the area the enemy bombed the R.A.F. Station, where some damage and injuries to personnel resulted. No alarm was sounded for this attack until after the 'plane was well on its way towards Germany, and thus the general public became convinced (if at this stage it needed convincing) of the inadequacy of the warning system. Those "in the know" were perhaps better able to appreciate the difficulties that might occur in detecting the approach of the single or sneak raider.

★   ★   ★   ★   ★

After July, 1941, Caithness was, more or less, left alone by the *Luftwaffe,* the county entering on what was to be a comparatively uneventful period. Enemy 'planes that visited Caithness were reckoned to have been stationed in Norway. When the war concluded the discovery was made that the Germans had three million bombs stored in that unhappy country. Who in Caithness would have slept so peacefully or moved around so unconcernedly at times had this fact been known?

The Norway hoard of bombs may well have been intended for Scottish soil, but when the invasion of Russia began (June 22, 1941) the outlook for the North of Scotland improved. Germany required bombing strength for the Eastern front. Thus the "scene was changed" and the people of our northern county, in unison with their sisters and brothers in the South, might be pardoned for heaving a temporary sigh of relief.

Youth had a duty.

Pre-Service Units Formed in Caithness.

BRITAIN determined to build a great air force for purposes of attack as well as defence. To maintain this force a continuous flow of manpower was required, and much of the flying personnel was trained in Canada and Rhodesia, far from likely scenes of war activities. At home was established the first pre-Service unit, the Air Training Corps. This was in the Spring of 1941 and had as its object the

fitting of youth through preliminary training to take a ready place in the senior Services when the required age was attained.

Flights were formed at Wick and Thurso of 1285 (Caithness) Squadron A.T.C., and in the summer of 1943 Thurso formed a separate squadron (1769) to serve the western district of the county. In March, 1945, it was revealed that 40 former cadets of Thurso Squadron were serving with the R.A.F., 22 of them on aircrew duties. A flight formed at Lybster linked up with Wick, as also did sections at Keiss and Dunbeath.

The 1285 (Caithness) Squadron was under command of Flying Officer David Robertson, who succeeded Flight.-Lieut. J. Stewart. The commanding officer at Thurso was Flight.-Lieut. A.E.N. Williams. Several R.A.F. officers and others gave helpful and enthusiastic support and the A.T.C. became a valuable institution. In Wick the Corps acquired their own commodious premises for training and recreation. These were situated in Stafford Lane and were opened by Air Commodore Chamier. The Caithness flights were inspected on more than one occasion by the Duke of Hamilton, A.F.C., Commandant of the A.T.C. in Scotland, who expressed himself as well pleased with the training and appearance of the lads.

★   ★   ★   ★   ★

Caithness had a special interest in flying because of the 'dromes situated here, and the eyes of the youth of the county were often turned skywards. The young lads were very observant and different designs of machines were readily distinguished in the air. To them, aircraft recognition became easy — they grew up with it, so to speak. Service in the Corps was to them an interesting and educative apprenticeship, and theoretical knowledge acquired was but to help them when practical work was undertaken. Now and again they were billeted on the 'drome and permitted berths in aeroplanes on flights around our coasts. These were outstanding days in young lives.

Caithness youth made a fine response in numbers and enthusiasm, and about 80 per cent of the lads enlisting from 1285 Squadron were accepted by the R.A.F. Air Force losses, however, were latterly much below estimated calculations, with a consequent lessening demand for replacement personnel. Hence the guarantee of automatic transfer of Training Corps cadets to the Air Force proper was abandoned. Demands by the infantry became heavier and the call for youths for the coal-pits insistent. To these services boys were drafted. To be given a shovel under the coal-mining scheme instead of

A section of Wick Flight A.T.C. (1944). Seated in the centre of front row are Flying Officer P. Halcrow, Flying Officer D. Robertson, and Pilot Officer W. Robison.

work (or wings) for which voluntary preparatory training had fitted them was not appreciated by youth or by their instructors, all of whom had sacrificed much time on the movement. Thus the A.T.C. in part lost its impetus. In some centres indeed it was discontinued.

* * * * *

The Caithness area (when formed 1941) was governed by the following committee:– Comdr. R. R. Gore Browne Henderson (chairman), Provost T. W. Anderson, Provost W. M. Brims, Mr John S. Banks, Mr Alexr. Robertson, Colonel J. J. Robertson, Mr R. Scott (secretary), and Mr C. H. Thomson (treasurer). These were elected from a larger committee composed of representatives of the various public bodies in the county.

The Wick Corps was first under the instruction of Flying Officer A. Plant, and at Thurso Flight. Lieut. Williams was assisted by Pilot Officer W. Laing. The Thurso Flight had a section at Halkirk.

* * * * *

The logbook of an ex-member of the A.T.C. who joined the R.A.F. shows that he took part in some two dozen operational flights in which more than a hundred of the attacking 'planes were lost. The record may not be exceptional, but it is inter-

esting. The squadron was stationed at Skellingthorpe, Lincoln, and the targets *strafed*, included railway marshalling yards, shipping, U-boat pens, gun positions, troop concentrations, pockets of resistance, canals, and synthetic oil plants.

The flights were made mostly at night-time and the machine flew on bombing missions to Norway, Holland, France, Germany, and even Czechoslovakia – "a very long and tiresome operation." "The machine," it is said; but different machines were used – Easy, Love, How, Johnny, Fox, Able and George; sometimes they suffered damage from flak; entries read, 7 holes in aircraft, and even 28 holes, but ever they made home, and the closing observation ever reads, "landed at base without incident."

One passage in the logbook caught the eye. It read – "This trip (to Bergen, Norway) was a bind all the way there and back owing to the terrible weather we had to fly through . . . Light flak was very intense and two of our Lancs. had to land at Wick owing to flak damage."

Another passage is even more interesting. Here it is:– "Our first brush with Jerry nightfighters (21.2.45, when Gravenhorst was visited). . . Just as we were crossing the battle front the 'Skipper' saw a

JU.88 on the starboard bow up. He crossed over to port and started to make an attack from the port beam. . . Pete and I opened fire. . . We scored hits and saw flashes of flame come from the 88's tail. This combat was later confirmed . . . and gave us a JU.88 to our credit."

The logbook from which the above extracts are culled belonged to Flight-Sergt. (later W.O.) Thomas Farmer, whose home address is 12 Vansittart Street, Wick; and with him as another member of the crew was Flight-Sergt. Peter Macdonald, Henrietta Street. Two "townies" on one aircraft, and both gunners. Macdonald is the "Pete" referred to in the air combat recorded above.

* * * * *

What was true of the A.T.C. as a training unit was equally true of the Sea Cadets. This pre-entry unit for the Navy was very popular in Wick, and many lads passed through its ranks. Like the A.T.C., the Sea Cadets acquired their own premises. These were in Breadalbane Terrace.

The function of the Corps was to give technical sea training to, and instil naval traditions in, boys who intended to serve in the Royal and Merchant Navies both in war and peace, and to impart knowledge to sea-minded lads not wishing to follow a sea career in order that they might form a valuable reserve for the Navy. The Corps aimed to provide for the spiritual, social and educational welfare of cadets and to develop character and good citizenship in its widest sense.

The Corps at Wick was formed under the guidance of Lieut.-Comdr. Chilcott, R.N., and was open to youths aged 14-17. A local administrative committee was appointed in January, 1943. Members were:– Rev. Samuel Ballantyne, B.D. (chairman and padre); Mr William Sinclair, Harbour Office (hon.-secretary); Mr F. R. Cochran, British Linen Bank (hon. treasurer); Captain G. Sutherland, harbourmaster; Lieut. Baker, R.N.; and Messrs D. B. Alexander, Thomas Budge, Donald Budge, J. R. M'Robbie, Alexr. Robertson, M.A., and Neil Stewart, jun.

Mr G. S. Jenkins, fishery office, became commanding officer; Mr Wilfred M'Keown (now of Loch Street), administrative officer, and Dr Leask, medical officer.

The untimely death of Lieut. Jenkins (in July, 1943) was widely regretted. He was succeeded in command of the Sea Cadets by Lieut. W. H. M'Donell.

* * * * *

Some 60 boys enrolled at the first meeting in the High School on February 3, 1943, and within a few weeks the number almost doubled.

The Cadets simply loved the navy blue. Anyone could see that. They dreamed of ships, big ships, just as their brothers of the A.T.C. dreamed of wings. They were happy, too, with training arrangements, as these sometimes took them to southern coastal towns. They longed for the quarter-deck and did not appreciate being drafted to the infantry and much less sent to the mines. Indeed no Caithness lad had any inclination to become a coal-miner and most of them abhorred the prospect. With the removal of assured prospects of service in the Navy, the Cadet movement dropped considerably in strength although it still continues.

* * * * *

A third pre-entry training service formed was the Army Cadet Force. It was the youngest of the three pre-service units available to youths but in peace-time may well become the strongest numerically. There were at least three companies in Caithness – at Wick, Thurso and Halkirk, with sections at Watten and Lybster. Administration was good and the training sound and youths drafted to the Army found that progress was hastened through early initiation into soldiering ways and the handling of arms. Officers generally were men of experience, ready with advice and assistance, tactful and efficient, and able to maintain discipline without having to enforce it.

The Army Cadet Force was organised in the autumn of 1943. Major W. Reid, Halkirk, was responsible for the formation arrangements within our county and the movement started well. Lads took quickly to the familiar khaki battledress and there was no lack of "rookies." Early numbers were encouraging but figures fluctuated; at Wick the company has had as high as 85 youths in its ranks, and in post-war years may expect to average more than 50.

The Wick company had the good fortune to come under the command and tuition of Captain George Gunn, who formerly held a key position in the Home Guard, and although its composition has changed with the years he still continues as its officer. There have been changes in the leadership of the other companies.

Six of the Wick Army Cadets attended the Victory Parade in London, as also did Lieut. J. Budge, Thurso. The first Caithness cadet to attain the rank of sergeant-major was George Durrand, whose father was R.S.M. with the 5th Seaforths on service abroad.

★ ★ ★ ★ ★

War-time produced an organisation for juvenile girls as well. This was the Girls' Training Corps. Headquarters were at Wick, and there were sections at Thurso, Halkirk, Reay, Bower and Keiss. The chairman of the county committee was Miss Sinclair, Thurso Castle, who also served on the national executive committee.

Mrs Kenneth Duff-Dunbar, chairman of the local committee, presided at the inauguration meeting at Wick (October, 1942), and Miss Isobel Budge, Lybster, attended in uniform and told of her experiences when, along with Miss Ryrie, Thurso, the county secretary, she had attended classes at St. Andrews. Fifty cadets enrolled in 1943, but the number rose to more than eighty in later years. Physical training formed part of the curriculum, but cooking, first-aid, messenger work for Civil Defence etc., were undertaken.

Three thousand cadets of the Girls' Training Corps took part in a national rally in Edinburgh, where the Salute was taken by H.R.H. Princess Elizabeth. Five members of the Caithness companies were present – two from Wick, two from Thurso, and one from Reay.

Our folks supported all causes.

Savings Reached Peak Point.

THE war was said to be a civilian war in that it could be won or lost on the home front. Anyhow, the civilian had an important part to play – there was a wide choice of outlets for patriotic activities apart from essential duties entrusted to able-bodied men and women.

There were three "M's" in the forefront – men, munitions, and money. Wealth has been dubbed a weak anchor but in war-time it was more of a sure shield; money was needed to clothe, feed, equip, train and transport the fighting Forces; to build ships, aircraft, factories and living quarters – all on a scale hitherto unknown. Money was required to buy abroad: currency was all important. Britain's expenditure ultimately reached the amazing figure of 14 million pounds per day. Always a virtue, saving within the nation became a vital necessity; and expenditure by the individual on non-essential articles was discouraged. Taxation generally was increased, and a graded system of purchase tax introduced as a restrictive brake on spending. This system

affected almost every requirement, and reached as high as 100 per cent. on luxury articles. The lowering of income-tax allowances brought millions of wage-earners within the tax-paying scheme. This levy was deducted from weekly wages under a system known as "Pay as you earn," a weekly collection instead of the customary lump sum at the close of each half-yearly period. The citizen forcibly was made to realize the truth of the saying that war is mostly loss with a big L.

★ ★ ★ ★ ★

Caithness was regarded as a poor county. Its people were dependent mainly on two industries: both recognised as uncertain rather than as prosperous in pre-war years. Wealth (such as it was) in our county was accumulated by the consistent practice of industry, frugality and studied economy. Wages generally were below the country's average standard. War-time brought urgent national, international, as well as local appeals, yet Caithness responded to all with astonishing generosity. "The freedom and honour of our county is life itself to us" (said a lady speaker) "and we are prepared to give health, wealth and happiness for its sake." Maybe this was correct: a guid cause mak's a strong airm. Anyhow, a spirit of intense patriotism was maintained throughout the years.

War Weapons Week (1941) was the first big savings effort in Caithness when "Lend to Defend" was the slogan. The Week was supported enthusiastically. The target of £100,000 was surpassed before the half-way stage and finally £256,088 11s. 4d. was recorded as invested. This was a surprise result, being equal to £10 per head of the population. Money actually gifted totalled £629.

Lady Sinclair of Ulbster, who opened the campaign, sensed the position when she prophesied at the outset that the Caithness effort would be a huge success and would exceed the wildest hopes of the organisers – (1) that Caithness people were naturally generous; (2) that they were proud and that their pride would not allow them to give less than to the utmost limit of their capacity; (3) they were intelligent, and realized that nothing less than total effort would be enough to help overcome the German menace.

★ ★ ★ ★ ★

The county's savings effort in 1942 went to provide a destroyer. This was known as Warship Week and the target was set at £210,000 – more than double the aim of the previous year. Experience had

Caithness War Savings Committee snapped after meeting in Pavilion Picture-House, Wick (1943).

In front – Bailie J. Sinclair (Thurso), Provost W. M. Brims, (Thurso), Comdr. R. R. Gore Browne Henderson of Bilbster, Sir Archibald Sinclair, Lady Sinclair and Miss Sinclair; Mr James Robertson, county clerk; Mr Moffat, cinema manager.
Behind – Mr James Beath, town clerk, Thurso; Mr D. Polson, district clerk, Thurso; Mr Donald Sinclair, Halkirk; Mr D. Keith Murray, Thurso; Mr J. A. Moore, town clerk, Wick; Provost P. A. Sutherland, Wick; Bailie F. Robertson, Wick; Bailie D. W. Bain, Wick and Mr Mackenzie Miller, Wick.

indicated the response to expect and again the people did not fail. The amount invested was £233,202.

The destroyer adopted by Caithness was H.M.S. *Campbell* – named after the Thurso V.C. Plaques were presented by the Admiralty to commemorate the adoption and went to Wick and Thurso. Naval officers attended the unveiling ceremonies.

The *Campbell* was 26 years old and saw much service. "Not a dull moment" was said to describe her war career. And the crew had some exciting outings. In the spring of 1944, for instance, the *Campbell* was one of the British ships in action against enemy naval forces and obtained a direct hit on an E-Boat. Altogether, the *Campbell* steamed more than a hundred thousand miles on war duties. Officers and men on board were grateful for the thoughtfulness and kindness shown to them by Caithness and frequently expressed gratitude.

Writing under date July 3, 1945, to our county clerk, Lieut. B. W. Meaden, R.N., commanding officer of the *Campbell*, said the vessel was "paying off" that day and continued – "She's had a grand life and borne many a sailor safely through the war, and today when we gave three cheers for her these were most sincere and heartfelt. She had a glorious finish as the *Campbell* had the honour of escorting the Crown Prince of Norway to Oslo, and being the first destroyer there since the Germans capitulated . . . we flew the flag of the Admiral Commanding Norway, which was indeed an honour but well deserved. The plaque you sent us from Caithness has been sent to the Trophy Store at Chatham Barracks, and will probably adorn the next *Campbell*. My kindest regards to you and the rest of the kind people of Caithness."

★ ★ ★ ★ ★

The third big money-saving effort in Caithness was in May, 1943, under the "Wings for Victory" campaign. The county aimed at £150,000 and

**"Campbell"
Crest presented
to Caithness to
commemorate
adoption of the
ship.**

invested £28,303 more than the target figure, equal to £9 5s. 9d. per head. The county decided that the money should go towards the purchase of aircraft used for operations over the sea – two Sunderlands (costing £100,000); two Catalinas (£40,000); and four sea-rescue craft (£10,000).

"Salute the Soldier" Week was held the following year (1944) when the county aimed at £150,000 to equip an infantry battalion and a medical unit attached, the battalion chosen being the local Seaforths. Result – £220,628.

"Thanksgiving Week" was the designation of the 1945 savings effort. The county then aimed at raising £100,000 – and did it. The actual sum invested was £119,330. In each of these savings campaigns, although not mentioned except in reference to 1941, the county gave substantial sums as gifts, and in some cases investments were made free of interest.

★　★　★　★　★

The special savings week in 1945 brought the Caithness investments for the five separate weeks to more than a million pounds – a remarkably good response. The annual results are tabulated below so that figures can be seen at a glance:–

	Target.	Invested.
War Weapons	£100,000	£256,088
Warship Week	210,000	233,202
Wings for Victory	150,000	179,303
Salute the Soldier	150,000	220,628
Thanksgiving	100,000	119,330
	£710,000	£1,008,551

★　★　★　★　★

All these yearly money-saving campaigns were organised by the Caithness War Savings Committee under the chairmanship of Comdr. R. R. Gore Browne Henderson of Bilbster. Mr J. Robertson, county clerk, was hon. secretary, and Mr James M. Bremner, depute county treasurer, hon. treasurer to the Committee. The Town Councils of Wick and Thurso and each District Council in the landward area of the county were appointed sub-committees for the purpose of organising each Week in their respective areas.

Here it may be worthy of mention that the burgh of Wick alone contributed a million pounds in investments during the six war years. The towns-people responded generously to all recognised war charities and other deserving causes yet had the wherewithal to make the undernoted Investments: Savings Bank deposits, £437,000; Defence Bonds, £253,000; Savings Certificates, £217,000; Savings Bonds, £77,000; War Bonds, £16,000.

The small investor took a very prominent part. This statement is confirmed by the fact that the funds of Wick Savings Bank were trebled between the years of 1939-45, when these were returned as £570,000. Savings groups were active in all districts, ay, even in streets and business premises, and all met with some measure of success. A noteworthy return was made by Thurso Savings Group (95 members) with £8052. To show that the rural districts did equally well Reay can be quoted as an example. Here a savings group movement was started in October, 1940, and in two years had a membership of 128 and a savings record of £4570. This was hailed as "a grand lead from a little place."

★　★　★　★　★

Caithness patriotically presented the country with a Spitfire 'plane in the days of peril. A fund was opened for the purpose and contributions were made at the rate of £500 per week until the required £6000 was reached. The money came direct from the people's pockets and represented a weekly rate of 1s. 9d. per head of the population. These were not remarkable figures yet certainly very commendable.

The Spitfire was given the name "Caithness" and was soon in the sky attached to a famous Australian Fighter Squadron. It flew thousands of miles on bomber escort duty over German-occupied

Pilot seated in the cockpit of the Spitfire "Caithness."

Division, £360; Wick Cabin in Rosyth, £100; general donations, £53,000. These figures are not quoted as totals but to illustrate how well our county responded when the occasion arose. Never before had Caithness sent or lent on such a scale. Imagine peacetime efforts of this kind and the benefits that would accrue.

★　★　★　★　★

During the war years repeated appeals were made for blood donors – everywhere. The urgency grew as fighting and aerial bombardment increased, as cases of haemorrhage and shock requiring transfusions multiplied. The giving of blood was something almost new to Caithness people and it was stated that "for some peculiar reason or other" the inhabitants were reluctant to enrol as donors. The natives were advised that it was not a question of being willing when an emergency arose but of being examined and classified beforehand so that everything would be in readiness should the call come. The response may have beeen good or bad in proportion to population – unfortunately, inquiries made produced no figures. Miss C. Thain, 1 Breadalbane Cresent, Wick, was local organiser.

This much, however, can be said for Caithness: quite a number attended the hospitals in Novr., 1943, when a unit from Edinburgh visited the county to get from volunteers blood to be processed into dried plasma for use overseas. There were stated to be 120 civilian donors from the county, 90 of them resident in Wick and vicinity.

★　★　★　★　★

The war had not lasted a twelvemonth when the first salvage campaign was launched. The recovery of scrap metal and wastepaper was important, and as time went on aluminium, rubber, bones, rags, tins and other used material formerly regarded as rubbish, were added to the list of items given a new value.

The salvage campaign in Caithness opened in the summer of 1940, and within a fortnight the collection amounted to more than a hundred tons of

France, on shipping protective work, and on general convoy patrols. On one occasion it got separated from its squadron near the French coast on its way to base, and was attacked by two Messerschmitts. The pilot climbed and in the ensuing duel destroyed one of the enemy 'planes with a burst of gunfire. The aircraft went down in a steep dive and crashed into the sea.

It would be nice to know more of the record of the Spitfire "Caithness."

★　★　★　★　★

Writing of money matters, it can be stated that the five war years were all years of generous and continuing giving – everywhere. The response in Caithness was highly creditable. Searching for figures in substantiation of this assertion, one regretted at times the inclination of our county folk to follow the Bible injunction not to let the left hand know what the right hand doeth. Adherence to this (sometimes worthy) principle meant that many good deeds have been lost in the mists of Time. Yet there remained records sufficient to show that Caithness folk gave freely of their cash. They were counselled to "work, save and lend" – all of which they did handsomely – but they also gave without thought of reward. Research over a period brought the acknowledged total of £100,000 in gifts. These went principally to the undernoted funds:– Red Cross, £14,000; Penny-a-week, £9000; Fighter, £5778; Prisoner-of-war, £3500; Trafalgar, £3200; Russia, £1500; China, £950; Comforts to 51st scrap metal, 32 truck loads going south by rail. Wick made a special one-day door-to-door collection, and 14 railway trucks were loaded. Collectors were kept busy until 11 in the evening. A second county effort produced another 100 tons. Lybster contributed 11 tons of scrap metal and 30 cwt. aluminium.

The figures given are for 1940 but are not actually totals. These can be gauged from the revenue return – £1000 to the county in eight months. There was much work behind such an effort.

★ ★ ★ ★ ★

"Bundles for Britain" was the slogan used in the second salvage drive in Novr., 1941. Result: 31 tons scrap iron, 14 tons wastepaper, and much other material – bottles, rags, rubber, copper, lead.

Although collections continued until the end of the war, there was a noticeable falling-off in 1944, apart from used rubber. By then, however, shipping losses had been reduced to 65,000 tons in six months. In 1943 shipping losses averaged 246,000 tons a month.

Wick started off its wastepaper collection in rare style, averaging $2\frac{1}{2}$ tons per week, whereas the nation's aim was a ton a month per thousand of population. Moreover, the town maintained this high percentage for two years or longer. In the summer of 1941 Wick was officially complimented on a record collection of 11 tons per thousand of population – more than twice the average for the nation.

Wick collected 54 tons 3 cwts. wastepaper in the latter six months of 1940; 93 tons 6 cwts. in 1941; and in the month of January, 1942, 57 tons – equal to 17lb per head. Such a collection entailed much work, especially as all the material had to be baled – work that was undertaken voluntarily, mainly by ladies.

Thurso's wastepaper collection at one period (1942) averaged seven tons per month. The returns there were steady as well as abundant.

The collection of scrap was more difficult in the rural areas because there was not even a skeleton of a system to begin with. As in the towns, school pupils took a prominent part, and as well as collecting assisted Rural Institute members in sorting and grading the paper. Children everywhere were enthusiastic collectors of tinfoil and huge quantities were recovered for re-usage.

Central dumps for scrap iron and other metals were set up in the villages, and at intervals these dumps were emptied and the contents removed to the towns. Altogether, Caithness can look back with satisfaction on its salvage campaign.

The housewife was a worker, too.

Our Women Folk Accomplished Much.

WAR opens floodgates for the release of all that is vile in human nature. It provides, too, in balancing measure, an outlet for the best and highest instincts and qualities among those engaged actively in warfare and among non-combatants as well. Think on the multifarious services performed by women at home and all the many voluntary labours regularly and cheerfully undertaken, ofttimes at much inconvenience. Voluntary labour was synonymous with self-sacrifice. Thoughts were ever for the well-being of those braving the perils of the battlefronts.

Behind our fighting forces stood solidly the women of the country. Many were actually on service with the women's sections of the Forces, in Civil Defence organisations, in the Women's Land Army, or in the praiseworthy and indispensable role of nurses. Tribute has elsewhere been paid to them and to the females who manned the guns, who ferried the aircraft, who helped build the ships and make munitions, who assisted to maintain essential civilian services, and in divers directions undertook work usually assigned to males. In the home county we remember with gratitude our women of the Red Cross parties, of the First-aid Detachments, of the Women's Voluntary Service, of Rural Institutes, of church and town Guilds, and of working and knitting parties who toiled quietly and unceasingly in every town and village or scattered country district. All this was a labour of love and proved (if proof were needed) that work undertaken voluntarily can ever be accounted among the best performed. This great work was done mainly by housewives who also performed their daily tasks at home under unusually difficult conditions. There were war-time worries in every household.

★ ★ ★ ★ ★

The W.V.S. (Women's Voluntary Service) was inaugurated in the summer of 1940 and was known as the Housewife's Service. Lady Sinclair of Ulbster was the organiser for Caithness. The women's section of the British Legion gave it a good send-off with an enrolment of 85 members. The duties required the members to work in conjunction with the air raid wardens in their sectors, and in air raid evacuations were responsible for clothing distribution and feeding arrangements; the members became assistants for canteen services, rest centres, etc. – ay, even for salvage.

Canteens for the provision of meals to Servicemen were opened at Wick, Thurso and Halkirk in 1940, and the ladies of the county earned unstinted praise for a first-rate job – and everything done with a smile. These were comparatively good days. Eggs and sausages were plentiful and the canteen fryers had an exceedingly active four-hours' spell. A sausage and egg supper then cost the Serviceman sixpence (with two eggs, 8d.) with a penny for tea and a penny for bread – and trade was brisk. But the time came when sausages became less plentiful and eggs almost a luxury. Such substantial suppers ceased but the canteens retained a big measure of popularity until the end.

The Naval Canteen at Thurso Town Hall was among the first of its kind to operate at the beginning of the war, and among the last to close down. It continued active, ofttimes very active, for seven years. It was estimated that during that time over a million cups of tea, coffee or cocoa were served to grateful customers. The ladies' committee also provided at Mina Villa an excellent canteen service for a number of years during the war. This one catered in the main for the needs of those who travelled by train and in particular for travellers by the "Jellicoe," connecting with Scapa. It would be difficult (said a newspaper correspondent) to estimate the value of the grand work done voluntarily during seven years by a few dozen ladies in Thurso. One and all, they did a magnificent job of work.

Shipwrecked seamen landed at Thurso during the war were cared for by the Shipwrecked Fishermen's and Mariners' Society at a cost of £3143.

* * * * *

The women of Caithness did noble service under the Red Cross standard, providing working parties for the making (and latterly mending) of garments, remembering particularly the wounded and those who were prisoners in enemy hands, and always active in the ingathering of funds to maintain the services. First-aid detachments were efficient and well supported.

To get an idea of the work performed by the Red Cross, let's look at an ordinary year – the mid-year of war. The report for the twelve months ending August, 1943, stated that the Red Cross work parties made 4400 bandages and surgical dressings, supplied 700 garments (pyjamas, bedjackets and such-like) and also supplied local hospitals and the Home Guard. Money receipts were given as £5386 15s. 6d., and the Penny-a-Week Fund averaged £200 a month. Caithness contributed £2208 to the general fund, £500 to prisoners of war fund, £500 to the Russian fund, and £500 to the China fund. Seventy-seven Caithness men were known to be prisoners of war at that time and were provided for by the local branch of the Society. Hundreds of garments were sent to Russia in 1942.

* * * * *

War working parties were formed in the first month of war, and at the inauguration meeting each lady present contributed to form the nucleus of a fund for gifting comforts – socks, scarves, helmets, mittens, seaboot stockings, and, in the days of plenty, chocolate and cigarettes. The officials appointed at the inauguration meeting at Wick were Mrs K. Duff-Dunbar, president; Miss N. Connon, West Banks Terrace, secretary; and Mrs I. M'Hardy, Lilybank, treasurer. This party met regularly in the town hall for the making of comforts and also distributed wool for knitting. The material used could be measured in miles as more and more was ever needed. The appeal met with warm approval in all districts of the county and willing workers were found in all centres. While the Red Cross worked in the interests of the sick and wounded, the work parties opened comfort funds for those on service. Many thousands of garments were made and many an appreciated parcel was received by local lads on service. Wick War Work Party, for instance, distributed 2000 garments in its second year alone.

The cleaning of sphagnum moss was undertaken by these parties three days per week, and towards the end of 1940 darning depots were opened. Garments darned or mended numbered 2000 a week. "Make-do and mend" became the slogan as sewing and knitting materials became scarcer with the passing years.

Although Wick only is mentioned here all the women of the county were equally active in wartime work. For instance, Reay working party (inaugurated by Mrs Taylor of Sandside) in its first twelve months sent more than a thousand comforts. Mrs Horne of Thuster set an example to moss-cleaners by starting bi-weekly meetings and other districts followed.

* * * * *

Women were the principal money raisers.

Efforts in this direction were tireless and continuous and frequently yielded remarkable results. A Red Cross gift ship opened at Thurso met with phenomenal success. The shop service was maintained by women from rural areas on Tuesdays and by townswomen on Saturdays. In its first month (opening five hours daily and two days each week) the shop averaged an income of more than £100 per day: £197 was its first record. But in its second year (1944) drawings soared far beyond such figures, reaching to a new record of £287 in a day (average, £150). In thirty openings the total drawings were £3511 10s. 11d.

Good results were obtained everywhere in the county, and just to show how things were done here are a few gleanings at random:– £1049 12s (bazaar at Wick); £608 (Red Cross free gift scheme); £290 (Bower); £240 5s. (one-day carnival at Thurso); £171 3s. (Latheron); £160 (sale of work at Dunbeath for Nursing Association) and £50 at a dance; £132 3s (Forse bring-and-buy sale). The Penny-a-Week Fund also provided some astonishing figures. Berriedale, for instance, by this simple means, contributed in three years, £250 to the fund, and places like Dunbeath, Staxigoe, Reay and Watten had equally good or even better returns.

Church Guilds and Rural Institutes were very active in the providing of comforts and in the entertaining of Service men and women stationed in this area. Thurso Townswomen's Guild provided gifts to Thursonians in the Services (Christmas, 1944) at a total cost of £188 2s 9d. There were 23 Institutes in the county with a membership of approximately 600, and no appeal was allowed to go unanswered.

Many words of thanks reached the Institutes. Here are a few sentences from a typical letter:– " . . . of all the women's organisations that exist in this war the Berriedale W.R.I. party is one of the most highly esteemed by Servicemen. Do not think that the dull, uninteresting tasks you perform go unrewarded, for somewhere, possibly in this country or in the sand-swept desert or the damp-heat of the jungle, a lonely war-expelled man has his heart touched and his faith in humanity raised . . The thought behind the deeds is appreciated, and is characteristic of the warm-heartedness of the Berriedale people . . ."

There was unbounded enthusiasm in many an effort. Lybster Institute, to give only one example, distributed 765 comforts in a year.

Unbounded enthusiasm indeed. Instances of keenness could be quoted from every quarter but behind a smile we can content ourselves with one; a contretemps that really accentuates their keenness:

Warming to her work, one stallholder at a sale doffed her overcoat, and another stallholder promptly but unwittingly sold it! The error was not discovered until the ladies began to think of going home. Happily, all ended well.

★ ★ ★ ★ ★

Patriotic and anonymous workers were everywhere and among the most devoted were old folks and semi-invalids. Age had brought bodily weaknesses, but the spirit was undaunted and fingers still nimble. In Pulteney, for instance, were at least two industrious old ladies who knitted seaboot stockings of quality at a rate that surprised the grateful organisers. Another lady of 80 in the same area, though unable to move from her room, knitted 80 pairs of socks for Servicemen, and paid from her own purse for all the wool she used.

Away at the other end of the county (in Reay) a lady well over ninety passed her time in knitting and every week provided something for the soldiers. There were also three nonagenarians knitting in the parish. And at Gillock, Bower (in the heart of the county) a lady of 92 assisted in the making of garments as well as knitting comforts. She was said to make difficult jobs look easy. The old folks, however, didn't like publicity. "Huh, there's nothing wonderful about me," they would say in deprecatory fashion. And so, with a "Thank you!" to all, we'll leave it at that.

Sewing and knitting was only one department in which our ladies excelled. When voluntary jam-makers were called for in 1941 our women folks produced 4 tons, 7sts. 5 lbs. from home-grown produce, mostly rhubarb. This little lot was valued at £530. And all this was in addition to the usual household requirements. These were never neglected although the county suffered an injustice when denied an extra ration of sugar for making jam from rhubarb. The county grew much of this "despised" vegetable and the thrifty housewife always made good use of it. And all Caithness housewives are credited with being thrifty! No wonder some members of our many rural institutes were in rebellious mood concerning the exclusion of rhubarb from among the Food Ministry's favoured preserves.

★ ★ ★ ★ ★

Whisky was a sure winner at any war charity sale and when "snowballed" (bought and handed back repeatedly) added substantially to the drawings. For instance, during Wings for Victory Week (May, 1943) a bottle of this Scottish product fetched £23 when "snowballed" at Thurso Mart; a year earlier a half-bottle of rum sold in the same place made £7 for Red Cross funds. Other instances noted were a bottle of spirits sold at Lybster on behalf of a wounded soldier (Jan., 1945) – £22 3s.; and a bottle, auctioned at John O'Groats fetched £15 (April, 1945). In the auction room at Wick a bottle of whisky – the real stuff, 41 years old – left the auctioneer's hands at £6. Then tragedy – it fell from the purchaser's hands and smashed on the floor. There was no actual rush, but some genuine sorrow.

Sheep were always a popular sell for charity, and even little things like onions and matches were scarce commodities that could fetch fancy prizes. At a little function in Wick, for example, an onion changed ownership for 9s. 5d. when auctioned. Let's hope the knowledge of a good deed added to the flavour.

Death of a gallant and handsome Prince.

The Duke of Kent Killed in Caithness.

NOW and again, particularly in the earlier days, 'planes crashed on land and sea with a regularity that marked the happening almost as commonplace. Most of these were in or around the 'drome at Wick. When such cruel fate overtook the machines, the crash was audible within a wide radius; 'planes burst into flames, and the occupants, even if alive, were generally trapped. Sometimes the doomed airmen had become known to people in the district, and this added poignancy to the tragedy.

The Duke of Kent, described by Mr Churchill as a "gallant and handsome Prince," lost his life in a very lonely part of Caithness. The Duke was probably the most air-minded member of the Royal family and had flown thousands of miles, including the crossing of the Atlantic. He set out for Iceland on the afternoon of Tuesday, August 25, 1942, in a Sunderland flying boat carrying 16 in all, but the machine crashed on a mountain side miles from anywhere shortly after leaving the Cromarty Firth. The catastrophe was attributable (in part at least) to a dense fog that enveloped the countryside. Yet had the 'plane been flying but 15 feet higher it would have cleared the Eagles' Rock.

An angler plying his art three-quarters of a mile away was first to gauge what had happened. He forsook his hobby and made for the home of Mr James Macewan, gamekeeper, who communicated with police headquarters at Wick.

Search parties were formed from Wick and Dunbeath, but the density of the fog was such that members of the parties had difficulty in keeping in touch. Visibility on the moorland was within a range of only 15 feet.

Mr James I. Sutherland, farmer, first spotted the wreckage of a shattered 'plane near Cnoc Duin, about a mile north of Braemore Falls. He called to Mr James Gunn, shepherd, and others. The wreckage was still burning and there was some doubt about approaching it. Saying "To heck with bombs, there may be human beings yet alive," Dr Kennedy, Dunbeath, led the way, showing great courage and disregard of personal danger. He had come about eight miles by road in car and traversed the desolate moorland on foot about another four miles, yet this 70-year-old doctor was an industrious and inspiring leader. He was less squeamish when confronted with death than his fellows, who were shocked by the ghastly sights and the immensity of this hillside tragedy. All the occupants (15) were dead. Some were lying in the charred fabric of the 'plane and were badly burned. Others, including the Duke of Kent, had been thrown clear and lay scattered about. The difficult task of removing the bodies over the tracts and unbroken ground was undertaken next day when they were conveyed to Wick. The Duke's remains went to Dunrobin Castle, and later removed to London.

★ ★ ★ ★ ★

Twilight was gathering that autumn evening when the search parties concluded there were no survivors. The ground they had covered led them to believe all had perished. Standing on a hillside as they were about to depart, Constable Carter (Wick) exclaimed: "Listen, I heard a human cry. I'm sure I did." Quietness descended and the company became all alert, but no unusual sound was picked up by straining ears. There was the soft sigh of the wind, the call of birds, the rustle of the heather underfoot, and the movements of the wild – but no human cry, not even when the party spread again. The policeman was mistaken, they said. Just imagination. By the early hours of the following morning Army personnel were placed on guard duty at the scene of the tragedy.

Twenty-two hours after the crash came a surprise. There was a survivor – maybe the policeman had been right, but the victim had not called again. Anyhow, Flight-Sergt. A. W. S. Jack (21), Grangemouth, the rear gunner, had been thrown clear when the flying-boat crashed. He appeared dramatically three miles from the scene – barehead-ed, barefooted, his clothes in shreds, badly burned about the face and body, exhausted and suffering from shock, and almost unable to speak. He may at times have lapsed into unconsciousness or he may have wandered the hillsides all the long night. He was taken into the cottage of Mrs Sutherland, Ramscraigs, and tended to before the arrival of Dr. Kennedy, who happened to be passing that way. The doctor was amazed to find this sole survivor, and equally amazed that he had walked so far over the rough ground in his condition. He had him removed to the Bignold Hospital at Lybster, where he made a good recovery.

Although he could speak only with difficulty, Flight-Sergt. Jack said to Mrs Sutherland – "I am an airman and our 'plane has crashed. I am the sole sur-vivor." How did he know? Could it be that he had dragged the bodies away from the blazing machine, set off for help, lost his way and lapsed into uncon-sciousness?

By the way, there were explosives on the Sunderland, but none went off when the machine crashed and neither did they ignite from the fierce heat of burning oil and petrol or the flames from the surrounding heather.

★   ★   ★   ★   ★

Three weeks after this tragic occurrence H.M. the King came to Caithness to visit the scene of his brother's death. He came over the Ord by road, and was accompanied by the Duke of Sutherland and the Master of the Household. Mr W. K. Cormack, chief constable of the county, and officers of the R.A.F. were in attendance. Mr Macewan, game-keeper, was guide to the party over the tractless way to the hillside.

Some members of the search party were present-ed to the King. He conversed with them all, includ-ing Dr Kennedy, Mr David Morrison and his son, Hugh.

The Duchess of Kent visited Braemore in September, 1946.

It may be of interest to add that H.R.H. the Duke of Kent inspected Royal Air Force units at Wick Aerodrome on May 12, 1941. He was accom-paned by Her Grace the Duchess of Sutherland, who assisted in serving the troops with tea, cakes and chocolate from a mobile canteen, and extended her generosity to a number of appreciative workmen who were engaged nearby.

Escaped from peril on the sea.

Thurso Succoured Survivors from Sunken Ships.

SUNK at anchor in Scapa Flow. That was the fate of the *Royal Oak* at 1.30 on the morning of October 14, 1939. Eight hundred and ten officers and men lost their lives. Two of them belonged to Wick. There were 424 survivors.

The sinking of this battleship riding at the moor-ings in Scapa anchorage alarmed the country – it was almost unbelievable. An enemy submarine had penetrated the defences. This was described officially as a remarkable exploit of professional skill and dar-ing.

The survivors came to Thurso. Many had lost all their belongings, and the sailors were clad in a curi-ous assortment of garments. The authorities had asked for blankets to accommodate the men in halls, but the ladies of Thurso sensed the need of the occasion and the survivors were placed in private billets. Houses were thrown open to them and they were received into the family circle in scores of homes.

"Nothing has impressed me more in the course of my work than the spirit of the people in the North of Scotland," said Rev. B. P. Clayton, founder-padre of Toc H., then officiating in the Scapa area. "It has been wonderful. Take, for instance, the loss of the *Royal Oak*. Survivors were so overwhelmed with kindness from the good folk of Thurso that they asked the Admiralty to give spe-cial expression to their thanks. The citizens of Thurso literally turned out their homes in order to provide them with shelter."

The message from the Admiralty was couched in these words:– "The survivors wish to thank the people of Thurso who have so magnificently come to our assistance. The outstanding hospitality shown to us will never be forgotten, and our stay with you has been made exceptionally pleasant. We would especially like to thank those kind people who could ill afford the extra burden. For all this we wish to say how truly grateful we are to you all. May we meet again under more pleasant circumstances."

The survivors remained at Thurso for two days, and friendships that still endure were formed. The leave-taking was a memorable scene. From the train, as it moved out, rang out the strains of the best known of all Scots songs – "Auld Lang Syne."

★ ★ ★ ★ ★

Thursonians saw much of survivors. Did not 400 from the cruiser *Curlew* pass through in June, 1940? This is put in question form because of lack of authentic information. The "Silent Service" is worthy of its name!

Fifty American merchant seamen were landed at Scrabster by the s.s. *St. Ninian* on October 28, 1942. They were survivors of the crews of vessels sunk by enemy action on September 13 when the convoy of which they formed part was attacked by enemy submarines and bombers off Archangel when taking supplies to Russia. The vessels were:– *Christopher Newport* (6973 tons), *Kentucky* (5443 tons), and *Afrikander* (4400 tons). The seamen proceeded to Glasgow.

Three days previously (a Sunday) eight merchant seamen (seven Norwegians and a Dane) were landed at Scrabster. They were members of the crew of the Norwegian s.s. *Vestland* (1934 tons), which had foundered when being towed from Iceland to Newcastle.

Then again Thurso was the landing-place for 20 survivors (Danes, Norwegians and Swedes) from two Norwegian ships, the *Ariadne* and *Prince Olaf.* These vessels had been bombed off the coast of Norway (June, 1940) and the crews machine-gunned by 'planes when they took to the lifeboats, which later sank. The men had been in the water about an hour before being rescued by a British destroyer. One of the survivors had to go into hospital at Thurso, where he was detained because of a severe chill. The captain was suffering from a head injury.

★ ★ ★ ★ ★

The London steamer *Sea Venture* (1375 tons) was reported as "sunk off the north coast" in October, 1939. An early casualty. The vessel was made the target for gunfire by a submarine from three miles range, and went down after three hours.

There was a crew of 25. The first escape boat placed in the water was smashed by a shell, and the crew crowded into a second boat. They landed on an island, where they were fed, and were later taken away by lifeboat.

The lifeboat had been at sea 27 hours searching for the rescue boat. The sailors had dodged the lifeboat all night, and ignored signals flashed across the water. They had mistaken it for a submarine!

Answering a query, a Stroma correspondent wrote:– The only crew which landed on the island of Stroma was off the *Empire Parson,* which went ashore on January 12, 1942. There were Danish and Swedish steamers sunk off Duncansby Head, and the crews went through the Firth on rafts, and some of them were picked up by trawlers and taken to Wick or Thurso.

Norwegians Came to Our Shores.

Life in countries over-run by the German invader was an unhappy, precarious existence. The demands of the occupying forces were at all times unpleasant and sometimes so excessively unreasonable as to become intolerable. To oppose German measures was dangerous, to resist meant death. Every patriot who dared openly to oppose oppression was treated as a traitor and executed. Ofttimes good and honourable citizens were apprehended and just disappeared from ken – their fate unknown to friends. The absolute unfairness of such domination and such tyranny is beyond expression. No wonder German war leaders found themselves in the dock at Nuremberg that led in eleven cases to the scaffold.

Norway was ever a peace-loving country and its people industrious and law-abiding. It did not meddle in the affairs of any other nations. The same could with equal truth be said of Denmark, Holland, Belgium, and other subjected nations. But the day came (April 9, 1940) when Norway and Denmark were over-run by their then all-powerful neighbour and living conditions for all citizens (unless they became ready collaborators) were reduced to something never before known among men.

Escape was the readiest outlet. Thousands chose it as the gateway to freedom, and unknown numbers died in the attempt. The fact that men of all ages, and women too, were prepared willingly to leave everything behind them and venture secretly to lands unknown across the ocean testified beyond words to the tyranny of Nazi rule. The Norwegians set sail from their homeland in all sizes of craft, and that some of the smaller types crossed the ocean without mishap remains a tribute to their seamanship. Most of the escapees made for the Shetlands or for Caithness, and our county had much to do with them. They passed through the hands of the police here and were escorted south for interrogation by officials of their own country. This protective measure was essential because the German espionage system placed "representatives" among refugee parties from every country. It was a likely method of getting spies to Britain. Even Norwegian parties were not wholly genuine, but of all who landed in our county there was only one suspected as a Quisling. He was given no chance of assisting the enemy.

Norwegians generally set out hopefully from the fjords to this country in small parties. The first passed through Thurso in September, 1940, and the last arrivals reached Wick on April 23, 1945. It is recorded that a man with his wife and child made the crossing in a tiny open skiff. Six refugees (five men and a woman) reached Wick by small motor-launch on May 30, 1943. The female who joined in that precarious voyage was the wife of one of the men. Then there were three who made the trip in a small rowing boat in the autumn of 1941. They were picked up by a destroyer 60 miles east of Peterhead, transferred to the m.v. *Morialta* and landed at Scrabster. Further parties of four, seven and nine passed through about the same time, and ten came to Wick *via* Lerwick on the motor-boat *Svanen III*. That party came mostly from Bergen and included fishermen, two policemen, a student, post-man, clerk, and a factory worker. A Norwegian motor seine-net vessel named *Rundo* took about a week to make the trip. This boat was observed at John O'Groats on a Sunday in late September, 1941, and was taken to Scrabster. There were ten Norwegian nationals aboard, including one named Petter Rundo.

Refugee parties did not always arrive. When detected by the *Luftwaffe* the boats were made a target for ruthless bombing and machine-gunning, and frequently boats riddled with holes drifted ashore on the Scottish coast. It can be recalled that the Norwegian vessel *Dagney I* (from Spitzbergen) was bombed and sunk by the Germans on August 9, 1941, 30 miles east of the Faroes, and 61 survivors were rescued by a trawler and transferred to a destroyer, which landed them at Scrabster two days later. Twenty-two of the men were suffering from minor injuries, mainly burns. One man was wounded and landed at Faroes for hospital treatment. His name was Lauritz Johansen.

The Voice of the Enemy.

Broadcasting had an important role in war-time, especially for propaganda purposes. Enemy broadcasts were cleverly conceived. Always a certain truth was included – the remainder might be outrageously false. The aim was ever to undermine the faith of a nation in all its Allies and so divide them; to shake the confidence of a people in its leaders; to laud and enlarge upon successes and belittle or ignore setbacks. The radio was the main artery in the war of nerves. Britain issued bare statements as news or perhaps withheld information because of its value to the enemy. The German was quick to sieze on this and gave lucid and lurid details of British and Allied losses in all theatres of war and in the home country through bombing raids. Listening to the enemy (in his successful days) had the intended depressing effect, and was the main instrument in the spreading of rumour.

Exaggeration was a powerful weapon, but it had disadvantages as well. How often, for instance, did British people hear over the Hamburg radio of bombing damage caused in areas in this country. There was damage – very much of it regrettably – but the German ever exaggerated, and the people began again to understand the wisdom of the old maxim to "believe a third of what you hear."

These nightly harangues under the title "Review of the News" were usually given by one William Joyce, who, on account of a pronounced accent, gained a nation-wide notoriety as "Lord Haw-Haw". Joyce was a British subject who voluntarily had gone into the enemy camp. He was arrested in Germany on May 28, 1945, and later escorted to London on charges of treason on account of his anti-British broadcasts. He was found guilty and hanged.

Joyce only rarely alluded to our northern area –chiefly when Wick was bombed. He gave all details! Anyhow, he always gave place-names of areas bombed (withheld in British bulletins), and such information was not unacceptable.

Early in the war Germany (it was said) broadcast among other things that Thurso had been reduced to ashes. Or was that merely Rumour at work? Again, there was a German radio message for Caithnessians broadcast in May, 1940. It was to the effect that Caithness "had not yet been reached by the all-protecting hand of Hitler." The people were advised to be under no delusion for "this omission would shortly be remedied." No one at that time imagined Caithness was to become abode of 1600 Germans as prisoners of war!

The minister of a Caithness parish tells us (stated a writer in the *Glasgow Herald)* that he was visiting the home of one of his congregation at the hour when Lord Haw-Haw condoles with the "poor British worker" upon his inability to buy bacon.

The woman of the house was busy frying an ample supply of bacon and eggs for her man's supper when the Humbug of Hamburg made his usual remarks about our baconless state. This was too much for the good wife's patience. Forgetting the presence of the minister, she took the frying-pan off the fire, and, placing it as close to the wireless receiver as she dared, she snapped —"Ye son o' the deevil, smell that!"

They carried the goods.

Wondrous Work of Transport Services.

THE train service was an annoying yet an astonishing feature of the war years. Trains generally were badly overcrowded – as were the limited road buses. There was little comfort in travelling and still less for passengers, ofttimes weary and sleepy, who filled the draughty corridors – an everyday occurrence. Compartments did not warrant a mark for cleanliness and (for a time at least) remained unlit even after darkness fell as a precaution against bombing attack. Later restricted lighting was permitted. Black-out regulations made stations more dismal than usual, and the removal of sign-boards was the cause of much inconvenience. The dining-cars were withdrawn, but at certain stops tea was available to those in uniform. Such was the scarcity of cups, however, that latterly the buyer had to provide his own mug. The above is a bare outline of war-time travelling conditions.

The main railway lines were overtaxed with priority traffic, and time-tables for passenger trains were burst like the proverbial balloon. Services to the far north were ever dependent on, and affected by, the arrival of a series of connecting trains at Inverness, and these services were upset by varying needs.

Traffic to and from the North was remarkably heavy and generally much behind scheduled time – hours indeed seemed of small consequence. The afternoon passenger train reaching Wick and Thurso consistently crept alongside the platforms about or beyond the midnight hour, and it would be a hard heart that did not feel a measure of sympathy with strangers seeking destinations under black-out conditions. The police had many calls and responded with a knowingness and patience that did them credit. Many a weary traveller was found a billet or a bed at the end of a tiresome day, and even the popularity of the police cells as sleeping quarters was amazing. Women and children as well as Servicemen found refuge there. A hostel became a real necessity in Wick, but the town authorities failed to meet the need.

The withdrawal of the coastal steamer services and the restrictions on road traffic due to the shortage of both petrol and rubber, meant that every commodity, convenient or clumsy to handle, had to be distributed by rail. This entailed an enormous amount of work and long hours for the railwayman and it redounds to his everlasting credit that supplies were maintained unbroken under trying conditions over such a lengthy period of years.

★ ★ ★ ★ ★

With the coming of war, the sometimes despised and oft ridiculed old Highland railway became one of the key lines in the country. It was the main link between the South and Services' establishments in the northern counties. Such extraordinary traffic placed a heavy strain on the line capacity and on station and other terminal accommodation. Special trains with Forces personnel were ever on the move; urgent Government traffic, naval stores for the Fleet, material for use in connection with the erection and maintenance of new aerodromes and storage depots had to be conveyed; mines for the Admiralty at Kyle of Lochalsh, and the distribution of barbed wire and defence poles all formed new traffics – and all of considerable volume. Again, it is worthy of note that in five years the Highland Railway transported approximately two million tons of timber.

To cope with the unusual demands, more sidings and improved bank facilities had to be provided. Additional crossings had to be laid (of a total mileage of 440 only 41 miles were double track), loop lines for the reception of through trains were made, and a modern control office for the movement of traffic was opened at Inverness in 1942, where a new marshalling yard was constructed at Millburn. Additional staff accommodation was provided.

At Wick, a locomotive coaling plant and ashpit were erected, and even little wayside stations – Bilbster, for instance – became centres of activity and changed much in appearance.

Statistics showing the tonnage and passengers carried annually to and from Caithness are unfortunately not available, but it is known that the years 1939-45 constituted an all-time traffic record. The increase was enormous. Take Thurso, for example: in 1938 the number of passengers obtaining tickets and starting their journey at Thurso was 8231; in the year 1940 the number rose to 87,207. These figures represent only originating traffic, and at a conservative estimate the actual number of passengers carried to and from Thurso must have been double the numbers shown. Services' warrants and other vouchers exchanged for tickets in one month during the peak period weighed about one cwt.

★　★　★　★　★

Our northern railwaymen had their own difficulties to contend with during the war years. Freight trains required much handling, and long working hours with irregular meals were probably the worst enemies of the workers. There was a shortage of staff for the volume of traffic, and female workers were employed for platform and other duties. Engine-drivers had few nights of real rest. Locomotives and wagons that normally would have been withdrawn from service had compulsorily to be utilised to keep pace with the extraordinary transit of goods. The railwaymen, however, can look back with pride on the faithful and capable manner in which an essential job was accomplished by them.

Unforgettable difficulties were occasioned through a series of severe snowstorms. The worst of these are worth recalling. January, 1941, will be remembered in the Highlands as "the month of snowstorms," and strong winds and sharp frosts made them more deadly to traffic by road and rail. Stranded passengers and isolated communities began to feel the effects in the shortage of necessities. Passengers by train were marooned for days, as were workmen from Wick who went to their assistance, and food was dropped by parachute from a 'plane from Wick 'drome. Within ten days a second heavy snowstorm occurred, causing further dislocation of the transport services.

A third and even more serious snowstorm followed in March of the same year. Trains were again stranded for days, bus passengers marooned, communications by rail, road and telephone cut off. Wind reaching hurricane force accompanied the storm, and conditions became serious in all outlying areas, traders' vans being unable to get through. The worst railway drifts in all these storms were south of Scotscalder, at Altnabreac, Forsinard or Kinbrace, and the residents in these areas were very helpful, and rendered much kindness and assistance to unlucky victims of the storms.

Caithness was storm-bound for three days at the end of January next year (1942) when a blizzard raged for 24 hours. Road and rail traffic ceased and overland communications were interrupted. Two passenger trains were snow-blocked on the main south line and a 'plane was sent from Wick to drop food at Kinbrace. There were 200 passengers on the north-coming train. This was one of the fiercest of storms, and losses among sheep stock were heavy. A second storm followed on the night of 2nd February, and again transport services ceased. Quite a number of the roadways in Caithness had almost been cleared by working parties when the second storm undid all the labour entailed, to the disadvantage of small communities.

March came in like the proverbial lion in 1944, and Caithness people suffered inconvenience in consequence. There was a heavy snowfall and traffic on the road came to a standstill – some districts were cut off for more than a week. Sections which were cleared one day were filled in the next – and the restorative work had to be done again. It was a freak storm but a prolonged one. The roadmen were kept busy for ten days before completing their task. The main railway services were maintained uninterrupted, but the Lybster train was held by snow at Bruan for five days, and a goods train had to be released on the Thurso-Georgemas line.

In the last year of war (1945) all roads in Caithness were rendered impassable by snow in January. Roadmen had a heart-breaking time cutting through the drifts and then finding themselves stranded on the backward journey – drifts were filling in cuttings so quickly. Eight ploughs were in use on the roadways. Although trains were delayed, there was no actual stoppage. Telephone communication, too, was maintained.

★　★　★　★　★

The Ministry of Transport decreed it advisable to close the Wick-Lybster light railway service as a war-time measure. This action was taken in the Spring of 1944 "without prejudice to the post-war position." The assurance was given that it would be (to quote an optimistic phrase) "Good-bye until victory comes," but a railway on which much had been expended on replacement only months beforehand, and which had served the community for 41 years, was promptly dismantled and removed. There was no suggestion of removal of the permanent way in the Ministry's correspondence and an honest mind can only regard such action as scurvy treatment for a community which served the nation well. The local authority have been surprisingly silent anent the cessation and restoration of this railway service.

To the north of the railway gates at the road crossing at Lybster stands a roadway sign warning the public to "Beware of the trains." When last I saw it a humorist had obliterated the "t" in the last word. Or was he merely a humorist?

———————

Additions.

HONOURS.

FENELON, Major Michael Kevin, 2nd Battalion 10th Gurkha Rifles, British Indian Army. Mentioned in despatches for services in the Mediterranean theatre. Awarded American Silver Star for gallantry in action in Italy on October 11, 1944.

Citation stated – "Commanding the fighting to gain control of the precipitous slopes of Monte-Del-Erta, Major Fenelon led his men on an assault upon this vital objective, and displayed outstanding tactical ability, not only by completely annihilating the enemy, but laid plans for the successful advance beyond this point. Throughout this action, by his complete disregard for his personal safety, Major Fenelon was an inspiration to his men, and reflected the highest credit upon himself and the military service."

Major Fenelon is married to a daughter of Mr Alexander Tait, retired road foreman, 40 Dempster Street, Wick (formerly of Thurso).

APPENDIX.
Caithness – and the War 1939 - 1945

SEAMEN - MN RN RNR RNVR RM

The names of those who were killed or died during the Second World War have been abstracted from the full record which covers all the forces.

There are two aims:–

1. To verify and amplify the personal information on each person e.g. name, rank, ship, place of birth, age, other relationships.

2. To amplify the background information on each incident which resulted in the loss of life.

Norman Glass said in his Preface to the Record that there are many snags in collecting information. Written accounts do not always agree and, to quote him again, "there may well be errors of judgement." Since the Record was printed in 1948 other sources of information have become available and these are acknowledged in the list below.

Records at the National War Memorial, Edinburgh (NWM).

Chronology of the War at Sea by Rohwer and Hummelchen (CWS).

The Empire Ships by Mitchell and Sawyer.

Dictionary of Disasters at Sea by C. Hocking.

British Vessels Lost at Sea 1939-45 pub. P. Stephens.

Red Duster at War by John Slader.

ALEXANDER, WILLIAM GREEN, SEAMAN RN Patrol Service. Aged 30. Native of Wick. HMT Gloria. Trawler (formerly A169). (Built 1907; 187 tons. Requisitioned in Feb 1940 as a Barrage Balloon Vessel.) 19 March, 1942, drowned in the course of his duties at St Mary's Holm, Kirkwall. Buried Dornoch. .

ANDERSON, GEORGE, A.B., RN. Aged 24. Sept., 1940. Missing.

ANDERSON, JAMES, SEAMAN, RNR. Born Glasgow. Married. Home address – Old Schoolhouse, Thrumster. HMS Jervis Bay, Armed Merchant Cruiser. Former passenger liner (requisitioned from Aberdeen and Commonwealth Line; built 1922; 14,164 tons). 5 Nov., 1940, sunk by the Admiral Scheer in North Atlantic while defending the 37 ships of convoy HX84. Jervis Bay, the sole escort, engaged the enemy while the convoy scattered. Capt. Fogarty Fegen RN was awarded posthu-mous VC. Ship sank with the loss of 187 men, 68 survivors. Five merchant ships were sunk and the rest escaped.

ANGUS, CHARLES, SEAMAN RNR. Born Thurso. (In missing section.) H.M.S. Mosquito River gun boat. (Built 1939; 585 tons.) 1 June, 1940, sunk by aircraft during evacuation of forces from Dunkirk.

BAIKIE, DONALD J., ORD. SEAMAN, RN Patrol Service. Aged 21. Lybster. HMS Tranquil. Trawler. (Built 1912; 294 tons.) 16 June, 1942, sunk in collision off Deal. Body found seven weeks later at Deal. Buried in St. James Cemetery, Dover.

BAIKIE, WILLIAM C. CAPTAIN, MN. Born Mey. s.s. British Viscount (British Tanker Co.; built 1921; 6895 tons). 3 April, 1941, presumed killed when vessel was torpedoed 380 miles SSW of Iceland. Captain and 27 others lost. 8 U-boats attacked the 22 ship convoy SC26 whose only escort was the armed merchant cruiser Worcestershire, ex-Bibby Line. The escort was damaged and 10 ships sunk. CWS report; 'U73 sinks one tanker of 6895 tons along with U69.' ['On 17 Feb., 1943 the destroyer Viscount sinks U69 in the Atlantic.' 'On 16 Dec., 1943, U73 is sunk in the Med. by US Destroyers Woolsey and Trippe'].

BAIN, DONALD, PETTY OFFICER, RN. Aged 29. Born Wick. Ten years in Royal Navy. HMS Repulse. Battle Cruiser. (Built 1916; 33250 tons.) 10 December, 1941, set out to destroy Japanese army transports along Malay coast. Sunk by enemy aircraft. 27 officers and 407 ratings lost.

BAIN, JAMES, SEAMAN, RNR. Aged 27. Born Wick. HMS Jervis Bay, 5 Nov., 1940.

BAIN, JOHN McKENZIE, SEAMAN, RNR. Aged 27. Born Wick. HMS Jervis Bay, 5 Nov., 1940.

BREMNER, DAVID R., SEAMAN, RNR. Aged 29. Fisherman. Married. Born Wick. HMS Jervis Bay. 5 Nov., 1940.

BREMNER, ROBERT MACDONALD, SURGEON LIEUT: COMMANDER, George Medal, M.B., Ch.B. Aged 37. Joined RN in 1932. HMS Lynx (the Naval Base at Dover).

Killed in air raid on S.E. English town, 3 April, 1942. Buried Wick.

BREMNER, WILLIAM, SEAMAN, RNR. Aged 32. Born Wick. Fisherman. HMS Jervis Bay, 5 Nov., 1940.

BRIMS, ANDREW, CAPTAIN, MN. Born Thurso. (Taken from missing section.) s.s. Contractor (T. & J. Harrison Ltd. Built 1930; 6004 tons). 7 August, 1943, sunk by U371 in attack on convoy off Algerian coast near Bone. 5 killed including Captain. [CWS report; '4 May 1944. Under attack by Allied forces near Oran, U371 scuttles herself.']

BRUCE, JAMES R., PETTY OFFICER, RNR. Aged 33. Born Aberdeen. Seine-net fisherman. Married. HMT Cramond Island. Trawler [(formerly LH114). Built 1910; 180 tons. Requisitioned in November 1939 as a Boom Defence Vessel]. 3 April, 1941, vessel sunk by aircraft off St. Abb's Head. P.O. Bruce died in Berwick Infirmary of wounds received in action. Interred at Wick.

BRUCE, WILLIAM, LEADING STOKER, RN. Aged 25. Castletown. 5 years in Royal Navy. Missing, presumed killed. HMS Punjabi. Destroyer, (built 1937; 1870 tons). 1 May, 1942, escorting convoy of 25 ships to Russia, PQ15, collided with battleship King George V in thick weather and later sank.

BUDGE, JAMES ALEXANDER, A.B., MN. Native of Wick. MV Empire Gem. (Built 1941; 8139 tons.) 24 Jan., 1942, torpedoed by U66 off Cape Hatteras, USA, 49 crew lost. Captain and Radio Officer only survivors. ('6 May, 1944. U66 sunk west of Cape Verde Island, by US DE Buckley'.)

BUDGE, JOHN, BOY SEAMAN, RN. Aged 17. Native of Wick. HMS Royal Oak. Battleship, (built 1916; 29150 tons). 14 October, 1939, lost when vessel sank in Scapa Flow after being torpedoed by U47. 833 crew lost. ['7-8 March 1941. U47 sunk by the destroyer Wolverine in North Atlantic.']

CALDER, WILLIAM, CHIEF OFFICER, MN. Aged 38. Home in Dunnet. s.s. Arabistan (Strick and Co.; built 1929; 5874 tons). 14 August, 1942, ship sunk by Auxiliary Cruiser Schiff 28/Michel in South Atlantic, 550 miles ESE of Recife, Brazil. 57 crew and 10 gunners lost. The Chief Engineer, sole survivor, was later reported to be a prisoner of war in Japan. [CWS report. 'October 1943. In Japanese waters the Tarpon sinks the German auxiliary cruiser 28/Michel.']

CAMERON, ALEXANDER M., A/RIGGERS MATE, RNR. Aged 32. HMS Foss (official record at NWM gives his vessel as HMS Helicon, the name of the Naval Base at Aultbea). 9 June, 1942, died suddenly at Aultbea, Ross-shire.

CAMPBELL, DONALD, LEADING SEAMAN, RN Patrol Service. Aged 29. Born Wick. HMS Marshall Soult. (A monitor built in 1915; 6,400 tons. Disarmed and used as a Depot Ship for Patrol vessels at Portsmouth.) Died at Mount Vernon Hospital, Middlesex, 27 Nov., 1943. Interred Wick Cemetery.

CARTER, JAMES SUTHERLAND, SEAMAN RN Patrol Service. Aged 20. Lybster. (In missing section.) H.M.S. President III (s.s Carlier). (Belgian vessel built 1915; 7217 tons.) 11 Nov., 1943, bombed and sunk off Algeria. 67 lost.

COGHILL, GEORGE G. SECOND-HAND, RN Patrol Service. Aged 45. Native of Reiss, Wick. H.M.B. Matoya. Motor cruiser. (50ft long; built 1930. One of the 'little ships of Dunkirk' during the evacuation of troops from France in 1940. Later served as yacht patrol.) 29 Jan., 1941, killed on active service. Buried at Shotley.

COOPER, JAMES W. A., MARINE. Aged 24. Native of Thurso. HMS Hermes. Aircraft carrier. (Built 1919; 10,850 tons.) 9 April, 1942, sunk in air attack 20 miles east of Ceylon. 19 officers and 283 ratings lost.

CORMACK, ANGUS, A.B., RN. Aged 21. Native of Lybster. H.M.S. Hollyhock. Corvette. (Built 1940; 1010 tons.) 9 April, 1942, presumed lost when vessel was sunk by Japanese aircraft near Ceylon.

DAVIDSON, JAMES R., QUARTERMASTER, RNR. Native of Wick. HMS Patroclus (Requisitioned from A. Holt and Co.; Built 1924; 11314 tons). An Auxiliary Cruiser (Capt G.C. Wynter). 3 Nov., 1940, west of Ireland, Captain Wynter stopped his vessel to pick up survivors from the Auxiliary Cruiser Laurentic and became a target for another attack by the same submarine, U99 which was commanded by Lt. Cdr. Kretschmer. ['On 17 March, 1941, Lt. Cdr. Kretschmer of U99 was captured when his vessel was sunk by H.M.S. Walker. Early in 1947 along with others suspected of being Nazis he was sent to Watten POW camp in Caithness. After nearly two months he was sent south to a hospital in Wales. His release came a short time later. (cf. The Golden Horseshoe.)]

DUNDAS, CECIL, 3rd OFFICER, MN. Native of Stroma. s.s. Jumna (owners, J. Nourse; built 1929; 6078 tons). 25 Dec., 1940, killed by enemy action. The Jumna (Capt. N.R. Burgess) acting as Commodore vessel, was on a voyage from Liverpool to Calcutta. The ships of convoy WS.5A (Winston Special) carried 40,000 troops and were escorted by 3 cruisers and 2 aircraft carriers. 500 miles off Cape Finisterre they were attacked by the German heavy cruiser Admiral Hipper. The Jumna was sunk with the loss of all on board; 61 crew, 2 gunners and 48 passengers.

DUNDAS, GEORGE C., LIEUT. COMM., US NAVY. Native of Dunnet. Died at St. Albans Naval Hospital, N.Y. 14 Dec., 1945.

DUNDAS, JAMES, SEAMAN, RN Patrol Service. Native of Achscrabster, Thurso. H.M.T. Ganilly, (trawler completed May 1943; 545 tons). Sunk by mine in English Channel, 5 July 1944. Missing on war service connected with liberation of Europe.

DUNNET, THOMAS, A.B., MN. Born Mill of Mey. s.s. Ashworth (Owners, R.S. Dalgliesh; built 1920; 5227 tons). 13 October, 1942, the Ashworth (Capt. W. Mouat) was torpedoed and sunk by U221 when in convoy SC104 in the North Atlantic. The position was about 500 miles NE of St John's, Newfoundland. All hands were lost; 41 crew and 7 gunners. U221 went on later to sink the whale factory ship Southern Empress – see entry for Donald Ryrie.

FARQUHAR, DONALD, A.B., MN. Aged 42. Native of Wick. s.s. Giralda (owners, South Georgia Co., built 1924; 2178 tons). 30 January, 1940. The Giralda (Capt. J.E. Rasmussen), served as a Fleet Collier in Scapa Flow. She was bombed and sunk by German aircraft about 3 miles SE of Grimness, South Ronaldsay, Orkney. The crew took to the boats but none reached the shore. The Captain and 22 crew were lost.

FORBES, JAMES W., A.B., MN. Resident of Bower. Age 49. Born Edinburgh. s.s. Granta (Witherington and Everett; built 1927; 2719 tons). 12 January, 1940, the Granta, Capt. L.A. Sixt, was lost when she struck a mine in convoy in the North Sea off Cromer. 12 crew men were killed and one wounded.

FRASER, ALISTAIR, WIREMAN, RN. Aged 19. Native of Wick. H.M. L.C.T. 494. 18 October, 1944. Lost at sea off Land's End.

FYFE, PETER, LEADING SEAMAN. Aged 21. Born Reay. HMS Tervani. Trawler (formerly H260. Built 1930; 409 tons). Requisitioned May 1940 for Auxiliary Patrol and Minesweeping Duties. 7 Feb, 1943, sunk by the Italian submarine Acciaio off Cape Bougaroni, Algeria. [The Acciaio sunk on 13th July, 1943 by the British submarine Unruly.]

GEDDES, ROBERT, CHIEF PETTY OFFICER, RN. Born Wick. H.M.S. Pomona (the name of the Boom Defence Depot at Scapa). Died Military Hospital, Kirkwall, 12 May, 1944.

GUNN, ALEXANDER, A.B., MN. Aged 26. Native of Wick. s.s. Llanstephan Castle. 8 November, 1940, died at sea of pneumonia.

HARPER, JOHN, LEADING SEAMAN GUNNER, RNR. Native of Wick. 20 years service. HMS Camito, (Ocean Boarding Vessel. Requisitioned from Elders & Fyffes. Built 1915; 6611 tons). 6 May, 1941, torpedoed and sunk by U97 with all hands in North Atlantic. [16 June, 1943. U97 sunk in Eastern Med. by Hudson T of No 459 Sqdn. RAAF.]

HARROLD, JOHN MANSON, CHIEF PETTY OFFICER, ERA RN. Aged 23. Aberdeen and Wick connections. Died of wounds at Naples. HMS Penelope. Cruiser, (built 1935; 5270 tons). 18 February, 1944, torpedoed with an acoustic torpedo and sunk off Anzio beachhead by U410. 24 officers and 391 ratings lost. ['U410 sunk in USAAF attack on Toulon on 11th March, 1944.']

HARROW, WALTER, CHIEF ENGINEER, MN. Wick. Trained as engineer and emigrated to Australia. s.s. Berwickshire, (Scottish Shire Line. Built 1912; 7464 tons). 20 August, 1944, torpedoed and sunk by U861 between South Africa and Madagascar while in convoy DN.68. 7 killed.

HENDERSON, ALEXANDER, CHIEF PETTY OFFICER, RNR, Aged 36. Native of Wick. H.M.T. Lord Wakefield, Trawler (formerly H535. Built 1933; 825 tons. Requisitioned August 1939 for Anti-submarine duties). 29 July, 1944, sunk by enemy aircraft off Normandy.

HENDERSON, GEORGE ALLAN, RN. Joined Navy at outbreak of war. Seriously wounded in Med. Died Town and County Hosp., Wick, 26 Dec., 1946.

HENDRY, DONALD, CHIEF ENGINEER, RN Patrol Service. Aged 49. Born Thurso; Castletown connection. H.M.S. Avanturine. (official record at NWM says HMS Bacchante, the Naval Base at Aberdeen;) 19 Feb., 1943, died suddenly travelling on train to Glasgow.

INNES, JOHN, SEAMAN, RNR. Age 33. Born Clyth. HMS Jervis Bay. 5 Nov., 1940.

KENNEDY, CHARLES, FIRST RADIO OFFICER, MN. Born Dunbeath. Aged 32. s.s. British Chivalry, (British Tanker Co.; built 1929; 7118 tons.) 22 Feb., 1944, vessel torpedoed and sunk by Japanese submarine I-37 (Lt. Cdr. H. Nakagawa) in Indian Ocean. 7 men were killed in the explosion and 13 killed when they were machine-gunned after taking to the boats. Captain Hill taken prisoner. Survivors adrift 37 days before rescue. ('I-37 sunk near Palau Island, Pacific Ocean by US DE's on 19th Nov., 1944.')

KENNEDY, JOHN, FIRST RADIO OFFICER, MN. Born Edinburgh. s.s. Bristol City (Bristol City Line; built 1920; 2864 tons). 5 May, 1943, Convoy ONS5 contained 45 ships of which 12 were sunk. 8 U-boats were sunk by the escorts and 2 others sank after colliding. The Bristol City, Captain A.L. Webb, OBE, was bound for Halifax, Nova Scotia. She was struck by two torpedoes from U358 in Nos. 2 and 4 holds and went down in 9 minutes. 15 men killed. The Captain and 27 others were picked up by the corvette Loosestrife. [U358 sunk west of Ireland after a 38 hour hunt by UK 1st Support Group on 1st March, 1944.]

LEVACK, ALEXANDER, SECOND OFFICER, MN. Native of Brough. s.s. Courland (Capt. R.C. Smith). (Currie Line. Built 1932; 1325 tons.) 10 Feb., 1941, torpedoed and sunk (prob. by U37) SW of Cape St. Vincent while in convoy HG.53. 3 lost and 27 picked up by the Brandenburg (Currie Line) which was sunk (prob. by the same sub. U37) the following day leaving only one survivor who was landed at Gibraltar. [U37 was scuttled off Sonderburg on 8 May, 1945.]

LINDSAY, ANDREW R, ORDINARY SEAMAN, RN. Aged 19. Native of Thurso. H.M. M.T.B. 608. 29 March, 1944, killed in action.

LYALL, ALEXANDER SWANSON, A.B., RN. Aged 19. Native of Wick. H.M.S. President III (MV Rosewood; Oil & Molasses Tankers Ltd; built 1930; 5989 tons.) 9 March, 1943, vessel torpedoed and sunk by U409 in convoy SC121 in North Atlantic, about 300 miles west of Rockall. All lost; 33 crew and 9 gunners. [12 July, 1943; U409 sunk in the Med. by destroyer H.M.S. Inconstant.]

MACDONALD, HUGH KERR, ABLE SEAMAN, MN. Born Edinburgh. Aged 21. Later of Lybster. s.s. P.L.M. 14. (Built for French owners at Rouen in 1921; 3754 tons. Requisitioned after fall of France and managed by Salvesen for Ministry of Shipping.) 17 October, 1940, torpedoed by E-boat, about 30 miles ENE of Cromer. Vessel stayed afloat so Captain Hood and 8 volunteers went back aboard. Escort towed vessel to the Humber. Repaired later on the Tyne.

MACKAY, DENNIS L, LEADING STOKER, RN. Born Aberdeen. Edinburgh and Dunbeath connection. H.M.S. Fiji. Cruiser. (Built 1939;

8000 tons.) 22 May, 1941, bombed and sunk off Antikithira Island during evacuation of Crete. 17 officers and 224 ratings lost; 34 officers and 500 ratings picked up.

MACKAY, HUGH, A.B., MN. Born Kinlochbervie. s.s. Gretafield, 14 February, 1940. [See entry for Donald Sinclair who was on the same vessel.]

MACKAY, JOHN ALEXANDER, RADIO OFFICER. Aged 25 years. Native of Wick. Injured on board R.M.S. Ceramic en route to Australia. Died in Hospital, Inverness, 23 Sept., 1940.

MACKAY, ROBERT, PETTY OFFICER, RN. Home Address, Thurso. Born Kinlochbervie. H.M. B.V. Caliban. Trawler (formerly M277; built 1919; 277 tons. Requisitioned December 1939 as a Boom Defence Vessel). 21 December, 1940, accidentally drowned.

MACLEOD, DONALD McGILLIVRAY, A.B., RN. Born Wick. Aged 21. Joined Navy in 1937; later volunteered for submarine service. H.M.S. M.P. 314. 21 Dec., 1942. Died at sea. Interred Latheron.

MACLEOD, ERNEST R. (Rank not known). Aged 29. Native of Lybster. s.s. Sirikishna (South Georgia Co.; built 1936; 5458 tons). Left Clyde on 19th Feb., 1941 for Loch Ewe to join convoy OB288 for Halifax. 24 Feb., 1941, probably sunk by U96 500 miles West of Rockall. Crew of 35 and 2 gunners. Total of 10 vessels lost in this convoy. [30 March 1945; U96 bombed and sunk at Wilhelshaven by aircraft of USAAF.]

McLEOD, GEORGE FARQUHAR, A.B., RN. Aged 24. Born Thurso. Native of Strathy. H.M.S. Veteran. Destroyer. (Completed 1919; 1120 tons.) 26 September, 1942, lost at sea when his vessel was sunk by U404 while escorting convoy RB.1. in North Atlantic. All hands lost plus many merchant seamen survivors. [On 28 July, 1943 U404 is sunk in the Bay of Biscay by Liberator W of No 224 Sqdn. RAF.]

MACLEOD, NORMAN A., RADIO OFFICER. Aged 30. Born Stornoway. Ex-member Wick radio station. Interred Calais. s.s. Alert. Cable ship. (Built 1918; 941 tons.) 24 February, 1945. Vessel torpedoed off North Goodwin.

MCIVOR, WILLIAM, ORD. SEAMAN, RN. Aged 19. Born Latheron. H.M.S. Glowworm, (destroyer built 1935; 1345 tons). 8 April, 1940, vessel sunk by gunfire off Norway by German heavy cruiser Admiral Hipper. 7 officers and 105 ratings lost.

MCIVOR, WILLIAM J.D., RN Patrol Service. Aged 34. Native Latheronwheel. 12 April, 1941, killed at Portland during air raid. Buried Dorset.

MCKAIN, FRANCIS, SEAMAN, RNR. Aged 29. Native of Wick. H.M.S. Avenger. (Escort aircraft carrier. Built 1940; 13785 tons.) 15 November, 1942, torpedoed and sunk by U155 west of Gibraltar. 67 officers and 1438 ratings lost.

MCLEOD, DANIEL, A.B., MN. Born Wick. s.s. Zurichmoor (Moor Line; built 1925; 4455 tons.) 24 May, 1942, lost without trace on voyage in ballast from Halifax, N.S., to St Thomas. Position about 400 miles east of New York. 39 crew and 6 gunners lost. (Listed at NWM but not in Caithness Record.)

MCLEOD, HUGH, SEAMAN, RNR. Born Helmsdale. HMS Rawalpindi (requisitioned from P&O; built 1925; 16697 tons). 23 Nov., 1939, sunk by Scharnhost SE of Iceland. Capt. E.C. Kennedy lost and 38 officers and 226 ratings. 37 survivors.

MATHESON, HUGH SAMPSON, RADIO OFFICER. Born Caithness. s.s. St Catherine. (North of Scotland Line; built 1916; 1216 tons.) 14 Nov., 1940, voyage from Aberdeen to Kirkwall, torpedoed and sunk by German aircraft, ¼ mile S of Outer Buoy, Swept Channel, Aberdeen. 14 crew and 1 passenger lost. Vessel was previously named the Highlander, which achieved fame for bringing down two German aircraft.

MILLAR, RENWICK D.F., 3rd RADIO OFFICER, MN. Born Aberdeen. Aged 19. His first voyage. Grandson of former John O'Groat Journal editor, R.J.G. Millar. s.s. Port Hunter (Port Line; built 1922; 8826 tons). 11 July, 1942, bound for New Zealand, proceeding independently after first leg as part of convoy OS33. Vessel torpedoed and sunk by U-582, midway between the Azores and the Canary Islands. Captain J.B. Bradley, 69 crew, 14 gunners, 5 passengers lost. [CWS; '5-6 Oct., 1942, U582 sunk in air attacks by Catalina I of VP-73 and Hudson N of 269 Sqdn. RAF.']

MILLER, ANDREW, FIRST RADIO OFFICER, MN. Born Stroma. s.s. Empire Sun. (Managed by Cory for MOWT; built 1941; 6952 tons.) 7 Feb., 1942, 'On voyage from Portland, Maine to England. Torpedoed and sunk by U-751 about 60 miles south of Halifax. 8 crew, 2 gunners and 1 passenger killed.' [CWS; '17 July, 1942. Whitely H of No 502 Sqdn. and Lancaster F of No 61 Sqdn. sank U751 outward bound in Bay of Biscay.']

MILLER, FRANCIS, A.B., RN. Aged 20, Ulbster. 17 January, 1945. Died of wounds.

MILLER, JAMES, RNR. Aged 36. 16 June, 1942.

Died Liberton Hospital. Buried Wick.

MILLER, PETER, SEAMAN, RNR. Aged 23. 13 April, 1942. Reported missing later presumed lost at Singapore 16 February, 1942. Was a survivor from the cruiser 'Laurentic' which was torpedoed and sunk towards end of 1940.

MILLER, TEMPLE F., SECOND OFFICER, MN. Born Wick. MV Empire Spring. (Managed by Donaldson Bros. for MOWT; built 1941; 6946 tons.) 15 February, 1942. Vessel was a CAM (Catapult Aircraft Merchant) ship (Capt. A. McKechan.) Left the Mersey on 2 Feb. for Halifax. Sunk by U576 about 450 miles ESE of Halifax. Crew 42 and 5 gunners. [CWS report: '15 July, 1942, U576 attacked by aircraft of VS-9, rammed by steamer Unicoi and sunk.']

MILLER, WILLIAM, CHIEF ENGINEER, MN. Born Wick. s.s. Clan Maciver. Died at Capetown 12 June, 1941.

MILLER, WILLIAM BOOTH, SEAMAN, RNR. Aged 27. Born Wick. HMS Jervis Bay. 5 Nov., 1940.

MOWAT, GEORGE, A.B., MN. Born Thurso. Aged 57. Deep-sea sailor for forty years. MV San Arcadio (Eagle Oil Co. built 1935; 7419 tons). 31 Jan., 1942, torpedoed and sunk by U-107 about 400 miles south of Halifax. Capt. W.F. Flynn and 41 crew killed. [CWS: '18 Aug., 1944, U107 is sunk by Sunderland W of No 201 Sqdn. RAF in English Channel.']

MUNRO, JOHN CORMACK, SEAMAN, RNR. HMS Jervis Bay. 5 Nov., 1940. Aged 28. Posted missing, presumed lost. Fisherman. Keiss.

RICHARD, DAVID F., FIFTH ENGINEER OFFICER, MN. Aged 26, born Wick. MV Maja (Anglo-Saxon Petroleum Co.; built 1931; 8181 tons.) 15 January, 1945, vessel torpedoed and sunk (U1055?) 30 miles SW of Isle of Man. 17 crew and 8 gunners killed. Capt. W. C. Robinson.

ROBERTSON, JOHN S. MACK., BOATSWAIN MN. Born Thurso. s.s. Rhineland. (Currie Line; built 1922, 1381 tons.) 21 September, 1941, in convoy OG74 from UK to Gibraltar; vessel sunk by U201 with loss of 23 crew and 3 gunners. 17 Feb., 1943, U201 sunk by the Destroyer Escort H.M.S. Fame in North Atlantic.

ROBERTSON, MALCOLM, MARINE, RM. Aged 23. Born Stroma. 1st R.M. Group. MNBDO. 23 May, 1941, lost his life in the battle for Crete.

RYRIE, DONALD BREMNER, FIRST RADIO OFFICER, MN. Born Keiss. s.s. Southern Empress (Chr. Salvesen Co; built 1914; 12398 tons). 13 October, 1942, vessel sunk by U221, 400 miles S of Cape Farewell. 24 crew, 4 gunners, 20 passengers lost. Posted missing, presumed lost at sea. [CWS report: '27 Sept., 1943. U221 sunk in Bay of Biscay by Halifax 'B' of No. 58 Sqdn. RAF.']

SHEARER, JAMES, ORD. TELEGRAPHIST, RN. Aged 22. Born Wick, ex Wick Post Office. H.M.S. Barham, battleship. (Built 1915; 31100 tons.) 25 November, 1941, vessel torpedoed by U331 off Sollum, Egypt. 862 lost and 450 survivors. [U331 sunk by an Albacore of No. 820 Sqdn. FAA from the carrier Formidable and Hudsons of No. 500 Sqdn. RAF. on 17th Nov., 1942.]

SIMPSON, JOHN W., ORD. SEAMAN, RN. Aged 21. Native of Brough. H.M.T. Medoc. (requisitioned from Worms et Cie; built 1930; 1166 tons). 26 November, 1940, French vessel, flying British flag, on patrol near Eddystone Lighthouse in English Channel, torpedoed and sunk by German aircraft. 39 of her crew lost.

SINCLAIR, ALEXANDER S., A.B., MN. Aged 49. Born Thurso. s.s. Otterpool (Pool Shipping Co., built 1926; 4876 tons). 20 June, 1940. Capt. T. Prince. Cargo of ore. Torpedoed and sunk 90 miles SW of Scillies. 22 crew and 1 gunner.

SINCLAIR, DAVID SIMPSON, A.B., RN. Stroma. HMS Rawalpindi. 23 Nov., 1939.

SINCLAIR, DONALD, SEAMAN, MN. Aged 20. Born Wick. s.s. Gretafield (Northern Petroleum Tank Co.; built 1928; 10191 tons). 14 Feb., 1940. Capt. E. Derricks. Vessel carrying a cargo of fuel oil for Invergordon, torpedoed and sunk by U57 about 15 miles East of Wick. 11 killed. Set on fire; drifted ashore at Dunbeath. 27 survivors. [U57 sank in the Baltic on 3 Sept., 1940 after being rammed by the Norwegian s.s. Rona.]

SINCLAIR, JAMES, BOATSWAIN, MN. Aged 29. s.s Hartlepool (5500 tons). 5 July, 1940, in convoy OA178. Torpedoed and damaged 16 miles SSW of Portland Light by E-boat.

SINCLAIR, KENNETH, LIEUT., RNR. Castletown. H.M.S. Torrent (formerly the Yacht 'Anna Marie'. Built 1930; 336 tons). 6 April, 1941, vessel mined and sunk off Falmouth.

SINCLAIR, WILLIAM, SECOND ENGINEER OFFICER, MN. Aged 22. M.V. Stork. 7 October, 1945, accidentally drowned at Rouen.

SLATER, JAMES MCKENZIE, ORD. SEAMAN, RN. Native of Buckie (Rathven). Ex Fishery Office, Wick. H.M.S. Fleur de Lys (Corvette; built 1940; 925 tons). Took part in Malta con-

voys of 1941.) 14 October, 1941, torpedoed and sunk by U206 off the Straits of Gibraltar. 6 officers and 65 ratings killed. [On 30 Nov., 1941, U206 sunk in the Bay of Biscay by Whitely B of No 502 Sqdn. RAF.]

SMITH, DONALD, A.B., MN. Born Stroma. Brother of Nicol Smith (see below). s.s. Stockport (LNER; built 1911; 1683 tons). 23 Feb., 1943, rescue ship (Captain Fea) sunk by U604 in mid-Atlantic; Convoy ON 166, 51 crew, 9 gunners, 4 naval personnel lost. [On 11 August, 1943, U604 was scuttled after air attacks by US aircraft.]

SMITH, JAMES, A.B., RN. Aged 23. Thurso. H.M.S. Arethusa (Light cruiser). 18 November, 1942, killed in Eastern Med. Gunner and diver. While escorting a convoy for Malta from Alexandria the Arethusa was badly damaged by air attack when north of Derna. 155 of her crew were killed. Towed stern-first, the cruiser was got back safely to port.

SMITH, NICOL, STOKER, RN. Stroma. H.M.S. Grampus (Submarine; built 1937; 1520 tons). 16 June, 1940, after laying mines off Augusta, Sicily, vessel was sunk off Syracuse by Italian Torpedo Boats Circe, Cleo and Polluce. 5 officers and 54 ratings lost.

STEVEN, GEORGE BAIN, SEAMAN, MN. MV San Cirilo, (Eagle Oil Co.; 8012 tons.) Keiss connection. 10 Dec., 1944, died in hospital in Bombay. Vessel was torpedoed south of Colombo on 21 March, 1942 but succeeded in reaching Bombay to undergo temporary repairs. The voyage was continued via South Africa and Trinidad to New York where full repairs were effected. Ship in Russian convoys in spring 1944; JW56A and RA57.

STEVEN, WALTER J., CAPTAIN, MN. Born Canisbay. Aged 31. His first trip as captain. MV Australind. (Aust. S.S. Co.; built 1929; 5020 tons.) 14 August, 1941, left Adelaide on 8 July for Balboa, Panama Canal. Sunk by gunfire from German auxiliary cruiser Schiff 45/Komet, 200 miles SSW of Galapagos. [CWS report. '14 October, 1942. Schiff 45 sunk off Cape de la Hague by Motor Torpedo Boat 236 (Sublt Drayson).]

STEWART, HUGH, INSTR. LIEUT., RN. Aged 24. H.M.S. Royal Oak. Battleship. (Built 1916; 29,150 tons.) 14 October, 1940.

STEWART, WILLIAM, LEADING SEAMAN, RNR. Born Helmsdale. H.M.S. Minster. Netlayer. (Requisitioned from Southern Railway Co. Built 1924; 707 tons.) 8 June, 1944, sunk by mine in Seine Bay, Normandy.

SUTHERLAND, DOUGLAS S., RADIO OFFICER. Born Castletown. HMS Rawalpindi. Armed Merchant cruiser. 23 Nov., 1939.

SWANSON, JOHN, PETTY OFFICER, RN Patrol Service. Aged 34. Born Staxigoe. H.M.S. Astral. (Belgian pilot boat requisitioned by RN. Built 1930; 451 tons.) Used as Wreck Location Vessel 1944-45. 9 June, 1944, died Naval Hospital, Invergordon.

SWANSON, WALTER, SEAMAN. HMS Hood. Battle cruiser, (built 1920; 42100 tons). 24 May, 1941, sunk in action with the Bismarck. 95 officers and 1323 men lost, only 3 rescued. [27 May, 1941. Bismarck sunk by British forces. 2106 men lost, 115 survivors.]

TAIT, JOHN BRUCE, SUB. LIEUT., RNVR (Mentioned in despatches.) Aged 29. Native of Wick. Ex Metropolitan Police. H.M. L.C.T. 980. 6 June, 1944, killed in action on D-Day.

TAIT, JOHN CORMACK, MN. Aged 37. 27 Sept., 1945, died at Blyth.

WATT, DAVID A., LEADING STOKER RN, Aged 31. Native of Thurso. Wife resided Dunfermline. H.M.S. Vortigern. (Destroyer, built 1917; 1090 tons.) 15 March, 1942, vessel torpedoed and sunk by E-boat S.104, off Cromer. 7 officers and 140 ratings killed.

WEBSTER, ALEXANDER, SEAMAN-GUNNER, RNR. Born Wick. HMS Jervis Bay. 5 Nov., 1940.

MEN OF CAITHNESS CONNECTION.

BREMNER, DONALD, ENGINEER, MN. Aged 49. Born Nairn. s.s. Fort Babine. (Managed by Ben Line for Ministry of War Transport. Launched June 1942; 7135 tons.) 6 February, 1943, killed along with five other crew, when his vessel was torpedoed and damaged by aircraft near Algiers. Vessel survived this attack but was later sunk by bombing SW of Cape Finisterre on 13 September, 1943.

FLEMING, JOHN, SEAMAN. H.M. Trawler, Oswaldian. (Requisitioned for minesweeping in May, 1940. Formerly GY1104; built 1917; 260 tons.) 12 August, 1940, lost at sea through enemy action. BVLS report: 'Mined in Bristol Channel, 4 Aug., 1940.

M'LAUCHLAN, JOHN, A.B., September, 1942, reported missing, presumed drowned on convoy to Russia.

RANSON, ROBERT, CAPTAIN, MN. 20 December, 1942, reported missing, presumed lost.

ROBERTSON, JOHN W., A.B., RN Patrol Service. Born Forse. H.M.S. Remillo. (Requisitioned April 1940 as a Dan-layer and Auxiliary Patrol. Built 1917; 266 tons.) 11 October, 1940, died in RN Hospital, Grimsby. (The vessel was sunk by a mine off the Humber about 27 Feb., 1941.)

SINCLAIR, ROBERT MACKENZIE, SEAMAN RCNVR. Aged 26. November, 1940, lost off south coast of England.

SMITH, WILLIAM C., PETTY OFFICER, RNR. Born Rathven. H.M.S. Europa, (the name of the Patrol Service base at Lowestoft). 18 April, 1943, died in a Naval hospital, Dunfermline.

WALLACE, DANIEL M., A.B., RN. Aged 30. H.M.S. Egret. Sloop. (Built 1938; 1250 tons.) 27 August, 1943, vessel sunk by glider bomb in air attack by Do217s in the Bay of Biscay.

WHITELAW, WILLIAM A.B., RN. Aged 18. Born Kirknewton. H.M.S. President III (M.V. Polperro). 6 January, 1944, killed in action when his vessel was torpedoed during an attack by German E-boats 6 miles off the Longships. Vessel on passage from Manchester to Penryn; 8 crew and 3 gunners lost.

These notes researched by Douglas G. M. Cameron and Sutherland Manson. Details included from records at National War Memorial, Edinburgh, with the assistance of Lt. Col. I. Shepherd. 22 January, 1994.